COERCION

STUDIES IN MORAL, POLITICAL, AND LEGAL PHILOSOPHY

General Editor: Marshall Cohen

COERCION

Alan Wertheimer

PRINCETON UNIVERSITY PRESS
PRINCETON, NEW JERSEY

Copyright © 1987 by Princeton University Press
Published by Princeton University Press
41 William Street
Princeton, New Jersey 08540
In the United Kingdom:
Princeton University Press, Guildford, Surrey

All Rights Reserved

Library of Congress Cataloging in Publication Data
will be found on the last printed page of this book

ISBN 0-691-07759-2

Publication of this book has been aided
by the Whitney Darrow Publication Reserve Fund
of Princeton University Press

This book has been composed in Linotron Palatino

Clothbound editions of Princeton University Press books
are printed on acid-free paper, and binding materials
are chosen for strength and durability. Paperbacks,
although satisfactory for personal collections,
are not usually suitable for library rebinding

Printed in the United States of America
by Princeton University Press
Princeton, New Jersey

To my parents

CONTENTS

CONTENTS

CONTENTS

PREFACE

One way that people disclaim responsibility for their acts is to say that they were coerced—"Don't hold me responsible—I was forced to do it." Such claims, and their more technical analogues, are a general and important feature of our moral, political, and legal experience. Promises are not binding, rights cannot be waived, and punishment cannot be appropriately applied if the agent is coerced. In addition, (what I call) coercion claims are crucial to our views of various social practices and, in fact, to the adequacy of general social theories (for example, capitalism).

The purpose of this book is to develop a theory of coercion. I wish to explain what it is to be coerced, to act under duress, to be forced to do something, particularly in cases where coercion serves to nullify or mitigate one's legal or moral responsibility for one's actions. More specifically, I argue that an adequate philosophical theory of coercion emerges from an analysis of the way coercion claims have been adjudicated in the law.

Although this is, I think, a reasonably ambitious book, I do not, except tangentially, address the question of when individuals or the state are *justified* in using coercion, nor am I concerned with the grounds of such justifications. For reasons that will emerge in the book itself, in some contexts it is uncontroversial whether someone *is* coerced; there the question is whether the coercion can be defended. By contrast, I am primarily concerned with cases in which coercion is thought to be *un*justifiable and where it is problematic whether one is, in fact, coerced.

At the most general level, there are two views about coercion. One view holds that coercion claims are essentially value-free, that whether one *is* coerced into doing something is an ordinary empirical question. Another view holds that coercion claims are moralized, that they involve moral judgments at their core. I argue that the second view is correct.

In traveling towards my philosophical destination I have taken a demonstrably indirect route, one which, I hope, lends strength to the philosophical argument that follows. Because the distinction between the coerced and the voluntary has figured prominently in the law, I begin by studying the way American courts have adjudicated coercion claims across a range of legal contexts. I argue that, broadly understood, there is *a* theory of coercion which underlies judicial decisions across the full range of these contexts and that, properly understood and recast, this legal theory is philosophically sound.

In an early stage of this project, I considered the question whether plea bargaining coerces defendants into pleading guilty. I argued that the Supreme Court's answer to this question (it has held that plea bargaining, in general, does not coerce) contains ideas which are helpful to the development of a philosophical theory of coercion. Excited by what I found there, I made a leap of faith, to wit, that if the study of plea bargaining contributed to the development of a theory of coercion, a more extensive and comparative analysis of the law would provide even more help. This is the result.

I hope that readers will find the legal analysis of independent interest. To the best of my knowledge (to use a legal dodge) there are no other studies which examine the adjudication of coercion claims across a broad range of legal contexts. At the same time, I want to stress that this is not a legal treatise but a work in political philosophy. My goal is to develop a theory of coercion, and I do not, for the most part, attempt to bring a philosophical analysis of coercion to bear on the law. Quite the reverse. I use legal materials to cast light on what I take to be a central problem in political philosophy.

My philosophical goals have, therefore, directly shaped the way in which I, a nonlawyer, have used legal materials. Unashamedly, I move from state to federal law and back again, from lower appellate courts to the highest court in the land, and back and forth in time. I have taken (sometimes bits and pieces of) legal materials which I found to be of interest to the development of a theory of coercion and have organized their presentation in terms that serve those philosophical aims. I am not embarrassed about my exploitation of the law, but in the spirit of truth in advertising, the reader is hereby warned not to assume that I have always provided the best account of current law. *Caveat lector.*

A note on citations. Because I make extensive use of legal materials, I have used the legal method of citation throughout. There is an advantage in consistency, and that method conveys information quite economically. To illustrate, 400 U.S. 25, 26 (1970) refers to a case found in volume 400 of the U.S. Reports which begins on page 25, where the citation refers to material found on page 26. Similarly with 10 *Philosophy & Public Affairs* 121, 123 (1981).

Burlington, Vermont
December 1986

ACKNOWLEDGMENTS

Since much of this book concerns the ascription of responsibility, I should say something about my position at the start. I do not believe that responsibility is governed by some analogue to the conservation of energy. There is often plenty to go around. One can be fully responsible for a crime, even though others are responsible for having induced one to commit it. Similarly, I am fully responsible for everything that is written here, both its merits and its defects. At the same time, many others share its merits (I cannot explain but am willing to accept the principle that they bear no responsibility for its defects), and I am delighted to acknowledge their help.

Kim Ohnemus commented on the entire first draft with the kindness that task required. John Burke read several chapters and offered many helpful remarks. Although I make my home in a political science department, I am fortunate to count among my friends several philosophers whose advice and encouragement have been indispensable. Hilary Kornblith, Arthur Kuflik, George Sher, and Mark Wicclair read the entire second draft, and made more insightful comments than I knew how to handle. They will recognize the numerous places in which I took their advice, and, I hope, the less numerous places where I did not.

The first draft of this book was written during the 1984–85 academic year at the Institute for Advanced Study in Princeton while I was on sabbatical leave from the University of Vermont. Somehow, the Institute creates an environment which is both stimulating and distractionless. To the faculty of the School of Social Science and to my fellow members, I owe a special debt of thanks. I was able to complete this book while serving as chairman of my department. As my colleagues already know, this would not have been possible without the help of Barbara McGray and Candace Smith. Sandy Thatcher and the staff of Princeton University Press have been an author's dream—supportive, helpful, and unintrusive.

My wife, Susan, lived with this manuscript day in and day out. She made it possible in ways that she understands all too well.

COERCION

INTRODUCTION

> Since virtue is concerned with passions and actions, and on
> voluntary passions and actions praise and blame are be-
> stowed, on those that are involuntary pardon, and some-
> times also pity, to distinguish the voluntary and the invol-
> untary is presumably necessary for those who are studying
> the nature of virtue, and useful also for legislators with a
> view to the assigning both of honors and of punishments.
> —*Aristotle*

The Problem

The distinction between voluntary and involuntary actions is an essential feature of our moral, political, and legal discourse. "He
made me do it." "I was forced into doing it." "I did it under duress."
"He coerced me." "I didn't act of my own free will." "I had no
choice." Sometimes we accept (what I shall call) *coercion claims* quite
readily. At other times, we demur. "What do you mean—you had
no choice?" "You didn't have to do it." "Your situation was tough,
but you weren't *coerced*." It is not, of course, what we *say* that is important. Coercion claims are important because they have important bearing upon the moral and legal status of our actions.

Consider promises and agreements. A coerced promise is not
morally binding. A legal contract is voidable if made under duress.
A marriage may be annulled if it results from coercion. A will is not
valid if the testator was subject to "undue influence."

Consider rights. The right not to incriminate oneself can be
waived, but a confession is not valid or admissible as evidence if
made under duress. The right to a trial by jury can be waived by
pleading guilty, but a coerced guilty plea is not valid. A biological
parent can waive her right to her child, but an adoption can be
voided if the mother was coerced. One can waive a right to sue in
tort by voluntarily assuming a risk of injury (*volenti non fit injuria*),
but duress invalidates the waiver and makes recovery possible. One

3

can consent to a surgical procedure, but if the consent is not voluntary, even competent surgery may constitute battery.

Consider blame and punishment. A defendant can seek acquittal by claiming that he was coerced into performing a crime. Prisoners have argued that they were coerced into "going over the wall" by threats of homosexual rape or other intolerable conditions of prison life. Moreover, just as coercion can excuse bad actions, it can also rob good (or "evil-canceling") actions of their moral or legal credit. One who voluntarily abandons a criminal attempt will normally escape prosecution, but one who is coerced into doing so may be convicted.

At the most general level, all of this is uncontroversial. Our moral and legal responses to individual behavior are typically based on (what I shall call) *the voluntariness principle*. The general assumption is that promises are binding, rights can be waived, and punishment appropriately applied if, but only if, the relevant actions are voluntary. There are, of course, several conditions which can compromise the voluntariness of one's action—for example, fraud, mistake, and insanity. Here we are interested in coercion. But while the principle that coercion undermines voluntariness may be uncontroversial, it is less clear what *constitutes* the coercion or duress that violates the voluntariness principle. What sort of coercion invalidates an agreement or waiver of a right? What kind of coercion will excuse wrongdoing or rob agents of praise? Those are more difficult questions. To answer them, it would seem that we need a theory of coercion.

Our understanding of coercion underlies not only our response to individual action but also our view of various social practices. A recent proposal to establish a market for kidneys has been criticized on the grounds that sellers are likely to be extremely poor and that such poverty precludes voluntary consent. A similar point has been made about prisoners who agree to participate in testing new drugs in exchange for monetary benefits or in the hope that their sentences might be reduced. So, too, for plea bargaining, where it has been said that a prosecutor's proposal "Plead guilty or risk a harsher sentence if you are convicted at trial" is no less coercive than the paradigmatic gunman's proposal, "Your money or your life." To know which practices coerce and which do not, it would seem that we need a theory of coercion.

At a still more general level, an entire social theory may be based upon a theory of coercion. Capitalist theory typically assumes that market transactions are voluntary and uncoerced, even if they are made against a background of economic necessity. To sustain that position, Robert Nozick argues that there is an important and sharp distinction between "circumstances" that limit alternatives *non-coercively* and specific interpersonal threats that coerce.[1] That capitalist theory *needs* to make such a distinction is clear; the viability of the distinction is less so. It can, after all, also be argued that the distinction between pressures generated by specific threats and those arising out of general social conditions cannot be sustained, that the distinction is, at least, of little or no moral significance. Which of these views is correct? To answer that question, it seems that we would need a theory of coercion.

A similar problem is central to John Rawls's theory of justice. Rawls assigns the highest priority to the principle of maximum equal liberty. Although other elements of Rawls's theory are strongly egalitarian, the maximum equal liberty principle is compatible with considerable economic inequality. For, according to Rawls, while poverty reduces the value or "worth of liberty," it is not, in itself, a constraint on *freedom*. Poverty does not coerce.[2] But if, as some have argued, the distinction between the worth of liberty and liberty itself cannot be sustained—if poverty can coerce—then a commitment to equal *liberty* will require a greater degree of economic equality than Rawls supposes.[3]

These are the sorts of problems which create the need for a theory of coercion. The purpose of this book is to develop such a theory. In what follows, I hope to explain what it is to be coerced, to act under duress, to be forced to do something.

Basic Issues

Coercion Claims. In "technical" terms, I am interested in the truth conditions of the sorts of coercion claims noted at the outset of this chapter, where A (an alleged coercer) is said to coerce B (the alleged subject of the coercion) to do X (some act). I shall, for present purposes, refer to *all* such expressions as *coercion* claims, although they do not all invoke the *word* "coercion." I do not, of course, want to deny that the various locutions ("coercion," "duress," "force," "compulsion," and so forth) may reflect distinctions of some im-

---

[1] *Anarchy, State, and Utopia* (New York: Basic Books, 1974), 262–63. Also see *Philosophical Explanations* (Cambridge: Harvard University Press, 1981), 49.

[2] *A Theory of Justice* (Cambridge: Harvard University Press, 1971), 201–5

[3] For example, see Norman Daniels, "Equal Liberty and Unequal Worth of Liberty," in *Reading Rawls*, ed. Norman Daniels (New York: Basic Books, 1976), 253–81.

portance. It does, for example, seem easier to say "B does X under duress" when B is subject to circumstantial pressures than to say that such pressures "coerce B to do X." Yet it seems wise not to draw sharp distinctions now. At this point, I think it best to use the family of coercion terms in a rough way. If we find it necessary to draw terminological distinctions, that can be done later.

Coercion Contexts. Coercion claims are (explicitly or implicitly) used in many descriptive and normative contexts. I shall have much more to say about this in Chapter 10. For the most part, however, I shall be primarily interested in two types of situations. In the first type of situation, A proposes to do Y unless B *agrees* to do X or waives his right not to do X, where B has no prior obligation to do X. In these cases, B's agreement to do X ordinarily changes B's moral or legal status in some way—B becomes bound by his promise to do X, B's right not to do X is waived. In the second type of situation, A proposes to do Y unless B does X, where B has a prior obligation not to do X. Here the question is whether B deserves blame or punishment for doing X. While there may be interesting differences between these two types of situations, they exhibit an important unifying thread. In both cases we can ask: Is B *responsible* for the normal moral or legal effects of his action? Does A's proposal constitute the sort of coercion that nullifies or mitigates B's responsibility for his action?

Theories of Coercion. The purpose of this book is to develop a theory of coercion for these sorts of *responsibility-affecting* contexts. What are the theoretical problems which such a theory is meant to resolve? Consider some paradigmatic examples of such coercion. A gunman says to Jones, "Your money or your life." Jones, preferring his life to his money, turns over his wallet.[4] Suppose the gunman says, "You don't have enough money, but I'll spare your life if you sign this contract to pay me $1,000 next week." Jones signs. Few would doubt that the agreement had been coerced, so that Jones is not morally or legally bound to pay. Or suppose that someone kidnaps Jones's children and makes a credible threat to kill them unless Jones embezzles some money from his employer. Jones does so. Few would say that Jones should be punished for the embezzlement.

It is easy to say that Jones is coerced in these cases (or they would not be paradigmatic). It is less easy to explain what *makes* them coer-

---

[4] It was not such an easy problem for Jack Benny. In response to the proposal, he replied, "I'm thinking, I'm thinking."

cive. Is it the psychic pressure on Jones? Is it that Jones (feels that he) has no reasonable alternative? Is it that there are threats to violate Jones's rights? What best explains such coerciveness? That, in brief, is the theoretical problematic of this book.

In scouting the philosophical terrain, one finds two principal types of theories of coercion, although there are important variations within each type. One view maintains that a coercion claim is essentially *empirical* or value-free.[5] A second view maintains that the truth of a coercion claim is fundamentally *moralized*. An empirical theory maintains that the truth of a coercion claim rests, at its core, on ordinary facts: Will B be worse off than he now is if he fails to accept A's proposal? Is there great psychic pressure on B? Does B have any "reasonable" alternative? Would virtually all (rational) persons accept such a proposal? By contrast, a moralized theory holds that we cannot determine whether A coerces B without answering the following sorts of questions: Does A have the *right* to make his proposal? *Should* B resist A's proposal? Is B *entitled to recover* should he succumb to A's proposal?

It is important not to make too much of the particular labels that I have adopted. Consider, first, the notion of an empirical theory of coercion. Our interest in an empirical criterion may be motivated by the desire to make certain sorts of moral (or normative) judgments. Whether someone *is* insane, for example, may depend on facts about the person. Yet the *criteria* for insanity are motivated by moral considerations and serve a moral purpose. On the one hand, we must determine just which mental states are sufficient to bar the ascription of responsibility. On the other hand, we are interested in a person's mental state precisely because we think that some mental states should bar the ascription of responsibility. Similar things might be said about coercion, even on an empirical account of that concept. In addition, the application of many uncontroversially descriptive terms (for example, "tall") requires a reference to standards or norms (although these may not be *moral* norms). We would, of course, need to make similar "normative" judgments within the framework of an empirical theory of coercion: How worse off? How much psychic pressure?[6]

While an empirical criterion can serve moral purposes and re-

[5] There are many who make this claim, and their views will be discussed in Part Two, particularly in Chapter 14. See, for example, David Zimmerman, "Coercive Wage Offers," 10 *Philosophy & Public Affairs* 121 (1981).

[6] I thank Richard Wasserstrom and David Zimmerman for pressing me on this point.

7

quire normative judgments, a moralized theory does not deny that morality is supervenient on facts. Nonetheless, a moralized theory does insist that we cannot assess the validity of a coercion claim without making moral judgments. On a moralized theory, unlike on an empirical theory, the truth of a coercion claim requires moral judgments at its *core*. And whatever we want to call these two sorts of theories, there is, I believe, an important difference between them.

Of the two, it must be said that an empirical theory would be more attractive—if it turned out to be true. One reason is this. In the contexts in which I am interested, a coercion claim typically works as a premise in a moral argument. For example:

(1) Coerced agreements are not binding.
(2) A coerces B into an agreement.
(3) Therefore, B is not bound to keep his agreement.

or

(4) One is not punishable for acts one is coerced into performing.
(5) A coerces B into performing an act.
(6) Therefore, B is not punishable for his act.

Now if coercion turned out to be essentially empirical, then we could generate moral conclusions ([3] and [6]) from noncontroversial moral premises ([1] and [4]) and ordinary facts ([2] and [5]). And that would be a satisfying result. On the other hand, if the claim that A coerces B presupposes complex moral judgments, the respective moral arguments may seem trivial, if not somewhat circular. For on a moralized theory of coercion, it is possible that the relevant coercion claims ([2] and [5]) presuppose (something like) the moral judgments contained in the conclusions ([3] and [6]). And then, it could be argued, the coercion claims themselves would do relatively little work. If, for other reasons, we are led to prefer a moralized theory of coercion, the question whether such putative circularity or triviality can be avoided will remain.

Coercion and Voluntariness. Whether fundamentally empirical or moralized, an adequate theory of coercion will provide the criteria for a valid coercion claim. There is, however, another important issue, raised by the first sentence of this chapter. What I called the voluntariness principle presupposes that coercion compromises or negates the voluntariness of an act, that we do involuntarily what we are coerced to do. That claim can be denied. It may, for example, be said that Jones *could* refuse to turn over his money to the gunman or to succumb to the kidnapper's demands, that it is *literally* false that he has no choice. And if that appears to push the notion of having a choice too far, recall that when at Nuremberg those accused of war crimes claimed that they were "only following orders" under a threat of death, it was said that they could and should have refused, that they acted voluntarily.

It may be argued that in holding that coercion runs afoul of the voluntariness principle I have begged the question of whether coerced acts are involuntary. Although I do not want to beg the question, I shall, for present purposes, continue to use "voluntariness" in a rough, broad, and nontechnical way—one that is, I should say, consistent with both ordinary language and the language of judges in a broad range of legal contexts. At the same time, I am prepared to grant that it is premature to say that acts performed under duress are, in a more technical and important sense, *properly* described as involuntary and, if so, in just what way.

Whatever we conclude about the relation between coercion and voluntariness, it will prove useful to distinguish between three senses of involuntariness, broadly construed. First, we may call involuntary those bodily movements such as twitches, seizures, spasms, reflex actions, and the like which are autonomic or virtually divorced from a person's will. Because these are arguably not acts at all, we might refer to them as "involuntary *movements*."[7] Second, we may call involuntary those acts which proceed from the actor's will, but where the will is "impaired" or "overborne" by some internal condition (For example, insanity, retardation, or uncontrollable urges) or by external pressure (as in torture or intimidation). In either case, the agent is, for some reason, unable to make a rational choice that reflects his underlying long-term preferences. These two senses of involuntariness are not identical. Involuntary *movements* involve the *absence* of volition; involuntary *acts* involve a *defect* of volition. It will, nonetheless, be helpful to refer to *both* as types of *nonvolitional* acts.

Nonvolitional acts can be contrasted with a third type of act, one where the agent is confronted with unwanted alternatives, but is quite capable of making rational choices among them.[8] Call these cases of *constrained volition*. It is, of course, a tautology that all

---

[7] Hyman Gross, *A Theory of Criminal Justice* (New York: Oxford University Press, 1979), 68. This category may also include unconscious acts such as somnambulia and acts performed under hypnotic suggestion.

[8] See Michael Philips, "Are Coerced Agreements Involuntary?" 3 *Law and Philosophy* 133 (1984).

choices are constrained. We *always* choose from among a limited set of options. Nonetheless, some sets of options are more constrained than others, and it is these relatively highly constrained choice situations that I have in mind.

Some coerced acts may be nonvolitional. They may involve overborne or impaired wills. The *standard* cases of coercion are *not* like this. They are cases of constrained volition. In the standard case of coercion, B does X because B rationally regards X as the most attractive alternative—under the circumstances. B knows what he is doing and means to do it. We can, then, ask this question: are cases of constrained volition properly described as *involuntary*? There are, I think, two positions we could adopt. On the first view, the involuntary is identical with the nonvolitional, and coerced acts of constrained volition are therefore voluntary. On the second view, the involuntary straddles the volitional and the nonvolitional, and coerced acts of constrained volition are involuntary. The question of which of these two views is most plausible is one we shall encounter throughout and consider in more detail in Chapter 16.

From Philosophy to Law

My aim is to provide a theory of coercion. Yet given that I begin with the law and devote about half the book to it, I should say something about what I, a political philosopher, can hope to gain from such an enterprise. The typical and perfectly reasonable strategy for developing a theory of coercion is to engage in the traditional forms of philosophical analysis, testing our theories for coherence, consistency, and compatibility with our linguistic and moral intuitions in a variety of hypothetical examples. We then try to abstract from our intuitions to a more general account of coercion. Consider a few examples from the contemporary philosophical literature.

A. ". . . suppose . . . that a woman needs a job to support her children and avoid eviction, there is no public assistance available, someone offers her a job if, but only if, she will go to bed with him, and that this is the only job offer she has. This case strikes me as involving coercion but not as involving a threat . . ."[9]

B. "Suppose opportunistic A holds out to unfortunate B the prospect of rescue or cure—but for a price. B is in an otherwise hopeless condition from which A can rescue her if she gives him what he

9 Theodore Benditt, "Threats and Offers," 58 *Personalist* 382, 384 (1977).

wants. He will pay for the expensive surgery that alone can save her child's life, provided that she becomes for a period his mistress . . . [such proposals] are coercive because they manipulate a person's options in such a way that the person has 'no choice' but to comply or else suffer an unacceptable alternative."[10]

C. "Suppose Q is about to lose a large sum of money in the stock market. P realizes this, informs Q of his predicament, and says that he will help if Q will give him 15 percent of the money he would have lost . . . P is not threatening Q. He is offering to help."[11]

D. ". . . you arrive home one evening to find that an intruder has broken into your house and is assaulting your wife. Before you are noticed, you grab your pistol from the desk drawer and threaten to shoot him if he does not immediately leave. He leaves. According to [many] analyses . . . you have COERCED him into not raping your wife. This seems absurd."[12]

Working with these sorts of hypotheticals is a plausible philosophical strategy. Indeed, I shall myself make some use of such examples in Part Two. I propose, however, to begin in a different way, by examining, in some detail, the way coercion claims have been adjudicated in a wide range of legal contexts. I choose this strategy for several reasons. First, the law presents a remarkably diverse set of cases in which questions of coercion and duress are raised. The philosopher does not need to develop hypothetical cases; the real ones will suffice. Some of the cases are intrinsically exciting. Some are mundane. But even relatively mundane cases, and arguably *especially* the mundane cases, have required courts to wrestle with precisely the sorts of arguments and problems that are of concern to philosophers. Consider these examples:

1. As part of a divorce agreement, Kaplan signed over his property to his wife. He later claimed that he had done so under duress because she had threatened to publicize his extramarital affairs. The court ruled there had been no duress: "Even if we assume . . . that the threat of an outraged and humiliated wife to publicize the affair of her husband is wrongful . . . we are not prepared to say . . . that a threat of personal embarrassment . . . was such as to control the

---

[10] Joel Feinberg, "Noncoercive Exploitation," in *Paternalism*, ed. Rolf Sartorius (Minneapolis: University of Minnesota Press, 1983), 208.

[11] Martin Gunderson, "Threats and Coercion," 9 *Canadian Journal of Philosophy* 247, 258 (1979).

[12] Cheney C. Ryan, "The Normative Concept of Coercion," 89 *Mind* 481, 483 (1980).

will of the plaintiff, or to render him bereft of the quality of mind essential to the making of a contract."[13]

2. A natural mother had given up her child for adoption, as she was under great emotional and financial stress. She was nineteen, had just been divorced, and lived with her parents, who fought bitterly—and that is only part of a very sad story. She later sought return of the child, claiming that her previous decision had been made under duress. The court stated: "We must hold . . . that as a matter of law, mere haste coupled with environmental stress does not constitute duress."[14]

3. Alford was accused of first-degree murder, for which he could have received a death sentence if convicted at trial. He was offered an opportunity to plead guilty to second-degree murder, for which the maximum sentence was thirty years. When Alford appeared in court to plead guilty, the judge asked him about the crime. Alford said that he had not killed anyone: "I just pleaded guilty because they said if I didn't they would gas me for it . . . I'm not guilty but I plead guilty." The court accepted Alford's plea. Alford subsequently claimed that his guilty plea had been made under duress because its principal motivation had been fear of the death penalty. The Supreme Court ruled that Alford's plea was both voluntary and valid.[15]

These are but a few examples. We shall encounter many more. But it is not just that the law supplies a ready-made body of examples; there are several additional reasons for thinking that working with the law is a good way to begin. Judges not only adjudicate coercion claims, they give *reasons* for their decisions. The adjudication of coercion claims has, in effect, required the courts to develop a theory (or theories) of coercion, even if that theory has not always been consciously held or explicitly articulated. And even if, as some might argue, the stated reasons for a decision may not reflect a court's true motivations, that a rationalization is *plausible*, that it constitutes a justification that is thought to be consistent with the community's morality, is not unimportant, and suggests that judicial reasoning should prove interesting grist for the philosophical mill, even if (on legal or philosophical grounds) some of that reasoning is ultimately rejected.

Beginning with judicial reasoning has two other advantages over

[13] *Kaplan* v. *Kaplan*, 182 N.E.2d 706, 710 (1962).
[14] *Regenold* v. *Baby Fold, Inc.*, 335 N.E.2d 361, 365 (1976).
[15] *North Carolina* v. *Alford*, 400 U.S. 25 (1970).

the traditional philosophical strategy. First, working with hypotheticals works best when they yield intuitions on which there is a relatively high consensus. I think this is *not* characteristic of the philosophical literature on coercion. If, as Justice Holmes once said, "hard cases make bad law,"[16] it might also be said that hard moral cases may make for bad philosophy. Yet hard legal cases have a distinct advantage: they have been decided on the basis of arguments presented on both sides, and they have been subject—over time—to extensive criticism.

Second, and more importantly, while philosophers worry about what to *say* about coercion claims, judges must decide what to *do* about them. When a philosopher says, about a given hypothetical, it "seems right" to say "A coerces B" or "B did X under duress," the linguistic intuitions are often detached from their moral consequences. If, on the other hand, a judge says "A coerced B," that claim is almost always a premise in a decision that has important effects: B's contract may be voidable, B's guilty plea may be reversed, B's marriage may be annulled, B's child may be returned from its adoptive parents.

Consider a standard hypothetical. A offers B a job. B is in great poverty. Although B would otherwise prefer not to accept the job, B feels he has no acceptable alternative. Is B's contract made under duress? As a philosopher, one is tempted to think primarily about B's choice situation. Nothing in the philosopher's situation requires him to think through to the *consequences* of saying that such proposals are coercive. If, on the other hand, a judge finds that B was coerced, he is, in effect, deciding that B is *not* bound by his contract. Perhaps this is as it should be, perhaps not. But it is a consequence that a theory of coercion must confront. I want to be careful. My point is *not* that judges operate in the "real world" where their decisions have "practical consequences" whereas philosophers only "play with words." My point is smaller, and, I hope, more sensible. It is simply that there are constraints on judicial reasoning from which a philosopher can learn.

The general rationale for my strategy might be put this way. For better or worse, our moral views about coercion are somewhat inchoate. The law, by its very nature, attempts to make those inchoate beliefs reasonably consistent and explicit. True, judges discuss coercion "in the law," whereas philosophers are concerned with

---

[16] *Northern Securities Co.* v. *U.S.*, 193 U.S. 197 (1904).

"morality." It would, however, be wrong to make too much of this. The law's interest in coercion reflects our moral views about the conditions under which persons should be held responsible for their acts. And thus the law gives us a lens through which we can see and analyze these moral notions at work.[17]

There are several plausible objections which might be raised against the strategy I propose.[18] It may be said that we should not take the law too seriously. It may be argued that what I take to be a virtue of the law is better understood as a liability. Precisely because a court's account of coercion must be compatible with what it (or the society) takes to be an acceptable result in a given case, courts will be driven to adopt accounts of coercion that yield the conclusions they want. In particular, the theory of coercion that underlies the law (if there is *a* theory) may derive from practical or policy considerations that would be ignored or rejected by the best philosophical account. The law, it may be argued, is inherently conservative, and my strategy is bound to yield a conservative account of coercion.

Now even if, as I believe, there is something to these objections, the law is still a good place to start. If, on the one hand, what we take to be the best account of the law's theory of coercion is consistent with our preferred philosophical theory, we should have greater confidence that the philosophical theory is correct. If a theory can account for law as well as morality, that should count in its favor. If, on the other hand, the theories appeared to be inconsistent, that, too, would be important. For if the preferred philosophical account of coercion seems to entail a conclusion at variance with the law, we could then go one of two ways. We could decide that the law has come to the wrong conclusion and that the law must be revised. Or we could decide that the law is correct and that the preferred philosophical theory must be revised.

But whatever our ultimate view, it will still be enormously helpful to begin with the law. Simply put, there are few philosophical problems about which we can find a practical literature so extensive, so deep, so rich in discussion of concepts at home in philosophical discourse, and so much the product of the kind of dialogue and argumentation characteristic of the best philosophy. A philosopher interested in coercion ignores the law at his peril.

---

[17] As Charles Fried has written, "because the law derives from and mirrors our considered moral judgments . . . there is a tendency for the deepest structures in both domains to converge." See "Right and Wrong: Preliminary Considerations," 2 *Journal of Legal Studies* 165, 184 (1976).

[18] For a more extended discussion of these objections, see Chapter 10.

Plan of the Book

This book consists of two major parts: "Law" and "Philosophy." Part One undertakes a general examination of the adjudication of coercion claims in the law, with a view to unraveling the theory (or theories) of coercion that underlie the decisions. I do not, of course, merely "read off" a theory of coercion from the decisions I discuss. I frequently enter into a more dialectical mode—interpreting and criticizing the law as I go forth. Nonetheless, my general aim in Part One is to see whether we can abstract a general legal theory of coercion from a consideration of the various legal contexts.

Although the ordering of the chapters is, perhaps, not crucial, there is a logic to it. I begin with contracts, because this area provides the most fully developed account of coercion in the law. I follow with two additional chapters on the *civil* law. I then shift to the *criminal* law, beginning with an analysis of blackmail and coercive speech, where the very making of a coercive proposal is said to constitute a crime. I follow with two chapters on criminal *process*, examining contexts in which defendants have claimed that they were coerced into waiving their procedural rights. I then examine duress as a defense to a crime.

We shall see that the general attitude of American law towards coercion has changed over time. Courts were once much tougher—generally taking a dim view of what one judge called "the womanish plea of duress."[19] And yet I believe that, at its deepest level, there is *a* theory of coercion that has shaped the law's adjudication of coercion claims, that the *structure* of the law's understanding of coercion has remained remarkably stable.

In Part Two, I step back from the law and address from a philosophical perspective the issues that have surfaced. I want to see whether the theory of coercion that emerges from the law can be given a philosophical justification that is appropriately deep and satisfying. At the broadest level, I shall argue that the structure of the law's theory of coercion is correct, although it needs to be recast in some important respects. I do not, for the most part, anticipate that recasting in Part One. The book follows the genesis of my own thinking about coercion, and I have not revised what comes before in the light of what I now know to have come later.

[19] *Wood* v. *Kansas City Home Telephone Co.*, 223 Mo. 537 (1909).

15

PART ONE

LAW

T W O

CONTRACTS

The law is always more complicated than one would suppose, whether or not, as some say, lawyers designed it that way. One assumes that contract law is rooted in the obligation to keep a promise, only to find that some lawyers disagree. They maintain that the obligation to keep a contract is based on notions of mutual benefit, fairness, or efficiency.[1] On one such view, a contract must be honored because the other party has reasonably relied to his detriment on one's performance; the obligation to keep a contract is derived from the general obligation not to inflict *harm*. Indeed, on some such views, contract law is better regarded as a subfield of torts than as an independent body of law.[2] Some features of contract law (and the practice of promising) may support such a theory. At its deepest level, it may even be correct.[3] I shall assume, however, that whatever its deepest rationale, a fundamental problem of contract law is to specify the conditions under which individuals can voluntarily undertake mutual obligations that they otherwise would not have.

It would, however, be a mistake to emphasize the obligation-creating dimension of contracts. When viewed from a slightly different perspective, the ability to obligate oneself by creating a binding contract is an important aspect of our freedom. As Charles Fried puts it, there is a conservative and a creative dimension to the principle of liberty: the conservative dimension prohibits others from imposing on us and is expressed in the law of torts; the creative dimension allows us to join others on terms which are mutually agreeable, and

---

[1] For a review of several different accounts, see Randy Barnett, "A Consent Theory of Contract," 86 *Columbia Law Review* 269 (1986).

[2] See, for example, Grant Gilmore, *The Death of Contract* (Columbus: Ohio State University Press, 1974), and P. S. Atiyah, *Promises, Morals, and Law* (Oxford: Oxford University Press, 1981).

[3] By this I mean that the obligation to keep a promise may be derived from a consequentialist, although not necessarily utilitarian, defense of the practice of promising. See, for example, Thomas Scanlon, "Liberty, Contract, and Contribution," in *Markets and Morals*, ed. Gerald Dworkin et al. (Washington: Hemisphere, 1977).

is expressed in the law of contracts.[4] In slightly different terms, it might be said that to be *free* is not to be interfered with, but to be *autonomous* is to be able to plan and control one's life. And to be autonomous, in this sense, one must be able to form binding relationships with others.

It might be objected that while legal *prohibitions* (such as the criminal law) limit one's freedom, the mere inability to create a binding contract does not. As Joel Feinberg has written, "a legal disability consequent on the state's failure to produce a service (or confer a 'legal power') is not the *same* as a legal duty to desist enforced by the threat of punishment for disobedience."[5] Feinberg is right. A legal disability is not the *same* as a prohibition. Nevertheless, its effect may be virtually identical. We can attain some of our ends only through agreements with others, and they may be willing to make agreements with us only if they can count on our performance.[6] Consider two examples. Prohibiting teenagers from working is not identical to not allowing them to contract to work for less than the minimum wage, yet the state's failure to allow or uphold such labor contracts may effectively deny some teenagers the possibility of employment (which is not to deny that minimum-wage laws may be justifiable). Prohibiting usurious loans is not identical to not enforcing their terms, but the latter effectively prevents those to whom no one will lend at nonusurious rates from borrowing money through legal means. Thus the distinction between not permitting and not enforcing an agreement cannot sustain too much pressure. If the state refuses to enforce our agreements, if it is unwilling to hold us to our word, then if we have not lost our *liberty*, we have lost a very close analogue indeed.

If respect for liberty requires that one be permitted to make binding agreements, it also demands that binding agreements reflect one's *voluntary* choices. It is, as H.L.A. Hart points out, just because the civil law exists to render our preferences effective that the civil

---

[4] "Is Liberty Possible?" in *Tanner Lectures on Human Values* (Salt Lake City: University of Utah Press, 1982), 95–96.

[5] "Autonomy, Sovereignty, and Privacy," 58 *Notre Dame Law Review* 445, 465 (1983) (emphasis added).

[6] Thomas Schelling has pointed out that we might want to bind ourselves as a way to attain a purely *personal* goal, for example, to stop smoking. See *Choice and Consequence* (Cambridge: Harvard University Press, 1984), 27ff.

[7] Fried puts it this way: "By recognizing and enforcing promises society enlarges liberty. By selectively refusing to enforce some promises because of how the promisors use their liberty, or because of who ends up better off because of them, or who the promisor is, the collectivity is again asserting an authority over individuals which is incompatible with their liberty." "Is Liberty Possible?" 112.

law also includes *"invalidating* conditions" such as mistake, fraud, and duress—the sorts of conditions implied by the voluntariness principle.[8] To enforce agreements made by fraud or coercion would nullify the point of allowing binding agreements in the first place.

To say that only voluntary contracts can create obligations does not entail a libertarian theory of obligations; it does not entail that voluntary agreement is necessary or sufficient for obligation.[9] Voluntary agreement may not be necessary for obligation because there is no reason to assume that all obligations arise from contract. Some obligations arise from one's status, for example, as parent or citizen. And we may have, to use Rawls's locution, other "natural duties," such as a duty of mutual aid.[10] Voluntary agreement is not sufficient to create an obligation because it may be that obligation-creating agreements are justifiably restricted for reasons other than involuntariness—for example, to ensure their fairness, to prevent someone from harming himself, or to reduce negative externalities on third parties.[11] But these qualifications aside, voluntariness—and, in particular, the absence of coercion—is still a necessary condition of obligations grounded in agreement.

I observed, in passing, that we might want not to enforce unfair as well as coerced agreements. It will help to sharpen our understanding of duress if we pursue this point in more detail. We can, it seems, evaluate an agreement or contract in terms of its *process* and its *result* (or content). While we would expect that a legitimate process would tend to produce legitimate results, process and result capture different dimensions of the morality of agreements.[12]

Early English law was relatively unconcerned with process. Prior to the nineteenth century, the governing principle of contracts was some conception of fairness.[13] A contract was valid if both parties received adequate consideration or value, a view exemplified by the Roman law principle *laesio ultra dimidium vel enormis*, under which a

---

[8] "Legal Responsibility and Excuses," in *Punishment and Responsibility* (Oxford: Oxford University Press, 1968), 29 (my emphasis).

[9] It does not (in Justice Holmes's words) "enact Mr. Herbert Spencer's *Social Statics." Lochner* v. *N.Y.*, 198 U.S. 45, 75 (1905) (dissenting opinion).

[10] John Rawls, *A Theory of Justice* (Cambridge: Harvard University Press, 1971), 333ff.

[11] Michael Walzer discusses several justifications for "blocking exchanges" in *Spheres of Justice* (New York: Basic Books, 1982), 100ff.

[12] For a discussion of this distinction, see Michael Sandel, *Liberalism and the Limits of Justice* (Cambridge: Cambridge University Press, 1982), 106ff. Also see Anthony Kronman, "Contract Law and Distributive Justice," 89 *Yale Law Review* 472 (1980).

[13] See P. S. Atiyah, *The Rise and Fall of Freedom of Contract* (Oxford: Oxford University Press, 1979), 435.

contract could be avoided if a party received less than one-half the value of what was exchanged. As liberal individualism became more entrenched in the law, fairness and consideration became less important, and voluntariness took their place. Indeed, in the strongest version of this view, voluntariness *eliminates* an independent notion of fairness. Hobbes, for example, says that a voluntary contract *cannot* be unfair: "The value of all things contracted for, is measured by the appetite of the contractors: and therefore the just value, is that which they be contented to give."[14]

Assuming that Hobbes's view is not tautologically true, I see no reason to believe that it is true at all—at least with respect to discrete exchanges. While it may be difficult to establish the independent value of goods and services, it may be said that "right you are as right you think you are" is no more valid here than anywhere else. An unfair exchange may, for example, result from market imperfections or from one's desire to show affection for the other party. Thus, just as a *coerced* agreement can be *fair* (with respect to the value exchanged), a *voluntary* agreement can be *unfair*.

Of course, even if voluntariness and fairness are independent criteria, it could still be argued that the fairness of an exchange is only as important as the parties want it to be. It may be thought that one indicator of a society's respect for autonomy is precisely whether its members can bind themselves through contracts which are arguably *un*fair. In the famous words of a nineteenth-century case, "A cent or a peppercorn, in legal estimation, would constitute consideration"—if the parties believe a peppercorn is adequate.[15] And that is for them to decide.

Let us assume, *arguendo*, that there should be a reasonably strong presumption that a contract should be enforced if it is voluntary, putting aside the question of just how strong that presumption should be. We shall assume, in particular, that the contract is not made under duress. What does that mean? According to Hobbes, not much. The Hobbesian position is that one acts involuntarily only when one acts against one's will, and one wills whatever one does intentionally. In particular, says Hobbes, "Fear and liberty are consistent; as when a man throweth his goods into the sea for FEAR the ship should sink, *he doth it nevertheless very willingly, and may refuse to do it if he will*."[16] On this account, duress is limited to nonvolitional coercion. Even the gunman's victim acts voluntarily, for un-

---

[14] *Leviathan*, chap. 15.
[15] *Whitney* v. *Stearns*, 16 Me. 394, 397 (1839).
[16] *Leviathan*, chap. 21 (emphasis added).

der the circumstances, he intends and wants to turn over his money.[17]

If we turn from political theory to the law, we find that duress was only slightly easier to establish. In the eighteenth century, one could avoid a contract on grounds of duress if it was caused by actual imprisonment or the fear of loss of life or limb.[18] The *threat* of imprisonment was not sufficient, and one could not claim economic duress or "duress of goods." Blackstone's *Commentaries* says this: "A fear of battery . . . is no duress; neither is the fear of having one's house burned, or one's goods taken away or destroyed, because in these cases, should the threat be performed, a man may have satisfaction by recovering equivalent damages: but no suitable atonement can be made for loss of life or limb."[19] In the words of an important English case, whereas threats to one's person can deprive one of free agency, threats to one's property do not, or will not if one "possesses that ordinary degree of firmness which the law requires all to exert."[20]

Although this account of the criteria of duress seems unduly restrictive by modern standards, it is also understandable—given its underlying rationale. For if duress is defined in terms of an "overborne will," it is extremely difficult to develop criteria which are neither over- nor underinclusive. If, on the one hand, threats of imprisonment or threats to one's property cannot overcome one's will, duress so defined seems much too narrow; it fails to invalidate contracts that ought to be invalidated. If, on the other hand, a rational fear of the alternatives overcomes one's will, duress so defined seems much too broad; it invalidates contracts that ought to be enforced. The task for the law was to develop an account of duress according to which some deliberate and rational agreements are made under duress whereas others are not.

A Sample of Cases

To adopt the strategy for which I argued in Chapter 1, let us ask this question: When do courts *find* that contracts are made under du-

---

[17] Hobbes says this: "Covenants entered into by fear, in the condition of mere nature, are obligatory . . . And even in commonwealths, if I be forced to redeem myself from a thief by promising him money, I am bound to pay it, till the civil law discharge me." *Leviathan*, chap. 14.

[18] John Calameri and Joseph Perillo, *Contracts* (St. Paul: West, 1977), 261.

[19] *Commentaries*, *131.

[20] *Skeate* v. *Beale*, 11 A. & E. 983 (1840), cited in Atiyah, *The Rise and Fall of Freedom of Contract*, 435.

ress? While I shall not follow this approach in subsequent chapters, at this point I think it best to simply examine a sample of cases (arranged chronologically) in some detail. In this way, we can get a feel for the sorts of controversies which make up the stuff of contractual duress and for the way the courts have attempted to respond to those problems. I invite readers to ask, about each case, whether they would hold that the contract was made under duress. And why?

1. *Hackley* v. *Headley* (1881). Headley sued Hackley to recover compensation for hauling and delivering logs in the Muskegon river. There was dispute over some terms of the contract (the measurement of the logs). Hackley offered to pay less than Headley thought he was due. Because Headley was in financial straits and would be "ruined" if he were not paid quickly, he agreed to the lesser amount and signed a receipt stating he had been paid in full. Headley later claimed his receipt had been signed under duress, as Hackley had knowingly taken advantage of Headley's difficult situation. Headley won. On appeal, the court conceded that Hackley "took a most unjust advantage of Headley," but held that such injustice did not constitute duress. "Duress exists when one by the unlawful act of another is induced to make a contract . . . under circumstances which deprive him of the exercise of free will . . . In what did the alleged duress consist . . . ? Merely . . . that [Hackley] refused to pay on demand a debt already due, though [Headley] was in great need of the money . . . It is not pretended that Hackley . . . had done anything to bring Headley to the condition which made this money so important . . . or that [Hackley was] in any manner responsible for [Headley's] pecuniary embarrassment . . ."[21]

2. *DuPuy* v. *United States* (1929). The Internal Revenue Service believed that DuPuy had underpaid his taxes. The IRS threatened to sue. DuPuy entered into a settlement and then claimed that he had settled under duress. The court maintained there had been no duress: "the fact that one of the parties signed the settlement to avoid the trouble and expense of a law suit does not amount to intimidation or duress for that is ordinarily the purpose of a settlement . . . If the counsel for the government had acted in bad faith, the conclusion would be different . . ."[22]

3. *United States* v. *Bethlehem Steel* (1938). In early 1918, the United

[21] 8 N.W. 511, 512, 514 (1881).
[22] 35 F.2d 990, 1003 (1929).

States contracted with the Bethlehem Shipbuilding Corporation, a subsidiary of Bethlehem Steel, to build warships. The United States attempted to negotiate a fixed-sum contract, but eventually acceded to Bethlehem's demand for a cost-plus-fixed-fee contract. The United States paid the costs, the fixed fees, and some additional sums by way of bonus, but refused to pay a balance of $5 million. The United States sued for a refund of amounts paid in excess of what it regarded as fair compensation, maintaining that the contract had been signed under duress—the government needed the ships to fight the war, there were few shipbuilding facilities in the United States, and Bethlehem was the largest shipbuilder in the world. Bethlehem successfully countersued for full payment under the terms of the contract. On appeal, the Supreme Court found no duress: "The word duress implies feebleness on one side, overpowering strength on the other. Here it is suggested that feebleness is on the one side of the government . . . overpowering strength on the side of a single private corporation . . . there is no evidence of that state of overcome will which is the major premise of the . . . argument of duress."[23]

4. *Caivano* v. *Brill Contracting Corp.* (1939). Brill was installing plumbing as a subcontractor to the Wheeler Engineering Company. Caivano, a plumber, was hired by Brill for $61.25 per week. Employment was conditioned on the payment of $25.00 per week by Caivano to Brill. The kickback payments were made until Caivano's employment ended, when he sued on grounds of duress to recover what he had paid. The court found for Caivano, holding that the agreement "was consented to . . . under the pressure of a general economic depression, scarcity of employment and . . . other factors which combine to create the unequal position between employer and employee . . . We realize that . . . under present day economic conditions the employee may be forced to accept terms which he would not accept under normal economic conditions; that the fear of economic distress is a compelling force which, when combined with the superior position of the employer, destroys the free agency of the employee . . . [such] payments made . . . under economic conditions such as exist today, are clearly involuntary payments made under duress . . ."[24]

5. *Hochman* v. *Zigler* (1946). Hochman held a lease from Zigler on premises where Hochman ran a business. Zigler refused to renew

[23] 315 U.S. 289, 300, 301 (1938). Justice Frankfurter dissented.
[24] 11 N.Y.S.2d 498, 502 (1939)

Hochman's lease. Zigler told Hochman to vacate and suggested that Hochman sell the business and that if he (Zigler) approved of the purchaser, he would give the new purchaser a lease. Hochman found a purchaser, who agreed to buy the business for $7,800, but only if he could get a lease. Zigler told Hochman that he would not execute the lease unless Hochman gave him $3,500. Hochman paid Zigler $3,500, and subsequently sued to recover on grounds of duress. The court found for Hochman: "Judgment whether the threatened action is wrongful or not is colored by the object of the threat. If the threat is made to induce the opposite party to do only what is reasonable, the court is apt to consider the threatened action not wrongful unless it is actionable in itself. But if the threat is made for an outrageous purpose, a more critical standard is applied to the threatened action . . . Zigler . . . was under a moral obligation to execute the lease."[25]

6. *Meier* v. *Nightingale* (1946). Meier agreed to pay Nightingale for repair work on his car. Nightingale wanted more money than Meier believed they had agreed upon and told Meier that he would not return the car unless he received more than the original amount. Meier paid the additional amount, got his car back, and then sued to recover the excess amount on grounds of duress. The court held that because Meier had had other options, the payments had not been made under duress.[26]

7. *Ewert* v. *Lichtman* (1947). Ewert had a business on property that he rented from Lichtman. Ewert decided to sell his business because he was ill. Ewert located a potential buyer who said that he would not buy without a ten-year lease. Lichtman told Ewert he would give the purchaser a ten-year lease if he (Lichtman) received $1,000 from the purchase price of the business. Ewert paid and then sued to recover, claiming the payment had been made under duress. The court disagreed: "It has long been our conception of competitive business activities that 'he who comes first to the top of the hill, may sit where he will' [unless he] resorts to fraudulent, inequitable, or unconscionable practices . . . The failing health of the complainants was doubtless the most influential factor in their ambition to retire from business. The prime obstructions were of their own making."[27]

8. *Shasta Water Co.* v. *Croke* (1954). Shasta accused Croke of stealing from the company. Croke signed a contract in which he prom-

[25] 50 A.2d 97, 100 (1946).
[26] 46 A.2d 785 (1946).
[27] 55 A.2d 671, 674 (1947).

ised to repay the money in exchange for a promise by Shasta not to prosecute. Croke then breached the contract. Shasta sued to require Croke to perform his part of the contract. Croke claimed he had signed the contract under duress. The court ruled: "An agreement obtained through threat of criminal prosecution is void even if the amount agreed to be paid was due, because the use of criminal prosecution as a means of collecting a debt is against public policy; such threats . . . constitute a menace destructive of free consent."[28]

9. *Austin Instrument* v. *Loral Corp.* (1971). Loral was awarded a contract by the Navy to produce radar sets. It subcontracted with Austin to produce twenty-three (of forty) precision gear components. Loral later received a second Navy contract for additional radar sets. Austin bid on all forty components, but Loral said it would award all subcontracts to the low bidder. Austin refused to accept an order for less than all forty components, and told Loral that it would stop delivery of components due *under the existing contract* unless Loral (a) agreed to substantial price increases for the parts ordered under the existing contract (including parts already shipped), and (b) agreed to order from Austin forty components that Loral needed under the second Navy contract. Loral refused. Austin stopped shipments. Loral could not find alternative suppliers who could produce the parts in time for Loral to meet its deadline. Loral then agreed to Austin's demands: "we are left with no choice or alternative but to meet your conditions." Loral subsequently sued to recover the excess price paid. The trial court found that Loral had agreed under duress, and Austin appealed. The judgment was affirmed: "Loral . . . had no choice . . . except to take the gears at the 'coerced' price and then sue to get the excess back . . . Loral agreed to the price increases in consequence of the economic duress employed by Austin."[29]

10. *Smedley Co.* v. *Lansing* (1978). Smedley stored and moved household furniture owned by Lansing. Lansing claimed that he did not owe Smedley for storage, because the goods had been stored under direction of his estranged wife, and their storage had not been authorized by him. Before unloading the goods, the truck driver demanded a check for the amount due. Lansing wrote a check on which he typed "Under Duress—without prejudice to any claims Joseph D. Lansing has or may have." Lansing got his furniture, then stopped payment on the check. Smedley sued for the

[28] 276 P.2d 88, 91 (1954).
[29] 29 N.Y.2d 124, 133 (1971).

27

amount due. Lansing claimed that the original check had been written under duress, for he could not otherwise have recovered his furniture. The court held for Smedley: "Where one [Smedley] insists on a payment which he honestly believes he is entitled to receive, certainly unless that belief is without any reasonable ground, his conduct is not wrongful and does not constitute duress."[30]

11. *LaBeach* v. *Beatrice Foods Corp.* (1978). LaBeach was employed by Beatrice as manager of Nigerian operations. His employment was terminated by Beatrice. LaBeach met with Dutt (president of Beatrice) to settle various claims. Dutt agreed to pay $122,210 if LaBeach signed a release that this constituted payment in full settlement of all claims against Beatrice. LaBeach claimed that the release had been signed under duress because (1) Beatrice would not pay him unless he signed the release; (2) Beatrice had vast economic power; and (3) his bank was pressuring him for payment of a $100,000 personal loan. The court ruled there had been no duress: "The mere presence of economic power, without some wrongful use of that power, does not . . . . constitute economic duress . . . Even assuming Beatrice had knowledge of this loan and the pressure being asserted on LaBeach for repayment . . . Beatrice cannot be held responsible for economic pressure put on LaBeach by a third party."[31]

Preliminary Observations

While these cases do not present a unified picture of contractual duress, several points can be made at the outset. First, none involves the absence of or even a defect in the agent's volition. In each case the party claiming that he acted under duress knew what he was doing and meant to do it. Second, none involves the threat of imminent physical injury; no one demanded money at the point of a gun. As in the overwhelming majority of cases of contractual duress, the pressure is "merely" economic. Third, and most important for our theoretical purposes, cases analogous in one crucial respect yield different results. In virtually all of the cases, the party claiming duress can plausibly claim to have had "no choice" but to make the contract under dispute. In some cases, the court found duress, in other cases not. What explains this? The *date* of the case is obviously significant. The period from the middle of the nineteenth century to the middle of the twentieth century witnessed a broadening of the

[30] 398 A.2d 1208, 1209 (1978).
[31] 461 F. Supp. 152, 157, 158 (1978).

criteria for duress. Moreover, some courts are more conservative (or economic libertarian) and are (generally) less likely to find duress. And yet date and ideology do not explain it all. For the apparent inconsistencies may strike us as eminently *reasonable*. Perhaps La-Beach and DuPuy had no other alternative, but it seems that their contracts should stand. On the other hand, it seems that Loral and Hochman are entitled to be released from their contracts. Can this be explained? And how?

The Current View: The Restatement of Contracts

It cannot be explained, or so it seems, on the old view. For despite frequent *references* to "overborne wills," that notion *seems* to do relatively little work.[32] The reason, I think, is this. While the courts want to invalidate some contracts which B makes under pressure, they also want to enforce many agreements to which B (even very) reluctantly gives his consent.[33] Because the "overborne will" theory does not help to make this sort of distinction, courts tend to focus on the nature of *A's proposal* and only secondarily on *B's state of mind*.

The rejection of the will theory, at least as a complete account of contractual duress, is now enshrined in virtually all the standard texts and in the major treatise which attempts to summarize and explain the accepted doctrines of contract law. The American Law Institute's *Restatement of Contracts* says this:

Sec. 492. DEFINITION OF DURESS.
Duress in the Restatement of this Subject means
(a) any wrongful act of one person that compels a manifestation of apparent assent by another to a transaction without his volition, or
(b) any wrongful threat of one person by words or other conduct that induces another to enter into a transaction under the influence of such fear as precludes him from exercising free will

---

[32] I say that the current view *seems* to reject the "will theory" because it may survive as *part* of the current view. It is also possible that there is a deep connection between the "will theory" and the part of the current view which, on its face, rejects it.

[33] As Atiyah notes, "It is a common part of the judicial process for persons to give undertakings of various kinds to judges, for example, to be of good behaviour . . . if promises of this nature are to be treated as creating binding obligations, the conventional will-theory explanation of . . . duress will not do." *Promises, Morals, and Law*, 23.

and judgment, if the threat was intended or should reasonably have been expected to operate as an inducement.[34]

The *Restatement* identifies two types of duress: type (a) corresponds to what I called nonvolitional duress; type (b) to what I called constrained volition. In illustrating type (a) duress, the *Restatement* refers to cases in which A "is a mere mechanical instrument or wholly unaware of what he is doing," as when A physically forces B to sign a document by moving B's hand or when A gets B to sign a note under hypnosis.[35] Interestingly, the *Restatement* says that such acts of compulsion must be "wrongful," implying that there might be *non*wrongful acts which preclude B's volition but which do not constitute duress. But that receives no comment, and I am inclined to think that the adjective "wrongful" is unnecessary. If B has no volition at all, it seems that the contract *must* be void.

The *Restatement* also says that cases of type (a) duress are "rare." Virtually all contract law duress cases are of type (b), where "duress consists of threats that cause such fear as to induce the *exercise of volition*, so that an undesired act is done." And it is upon these sorts of cases that my analysis will focus. Here the *Restatement* adopts what I shall call a *two-pronged theory* of duress, although it is not advanced or discussed (in the scholarly literature) in quite these terms. The essential and structural feature of the two-pronged theory is that it consists of two *independent* tests for duress, each of which is necessary and which are jointly sufficient. I shall refer to the first test as the *choice prong*. Putting aside, for now, precisely how the choice prong is to be defined, the point is that A's proposal must prevent B from "exercising free will and judgment," or, as it is sometimes put, that B has "no reasonable choice" or "no acceptable alternative" but to succumb to A's proposal. I shall refer to the second test as the *proposal prong*. To show that B acts under duress, it is also necessary, but not sufficient, to show that A's proposal is wrongful. And A's proposal cannot be wrongful simply because it deprives B of "free will and judgment" (under the choice prong), or it would be pleonastic to speak of wrongful compulsion.

Interestingly, the *Restatement* provides relatively little discussion of the criteria for applying the choice prong, of what is meant by an exercise of volition which compromises one's "free will and judgment." We can say this. First, Blackstone's limitations are no longer in force. A can coerce B through threats of battery or threats to B's

---

[34] St. Paul: West, 1932 (Sec. 492).
[35] Ibid.

property (or duress of goods).[36] Second, duress is "individualized." The question is not whether A's proposal would coerce a "brave man" or a man of "ordinary firmness," but whether it coerces B.[37] Third, the *Restatement* explicitly indicates that "coerciveness" is a matter of degree, although it does not state of *what* it is a degree. A court must, in any case, decide whether the degree of pressure is sufficient to constitute duress.

With respect to the proposal prong, the *Restatement* holds that a "nonwrongful threat" does not constitute legally recognizable duress, implying that its conception of "wrongful" is at least not parasitic on the traditional distinction between *threats* (which coerce) and *offers* (which do not).[38] What qualifies as a *wrongful* threat? Rather than provide an intensive definition, the *Restatement* chooses to work primarily by illustration, and mentions threats of "personal violence," "imprisonment," "physical injury," "imprisonment of a husband, wife, or child," "wrongfully destroying, injuring, seizing or withholding land or other things," and "any other wrongful acts." It would be a crucial mistake, in this connection, to think that the *Restatement* relies on a special legal or nonmoral account of wrongness. Quite the contrary. It refers to "acts that are wrongful in a moral sense."[39] In particular, A's threat can be wrongful—and therefore constitute duress—even if A threatens to do something which is not otherwise illegal.

At a more general level, there is one further observation we might make. Nonvolitional (type [a]) duress is essentially empirical. Whether or not B acts without volition is, it seems, fundamentally a matter of *fact*. On the other hand, the two-pronged theory of (type [b]) duress is at least partially moralized. Whether the choice prong is essentially empirical or moralized is a question we shall have to resolve. But the whole point of the proposal prong is to distinguish between morally permissible proposals, which do not constitute duress, and morally impermissible proposals, which do.

The Choice Prong

Though the *Restatement*'s two-pronged theory of contractual duress may have to be revised, it will be useful to adopt its framework as

[36] A can be bluffing, yet coerce. The question is not whether A has the ability to carry out his threat, but whether B can reasonably regard it as credible.

[37] "Persons of a weak or cowardly nature are the very ones that need protection. The courageous can usually protect themselves . . ." Ibid.

[38] I argue that this is misleading in Part Two.

[39] 941.

we examine the case law in more detail. The two-pronged theory can be understood as claiming that whereas the choice prong defines duress *simpliciter*—whatever that might be—there is wrongful and nonwrongful duress (as distinguished by the proposal prong), that only wrongful duress constitutes *legally recognizable* duress, and that only wrongful duress will invalidate a contract. Understanding contractual duress in this way was (perhaps too) liberating for the courts. For once courts held that nonwrongful duress would *not* invalidate a contract, they had less need to provide a satisfactory account of the choice prong itself. As John Dawson suggests, judges came to assume "that the wrongfulness of the means used made unnecessary any inquiry into their precise effects on the party coerced."[40] Yet some account of the choice prong seems necessary. A proposal, such as bribery, can be wrongful even if it does not coerce. We must be able to distinguish between wrongful coercive and noncoercive choice situations. And that seems to be the job of the choice prong.

The case law includes some clearly unsatisfactory accounts of the choice prong. *United States* v. *Bedford* concerned a breach of a lease agreement which Bedford had made with the General Services Administration, but which Bedford alleged had been made under duress.[41] In finding for Bedford, the court maintained that although it is "generally true that threatening to exercise a legal right does not constitute duress . . . such action may constitute duress *if the threat is made primarily to coerce someone into doing something he would otherwise not do.*"[42] If we ignore the first part of this statement, which refers to the proposal prong, the second part of the statement is clearly wrong. The point of virtually *all* proposals—coercive and noncoercive alike—is to get someone to do something he *otherwise* would not do. So that criterion will not help.

Although it is frequently (albeit sometimes only nominally) invoked, the "overborne will" theory does not fare much better. Recall the plight of Mr. Kaplan, who entered into a property settlement because his former wife had threatened to publicize his extramarital affair.[43] In finding no duress, the court held: "Even if we assume . . . that the threat is wrongful . . . we are not prepared

---

[40] "Economic Duress—An Essay in Perspective," 45 *Michigan Law Review* 253, 256 (1947).

[41] 491 F. Supp. 851 (1980). To extract favorable terms, the GSA had threatened to exercise a renewal option, knowing it would be financially disastrous to Bedford. In fact, the GSA had no intention of exercising the option.

[42] Ibid. (emphasis added).

[43] 182 N.E.2d 706 (1962).

to say as a matter of law that a threat of personal embarrassment . . . was such as to control the will of the plaintiff . . ." Duress, said the court, must be more than "annoyance or vexation," and Mrs. Kaplan's threat did not meet this more exacting standard. What would qualify? The court does not say.[44]

Or consider the case of Robinson, who contracted to pay his employer to avoid prosecution for embezzlement.[45] In finding against Robinson, the court said this: "The question . . . must be whether the person threatened was deprived of his freedom of will; and that is a question of fact . . ." But what facts? The court held that "the mere fact that one acts with reluctance or . . . in a mental state of perturbation . . . is not sufficient." And that seems right. But the court went on to say that duress "is tantamount to compulsion which is an impulse or feeling of being irresistibly driven toward the performance of some irrational action."[46] And that seems wrong. For even in the paradigm cases of duress, the party who acts under duress is engaged in volitional and rational action. Recall, for example, *Caivano* v. *Brill*. In holding that Caivano agreed to the kickback arrangement under duress, the court argued that the prevailing economic conditions and the superior position of the employer combined to destroy his "free agency."[47] Perhaps. But not because Caivano was "irresistibly driven" to an "irrational action."

While it is a mistake, then, to view all cases of contractual duress as nonvolitional, *Gallagher* v. *Robinson* was responding to a genuine difficulty. If the choice prong is understood in terms of B's "will," and what overbears B's will is a matter of *psychological fact*, it is difficult to identify the psychological facts to which it should refer. To say that a promisor is not coerced merely because he acts intentionally and rationally sets the standards for duress too high. At the same time, "to say that a choice is free enough to ground a promise only if it is in some sense gratuitous or unmotivated" sets the standards too low (if the notion of an unmotivated promise is coherent at all).[48]

One alternative, which the law has occasionally adopted, is to focus on the "will" of an artificial construct. On this account, B acts

---

[44] Also see *Dunham* v. *Griswold*. "It is not sufficient . . . that the threats were uttered . . . it must also be shown that they *constrained the will* . . ." 3 N.E. 76 (1885) (emphasis added).

[45] *Gallagher* v. *Robinson*, 232 N.E.2d 668 (1965).

[46] Ibid., 670, 671.

[47] 11 N.Y.S.2d 498, 502 (1939). Note that the court did not say that Caivano should recover his money simply because such kickbacks are immoral.

[48] Fried, *Contract as Promise* (Cambridge: Harvard University Press, 1981), 94.

under duress if A's proposal would overcome the will of "the reasonable man," "the brave man," or "the person of ordinary firmness."[49] Whether this provides an adequate account of the choice prong is a question to which I shall return. Here I want to make two points. First, to substitute the will of a "person of ordinary firmness" for the will of the person claiming duress does not modify the will theory; it abandons it. Second, to say that B acts under duress if A's proposal would overcome the will of a person of "ordinary firmness" (for example) is to employ an account of the choice prong which is transparently normative.

It is precisely these sorts of difficulties that have prompted P. S. Atiyah to remark that the " 'overborne will' theory should be consigned to the historical scrapheap." Indeed, he and others have suggested that we should abandon the entire concern with this dimension of duress and confine our attention to the morality of A's proposal.[50] Nicholas Rafferty, for example, approvingly quotes a nineteenth-century English case: "If a party making the payment is obliged to pay, in order to obtain possession of things to which he is entitled, the money so paid is not a voluntary, but a compulsory payment . . . whether there was a pressing necessity or not, he has a right to recover it back."[51] Making a similar point, Richard Epstein offers the following example of contractual duress: "Suppose that [A] has agreed to clean [B's] clothes for $10. After the work is done, [A] tells [B] that he will return the clothes only if [B] pays, or promises to pay, him $15. If [B] pays the $15, it is quite clear that he has an action to recover the $5 excess . . . [A] has required [B] to abandon one of his rights to protect another."[52]

There are two reasons for resisting the sort of proposal which Rafferty and Epstein advance and for insisting that some version of the choice prong be included in an account of duress. First, on conceptual grounds, it seems premature, if not simply wrong, to divorce the urgency of B's situation from a finding of duress. With reference to Epstein's case, for example, it simply begs the question to assume that B has been *required* to pay anything, particularly given that he could sue B to recover his clothes.

---

[49] "[D]uress . . . means that degree of constraint or danger . . . which is sufficient, in severity or apprehension, to overcome the mind and will of a person of ordinary firmness." *Pierce* v. *Brown*, 7 Wall 205 (1868).

[50] "Economic Duress and the 'Overborne Will'," 98 *Law Quarterly Review* 197 (1982).

[51] *Shaw* v. *Woodcock*, 108 E.R. 652, 657 (1827), cited in "The Element of Wrongful Pressure in a Finding of Duress," 18 *Alberta Law Review* 431, 440 (1980).

[52] "Unconscionability: A Critical Reappraisal," 18 *Journal of Law and Economics* 293, 296 (1975). I have changed Epstein's letters to correspond with my usage.

Second, the choice prong captures at least two important moral points. One moral point is this. People frequently have disputes in which they make threats of legal action. In some cases, A knows B is in the right and is merely trying to get something to which he is not entitled. In other cases, however, each side has a good-faith belief that its claim is justified or at least that it might be upheld. If A and B settle, each has foregone the opportunity to press his claim in court. In this sense, a settlement represents a genuine compromise even by one who may expect (statistically) to lose. And, it can be argued, the law should be very reluctant to undo such genuine compromises—particularly if B had a reasonable alternative to succumbing to A's proposal.

Another point is this. If B surrenders to A's threat and later seeks to have the contract voided, B is, in effect, asking the court to ignore that he acted with the deliberate intent that A should rely on his promise. As John Dalzell suggests, "There may have been serious wrong in the threat; but there is also something objectionable in the shift of position by [B] between the time he yields to the pressure and makes promise or payment, and the time he subsequently attacks the transaction in the courts for duress."[53] The point might be put this way. Our legal system is designed to provide remedies for (some) private wrongs. If one decides to forego what is an adequate remedy, it is arguable that society has done all that it needs to do.

Not only are there good reasons to retain some account of the choice prong in an account of contractual duress; I believe that the law has developed an account of the choice prong which (implicitly) responds to these very points. Recall *Austin* v. *Loral*. The court said not that Loral's will had been overborne but that "Loral . . . had no choice . . . except to take the gears at the 'coerced' price and then sue to get the excess back."[54] Now it is obvious that in *some* sense, Loral had a choice—it could have defaulted under the Navy contract and sued Austin for breach of contract. But the court understood that "no choice" should not be taken literally. It did not mean that it was logically or psychologically impossible for Loral to have done otherwise or that Loral had been driven to undertake some irrational action.[55] It meant that Loral had had "no *reasonable* choice" or "no *acceptable* alternative."

[53] Dalzell, "Duress by Economic Pressure: II," 1 *North Carolina Law Review* 341, 368 (1942).

[54] 29 N.Y.2d 124 (1971).

[55] As Justice Holmes once observed: "It is always in the interest of a party under duress to choose the lesser of two evils. But the fact that a choice was made according to interest does not exclude duress. It is the characteristic of duress properly so

I believe that some version of the "no reasonable choice" theory provides the best account of the choice prong in contract law and is consistent with most (although not all) of the cases, including those which nominally refer to "overborne wills." The "no reasonable choice" account helps, for example, to explain cases in which payments to utilities have been held to have been made under duress. Some argue that these cases demonstrate that contractual duress is rooted in the "inequality of the bargaining position" between the parties.[56] But inequality, per se, is not the gravamen of duress, as several of the sample cases make clear (for example, *LaBeach* v. *Beatrice*). The point is that utilities provide an essential service for which there is no alternative supplier, and it is often unreasonable to expect the customer to refuse to give in to a utility's demand and sue later in an attempt to recover.

This account of the choice prong also helps us to understand cases in which courts have rejected coercion claims. Recall *Meier* v. *Nightingale*. Meier had not paid to recover his car under duress, said the court, because Meier had had a reasonable alternative—to sue for breach of contract.[57] When a husband threatened to discontinue support for his wife if she did not agree to a divorce, the court ruled that the agreement had not been made under duress because the wife had known, or at least should have known, that the threat was specious.[58] As the Supreme Court held in one of its rare discussions of contractual duress, "Before the coercive effect of the threatened action can be inferred, there must be evidence of some probable consequences of it to person or property for which the remedy afforded by the courts is inadequate."[59]

Although courts are generally reluctant to find duress, they do understand that even when legal remedies are nominally available, they are not always adequate, that situations may arise in which one has no reasonable choice but to agree first and then sue to recover. Consider *Miller* v. *Eisele*, a complex case involving the stock

---

called." *Union Pacific Railroad Co.* v. *Public Service Commission of Missouri*, 248 U.S. 67, 70 (1931).

[56] Nicholas Rafferty, "The Element of Wrongful Pressure in a Finding of Duress," 435.

[57] 46 A.2d 785 (1945). Similarly, in *Tri-State Roofing Co.* v. *Simon*, the plaintiff threatened to breach its contract if the defendant refused to release it from liability for delay of performance. 142 A.2d 333 (1958). Simon signed a release, then claimed duress. The court found that Simon had had adequate legal remedies, and therefore there had been no duress.

[58] *Oberstein* v. *Oberstein*, 228 S.W.2d 615 (1950).

[59] *Hartsville Oil Mill* v. *U.S.*, 271 U.S. 44 (1925).

market crash of 1929.[60] Miller believed that his broker had opened an unauthorized account in his name and had made improper charges against it. The broker insisted otherwise. The market began to tumble. The broker indicated that unless Miller came forth with additional cash, it would sell some of his securities to cover his margin debt. Miller threatened to hold the broker responsible for the outcome, but it went ahead and sold half his securities and demanded additional cash payments if it was going to be barred from selling more. The market continued to fall, and in order to regain control of his stock, Miller reluctantly made the payments. He later claimed he had done so under duress. The court agreed. It might be objected that Miller had not made the payments under duress because he could have sued to collect the value of his stock. The court saw things differently: "in light of the developments since 1929," Miller should not have been required to "rely on his questionable remedy against the brokers . . . Time alone has since proven that his fears were those not only of a reasonable man, but those of a wise man."[61] Since Miller had had a reasonable fear that the broker would not be in business some years hence, a fear confirmed by the events of the Great Depression, the court upheld his claim.

Even if the "no reasonable choice" account of the choice prong is, at least in a rough way, on the right track, it does not follow that it is easily or always correctly applied.[62] Bluhm was threatened by Wolff's father with criminal prosecution (this was 1897) unless he signed a note to provide for the child he had allegedly fathered. After consulting with friends who advised him to settle, Bluhm signed the agreement. He subsequently claimed he had done so under duress. The court said this: "It is not the threat of criminal prosecution . . . that constitutes duress, but the condition of mind produced thereby . . . a threat of lawful arrest . . . where . . . there is no danger of the threat being immediately carried out does not constitute duress."[63] Despite the nominal reference to a psychological account of duress, the court's reasoning does not turn on references to Bluhm's state of mind. The court said, in effect, that since there had been no "immediate" threat of incarceration, Bluhm could not

[60] 168 A. 426 (1933).

[61] Ibid., 432.

[62] In *Neely's Appeal*, a prospective groom threatened not to go through with the marriage unless his fiancée signed a property settlement. The invitations were already out. The bride signed, tearfully, and later claimed she had done so under duress. The court ruled that because calling off the wedding was a reasonable alternative, there had been no duress. 16 A. 833 (1889).

[63] *Wolff* v. *Bluhm*, 70 N.W. 73 (1897).

37

reasonably claim he had had no acceptable alternatives (whatever his state of mind), and therefore could not claim that he had acted under duress. Perhaps, perhaps not.

A plausible theory can be not only misapplied but even put to rather perverse ends. It is arguable that this is just what happened in *King* v. *Lewis*. Lewis, a "negro" farmer, made unfavorable remarks about a local sheriff (King) before a grand jury. Lewis came to believe that King would sue him for slander unless he settled out of court, although King claimed that no direct threats were ever made. Lewis paid, then sued to recover, claiming he had paid under duress. Lewis won. King appealed. The court said:

> With an appreciation of the veneration and sometimes fear in which the "high sheriff" is held, especially by some members of the colored citizens in this southern country, we can well understand how the plaintiff, when he began to hear rumblings of the sheriff's wrath, could have become frightened and fearful of the consequences to himself . . . But apprehension . . . as to what the sheriff might do, even if it resulted in his signing notes which but for the fear thus generated he would not have signed, does not measure up to the legal definition of duress . . . It must be exerted by the other person or his agent, and can not be a creation of the mind of the person claiming his will has been restrained by fear.[64]

The court held, quite plausibly I think, that duress is a feature of the choice situation and not of one's state of mind, that it "must come from without, and not from within." The court was right to hold that Lewis was not coerced just because he *felt* coerced. On the other hand, it is by no means clear that Lewis was not coerced, even on the court's own criteria.

The Proposal Prong

On the two-pronged theory, B's contract is made under duress only if B has no choice—under some interpretation of the choice prong. We have seen, however, that this is not sufficient. B's contract is not made under duress unless A's proposal is "wrongful." Now a proposal is not wrongful—under the proposal prong—just because it is morally objectionable in some broad sense. Not any wrongfulness will do. What would do? The most important principles are these.

[64] 4 S.E.2d 464, 468 (1939).

First, it is wrong to propose to do that which is independently illegal. Second, and a corollary of the first principle, it is generally not wrong to propose to exercise a legal right: "It is not 'duress' to threaten to do that which a party has a legal right to do."[65] Third, there are exceptions to these two principles.

Causing and Taking Advantage. In distinguishing between wrongful and nonwrongful proposals, contract law holds that it is one thing for A to *cause* B's dilemma and quite another for A to take advantage of—to exploit—background circumstances for which A is not responsible.[66] Recall *Hackley* v. *Headley*, where Headley accepted less than he thought due him because he was in acute financial distress. In rejecting Headley's claim of duress, the court said: "It is not pretended that Hackley . . . had done anything to bring Headley to the condition . . . or that [Hackley was] in any manner responsible for [Headley's] pecuniary embarrassment."[67] Although many commentators and judges now disagree with *Hackley's* conclusion, its general *premise* is still largely accepted: "It has become settled law that the mere stress of business conditions will not constitute duress where [the other party] was not responsible for the circumstances."[68]

The distinction between causing and taking advantage of another's dilemma helps to reconcile arguably incompatible decisions. Recall *Ewert* v. *Lichtman* and *Hochman* v. *Zigler*. There is no reason to believe that Ewert was under less stress than Hochman or that he had more viable alternatives. There was, however, this difference. The Ewerts decided to sell their business because Mr. Ewert had taken ill. Lichtman used the situation to obtain a part of the sale price for himself.[69] In finding no duress, the court said: "The failing health of the complainants was doubtless the most influential factor in their ambition to retire from business. The prime obstructions were of their own making." Putting aside the doubtful notion that Ewert was responsible for his illness, it seems fair to assume that Lichtman was not. Zigler, on the other hand, precipitated Hoch-

---

[65] *Ellis* v. *First Nat. Bank*, 260 S.W. 714, 715 (1924). Or, "A lawful assertion of a legal right is not duress no matter how harsh that may be in its effects." *Molloy* v. *Bemis Bag Co.*, 174 F. Supp. 785, 791 (1959).

[66] "The assertion of duress must be proven to have been the result of the defendant's conduct and not by the plaintiff's necessities." Williston, *Contracts*, 3d ed. (New York: Baker, Voorhis, 1938), sec. 1617.

[67] 8 N.W. 511, 514 (1881).

[68] *Fruhauf Southwest Garment Co.* v. *U.S.*, 111 F. Supp. 945 (1953). See *Johnson, Drake, and Piper* v. *U.S.*, 531 F.2d 1037 (1976), and *Higgins* v. *Brunswick Corp.*, 395 N.E.2d 81 (1979).

[69] 55 A.2d 671 (1947).

man's dilemma by refusing to renew Hochman's lease.[70] Given that he had created Hochman's situation, Zigler, the court maintained, had had a "moral obligation to execute the lease" to the new buyer. Zigler's cut had been obtained under duress because Zigler had acted wrongly.

It might be objected that the distinction between causing and taking advantage of another's dilemma cannot be sustained or, at least, that it is of little significance. Dalzell, for example, maintains that when someone consciously takes advantage of another's adversity, "the fact that he did not create [it] should be treated as of little importance."[71] Now there is *no* reason to think that the *degree of pressure* on B at the time he contracts with A or the adequacy of the alternatives available to B is contingent on whether A, B, or anyone in particular caused B's dilemma. In that sense, Dalzell is correct. But if the point of the distinction is essentially moral, the distinction is not obviously unimportant. It may be argued that whatever might be said about B's choice situation itself, it is less wrong for A to take advantage of B's situation than to cause it (or even not wrong at all). And because it is less (or not) wrong, it does not constitute legally recognizable duress.

Exploitation or unconscionability can, of course, serve as grounds to invalidate a contract independent of considerations of duress. At the same time, it seems that a liberal theory of contract needs to presuppose *some* moral distinction between pressures which A exerts on B and those which are (at least with respect to A) simply part of B's background circumstances (even if they are caused by other persons). To the extent that the distinction between causing and taking advantage serves to capture this moral point, it seems to be on safe conceptual ground, although there can be reasonable disagreement as to just how *much* moral weight the distinction can bear.

There are, it should be noted, at least some cases which suggest that A's proposal may be coercive even if A has not caused B's dilemma. Recall *Caivano* v. *Brill*. Brill did not create Caivano's unemployment and did not have to offer him a job. Still, Caivano had no viable alternative but to accept Brill's offer, and because (according to the court) the proposal was wrongful, the court held that the kickbacks had been paid under duress.[72] Is *Caivano* consistent with

[70] 50 A.2d 97 (1947).

[71] "Duress by Economic Pressure," 1 *North Carolina Law Review* 240, 257 (1941).

[72] 11 N.Y.S.2d 498 (1939). Similarly, to make a waiver of workmen's compensation a condition of employment was held to constitute coercion, even if the company did

the distinction between causing and taking advantage, between duress and exploitation? One possibility is that it is not and that it was wrong to find duress, even if it might not have been wrong to invalidate the agreement on other grounds. It could, however, be argued that taking advantage of another's situation, although not prima facie wrong, could nonetheless be sufficiently wrong in a particular case to qualify as immoral and therefore as legally recognizable duress.

Nonwrongful Threats. The question of causation aside, there is generally no duress if A's proposal is not wrongful—even if it serves to *create* B's dilemma. B.I.C. had a contract with Sony under which B.I.C. would be paid a commission for securing customers to use Sony products as business incentives. The contract was terminable by either party. Sony told B.I.C. that it would terminate the relationship if B.I.C. did not agree to new terms. B.I.C. agreed and then claimed it had done so under duress. The court ruled that there had been no duress because Sony had merely proposed to exercise a preexisting right.[73] In *Simmonds Precision Products, Inc.* v. *United States*, the plaintiff had not met the conditions of its contract, and the government's contracting officer had gotten Simmonds to modify its contract by threatening to place it on the "Contractor's Experience List."[74] The modifications had not been made under duress, the court said, because "there was nothing offensively coercive or unfair in the threat." The court did not deny that the government's threat was (in some sense) coercive. Rather, it was not "offensively" coercive, therefore there was no duress.[75]

Yet the oft-cited rule that it "is not 'duress' to threaten to do that which a party has a legal right to do" is somewhat misleading.[76] It is misleading because, as Justice Holmes once remarked, "It does not follow that, because you cannot be made to answer for the act, you may use the threat."[77] Indeed, not only may it be wrongful for A to threaten to do what he has a *right* to do; it may be wrong for A to threaten to do what he has an *obligation* to do, as when Shasta

---

not have to offer a job at all. *Red Rover Copper Co.* v. *Industrial Commission*, 118 P.2d 1102 (1941).

[73] *Business Incentives Co. Inc.* v. *Sony Corp.*, 387 F. Supp. 63 (1975).

[74] 546 F.2d 886 (1976).

[75] Also see *Mills* v. *U.S.*, 410 F.2d 1255 (1969).

[76] *Ellis* v. *First Nat. Bank*, 260 S.W. 714, 715 (1924).

[77] *Silsbee* v. *Webber*, 50 N.E. 555 (1898). It is now settled law that it may be wrongful to propose to carry out an action which is independently legal. Williston, *Contracts*, sec. 1606. Also see *The Restatement of Contracts*, Sec. 492.

threatened to report Croke's crime to the authorities if Croke did not make an agreement with Shasta.[78]

Consider the threat to sue. Assuming that a threat to sue meets the choice prong of contractual duress, it will generally not meet the proposal prong. The threat to sue is, after all, arguably nothing more "than a statement of intent to refer a private dispute to a public tribunal for orderly settlement; how can it be duress to tell the adverse party that these tribunals are to be called in to administer justice according to established law?"[79] As the court said about DuPuy's settlement with the IRS, "the fact that one of the parties signed the settlement to avoid the trouble and expense of a law suit does not amount to intimidation or duress for that is ordinarily the purpose of a settlement . . ."[80]

The threat to sue is not wrongful and does not constitute contractual duress if it is not abused.[81] What constitutes abuse? The distinction between good-faith and bad-faith suits is certainly important. If A *knows* he has no valid cause of action against B, the contract can be voided for duress.[82] Recall, for example, that in *DuPuy* the court said, "If the counsel for the government had acted in bad faith, the conclusion would be different."[83] On the other hand, a good-faith suit will generally not constitute duress, even if it is unmeritorious. When A's executor, mistakenly believing that B had not already paid, got B to pay a debt a second time by threatening to sue, the court found no duress.[84]

Now it might be thought that if A induces B to contract with him by threatening an unmeritorious suit, something wrong has occurred. But that would be to substitute hindsight for reasonable foresight. Suppose that A threatens to sue B for $1,000,000, but is willing to settle for $100,000. B believes he has a 70 percent chance

---

[78] *Shasta* v. *Croke*.

[79] Dalzell, "Duress by Economic Pressure: II," 344. In *Campbell* v. *Parker*, the court held that a promissory note induced by a threat to sue was not duress, since the plaintiff "was informing defendant of his lawful rights." 209 So.2d 337 (1968).

[80] *DuPuy* v. *U.S.*, 35 F.2d 990, 1003 (1929).

[81] For a general discussion of this issue, see Dawson, "Duress through Civil Litigation," 45 *Michigan Law Review* 571 (1947).

[82] For a discussion of such cases, see Dalzell, "Duress by Economic Pressure: II," 345. Here, we might say there is a union of fraud and duress.

[83] 33 F.2d 990, 1003 (1929).

[84] *Shockley* v. *Wickliffe*, 148 S.E. 746 (1929). Or, in the words of *King* v. *Lewis*, "an agreement is valid and binding, not because it is a settlement of a valid claim, but because it is a settlement of a bona fide controversy." 4 S.E.2d 464, 468 (1939). Similar reasoning was advanced in *Smedley* v. *Lansing*, where it was held that there was no evidence that Smedley's belief that it was entitled to be paid "was not honestly held or was so patently untenable as to be groundless." 398 A.2d 1208, 1209 (1978).

of winning and not paying anything. Ignoring litigation costs on both sides (which, of course, provide additional motivation to settle), the *ex ante* cost of the settlement to B is $100,000 and the *ex ante* cost of a suit is $300,000 (30 percent times $1,000,000), so the expected benefit to B from the settlement is $200,000. A system which frequently voided such agreements for duress would discourage A from proposing such settlements in the first place—a consequence which B would clearly want to avoid.

Interestingly, just as A can make a good-faith threat to sue although he lacks a valid cause of action, A can make a bad-faith threat while having a valid cause of action. A textbook case concerns a creditor who procured a writ of attachment against the debtor's ice wagon in the predawn hours when it was already loaded with ice. To reclaim his wagon, the debtor paid. His only alternative was to post a bond. That process would have taken him three days, by which time his ice would have been lost.[85] Because the creditor had initiated his action at a time when the defendant was helpless, the court ruled that the debtor had paid under duress.

The principle that it is wrong to abuse what would otherwise be a legal right is perhaps most evident when A proposes to exercise a right that he has in virtue of the criminal law. In *Shasta* v. *Croke*, the court ruled that Shasta's threat to press charges against Croke for embezzlement "as a means of collecting a debt is against public policy . . ."[86] In another case, Thompson had been injured in Niggley's saloon and wanted compensation from Niggley. Thompson also knew that Niggley was selling liquor illegally, and threatened to press charges against Niggley unless Niggley settled the dispute over compensation on terms acceptable to Thompson. Niggley settled, then sued to recover. The court held that Niggley had acted under duress, because it was not "inclined to encourage a resort to such pressure . . . to compel the settlement of private demands."[87]

The abuse of the right to sue and the abuse of the right to press charges for a crime can be seen as violations of a more general principle, to wit, that legal processes should not be used outside their proper sphere or to secure an unrelated or improper benefit.[88] Thus in a 1909 case the court ruled that a deed obtained by a threat to press charges against one's wife for adultery is duress (adultery was

[85] *Chandler* v. *Sanger*, 114 Mass. 364 (1874).
[86] 276 P.2d 88 (1954). Also see *Gallagher* v. *Robinson*, 232 N.E.2d 668 (1965).
[87] *Thompson* v. *Niggley*, 35 P. 240, 241 (1894).
[88] There is a strong parallel here between the legal notion of wrongfulness and the account of justice developed in Michael Walzer's *Spheres of Justice*.

then a criminal offense).[89] Similarly, a transfer of stock from wife to husband was voided for duress because it had been obtained by the husband's threat to sue for sole custody of their children, a threat made more credible because the wife had confessed to adultery.[90] In *Lafayette* v. *Ferentz*, the court held that a threat to strike is a legitimate means to secure higher wages, but not to force the employer to hire unwanted and unneeded employees.[91] As the court held in *Hochman* v. *Zigler*, "if the threat is made for an outrageous purpose, a more critical standard is applied."[92]

Does a threat to breach a contract constitute duress? Interestingly, it often does not. There are two reasons for this. First, as we have already seen, A's threat to breach will not always meet the choice prong. B ordinarily has an adequate remedy for which the law provides—to sue for breach of contract. But suppose that the remedy is not adequate. Would a threat to breach then constitute duress? Often, yes; sometimes, no. Circumstances change, and it might be more reasonable for both parties to agree to modify their contract than for A to breach and B to sue for damages.[93] Suffice it to say that some threats to breach are *not* reasonable, and therefore may constitute duress. Rosellini, a building contractor, needed installment payments to pay his subcontractors. Banchero knew Rosellini needed the payments, and told Rosellini it was dissatisfied with his work and would withhold payments unless Rosellini lowered the ceiling price on the job. Rosellini agreed to the modification and then sued to recover the full price. The court invalidated the modification because Banchero's expression of dissatisfaction had been disingenuous and because Banchero could have made the installment payments without exceeding what it claimed to be a reasonable price.[94]

Internal and External Wrongs. More could be (and has been) said about the kinds of proposals that courts consider wrongful, but given my philosophical purposes, it is not necessary to say more here. Instead I want to raise a different and more general problem

[89] *Kwentisky* v. *Sirpovy*, 121 N.W. 27 (1909).

[90] *Link* v. *Link*, 179 S.E.2d 697 (1971).

[91] 9 N.W.2d 57 (1934)

[92] 50 A.2d 97, 100 (1946).

[93] See Henry Mather, "Contract Modification under Duress," 33 *South Carolina Law Review* 615 (1982).

[94] *Rosellini* v. *Banchero*, 517 P.2d 955 (1974). In fact, the court ruled on the ground that Rosellini had received "no new consideration" for the modification, but the decision could and (probably) should have been grounded on duress. See "Modification Agreements: Need for New Consideration," 50 *Washington Law Review* 960 (1975).

about the way moral criteria figure in the theory of contractual duress. Roughly speaking, there are two moral questions that might be raised about a contract: (1) Would it be wrong to enforce the contract because of some problem *internal* to the contract itself (that is, its process or its result)? (2) Would enforcing the contract have undesirable *external* consequences for the society as a whole? While the standard analyses of contractual duress typically focus on *internal* moral criteria, some cases seem to turn on a court's concerns about *external* or *public policy* considerations. In upholding Headley's agreement with Hackley, for example, the court argued that to find duress because of Headley's unfortunate financial difficulties "would be a most dangerous . . . doctrine . . . no one could well know when he would be safe in dealing on the ordinary terms of negotiation with a party who professed to be in great need."[95] When the Georgia Pacific Corporation got Capps to accept less than his due because he was in financial straits and the company threatened to tie him up in court, the court found no duress. A concurring opinion said: "This seems to be as strong a case for the operation of the doctrine of economic duress as can be made. Nevertheless, I believe it would be judicially unwise to hold that these allegations constitute economic duress . . . because . . . a substantial number of business transactions today have these same basic ingredients."[96]

Is the two-pronged theory of contractual duress consistent with the appeal to such external considerations? It depends. The appeal to policy considerations might be rooted in epistemological difficulties. It might be argued that because it is difficult to determine just when B acts under duress, it is (generally) better to make a very strong presumption that he does not. This view does not appeal to public policy criteria in determining whether B in fact acts under duress. It maintains only that it might be best to *hold* that someone does not act under duress—even if he does—just as it might be better to acquit someone of a crime even if he is guilty than to find someone guilty when he is not. A more interesting question is whether, as some cases suggest, public policy considerations are properly considered within the framework of the proposal prong of contractual duress. In *Shasta* v. *Croke*, the court remarked that using a threat of criminal prosecution to secure an agreement is "against public policy; such threats . . . constitute a menace destructive of free consent." It is not clear whether the court meant to provide two

---

[95] *Hackley* v. *Headley*, 8 N.W. 511, 514 (1881).
[96] *Capps* v. *Georgia Pacific Corp.*, 453 P.2d 935 (1969).

independent rationales for its decision or whether it believed that there was a relation between them. On the latter view, whether B in fact acts under duress is dependent upon the policy consequences of holding that he does. Whether such a view can be defended is a question to which I shall return.

The Voluntariness Problem

Let us suppose that my formulation of the principles of contractual duress is essentially correct. Properly defined and applied, the two-pronged theory yields the conclusion that a contract is binding if and only if it ought to be binding. There are, nonetheless, two related objections that can be raised about the theory, and in particular about the notion that B is coerced only if A's proposal is wrong. The first objection may be put this way. Even if we need something like the proposal prong to tell us when a contract should be legally *enforced*, that may only show that some coerced contracts should be enforced despite their being coerced. The two-pronged theory may yield the right legal consequences, but it does not provide a satisfactory account of *coercion*. For coercion has to do with freedom and not enforceability. The second objection might be put this way. Perhaps, it may be said, there is a distinction between being coerced and acting involuntarily. Even if the two-pronged theory gives a satisfactory account of *coercion* or *duress*, that only goes to show that coercion does not, in fact, compromise the *voluntariness* of an action. How, it might be asked, can the *voluntariness* of B's action have anything to do with A's right to make his proposal? On either argument, then, the two-pronged theory of coercion is incompatible with the view that coerced agreements should not be enforced because they are involuntary. Call this the voluntariness problem.

The voluntariness problem is raised by at least two additional features of contractual duress. We noted above that the *Restatement of Contracts* distinguishes between volitional and nonvolitional coercion. It seems that these two types of contractual duress have different legal upshots: nonvolitional contracts are said to be *void*; contracts made under volitional duress are said to be *voidable*. To say that a contract is *void* is to say that it is invalid and no subsequent acquiescence will change its original status. To say that a contract is void*able* is to say that if B makes an agreement under duress but does not challenge it when the duress is no longer operative, B cannot subsequently seek to have it invalidated. B's acquiescence removes the stigma attached to the original contract. If, as on the two-pronged theory, a contract is voidable only if A acts wrongly, and if B acts wrongly in first benefiting from the contract and subsequently challenging it, then B's later wrongness may cancel the force of A's earlier wrongness—thereby eliminating the finding of duress. While this move may explain the principle that a contract made under volitional duress is voidable, but not void, it also suggests that volitional duress does *not* undermine the voluntariness of one's contract. For if volitional duress does undermine the voluntariness of one's contract, it is difficult to see why we should distinguish between the enforceability of volitional and nonvolitional contracts in the first place.[97]

Consider, too, the problem of third-party duress. The ordinary case of contractual duress involves two parties: A coerces B into making a contract with A. But suppose that A coerces B into making a contract with C. The standard rule about three-party cases is that "the contract is voidable by the victim unless the other party to the transaction in good faith and without reason to know of the undue influence either gives value or relies materially on the transaction."[98] If C has not acted wrongfully, then B is bound by his contract with C—whatever cause of action B may have against A. When a young man executed a mortgage to secure a loan to his father and subsequently claimed that his father had coerced him into doing so, the court held that the bank should not lose its money because of a dispute between the man and his father.[99] By contrast, B's contract with C is voidable if C has *not* relied to his detriment on the agreement. So, too, if C knows of or conspires with A's coercion.[100]

Now I see nothing inherently problematic about the principle that A's coercion of B should not undermine B's contract with an innocent C. Its legal result seems correct. The principle presents an interesting problem because it threatens to undermine the principle that only voluntary contracts are binding.[101] It could, of course, be argued that while B's agreement *is* involuntary, it should be upheld, nonetheless, because it would be unfair to make C bear the costs of A's wrongdoing. But even if that argument justifies the rule on three-party cases, it does so by abandoning the notion that a coerced contract cannot be binding. Another argument attempts to

---

[97] See Atiyah, "Economic Duress and the 'Overborne Will'," 201.

[98] Williston, *Contracts*, sec. 1622A.

[99] *Detroit National Bank* v. *Blodgett*, 115 Mich. 160.

[100] *Restatement*, Sec. 496.

[101] In reviewing the literature, I have not found *any* attempt to square the rule on third-party duress with the principle that a valid contract must be voluntary or even any sensitivity to the fact that this might be a problem.

square the rule on third-party duress with the principle that coerced contracts are not binding. There are at least two possible versions of this argument. It might be held that coercion is a *relational* concept, that people coerce, but circumstances do not. On this view, B's agreement is *coerced* vis-à-vis *A*, but it is *not coerced* vis-à-vis *C*. A second version argues that the requisite wrongness must be due to the party with whom the contract is made. Although the proposal prong may be satisfied with respect to A, it is not satisfied with respect to C, and hence there is no duress. Yet, once again, even if these arguments serve to justify the *rule* on third-party duress, it is arguable that they do so by abandoning the connection between coercion and involuntariness.

Economic Analysis of Duress

The voluntariness problem can also be seen from the standpoint of what has become an important if not the dominant intellectual approach among contemporary legal scholars—the economic analysis of law. Roughly speaking, this approach involves both a descriptive and a prescriptive thesis. The *descriptive* thesis holds that the content of and changes in legal rules are best explained by the premise that the law attempts to promote economic efficiency or the maximization of wealth. The *prescriptive* thesis maintains that whatever the actual effect of legal rules and principles, they *should* serve to promote economic efficiency or maximize wealth. The two theses are independent. Whether or not the descriptive thesis provides the best account of American law, it does not follow that economic efficiency *should* be the law's primary objective. Whether or not the law has historically served to promote economic efficiency, it may be that it should do so.[102] The prescriptive thesis is clearly the more interesting for our purposes.

The economic analysis of law maintains that persons will ordinarily make agreements only if they expect to be better off. Because voluntary agreements are typically efficient (or Pareto-superior), at least as between the parties involved, the law should encourage such contracts by enforcing their terms. What of contracts made under duress? Nonvolitional agreements present no difficulties for the

[102] There is a large and growing literature on the economic analysis of law. Perhaps the single most important work is Richard Posner's *Economic Analysis of Law* (Boston: Little, Brown, 1977). A good collection of essays for philosophers is *Law, Economics, and Philosophy*, ed. Kupperberg and Beitz (Totowa, N.J.: Rowman and Allanheld, 1983).

economic analysis of law. If B is not exercising his volition or is incapable of making rational judgments about his interests, then according to the leading advocate of this school, there is no "presumption that the contracts he makes increase value."[103] Nonvolitional agreements should not be enforced, not because they are involuntary, but because we cannot assume that such agreements promote economic efficiency (even if they fail to promote efficiency because they are involuntary).

But what of constrained volition? What of those cases where, under the circumstances, one's decision "increases value"? Will economic analysis insist that such agreements be enforced? Probably not. Economic analysts of law maintain that the general (capitalist) scheme of rights in one's person and property is economically efficient. Contracts made under duress interfere with that scheme because they require an individual to abandon one of his rights to protect another.[104] When the gunman says, "Your money or your life," the victim is required to abandon his right to his money in order to protect his life. The contract should be set aside, but not because the victim acts involuntarily. To the contrary. Richard Posner argues that the gunman's victim is, in fact, "extremely eager" to exchange his promise of money for the gunman's "forbearance." The point, says Posner, is that enforcing such agreements "retards rather than advances the movement of resources to successively more valuable uses."[105]

The economic theory of law can also be applied to contractual duress in a slightly different way. Anthony Kronman has observed that in the process of bargaining, individuals may make use of various characteristics, abilities, or "advantages"—for example, charm, business acuity, beauty, information, rectitude, and physical strength.[106] As things stand, the law allows people to exploit some of these advantages (for example, intelligence), but not others (for example, physical strength). Why? On one traditional view, the assertion of some advantages (for example, physical strength) interferes with the other person's liberty, whereas the assertion of other advantages (for example, intelligence) does not. The economic analysis of law would see this differently. It would argue that there is no

---

[103] Posner, *Economic Analysis of Law*, 49.

[104] "The defense of duress allows . . . a defendant in a contract action . . . to vindicate *both* his initial entitlements, even though he has yielded to the force of the moment . . . consent has been given, but there is good reason to set it aside." Epstein, "Unconscionability: A Critical Reappraisal," 296.

[105] *Economic Analysis of Law*, 49.

[106] "Contract Law and Distributive Justice," 480.

inherent or liberty-based distinction between the different forms of advantage taking, but that whereas a rule permitting contracts generated by physical coercion would be nonproductive, a rule which allows well-informed parties to exploit their knowledge and information enhances efficiency.[107]

The economic analysis of law is, at least potentially, compatible with the two-pronged theory of duress. For a conception of immorality (as inefficiency) does underlie its account of duress. Unfortunately, this potential compatibility with the two-pronged theory also serves to reinforce the previous doubts about the connection between contractual duress and involuntariness. For the whole point of the economic analysis of contractual duress is that duress typically does *not* involve a deprivation of voluntariness; rather, it interferes with the maximization of wealth.

Of course, all this is of concern only if the economic analysis of law is true, and that is a question I prefer not to pursue. This much can be said. Whatever insights might be gained from the economic analysis of duress, that approach does not seem to properly *locate* the wrongness of using the threat of physical harm, as illustrated by its account of the gunman case.[108] But my point is not just that its explanation of coercion is intuitively unsatisfying, but that the intuitive oddness of this explanation lends credence to the view that a proper account of duress must show that and how duress undermines freedom and is not simply inefficient or otherwise wrong.

Duress, Fairness, and Autonomy

I noted, at the outset of this chapter, that some scholars argue that contract law is rooted in considerations of fairness and reciprocity, not of promise, voluntariness, and autonomy.[109] Recall, in this connection, Kronman's observation that in bargaining with others, one is permitted to exploit one's information, knowledge, and financial resources, but not one's capacity for deception or one's superior

[107] Ibid., 490.

[108] If its account of contractual duress seems intuitively unsatisfying, consider its account of exploitation. Suppose, says Posner, that A finds B wandering in the woods, lost in a snowstorm; A refuses to help B unless B promises all his wealth to A. A court should refuse to enforce such a promise. Why? Not because A's proposal is coercive. The point, says Posner, is that "if we permit monopoly profits in rescue operations, an excessive amount of resources will be attracted to the rescue business." *Economic Analysis of Law*, 49.

[109] Atiyah, in fact, argues that the obligation to keep a *promise* is rooted in reciprocity rather than in some notion of a voluntary undertaking. See *Promises, Morals, and Law*.

strength—although superiorities in intelligence, information, and financial resources are, at least in principle, no less *powerful* than superiorities in physical strength. What does this show? According to Kronman, it shows that the fundamental question is *not* what constitutes duress or coercion but which forms of advantage taking are consistent with distributive *justice*—at least on an account of distributive justice which emphasizes considerations of equality and fairness in result.[110] It shows that the conditions under which contracts are valid are a matter of *public policy*, and not a function of the quality of the private relationship. Kronman draws a radical conclusion from this:

> no one should be allowed to exploit his financial resources in transactions with others to any greater extent than he should be allowed to exploit his superior intelligence, strength, or information . . . each of these represents wealth of a different kind . . . but it is unclear why any importance should be attached to differences of this sort. If . . . advantage-taking . . . based on superior information . . . must be justified by showing that it is consistent with a particular conception of distributive justice, other kinds of advantage-taking, including those attributable to inequalities of a financial sort, should be justified in the same way. *It is simply arbitrary to assert that some forms of advantage-taking need to be justified but others need not be.*[111]

The view that the fundamental criteria for evaluating contracts are based on considerations of justice rather than of process might be supported in another way. I argued at the outset of this chapter that the ability to contract is a crucial dimension of our freedom, and that this creative dimension of contract requires intervention—by way of enforcement—by the state. It might be said that because private contracts require state enforcement, contracts are not essentially private. Since the state is implicated in private contract from the beginning, it would be arbitrary to restrict the state's intervention to assuring that the contract satisfied certain private criteria, such as the voluntariness principle. Precisely because there is no

---

[110] It is possible, of course, that considerations of freedom and autonomy are crucial to a fully developed theory of justice, as they are for Rawls. Similarly, even a theory which places equality at its core may provide considerable room for traditional notions of freedom and autonomy. See, for example, Ronald Dworkin "What Is Equality? Part 1: Equality of Welfare," 10 *Philosophy & Public Affairs* 185 (1981), and "What Is Equality? Part 2: Equality of Resources," 10 *Philosophy & Public Affairs* 283 (1981).

[111] "Contract Law and Distributive Justice," 497 (emphasis added).

"bright line" between the public and the private, it is legitimate for the state to see that contracts meet public or societal standards of acceptability. On this view, the distinction between unconsciona-bility and duress is largely collapsed; the entire point of the doctrine of duress is that it is designed to "police the limits of 'fair' bar-gain."[112]

Now there is, at least potentially, a good deal at stake here. If dis-tributive justice or other standards of public acceptability are the primary criteria for evaluating contracts, there may be little left to the notion of freedom of contract.[113] Perhaps this is so. Perhaps lib-erty and autonomy are not independently valuable or are less val-uable than we typically suppose. It would, however, be premature to conclude that duress is assimilable to unfairness or that if it is, Kronman's conception of fairness is correct. First, even if, as Kron-man suggests, force and fraud generate inequalities in advantage taking, the motivation for their condemnation may have little to do with eliminating such inequalities. Second, although Kronman rightly observes that it "is simply arbitrary to assert that some forms of advantage-taking need to be justified but others need not be," it is not arbitrary to assert that some forms of advantage taking *can* be justified and others *cannot* be. It is, at least in principle, possible that the distinction between legitimate and illegitimate forms of advan-tage taking can be made by a theory which does not appeal (pri-marily) to considerations of equality or fairness in result.

We could put the point this way. It is correct to point out that the argument that contracts preserve autonomy must not presuppose what it seeks to prove. If we wish to argue that individuals are free to enter into contracts with each other so long as their agreements are voluntary, we must start from some conception of the individ-ual, and the notion of autonomy cannot define that conception without begging the question at hand. In particular, we must be able to distinguish between factors which constitute an individual's situation and those which can be regarded as external forces. It would, however, be a mistake to assume, without argument, that the proper conception of an individual's situation derives solely from (result-oriented) considerations of distributive justice. For it is

---

[112] Clare Dalton, "An Essay in the Deconstruction of Contract Doctrine," 94 *Harvard Law Review* 997, 1024 (1985).

[113] Fried puts it this way: "if there is not even any stable way to define what a per-son's entitlements or rights are before we proceed to consider redistributing . . . then liberty is not possible in the deep, philosophical sense. It is not an independent con-cept at all." "Is Liberty Possible?" 91.

possible that the best theory will define an individual's position in terms of personal and property *rights* that give an individual considerable scope for action, including rights which produce unequal—indeed, unfair—results.

Conclusions and Questions

Because contract provides a model for a variety of legal contexts in which a party claims that he acted under duress, it was necessary to consider many issues in some detail. What have we found? First, contract law distinguishes between nonvolitional duress and constrained-volition duress. Second, in the standard cases of duress, contract law employs a two-pronged theory of duress. B acts under duress if, under the choice prong, A creates a choice situation for B in which B has no choice but to accept A's proposal and if, under the proposal prong, A acts wrongly in creating B's choice situation. Although there is considerable consensus about the structure of that theory, there is less consensus on the appropriate criteria for the choice and proposal prongs.

If we step back from the two-pronged theory, there are two additional and related points that can be made. First, we have seen it argued that contractual duress has little to do with freedom and voluntariness, and everything to do with wrongness or unfairness. Although it seems wise not to assume that the two-pronged theory cannot be connected with the voluntariness of an agreement, this is a problem that will demand our attention.

Second, given the distinction between "empirical" and "moralized" theories of coercion, it is clear that the two-pronged theory of contractual duress is at least partially moralized. That the proposal prong is moralized is clear. In subsequent chapters, I shall argue that the choice prong is also thoroughly moralized, and not just in the relatively trivial sense that what constitutes a "reasonable" alternative involves the application of some normative criteria. In any case, it is evident that either the right philosophical theory of duress is a moralized theory or the two-pronged theory of contractual duress is not philosophically defensible.

T H R E E

TORTS: ASSUMED RISK AND
INFORMED CONSENT

Although contracts and torts are closely related, there is this structural difference between them. In *contracts*, B undertakes an obligation that he otherwise would not have. If B's contract is made under duress, B is released from his obligation. In *torts*, A begins with an obligation not to harm B (or impose a *risk* of harm on B), an obligation which B can waive. If B waives A's obligation not to harm him under duress, A is still under an obligation and B can recover should he be injured.[1]

A priori, there is no reason why B should not be permitted to assume risks he has no obligation to assume. The principle that one can voluntarily consent to what would otherwise be an intentional or unintentional wrong is captured by the maxim *volenti non fit injuria* (to one who consents no wrong is done).[2] Sometimes it will be rational for B to assume such risks, although that will not always be true. But respect for autonomy requires that people be given (at least some) latitude to risk injury they need not (or even should not) risk.[3]

As with contracts, the *volenti* principle requires that consent be

[1] As I noted in Chapter 2, legal scholars disagree as to the significance of the distinction between contracts and torts, and these debates are not without philosophical interest. Fortunately, the debate has little bearing on the theory of coercion.

[2] *Injuria* is a *normative* term. Although one can obviously be *physically* injured even with one's consent, such an injury is not a legal *wrong* if the risk of injury is voluntarily assumed. The *volenti* principle is closely related to the "harm principle," which holds that the state is justified in using the criminal law to prevent one person from harming another. A harm does not count as a harm—for the purposes of applying the harm principle—if B has consented to the risk of harm. The literature on the harm principle is, of course, enormous. Two recent and extended discussions are John Hodson, *The Ethics of Legal Coercion* (Dordrecht: D. Reidel, 1983), and Joel Feinberg, *Harm to Others* (Oxford: Oxford University Press, 1984).

[3] As Francis Bohlen puts it in his classic article, the *volenti* principle is "a terse expression of the individualistic tendency of the common law, which [holds that] each individual is left free to work out his own destinies; he must not be interfered with from without, but in the absence of such interference he is held competent to protect himself." "Voluntary Assumption of Risk," 20 *Harvard Law Review* 14 (1906).

voluntary, that it not result from coercion or duress. In the sections that follow, I shall focus on applications of this principle in three contexts: assumed risk; informed consent to medical procedures; and informed consent by the poor and the institutionalized.

Assumed Risk

The standard view of assumed risk is advanced in the American Law Institute's *Restatement of Torts*:

> The plaintiff's acceptance of the risk is to be regarded as voluntary even though he is acting under the compulsion of circumstances, not created by the tortious conduct of the defendant, which have left him no reasonable alternative. Where the defendant is under no independent duty to the plaintiff, and the plaintiff finds himself confronted by a choice of risks, or is driven by his own necessities to accept a danger, the situation is not to be charged against the defendant.[4]

The appeal to the two-pronged account of duress is less explicit in the *Restatement of Torts* than in the *Restatement of Contracts*, but the underlying theory is virtually identical. When the *Restatement of Torts* says that an assumption of risk "is to be *regarded* as voluntary," it implies that meeting the choice prong of duress does not invalidate the waiver of one's right. It may be true, says the *Restatement*, that the plaintiff is led to assume a risk because of "the compulsion of circumstances," but assuming that the defendant did not act wrongly, the plaintiff "assumes the risk notwithstanding the compulsion under which he is acting."

The account of the choice prong in the *Restatement of Torts* is even more underdeveloped than the corresponding account in the *Restatement of Contracts*.[5] As with contracts, the proposal prong does most of the work. Indeed, some say that it does it all. As one text puts it, "If . . . defendant is not privileged to put plaintiff to the choice of taking or leaving a danger, the mere *posing* of the dilemma

---

[4] *Restatement of Torts*, Sec. 496E, Comment (b).

[5] However, the relevant case law and scholarly literature are not, as with contracts, correspondingly rich. One finds considerable discussion as to what constitutes an "assumption of risk," but little debate as to what constitutes a *coerced* assumption of risk. A standard text includes only one index citation to duress, and that section, entitled "Fraud or Duress" (it is not clear whether the authors believe there is no distinction), cites several cases of fraud, but none of duress. See Charles Gregory, Harry Kalven, Jr., and Richard Epstein, *Cases and Materials on Torts* (Boston: Little, Brown, 1977), 13.

takes away the voluntary character of any assumption there may be of the risk."[6]

But even if the choice prong is relatively unimportant, it cannot be ignored. Consider, for example, a case in which A sets B's house on fire, and B incurs serious burns while trying to save his television. The law, says William Prosser, will regard B as voluntarily assuming (at least some of) the risk. If the danger to B (greatly) exceeds the value of the endangered interest, then B "may be charged with contributory negligence in his own unreasonable conduct."[7] It is generally true, says Prosser, that if A's negligence puts B's property at risk, injuries that B suffers while trying to save his property can be charged to A.[8] On the other hand, if there is a "reasonably safe alternative" (for example, to let the television burn and sue later), B's choice of "the dangerous way is a *free one* . . ."[9] His assumption of risk is not coerced.

The "proposal prong" also has its analogue in torts, although here the term is a slight misnomer, for there may be no specific proposals at all.[10] The general idea is that A's conduct, broadly construed, does not constitute coercion unless it is wrongful (in the relevant sense). There is, of course, considerable debate as to what constitutes wrongful or tortious conduct. It seems, for example, that B's assumption of risk will be treated as voluntary if there is no *prior* relationship between A and B such that A has some special responsibility for or "independent duty" to B. The *Restatement* maintains, for example, that "a plaintiff who is forced to rent a house which is in obviously dangerous condition because he cannot find another dwelling, or cannot afford another, assumes the risk notwithstanding the compulsion under which he is acting."[11] The landlord may be taking advantage of his tenant's need for housing, but assuming that he is not responsible for the tenant's need, there may be nothing tortious in his behavior. As one text puts it, "The plaintiff takes a risk voluntarily . . . where the defendant has a *right* to face him with the dilemma of 'take it or leave it'—in other words,

[6] Foler V. Harper and Fleming James, Jr., *The Law of Torts* (Boston: Little, Brown, 1956), repr. in *Experimentation with Human Beings*, ed. Jay Katz (New York: Russell Sage Foundation, 1972), 603 (emphasis added).

[7] *Handbook of the Law of Torts* (St. Paul: West, 1941), 391.

[8] Ibid., 388.

[9] Ibid. (emphasis added).

[10] The *Restatement of Torts* says that an *involuntary* assumption of risk must be "created by the tortious conduct of the defendant." Sec. 496E.

[11] Ibid.

where defendant is under no duty to make the conditions of their association any safer than they appear to be . . ."[12]

It is important to note, in this connection, that what counts as tortious conduct can be changed by judicial decision and statute. Landlords may now have obligations to tenants they once lacked, and thus conduct that once did not constitute duress may do so now. Even so, the more general and conceptual point has not changed, to wit, that whether B is coerced to assume a risk will depend on whether A has a duty to B such that A's behavior is regarded as wrongful.

Cases. Many of the relevant cases occur in the context of what the law refers to as "master/servant" relations. The general question is whether an employee has voluntarily assumed certain job-related risks of injury and what sorts of pressures would constitute coercion. The courts do not seem to have developed a consistent view about this matter. Some decisions hold that a risk is not voluntarily assumed when an employee acts under an explicit or implicit threat of dismissal for disobedience, while other decisions hold that whereas an explicit threat might coerce, a generalized fear of loss of one's livelihood does not.[13] Still other decisions suggest that even a specific threat to dismiss an employee if he does not assume a certain risk would not coerce, on the grounds that the job belongs to the employer and the employee can always quit and suffer the consequences.

Consider *McKee* v. *Patterson*.[14] McKee, a construction worker, was working on a ladder placed on a floor that he knew to be quite slick. The ladder slipped and McKee was injured. McKee claimed that his assumption of the risk of injury had not been voluntary because he had feared that he would lose his job if he refused to perform the work. Although a dissenting opinion accepted McKee's claim, the majority disagreed: "the courts of this state have never held that the necessity of performing his duties and earning a livelihood was such economic compulsion or constraint as to render involuntary the workman's choice of *accepting or retaining* employment in the face of known and appreciated dangers."[15] It is not clear whether McKee had been told he would be fired if he refused to perform what he took to be a risky job, but it appears that it would not have

---

[12] Harper and James, *The Law of Torts* repr. in *Experimentation with Human Beings*, ed. Jay Katz, 603 (emphasis added).

[13] Prosser, *Handbook*, 391.

[14] 271 S.W.2d 391 (1954).

[15] Ibid., 396 (emphasis added).

mattered. The court held that there is no difference between the assumption of risk by those already employed and the assumption of risk by those of whom it might be demanded as a condition of employment. Since, *ex hypothesi*, the demand that employees assume risks would not be coercive in the latter context, it was not coercive with respect to McKee.[16]

Contra *McKee*, other cases sharply distinguish between the "economic compulsion" that causes one to *accept* a job (which does not constitute coercion) and the specific compulsion generated by a fear of being *dismissed* (which might). Draper, an electrician, was electrocuted while installing a switch on an energized line.[17] It appears that Draper had a reasonable fear that he would be dismissed for refusing to do "hot taps." His widow successfully sued for wrongful death. On appeal, the defendants noted that Section 496E of the *Restatement of Torts* states that the fear of economic deprivation concomitant with unemployment does not make an assumption of risk involuntary. In rejecting the appeal, the court argued that Draper's action was caused not by a generalized fear of economic deprivation, but by a direct fear of being fired: "One who undertakes a dangerous work task for fear of being fired . . . can hardly be said to have undertaken the risk voluntarily. To hold that economic duress of this sort does not vitiate the voluntariness of an assumption of risk would not only ignore reality but would also greatly decrease the likelihood of employees' obtaining just compensation in cases such as this."[18]

On closer inspection, *Draper* seems to contain two different lines of argument. The court could be arguing that a realistic understanding of economic duress (the choice prong) together with the arguably negligent conduct of the employer (the proposal prong) combine to make Draper's actions legally involuntary. Or the court could be understood as appealing to *public policy* criteria. In expressing its concern that to *hold* Draper's action to be voluntary would deprive him (and others) of *just compensation*, the court implies that its

---

[16] A similar decision was reached in *Fore* v. *Verneer Manufacturing Co*. Fore was injured while operating dangerous machinery. In finding that Fore had voluntarily assumed the risk of injury, the court said: "The mere fact that an employee exposed himself to an abnormal risk because he feared that he would lose his position is not considered evidence of legal constraint, and does not make his exposure to the risk involuntary." 287 N.E.2d 526, 528 (1972).

[17] *Draper* v. *Airco*, 580 F.2d 91 (1978). Also see *Hennigan* v. *Atlantic Refining Co.*, 282 F. Supp. 667, 681 (1967). There the court held: "It cannot be said, where a man is lawfully engaged in his work, and is in danger of dismissal if he leaves his work, that he wilfully incurs any risk which he may encounter in the course of such."

[18] 580 F.2d 91, 102.

adjudication of Draper's coercion claim decision may have been disingenuous, that it may have *held* that Draper had acted under duress even when he had not done so (on the accepted legal theory of duress) because the coercion claim was a useful legal lever by which the court could provide the compensation it thought that Draper deserved.[19]

While courts have frequently distinguished between the compulsion of circumstantial economic necessity and the threat of being fired, that distinction can be attacked from two sides. It might be argued that the threat to fire is no *more* coercive than the fear of unemployment by those now unemployed and that since the latter does not constitute duress, neither does the former. On the other hand, it might be claimed that the fear of unemployment by those now unemployed is no *less* coercive than the fear of being fired and that since the latter does constitute duress, so does the former. Thus Prosser maintains that the distinction between circumstantial pressures and direct threats writes into law an economic theory "based upon notions of a complete mobility of labor and an unlimited supply of work"—a theory which is "increasingly foreign to any realities."[20]

At the risk of taking issue with one of our most acclaimed legal treatises, I suggest that the distinction between a fear of unemployment and a fear of being fired need not rest on an *unrealistic* economic theory, or, indeed, on any (empirical) economic theory. To defend the distinction, one need not claim that the economic or psychic pressures on the unemployed are significantly less than those on the presently employed. One need only claim that employers have legal or moral responsibilities to their employees that differ from their responsibilities to others. This is a moral view, not an economic theory. It may or may not be a defensible moral view, but it need not presuppose any particular view about economic mobility and labor supply.[21]

---

[19] Also see *Mitchell* v. *C.C. Sanitation Co.*, 430 S.W.2d 933 (1969). When Mitchell was injured on the job, C.C. Sanitation asked to be released from its responsibility for Mitchell's injuries, and threatened to fire him if he did not sign a release. Mitchell did so, and subsequently claimed he had signed under duress. C.C. Sanitation argued that it had had the right to fire Mitchell, and that a threat to do what it had a right to do could not constitute duress. The majority of the court rejected the analogy with *McKee*, arguing that the pressures generated by circumstantial economic necessity can be distinguished from pressures caused by an employer's specific threat. A dissenting opinion accepted the analogy.

[20] *Handbook*, 391.

[21] It appears, for example, that in the late nineteenth century, British courts were more receptive to claims of involuntary assumption of risk than were American

To anticipate terminology I shall further develop later, we can say that the morality of an employer's conduct is evaluated in terms of the employee's *baseline* position. We might assume, for legal purposes, that the employee's baseline is that he is *always* potentially unemployed because the job belongs to the employer, who can dispense or withhold it at his discretion. On this view, each day (or moment) on the job is a new one, and being fired is equivalent to not being hired from that point on. And thus also on this view, assumptions of risk will tend to be regarded as voluntary. We might, however, assume that the employee's baseline is that he is employed and that he has certain rights in virtue of his present position. On this view, threats to fire an employee will tend to be regarded as compromising the voluntariness of the assumption of risk. In either case, the crucial factor is not how to judge the voluntariness of an employee's act given a certain view of his baseline, but how to set the employee's baseline in the first place. It is the baseline that does the work.

From a somewhat broader and perhaps more political perspective, the previous cases can be seen as raising two different issues: (1) the *voluntariness* of the assumption of risk and (2) the provision of safe working conditions for employees. We could try to make a tight connection between (1) and (2). We *could* say that if an employee assumes the risk of unsafe working conditions, it must be due to some flaw in the voluntariness of his action. On the other hand, even if we assume, for the sake of argument, that the assumption of the risk of unsafe working conditions is voluntary because the employee knows what he is doing and the job belongs to the employer, we could still insist that this is precisely the sort of risk that employees should not be allowed (even voluntarily) to assume.[22]

Interestingly, and somewhat ironically, critics of the sort of laissez-faire capitalism which generates these issues often seem to accept its basic philosophical premise. They say, in effect: "*properly understood*, the *volenti* principle is all that we need. If there is a social injustice, it must be due to some defect in the process of consent." I reject that view. There is no reason to assume that all cases in which

---

courts. Bohlen speculates that differences in economic conditions may have accounted for this difference. See "Voluntary Assumption of Risk," 115. If I am right, it is a question not so much of differences in economic conditions as of different conceptions of the responsibility of employers.

[22] In somewhat different terms, we might want to treat the right to safe working conditions as (technically) "inalienable."

employees assume the risk of unsafe working conditions (or other social wrongs analogous to this assumption of risk) must be traced to some defect in the voluntariness of their actions.

The last case to be considered under the rubric of assumption of risk confirms my earlier claim that philosophers do not have to invent hypotheticals.[23] Actual cases will suffice. Ranne's mad boar bit Marshall while Marshall was walking from his house to his car.[24] The boar's proclivities were known to Marshall, and he had often complained to Ranne about the animal. The trial revealed that Marshall was an expert marksman. The jury held that Marshall had voluntarily assumed the risk of being injured because he had failed to kill the boar when he had had the chance to do so. The appellate court reversed.

> We hold that there was no proof that plaintiff had a free and voluntary choice, because he did not have a free choice of alternatives. He had, instead, only a choice of evils, both of which were wrongfully imposed upon him by the defendant. He could remain a prisoner inside his own house or he could take the risk of reaching his car before the defendant's hog attacked him. Plaintiff could have remained inside his house, but in doing so, he would have surrendered his legal right to proceed over his own property to his car . . .[25]

Now it is not clear what a "free choice of alternatives" would amount to—the alternatives we face are never completely up to us. The court's argument is, I think, essentially this: (1) to remain a prisoner in one's own house or to kill the boar are not reasonable alternatives to risking injury in attempting to get to one's car; (2) because Marshall's options had been "wrongfully" imposed upon him, his assumption of risk had not been voluntary and he was entitled to compensation. Its bizarre details aside, *Marshall* supports the general view of coercion that we have encountered in contract law. In adjudicating questions of assumed risk, the law applies a moralized theory of coercion.

[23] Also see, in this connection, *Just* v. *Sons of Italy Hall*. A woman was injured falling down stairs while walking through a dark hallway in search of a restroom. The woman claimed that, given her situation, she had not acted voluntarily. The appellate court affirmed the trial court's judgment that she had acted voluntarily, but three judges dissented on the grounds that if the plaintiff felt "great physical urgency to get to the restroom," her need to relieve herself may have "vitiated the implied assumption of risk." 368 A.2d 308, 316 (1976).

[24] *Marshall* v. *Ranne*, 511 S.W.2d 255 (1974).

[25] Ibid. This case is discussed in Gregory, Kalven, and Epstein, *Torts*, 410.

Informed Consent

Therapeutic Contexts. The operative principle in therapeutic contexts is that a person has a right not to have his body touched without his permission.[26] Barring some special justification, a nonconsensual touching constitutes a battery. However, barring *other* special justifications for prohibiting such waivers, a person may allow his body to be touched by giving his informed and voluntary consent to such touching.[27]

The interesting question is not whether consent is required, but what is required by consent. Given that patients may have limited ability to understand the precise nature of the available options or weigh rationally the risks and benefits of the alternatives, and given that disclosure of information may be therapeutically unwise (as when it causes great psychic stress), there are serious legal and moral questions as to just what a physician must disclose.[28] One answer is developed in *Canterbury* v. *Spence*, where contrary to the wishes of many physicians, the court held that the extent of the physician's duty to disclose was *not* to be determined by accepted custom within the medical community.[29] Rather, said the court, "the patient's *right* of self-decision shapes the boundaries of the duty to reveal [and that] right can be effectively exercised only if

[26] This is not an absolute right. Compulsory vaccinations might be justifiably required by social utility, and other procedures may be justified by principles of paternalism. The problem of paternalistic medical procedures has given rise to several legal cases and a large philosophical literature. A well-known case is *J.F.K. Memorial Hospital* v. *Heston*, 58 N.J. 576 (1971), repr. in *The Philosophy of Law*, ed. Joel Feinberg and Hyman Gross, 2d ed. (Belmont, Calif.: Wadsworth, 1980).

[27] Mohr consented to an operation on her right ear. While under anesthesia for surgery on her right ear, Williams examined her left ear and then performed what he took to be the appropriate procedure on her left ear as well. Williams argued that because there had been no negligence or evil intent, there had been no battery. The court disagreed: "If the operation was performed without plaintiff's consent, and the circumstances were not such as to justify its performance without, it was wrongful; and, if it was wrongful, it was unlawful . . . every person has a right to complete immunity of his person from physical interference of others . . . and any unlawful or unauthorized touching of the person of another, except it be in the spirit of pleasantry, constitutes an assault and battery . . ." *Mohr* v. *Williams*, 104 N.W. 12, 13 (1905).

[28] For a general discussion of some recent legal developments, see Marjorie Shultz, "From Informed Consent to Patient Choice," 95 *Yale Law Journal* 219 (1985). Also see Alan Donagan, "Informed Consent in Therapy and Experimentation," 2 *Journal of Medicine and Philosophy* 307 (1977), and Ruth Faden and Tom Beauchamp, *A History and Theory of Informed Consent* (New York: Oxford University Press, 1986).

[29] 464 F.2d 772 (1972). The case involved postsurgical complications arising from an operation on the spinal column.

the patient possesses enough information to enable an intelligent choice."[30]

Canterbury v. *Spence* raises many questions of philosophical interest, and its requirements of disclosure have been widely debated. *Canterbury's* most interesting feature, for my purposes, is that it focuses exclusively on the *cognitive* dimension of the patient's consent and not on volition—on how much the patient *knows* about the procedure and not how much he *wants* it. As is the case with this entire body of law and most of the scholarly literature, *Canterbury* does not raise, much less answer, the question whether illness itself can compromise the voluntariness of a patient's consent.

Consider this hypothetical dialogue between P (patient) and D (doctor):

D: The result of my diagnosis is that you have breast cancer.
P: What are the options?
D: A radical mastectomy, with an 80 percent chance of long-term survival; no surgery, with a 0 percent chance of long-term survival.
P: I guess I don't have any choice.
D: I can't do the surgery without your consent.
P: But if I want to live, I *must* have the surgery.
D: That is true, so do you consent?

What does this dialogue show? It shows, I think, that while P's claim to have no choice (or no reasonable alternative) is perfectly understandable, her consent is still morally and legally important.[31] It would, after all, be quite wrong to forego obtaining her consent to the mastectomy on the grounds that she has no choice anyway. And if consent is important, it must be *possible*.

How is it possible for a patient to voluntarily consent to a procedure if she has no reasonable choice? From the law's perspective, it is possible because the fact that P's *circumstances* leave her with only one reasonable option is simply *not* the sort of duress or coercion of which the law will take note.[32] But why is this so? Why is it that the

[30] Ibid., 784 (emphasis added).

[31] William Schroeder, an early artificial heart recipient, when asked if he wanted to go ahead with the surgery, is reported to have said: "I really haven't got any other choice." *New York Times*, November 28, 1984.

[32] As a recent study suggests, "Consent is no less *legally* effective when it is unwillingly or reluctantly given; few patients would consent to major surgery if it were not for the force of surrounding circumstances, and the knowledge that health or even life may be in jeopardy if they do not consent." D. G. Skegg, *Law, Ethics, and Medicine* (Oxford: Oxford University Press, 1984), 97.

pressures generated by one's medical circumstances do not compromise informed consent?

Consider two examples we have discussed. In explaining why one who signs a consent form at the point of a gun does so under duress, whereas one who accepts unfavorable employment terms does so voluntarily, Samuel Gorovitz says that "one can refuse to accept the employer's terms."[33] Why? Because, says Gorovitz, the consequences in the latter case are not as unpalatable as the consequences in the gunman case. Still, even though he concedes that illness can "add up to a coercion as powerful as the gun," Gorovitz does *not* say that illness precludes informed consent. Indeed, he suggests that much *less* powerful pressure by a physician (for example, the implication that he would disapprove of a patient's decision not to follow his advice) might compromise the voluntariness of informed consent whereas the prospect of death does not.

The asymmetry between the noncoerciveness of illness and the coerciveness of the doctor's pressure cannot be explained on Gorovitz's account of coercion, by some (unspecified) metric of "pressure" or the degree of unattractiveness of the consequences. It can, however, be explained on the two-pronged theory of coercion. If B's unfortunate circumstances are not due to A and if A's proposal violates none of B's rights, B's agreement is not made under duress. By contrast, illicit pressures by a physician compromise informed consent.

Considered more generally, the medical context presents what is perhaps the clearest model of a situation in which unfortunate, nay *awful*, circumstances do not constitute the sort of coercion of which the law will take note. It is, perhaps, the paradigm case in which B's necessities are not due to any wrong on A's part or, for that matter, on anyone's part. Illness is unfortunate, but it does not violate one's rights.[34] Illness defines the conception of the person who may or may not be coerced, but it is not, in itself, an external form of pressure.

Informed Consent by the Institutionalized. Institutionalization raises two related issues. First, a prisoner or mental patient may have a condition which is thought to be treatable by a procedure such as psychosurgery. Indeed, release from institutional confinement may be conditional upon such treatment. Can an institutionalized person give genuine consent to such procedures? Second, a prisoner

[33] *Doctors' Dilemmas* (New York: Macmillan, 1982), 52–53.
[34] I ignore cases where the illness may be attributable to another's wrong.

may participate in experimental testing of new drugs in exchange for monetary rewards or special privileges, or in the hope that it will help him gain an earlier parole. Can a prisoner give genuine consent to participation in such experiments?

In what is perhaps the most famous case involving psychosurgery, the court started from the principle that "individuals are allowed free choice about whether to undergo experimental medical procedures."[35] But, said the court, "the state has the power to modify this free choice . . . when it cannot be freely given, or when the result would be contrary to public policy."[36] Now to prohibit choices when "free choice cannot be freely given" does not *modify* the principle of free choice; it applies it. And (the very important) questions of public policy aside, the issue here is precisely whether an institutionalized mental patient *can* give uncoerced and informed consent to such procedures.

Why should institutionalization be thought to preclude such consent? It might be thought that the patient's very *mental* disorder precludes genuine free choice because he does not have the mental abilities necessary to competently evaluate the alternatives. It is by no means clear that this is so, for a specific mental disorder may not, in fact, compromise the specific mental capacities needed to make this sort of choice. Moreover, this was *not* the *court's* argument. The court was concerned with the effect *of* institutionalization on the voluntariness of the patient's choice and not the reasons *for* it: "informed consent [for experimental psychosurgery] cannot be given by an involuntarily detained mental patient . . . the fact of institutional confinement has a special force in undermining the capacity of the mental patient to make a competent decision . . . even though he be intellectually competent to do so."[37] Although the court does not explain just why institutional confinement makes consent impossible, it comes closest to doing so in the following remark: "It is impossible for an involuntarily detained mental patient to be free of ulterior forms of restraint or coercion when his very release from the institution may depend upon his cooperating with the institutional authorities and giving consent to experimental surgery."[38]

---

[35] *Kaimowitz* v. *Department of Mental Health for the State of Michigan*, Circuit Court, Wayne County (1973), repr. in *Operating on the Mind*, ed. Willard Gaylin et al. (New York: Basic Books, 1975).

[36] Ibid., 193.

[37] Ibid., 195–97.

[38] Ibid., 198.

There is, no doubt, something intuitively plausible about the view that institutionalization is coercive and precludes the requisite informed consent. Nonetheless, this statement raises more questions than it answers. The court says, for example, that "special safeguards are necessary" in the case of an "experimental, dangerous, and intrusive procedure," but it is not clear whether those safeguards are required to protect the patient's interests, on the one hand, or his freedom of choice, on the other. The court also says that institutional confinement makes consent to a procedure impossible if the procedure is a precondition of release. But why should that be? If, as I have argued, one can noncoercively consent to a medical procedure when the only alternative is *death*, why should the prospect of permanent institutionalization be treated differently?

A similar problem arises in the debate over participation by prisoners in nontherapeutic pharmaceutical experiments. In quantitative terms alone, this is not a trivial problem. In 1975, some 3,600 prisoners in the United States served as the first subjects on whom the safety of new drugs was tested—about 85 percent of the total of such subjects.[39] In response to a complaint by the National Prison Project of the American Civil Liberties Union, the National Commission for the Protection of Human Subjects of Biomedical and Behavioral Research said this:

> It seems at first glance that the principle of respect for persons requires that prisoners not be deprived of the opportunity to volunteer for research . . . [but] . . . when persons seem regularly to engage in activities which, were they stronger or in better circumstances, they would avoid, respect dictates that they be protected against those forces that appear to compel their choices . . . although prisoners who participate in research affirm that they do so freely . . .[40]

The report (and the governmental proposals to which it led) noted several benefits which might make it attractive for an inmate to participate in experiments—for example, relief from boredom,

[39] Roy Branson, "Prison Research: National Commission Says 'No, Unless . . .' " from *Hastings Center Report*, vol. 7 (February 1977), repr. in *Medical Ethics*, ed. Abrams and Buckner (Cambridge: MIT Press, 1983), 548. It appears that the United States is quite alone, that few other nations permit clinical pharmacological studies on healthy subjects—in or out of prison.

[40] *Research involving Prisoners*, The National Commission for the Protection of Human Subjects of Biomedical and Behavioral Research, (1976) DHEW Publication No. (OS) 76–132.

money, good food, comfortable bedding, and medical attention.[41] And, it is argued, such inducements compromise the validity of the prisoner's consent. It is true, of course, that a prisoner would be unlikely to participate in such experiments if he were not in prison, or, as the commission puts it, if he were "in better circumstances." The question is what to make of that fact. For just as surely, a woman would not have a radical mastectomy if she did not have breast cancer. As a general rule, the law does not ignore a person's circumstances in determining what constitutes coercion or voluntary consent. Why, it might be asked, should it do so here? It may be argued, after all, that the prisoner is where he is, that his imprisonment defines his situation. If so, it may be thought that the real question for a theory of coercion is whether he should be prevented from improving that situation.

Organ Transfers. The increasing viability of organ transplant procedures has created a serious imbalance between demand and supply.[42] Consider, in particular, the case of kidneys. Because we are equipped with two kidneys and can survive with only one, a person can often relinquish one kidney without serious consequences. Given this, there are at least three ways a potential recipient might obtain a kidney (excluding cadavers): (1) someone might donate a kidney; (2) someone might sell a kidney; (3) the state might *coerce* people into giving up one of their kidneys.[43] We are inclined to think that (1) is noncoercive, while (3) is coercive by definition. The question here is whether (2) is (at least sometimes) coercive, and, if so, under what conditions.

Some say that it is. When Dr. Barry Jacobs formed the International Kidney Exchange to purchase and market kidneys, the president of the National Kidney Foundation said this: "It is immoral and unethical to place a living person at risk of surgical complication and even death for a cash payment . . . [to do so] . . . would make a travesty of informed consent, by introducing the temptation and

---

[41] "Protection of Human Subjects: Policies and Procedures," *Federal Register*, pt. II, 38 (November 16, 1973), p. 31743.

[42] In 1982, more than 10,000 Americans were awaiting kidneys, but only 5,358 transplants were performed. *New York Times*, September 24, 1983. As surgical techniques improve, and as new drugs inhibit the body's rejection of transplanted organs, the imbalance will probably worsen. Cadavers have served as the most important source of organs, but as I wrote the first draft of this paragraph, a baby girl had just received the heart of a baboon—suggesting a new potential source of organs, and touching off a new round of debates concerning the treatment of animals. *New York Times*, October 29, 1984.

[43] John Harris suggests in "The Survival Lottery," 50 *Philosophy* 81 (1975), that we might even want to kill people so that we can redistribute their organs.

bias of a cash award for consent."[44] Similarly, one bioethicist has argued that "dangling thousands of dollars in front of a poor person . . . is simply coercive—just short of putting a gun to someone's head and telling them to do something."[45]

But is that right? Is a poverty-stricken kidney seller coerced?[46] Certainly financial incentives are not always coercive. As one economist (all too predictably) commented, if all financial incentives are coercive, then "Fernando Valenzuela is being coerced into playing baseball for the Dodgers for a million dollars a year."[47] Yet it might be argued that while financial incentives are not coercive for most persons, they are coercive for the very poor. But even this is by no means obvious. For whatever we want to *say* about the coerciveness of such incentives, we need to confront the consequences of holding that such incentives are—in an important sense—coercive, to wit, that poor persons would be unable to better their economic position by selling their organs.[48]

Conclusion. It is frequently argued that institutionalization or poverty precludes genuine consent to medical procedures, experiments, or organ sales. Upon what theory of coercion is this argument based? It might be claimed that institutionalization or poverty compromises the *volitional* quality of decisions, that there is a general tendency for persons in such circumstances to underestimate the risks or overestimate the benefits. This may well be so, at least some of the time, and if it is so, the argument is clearly sustainable.

But I do not think that institutionalization or poverty always compromises the volitional quality of consent or that the coercion claim

[44] *New York Times*, September 24, 1983.

[45] Quoted in Fern Schumer Chapman, "The Life and Death Question of an Organ Market," *Fortune*, June 11, 1984, 108–18. Even Dr. Jacobs, the founder of the International Kidney Exchange, seems to think so. In defending his approach, he stated that the "voluntary approach" had not produced the needed organs. *New York Times*, September 24, 1983.

[46] Although financial incentives are said to compromise informed consent, donations seem much less problematic. Why is this so? Even if we grant that donations motivated by affection or a sense of moral responsibility are noncoerced, some may be produced by extreme familial pressure. One psychiatric study of unpaid kidney donors argues that informed consent is a "myth," that most donors make their decisions "irrationally," that they decide immediately upon being asked, and that subsequent information and consultation has little effect on their decision. See Carl H. Fellner and John R. Marshall, "Kidney Donors—The Myth of Informed Consent," 126 *American Journal of Psychiatry* 1245 (1970), repr. in *Experimentation with Human Beings*, ed. Jay Katz.

[47] Quoted in Chapman, "The Life and Death Question of an Organ Market," 114.

[48] Would we, for example, want to say that those who undertake dangerous construction work (in a tunnel or skyscraper) do so involuntarily—particularly if this would preclude persons from such employment?

assumes that it does. For it might be argued that even if the poor or institutionalized are capable of rationally weighing the alternatives and find it in their interest to undergo psychosurgery (or participate in an experiment, or sell a kidney), their consent is given under duress nevertheless, because they have no reasonable alternative but to consent.

Now we have seen that, by itself, the previous argument is highly problematic. By extension, it would not only invalidate many valid contracts but also preclude informed consent to a standard medical procedure by one whose only alternative is certain death. The argument would be more plausible, I think, if it were recast in terms of the two-pronged theory of coercion. It could be maintained that the circumstantial pressures of a life-threatening disease are merely unfortunate, are part of one's situation, and therefore do not coerce. By contrast, it could be maintained that the circumstantial pressures generated by institutionalization or poverty are immoral, are not simply part of one's situation, and therefore do coerce.

This is a *coherent* position. Is it defensible? At first glance, it seems that it is not. In both contracts and torts, the law puts considerable weight on the distinction between B's unfortunate circumstances and A's immoral threats. If the distinction is made in this way, institutionalization or poverty is an "unfortunate circumstance," and choices made within that environment are not for that reason made under duress. But the distinction might be made in a different way. It could be argued that although *most* circumstantial pressures are not akin to immoral threats, *some* circumstantial pressures create the sorts of immoral pressures which should invalidate consent. But even if we assume that certain circumstantial pressures are immoral, it still makes sense to ask whether people should be prohibited from consenting to something that would (by their own lights) improve their situation. If they should not be prohibited from doing so, we have two choices. We could say that we should recognize and enforce consent made under duress. Or we could say that even immoral circumstantial pressures do not coerce.

I want to stress that in raising these sorts of questions, I am decidedly *not* arguing that psychosurgery with the institutionalized should be permitted, that prisoners should be permitted to participate in drug experiments, or that we should permit a market in bodily organs. Just as we may not want to allow workers to assume certain risks or waive their right to compensation—even if such actions are voluntary—there may, in each case, be good reasons to prohibit the sorts of practices under discussion. I am, however, suggesting that the view that such practices should be prohibited on *grounds of coercion* needs much more defense than is often provided. Perhaps the coercion claim will work; perhaps not. But we should not assume that the only argument against such practices turns on coercion, and we should not ask an argument based on coercion to do more moral work than it can handle.

F O U R

MARRIAGE, ADOPTION,
AND WILLS

In this chapter I consider three legal contexts which are loosely related in that all are predominantly matters of family law. The law of marital duress, it should be said, is arguably and strikingly anachronistic. Nonetheless, for that very reason, it serves to demonstrate the extent to which the *structure* of the two-pronged theory of coercion has remained remarkably stable even as our moral views have changed. In the case of adoptions, we encounter a context in which circumstantial pressures are often particularly acute, but where the object of and parties to the agreement have important independent interests. In the case of wills, we encounter, for the first time, a context in which volition is of some importance.

Marriage

The song is wrong. Love and marriage do not always go together like a horse and carriage. It was not always assumed that they should. Consensual marriage is a relatively modern and by no means universal idea. Indeed, it continues to present special legal problems in Western societies where some residents (of non-Western descent) prefer a system of arranged marriages.[1] Here I am concerned with a different form of "arranged marriage." Although it is now rare for a reluctant bridegroom to look down the barrel of a firearm in the hands of an outraged father (it may never have been very

[1] See "Duress and Arranged Marriages," 46 *Modern Law Review* 499 (1983). In a recent British case, a Sikh attempted to annul his marriage to a girl who had come from India to marry him. *Singh* v. *Kaur*, 11 Fam. 151 (1981). He argued that failure to go through with the marriage would have resulted in disgrace to his family and he would have been unable to participate in his family's business. The court acknowledged his "sad position," but maintained that it "could not possibly . . . hold that this marriage is invalid by reason of duress." In a more recent case, the court of appeal annulled the marriage of a nineteen-year-old Hindu girl whose parents had ordered her to marry the person of their choice or leave home. *Hirani* v. *Hirani*, 4 Fam. 232 (C.A.) (1983).

71

common), it was a reality for Johnnie Cannon, a young country boy at work in the fields. Displaying a loaded shotgun, the father of Johnnie's bride-to-be said: "You God damn son of a bitch, you have ruined my daughter and I am going to kill you if you don't marry her."[2] Although Johnnie did so, the marriage was never consummated, and after it appeared that Mrs. Cannon was not pregnant, the couple separated. Johnnie was granted an annulment on grounds of duress.

While legalized abortions and the increasing acceptance of single parenthood have alleviated some of the pressures for shotgun marriages, there is something paradoxical in the notion that such marriages could ever have been legitimate—apart from whatever other forms of legitimacy they conferred. For if a contract between a gunman and his victim is paradigmatically coercive, the same should be true here. Strictly construed, it is and has been true. A marriage produced by the threat of violence has always been voidable in most American courts.

The more interesting questions, for our purposes, concern coercion claims in cases where shotguns were not displayed. Consider the view of the Catholic church, where annulment is especially important because of the church's refusal to recognize divorce. Canon 1087 of the Law of the Church of Rome says this: "Marriage is invalid when contracted because of force or grave fear, caused by an external agent, unjustly, to free oneself from which one is compelled to choose marriage. No other fear can bring about invalidity of a marriage."[3] On Catholic doctrine, the duress which will annul a marriage must originate from an external source and must be *unjustly* imposed. The standard accounts of marital duress in American law are not vastly different, and both are strikingly similar to the two-pronged theory we found in the law of contractual duress.[4] *Corpus Juris Secundum*, a standard summary of accepted American legal doctrine, says this: "the force or coercion must have been unlawful, and where a man marries under the threat of, or constraint

---

[2] *Cannon* v. *Cannon*, 7 Tenn. App. 19 (1928). For a general discussion, see L. Neville Brown, "The Shotgun Marriage," 42 *Tulane Law Review* 837 (1968).

[3] As cited in L. Neville Brown, "The Shotgun Marriage," 839.

[4] As with most cases of contractual duress, a marriage made under duress is voidable, not void. Since cases of marital duress typically involve three parties (unlike the typical contract), it might be noted that the rule regarding third-party contractual duress also seems to apply. Robert C. Brown says that the weight of the authority denies annulment where one was neither a party to nor aware of the duress, but adds that at least one case supports the opposite view. "Duress and Fraud as Grounds for the Annulment of Marriage," 10 *Indiana Law Journal* 471, 476 (1935).

from, a criminal prosecution arising from his illicit sexual relations, such as a prosecution for seduction or bastardy, he cannot avoid the marriage on the ground of duress but it is otherwise in the case of a prosecution which was instituted maliciously or without probable cause."[5]

In interpreting these principles, American law was once very rigid, particularly given its ambivalence towards the plight of the reluctant bridegroom.[6] While the law was committed to the view that marriage should be consensual, it was also thought that the unwilling husband got precisely what was coming to him—a point well illustrated by a nineteenth-century case of marital *fraud*. In this case, a woman knowingly and falsely accused her husband-to-be of causing her pregnancy, because she preferred marrying him to marrying the baby's father. Her husband came to know of her deception, and sued for annulment. The court held, in effect, that although the woman's deception had been wrongful, the husband would have known that her claim was fraudulent had he not himself transgressed. And thus the court refused to undo the marriage.[7]

The Choice Prong: The Motivation Problem. Although the law has applied something like the two-pronged theory to cases of marital duress, its use of that theory is less explicit in such cases than in the cases of contracts and torts. Nonetheless, the basic elements are there. It seems, for example, that the fear required by the choice prong must be genuine, specific, and supported by clear evidence. A New York court would not annul a marriage between "intelligent individuals of mature years" because the woman's father had said he "would do something" if the husband did not legitimize the expected child.[8]

Cases of marital duress do give rise to a special difficulty in this connection. In the paradigmatic case of marital duress, B (a groom) impregnates a woman (W) and is then confronted with external pressure from A to marry her. Suppose we assume that B has a moral obligation to marry W. If B marries W, there are two (not necessarily equally) plausible accounts of his decision: (1) B is responding to the external pressure, or (2) B is doing what he believes he has a moral obligation to do. If B is acting out of fear, his act may meet

[5] Vol. 5, Sec. 34, p. 875

[6] Robert C. Brown, "Duress and Fraud as Grounds for the Annulment of Marriage," 475.

[7] *States* v. *States*, 37 N.J. Eq. 195, 196 (1893).

[8] *Erickson* v. *Erickson*, 48 N.Y.S.2d 588 (1944). Also see the discussion of *Cooper* v. *Crane*, 12 P.D. 369 (1891), in L. Neville Brown, "The Shotgun Marriage," 846.

the choice prong, although there will be no legally recognizable duress if the proposal which generates the fear is not wrongful. But if B marries W for *moral* reasons, not even the choice prong applies. An act which one "has to do" because one believes it is the "right thing to do" is simply not an act performed under duress.

In most contexts in which a court must adjudicate a coercion claim, the motivations are simple and transparent. In cases of marital duress, the motivations are often complex and opaque. Sexual attraction, fortune hunting, social conformity, fear of imprisonment for seduction, the desire for children, fear of loneliness, family pressure, the desire not to hurt the other party—all these (and more) may play a part.[9] Unlike the other legal contexts we consider, here the courts must make a *judgment* as to what motivates B's decision. When a twenty-eight-year-old bridegroom faced his bride's father brandishing two loaded revolvers, the court held that he had yielded not to the father's threats, but to his better instincts to marry the woman that he had dishonored.[10] In another case, the husband married subsequent to his *promise* to do so, although the marriage did not take place until some additional threats were made. The court held that "where one marries another one impregnates and promises to marry, the court *assumes* that the marriage results from the promise, even though there may be threats."[11] That both courts *assumed* that the groom was motivated by *conscience* rather than *fear*, even in the face of contrary evidence, suggests, I think, that they were reading moral criteria into their application of the choice prong, thereby disregarding what is quite clear, namely, that B's motivations are essentially a matter of *fact*. It is arguable that a more honest approach would have been to concede that the men had been motivated primarily by fear, but refuse to annul on the grounds that they had had an independent obligation to marry.

The Proposal Prong. At the most general level, the law of marital duress accepts the contract law principle that there is no duress if one has the right to make the proposal in question.[12] When does the law regard a threat as sufficiently wrongful to support an annul-

---

[9] See L. Neville Brown, "The Shotgun Marriage," 847

[10] *Meredith* v. *Meredith*, 79 Mo. App. 636 (1899).

[11] *Shepherd* v. *Shepherd*, 192 S.W. 658 (1917) (emphasis added).

[12] A Rota decision annulled a marriage when a young woman's grandmother threatened to withdraw her (nonobligatory) financial support unless the young woman married the man chosen by her grandmother. The Papal Court argued that even though the grandmother had the right to withdraw her financial support, "she had no right to exact marriage by means of the threat." See "Marriage or Prison: The Case of the Reluctant Bridegroom," 29 *Modern Law Review* 622, 629 (1966).

ment? The violence of the traditional shotgun marriage will do. So will a groom's threat to kidnap and disfigure his wife and commit arson on her father's home.[13] And, so, too, perhaps, will a *wrongful* threat of imprisonment.[14] But unlike contract law, the law of marital duress has not always held that an otherwise legitimate threat to press criminal charges invalidates a marriage. In the words of an 1897 court, "marriage for the purpose of obtaining a release from imprisonment for a crime committed is not, in equity, to be considered a restraint."[15] Some twenty-five years later, a warrant for seduction was brought against Alfred Cox.[16] He was arrested and placed in the Atlanta police station. Berma Cox charged that Alfred had caused her pregnancy, and told him that she would dismiss the warrant if he married her. He did so, then sued for annulment on grounds of duress. The court said this:

> Duress will never be said to exist where two different courses of action are presented to the person who claims he was put in fear and he has free options to make a choice . . . The alternative presented him the right to have a trial before a jury of his peers; and if innocent, he should have been acquitted. No threat was made except to submit to petitioner the danger of conviction; and if he was conscious of his innocence, he should have been willing to stand trial. Mere threats cannot constitute duress.[17]

There are two ways in which the court can be understood. On one reading, the court is arguing that a choice between marriage and *actual* imprisonment may constitute duress, but the mere *threat* of imprisonment does not. On another reading, the court could be understood as arguing that the threat of *just* imprisonment, however credible, is not immoral, and that it therefore does not constitute *legally recognizable* duress. As late as 1962, *American Jurisprudence*, a standard summary of current legal doctrines, said this: "As a general rule a marriage will not be annulled on the ground that the marriage was entered into by the man to escape prosecution and imprisonment for bastardy or seduction, or because of threats of prosecution, arrest or imprisonment."[18] This view, however odd it

[13] *Fratello* v. *Fratello*, 193 N.Y.S. 865 (1922).
[14] See, for example, a 1965 English case, *Buckland* v. *Buckland*, 2 All E.R. 300 (1967).
[15] *Ingle* v. *Ingle*, 38 A. 953 (1897).
[16] *Cox* v. *Cox*, 127 S.E. 132 (1925).
[17] Ibid., 133.
[18] 2d ed., *Annulment of Marriage*, Sec. 25 (1962), as cited in L. Neville Brown, "The Shotgun Marriage," 854, 855.

may now appear, was consistent with other features of the law. Some state statutes specifically provided that a man could escape prosecution for seduction by marrying his victim—which indicates that such states not only were not averse to using legal pressure to induce marriages, but positively supported the idea, at least if the charges were brought in good faith.[19] In this vein, a 1952 New York court approved the use of legal pressure as "the right and proper course," saying that "to accede to the suggestion of duress would destroy a time honored method long used by society as a means of protecting itself against the evils of illegitimate children, unmarried mothers and 'ruined' womanhood."[20]

The interpretation of the proposal prong has, of course, changed considerably over time. Whereas illegitimacy was once considered worse than an unwanted marriage, the present view is better reflected by the words of a 1946 New York court: "shotgun marriages are partially doomed before they are entered upon, to explode and ultimately disappear. Only rarely do they work out advantageously to the people involved or to the community as a whole."[21] Similarly, it was once possible to sue for breach of a promise to marry, and consequently a marriage undertaken in response to a threat to sue was not made under duress.[22] So, too, today, albeit for a different reason: a promise to marry is no longer legally enforceable, and hence such a threat would not satisfy the choice prong.[23]

Conclusion. If we step back from the cases, it seems that the law's approach to the use of legal pressure to induce marriage has been motivated largely by public policy considerations: What sorts of marriages do we want to encourage? How important is consensuality? How important is the prevention of illegitimacy? Although courts have given different answers to these questions, and although those answers have changed over time, the courts have

[19] Just as contract law adopts the principle that "abuse" of process satisfies the moral prong, so too with the law of marital duress. A marriage induced by a criminal charge could be annulled if the woman brought the charges in bad faith, especially if the husband was "young and inexperienced." See Robert C. Brown, "Duress and Fraud as Grounds for the Annulment of Marriage," 478.

[20] *Figueroa* v. *Figueroa,* 110 N.Y.S.2d 550, 553 (1952). It should be noted that the case involved a Puerto Rican couple, a fact of clear relevance to the judge, who seemed pleased to support methods of reducing bastardy among a population that had "a large birth rate, and great poverty . . ."

[21] *Mills* v. *Mills,* 62 N.Y.S.2d 344 (1946).

[22] "The legal remedy exists precisely to impose this pressure to fulfill the promise of marriage." L. Neville Brown, "The Shotgun Marriage," 849.

[23] Ibid., 859. It is now considered better to disappoint those expecting the marriage than to give legal support to a marriage that seems doomed from the start.

generally held, in effect, that legal pressures which are compatible with "the public interest" do not constitute duress, whatever their effects on the parties involved. The law has attempted to accommodate changes in its view of the public interest by altering the way it interprets and applies the proposal prong of the two-pronged theory. The structure of its account of marital duress has changed little.

Adoption

For reasons that are not entirely clear, there is virtually no scholarly analysis of the conditions under which the surrender of a child by a natural mother can be avoided on grounds of duress (we shall simplify matters by ignoring the father).[24] At the same time, adoptions present an important legal context for working through the implications of different conceptions of coercion. The major reason is this. A mother's desire to keep her child is generally quite strong. She will ordinarily surrender a child only if she is under great environmental and emotional stress. If a valid surrender of a child must be voluntary and if environmental pressures could coerce, adoptions would be quite susceptible to invalidation. Yet to acknowledge this possibility is also to state the difficulty it would create. While the natural mother may have a claim on our sympathies, the children and adoptive parents also have a legitimate stake in the finality and irreversibility of the adoption process.

How might the law respond to this problem? There are three possibilities. First, the law might accept the consequences of its commitment to voluntariness and be prepared to invalidate a reasonable proportion of adoptions. Second, by legislation or judicial decision, the law might override its general commitment to the voluntariness principle in the name of other objectives, such as the "best interests of the child." Third, the law might hold that the pressures which typically cause a woman to surrender her child do not constitute legally recognizable duress. In general, and not surprisingly, the courts have adopted the third approach.

Cases. In *Drury* v. *Catholic Home Bureau*, a twenty-one-year-old "mentally ill" college graduate surrendered her child after discussions with representatives of an adoption agency.[25] She claimed

[24] The standard legal references, such as *Words and Phrases*, contain few or no references to the voluntariness problem in the context of adoption. I found but one brief law review article listed in *The Current Legal Index*. I suspect that the recent controversy over surrogate mothers will generate some relevant case law.

[25] 213 N.E.2d 507 (1966).

that the agency had exerted great pressure, and attempted to have the adoption invalidated on grounds of duress. It is not unusual for adoption agencies to argue strenuously on behalf of the desirability of adoption. Indeed, they may exert such pressure while genuinely (and accurately) believing that adoption is in the best interests of the natural mother and the child. For the most part, courts have been extremely reluctant to hold that such pressures constitute duress. As the *Drury* court put it, "Mere advice, argument or persuasion does not constitute duress or undue influence if the individual acts freely when he executed the questioned documents though the same would not have been executed except for the advice, argument, or persuasion."[26]

Aside from the question-begging claim that advice is not duress when the person acts freely, the court's general point is correct. A does not coerce B to do X if A provides B with what B decides are good reasons for doing X (""'stop smoking or you'll get cancer"), or, in slightly different terms, if A persuades B that the *consequences* of not doing X (for which A is not responsible) are such that it is better for B to do X. Assuming that the Catholic Home Bureau did not misrepresent the consequences of Drury's options, and assuming that its argumentation and advice did not distort Drury's cognitive or volitional capacities, it seems right to say that the *agency* did not coerce Drury, although it remains an open question whether Drury's *circumstances* may have done so.

Here, as in other legal contexts, the courts typically reject the claim that circumstances coerce. When destitute parents placed their child for adoption because they could not adequately support it, the court ruled that the fact that the parents "were penniless when they consented to adoption . . . did not constitute 'duress' which would render the consent invalid."[27] Adopting a version of the two-pronged theory, the court implies that there is *some* sense in which the parents acted under duress, but distinguishes *that* duress from the *legally recognizable* duress which would invalidate the adoption: "If consents to adoption were ineffective every time this sort of duress entered the picture, it is difficult to see how an adoption where consent is required could be allowed to stand, for what natural parents would ever consent to the adoption of his or her child in the absence of duress of circumstances?"[28] There are two ways in which this statement can be understood. The court might

---

[26] Ibid., 511.
[27] *Barwin* v. *Reidy*, 307 P.2d 175 (1957).
[28] Ibid., 185.

be arguing for a conceptual view according to which some sorts of circumstantial pressures do not constitute duress. The court might also be understood as making a consequentialist argument to the effect that while such pressures are—in some legitimate sense—properly described as coercive, such pressures do not constitute legally recognizable coercion because, but only because, the *consequences* of such a view (invalidating adoptions) would be unacceptable.

The latter position was ultimately explicitly defended in *Regenold* v. *Baby Fold, Inc.*[29] Linda Fay Regenold, a nineteen-year-old mother, contacted Baby Fold, a child welfare agency, about her fourteen-month-old son. A few days after her first meeting with Baby Fold, she signed adoption papers and surrendered her son, who was then placed with Richard and Priscilla Riley. After a few more days, Regenold contacted Baby Fold seeking the return of her son, and subsequently filed a petition for a writ of habeas corpus. A hearing was held, and the trial court ordered the son returned. Baby Fold and the Rileys appealed.

The facts about Regenold's dealings with Baby Fold were a matter of some dispute. She testified that in her first meeting with the agency, she had simply wanted to talk to someone about her situation. Her problems were many. She had just been divorced against the wishes of her ex-husband, her parents (with whom she lived) constantly argued, her mother was divorcing her father, her father threatened to force her and her child out of the home, she was adjusting to a new job, she argued with her mother over the responsibility for rearing her three-year-old brother, her brother was a threat to her son's physical well-being, she faced various financial difficulties, and she was under medication and feared a partial hysterectomy if the medication proved to be ineffective. Regenold claimed that on her first visit to Baby Fold, the agency had proposed adoption as a partial solution to her problems, and that "Baby Fold's hasty actions in accepting her surrender without exploring other solutions constituted fraud or duress which invalidated her surrender."[30] Baby Fold argued that Regenold had contacted it just for the purpose of surrendering her child, and that its counselor had discussed both permanent adoption and short-term foster care with her.

The trial court accepted Regenold's claim of circumstantial duress. In defending its decision, it said this: "The execution of the

---

[29] 355 N.E.2d 361 (1976).
[30] Ibid., 363

surrender was a reaction to the severe environmental stress and pressure under which the petitioner was operating. Her action in signing the surrender was neither voluntary [n]or understanding . . . The emotional disturbance that she was experiencing and the environmental stress and pressure upon her combined to produce a result which was the product of duress."[31] The court went on to argue that Baby Fold had acted hastily and thus had become an "active participant in the chain of events which denied . . . the exercise of her free will and deprived her of her infant son," suggesting that the agency's alleged *wrongful* participation was important to its finding and that neither the circumstantial pressures on Regenold nor concerns about the quality of her volition bore the entire burden of its decision.[32]

On appeal, it was held that the trial court's reasoning was "contrary to the manifest weight of the evidence."[33] In reaching the view that the sorts of circumstantial stress placed on Regenold did not invalidate the adoption, the court asserted that the standards for duress "must be determined in the context of the *public policy* favoring finality in the adoption process."[34] The court noted that the relevant legislation was designed to provide a stable and secure environment for the adopted child, and to "protect the parties from the complex psychological problems inherent in permitting a natural parent to *withdraw consent*."[35] The court's view was that these sorts of considerations defined the context in which the voluntariness of a surrender must be evaluated.

Now Regenold might have been claiming (1) that she had never given a valid consent or (2) that she should be permitted to withdraw her consent because it had been hastily given.[36] Although it is

---

[31] Ibid., 364

[32] Ibid.

[33] Ibid., 365. Before reaching that conclusion, the appellate court had to contend with a constitutional question. Adoptions in Illinois were governed by a statute which provided that "A consent . . . shall be irrevocable unless it shall have been obtained by fraud or duress *on the part of the person before whom such consent . . . is acknowledged* . . ." Ill. Rev. Stat. ch. 4, para. 9.1–11 (1975) (emphasis added). Regenold argued that this provision was *unconstitutional* (under due process and equal protection standards) because it legislatively precluded duress on the grounds of its *source*, rather than its *effect*. The court shared Regenold's doubts as to the provision's constitutionality, but concluded that the stress under which Regenold claimed to have acted, "*regardless of its source*, as a matter of law does not amount to the duress which is necessary to vitiate her consent." 355 N.E.2d 361, 364 (emphasis added).

[34] Ibid., 365 (emphasis added).

[35] Ibid. (emphasis added).

[36] Although there are "cooling-off" periods for installment loans (which allow the

not clear just what Regenold meant to argue, there is no *evidence* that she meant to rely (principally) on (2). And if she did not, then the court's argument is irrelevant. For even if such policy considerations justified prohibiting the *withdrawal* of an otherwise *valid* consent, it would not follow that they justify enforcing an original consent given under duress.

Yet it is likely that the court would also have rejected argument (1). Although it accepted Regenold's claim that there *could* be legal duress by persons other than the party receiving the consent to adoption, it held that duress requires *direct pressure* by *some* second party. Here *Regenold* was consistent with (although it did not cite) *Allen* v. *Morgan*: "Where normally the other party must exercise coercion, in adoption this is not so. If a woman consents to give her child up involuntarily, even though adopting parents did not coerce her, she may get the child back."[37] According to the court, there had been no direct pressure on Regenold at all. In defending its view, the court explicitly distinguished Regenold's case from *In re Sims*, where the mother's parents "conditioned their parental love of their daughter and their fulfillment of their legal obligation to support her during her minority on her consenting to the adoption."[38] In this case, Regenold's parents' behavior may have made it *desirable* for her to surrender her child, but they did not ask or command her to do so.

The last case to be considered here involves, if that is possible, even unhappier circumstances. A woman, who had never married, surrendered her children to the Massachusetts Society for the Prevention of Cruelty to Children (the Society).[39] The mother subsequently attempted to have her consent revoked, and the probate court held the surrenders void. The Society appealed. The background facts are these. The mother, who had an IQ of sixty, had been confined to a state school for six years (1949–55), and had been discharged against the recommendation of the school authorities. By March 1960, she had four children, who were living with her mother while, pregnant once again, she was in jail awaiting trial for

---

buyer to withdraw from the agreement within a specified period), there was, at least at the time, no such period for adoptions. The *Regenold* court specifically encouraged some such provision. Ibid.

[37] 44 S.E.2d 500 (1947). Although it is not clear whether this view is accepted as a general principle of the law of adoptions, it differs noticeably from the comparable principle about third-party duress in contract law. See pp. 47–48.

[38] 332 N.E.2d 36, 40 (1975).

[39] *In re Surrender of Minor Children*, 181 N.E.2d 836 (1962).

fornication. The woman talked with a representative of the Society, who told her that it would be in everyone's best interest to remove the children from the grandmother. Although "[n]o threats were made" when the mother spoke with the Society's representative, there "was talk of the mother's going to jail for two years."[40] Faced with the prospect of at least a two-year separation from her children, the mother signed the adoption papers. In voiding the consent, the probate court held that she had not been "in full possession of all her faculties and free from any influence, coercion or duress . . . [she was in] a state of mind where the slightest influence brought to bear on her to release said children for adoption, would be effective."[41]

Not so, said the higher court. The findings of fact, it said, require the conclusion that "the mother's act was voluntary and with a full understanding of every fact necessary to such consent."[42] There had been no "undue influence," because the Society's representative had acted properly in showing the mother the adverse effects on her children of her own conduct, the likelihood that her institutionalization would render her unable to care for them, and the grandmother's inability to properly care for the children. With respect to the claim that the mother lacked the mental ability to make a valid surrender, the court went on to stress that the mental capacities required by a valid surrender are not particularly demanding. The court conceded the mother's mental weakness, but argued that she had "understood precisely what she was doing . . . and acted for the paramount, sound reason that she believed she would be confined for some time and unable to care for her children."[43]

After dispensing with the claim that the Society's representative had coerced the mother or compromised the volitional quality of her consent, the court considered the probate court's finding that "circumstances coerced" her—that her mistaken view that she faced a two-year jail term (rather than noncriminal institutionalization) and the grandmother's inability to care for the children constituted legally recognizable duress. There was, said the court, no "*material* mistake of fact" with respect to the jail term because she

[40] Ibid., 837. Although the maximum *jail* sentence was three months, it was not at all improbable that the mother would be *institutionalized* for at least a two-year period. It is not clear whether the Society's representative intentionally did not distinguish between jail and institutionalization, or that this mattered much to the mother.
[41] Ibid., 838.
[42] Ibid.
[43] Ibid.

faced at least two years' institutionalization and separation.[44] With respect to the claim of emotional duress, the court said this:

> Contemplation of the surrender of one's own child is in many, if not all, cases a cause of emotional and mental stress. Many such surrenders are undoubtedly by mothers of children born out of wedlock and are contemplated because the trying circumstances tend to show that the welfare of the child calls for action at variance with that dictated by natural instincts of maternal love and affection. No statute has said that surrenders are valid only if executed free from emotion, tensions, and pressures caused by the situation. No principle of law requires the rule. *A balance of the interests of the persons concerned and of society weighs strongly against it.*[45]

If we examine this statement closely, we see that whereas the first part apparently refers (correctly or not) to the internal or conceptual requirements of duress, the last sentence suggests that external policy considerations played a crucial role in the court's decision. Indeed, in rejecting the claim of duress, the higher court specifically maintained that *"the welfare of the child comes first and the rights of society must be regarded."*[46]

In a spirited dissent, Justice Kirk argued that the majority's discussion of the children's welfare and the rights of society was irrelevant to the claim of duress, that it "beclouds the central issue which is simply the validity of the surrenders when executed."[47] On his view, even if such considerations might be appropriately taken into account should a mother petition for *revocation* of a valid surrender, they are not appropriate when the validity or voluntariness of the original surrender is itself at issue.

Conclusion. Adoption presents a unique context for the analysis of duress. On the one hand, the sorts of pressure which would lead a woman to surrender her child are frequently quite severe and might be thought to support a prima facie case that the surrender was made under duress. On the other hand, there may be good reasons to be extremely reluctant to invalidate adoptions. For even if we ignore the interests of the adoptive parents, it may still be in the child's interests that an adoption, once made, should be final. We

[44] Ibid. (emphasis added).
[45] Ibid., 839 (emphasis added).
[46] Ibid., 840 (emphasis added).
[47] Ibid., 843.

have seen that the courts have been very sensitive to the latter considerations, but they have not (at least nominally) abandoned the voluntariness principle in order to protect those interests.

Wills

What we have is ours to give. This was (and is) not universally so. Legal systems influenced by Roman law generally adopted "a set of guarantees aiming to ensure that close relatives of every owner will inherit a substantial, pre-determined share of his estate on his death."[48] Our view of the matter is different. Taxation aside, we believe that it is impermissible for the state to specify one's heirs. In the words of one judge, "every person of full age and of sound mind [has] the right to dispose of his property by will, within the limits fixed by statute, as he chooses."[49] If we now reject "forced heirship," we also reject heirship produced by force. In the special language of the law of wills, the testator must not be subject to "undue influence."

Undue Influence. But what constitutes undue influence?[50] And why does the law of wills refer to "undue influence" rather than "coercion" or "duress"? Let us consider the second question first. The answer is partly historical. Wills are adjudicated in special (probate) courts which have developed their own special terminology. Moreover, whereas contractual duress generally involves relations between nonintimates, undue influence generally involves a relative, friend, or advisor (such as a lawyer or priest).[51] As one decision puts it, undue influence involves taking "unfair advantage of another's *confidence.*"[52]

The different *sources* of pressure aside, does undue influence require *less* pressure or involve different *sorts* of pressure than coercion or duress? "Undue influence" *sounds* as if it should be easier to establish than "coercion" or "duress," a view supported by the observation that the first use of the phrase in Illinois produced an "av-

---

[48] John Dawson, *Gifts and Promises* (New Haven: Yale University Press, 1980), 29.

[49] *In re Rowlands*, 18 N.W.2d 290 (1945).

[50] Although undue influence is often conflated with fraud in the law of wills, we should distinguish between cognitive and volitional defects, between deceit and pressure. For a discussion of fraud, see *In re Budlong*, 27 N.E. 945 (1891).

[51] Milton Green, "Fraud, Undue Influence and Mental Incompetency," 43 *Columbia Law Review* 176, 182 (1943).

[52] *Buchanan* v. *Prall*, 167 N.W. 488, 489 (1918) (emphasis added).

alanche of litigation."[53] Yet, for several reasons, I do not believe that there is an important *conceptual* difference here. First, as in contracts, undue influence involves questions of process and not result. Just as a contract is not set aside for duress merely because the result appears to be unfair or unequal, "undue influence is not established by the inequality of the provisions of the will with respect to the natural objects of one's bounty, or by the injustice or unnaturalness of the will."[54] Courts will not substitute their judgment for that of a testator of "sound mind," although the terms of a will may constitute *evidence* of the testator's soundness of mind.[55]

Second, if undue influence were much easier to demonstrate than coercion or duress, one might expect that a relatively high proportion of wills would be set aside on that ground. Yet of 160 cases Willard King examined, the contestant won only 11 times, and there the emphasis was "as much on testamentary capacity as on undue influence."[56] Third, and perhaps most important, in explaining the meaning of undue influence, courts frequently appeal to the same phraseology used in explaining the meaning of duress in other legal contexts. "Undue influence which will invalidate a will must be such as to deprive the testator of free agency or destroy the freedom of his will and render it more the will of another than his own."[57] "The undue influence which will avoid a will must amount to coercion or fraud—an influence tantamount to force or fear, and which destroys the free agency of the party and constrains him to do what is against his will."[58]

Undue Influence and Mental Capacity. If there is no important conceptual distinction between undue influence and coercion or du-

---

[53] See Willard King, "Undue Influence in Wills in Illinois," 2 *University of Chicago Law Review* 457, 460 (1935). King points out that the word "undue" is used in daily discourse as the "mildest sort of epithet," as when we warn others not to attach "undue importance to our views."

[54] Atkinson, *Handbook for the Law of Wills* (St. Paul: West, 1953), 255.

[55] When a woman's niece was omitted from her will, the court maintained that she was not "the natural object of her bounty" just because she was her only near relative. *In re Rowlands*, 18 N.W.2d 290 (1945). When Joseph Bryan left all his wealth to a Roman Catholic school, his sister argued that it "was not his free and voluntary act." The court rejected the claim. *In re Bryan*, 25 P.2d 602, 603 (1933).

[56] According to King, the supreme court of Illinois first used the phrase in *Dickie* v. *Carter*, 42 Ill. 376 (1866), but it does not appear in its instructions to the jury. In the next case, *Brownfield* v. *Brownfield*, 43 Ill. 147 (1867), the words appear frequently. Subsequently, the pace of litigation accelerated. See "Undue Influence in Wills in Illinois," 459–60. "Undue influence" had already appeared in several English cases. See King, ibid., 457, 458.

[57] *Knudson* v. *Knudson*, 46 N.E.2d 1011 (1943).

[58] *Eastis* v. *Montgomery*, 9 So. 311 (1890).

ress, there is a difference in emphasis. In most legal contexts, coercion and duress raise questions of constrained volition. It is generally assumed that, under the circumstances, B can and does make a rational choice. Not so with wills, where courts are primarily concerned with the volitional quality of B's act, with establishing that the testator was, in fact, of "sound mind."

While the law often assesses an actor's mental state, those assessments do not always employ the same standards, nor are they used for identical purposes. Within the criminal law, for example, the criteria for sanity are not identical with the criteria for competence to stand trial. It is not just that "sanity" refers to B's mental state at the time of the offense, whereas "competence to stand trial" refers to B's mental state at the time of adjudication. Sanity and competence to stand trial are *different* mental capacities.[59]

The determination that a testator had the capacity to make a valid will is *chronologically* more akin to determination of sanity than to determination of competence to stand trial. It, too, requires a judgment about the agent's mental state at an earlier time.[60] *Substantively*, the determination is a function of two factors, each of which pulls in a different direction. Unlike the typical contract, wills are frequently made when the testator is old, ill, or weak. This leads probate courts to scrutinize the volitional quality of wills quite carefully.[61] On the other hand, A exerts undue influence over B only if he compromises the *specific* mental capacities necessary to a valid will, and the mental capacities required for a valid will are often said to be *less* than those required for other legal acts.[62] B may, for example, have the capacity to know that he wants A to inherit *everything* that he owns without understanding or being able to understand *what* he owns.[63]

[59] See Herbert Fingarette, *The Meaning of Criminal Insanity* (Berkeley: University of California Press, 1972).

[60] Of course, here the agent whose mental capacities we are interested in is no longer alive.

[61] "Probate" is, after all, derived from the Latin for "to prove."

[62] It has been argued that it takes less strength of mind to perform a one-party act, such as making a will, than to perform an act which requires bargaining, such as making a contract. Atkinson, *Handbook*, 239–40.

[63] When evidence suggested that Hobart Arnold's excessive consumption of alcohol had rendered him highly susceptible to "undue influence," the court said this: "A person who has mental power to understand and to transact the ordinary business affairs of life, doubtless, has capacity to make a will. But the converse is not necessarily true. Mental perception and power to think and reason of a lesser degree than that which is required in the understanding and transaction of ordinary business may be all that is requisite to the full understanding of everything involved in the execution of a will." *In re Arnold*, 107 P.2d 25, 32 (1940).

Unacceptable Motivations. Does the focus on the volitional quality of B's act mean that, unlike coercion according to the two-pronged theory, *undue influence* is essentially empirical? Yes and no. Yes, in that once the criteria for undue influence are set, the determination that A exerted undue influence over B essentially depends on psychological facts (although these may be difficult to ascertain). No, in that the notion of undue influence rests on an implicit and (I believe) moral view that some motivations are compatible with voluntary action and others are not.

Consider these two cases. (1) A has (not illicitly) caused B to fall madly in love with A, and B now wants nothing more than to provide A with as many material goods as he can. (2) D would prefer to leave his money to E, but C has badgered D into making C his only heir. It is entirely possible that B is less able to resist his desire to make A his only heir than D to resist his desire (under the circumstances) with respect to C. Nonetheless, C has exercised undue influence, but A has not. For A exercises undue influence over B only if A causes B to have *unacceptable motivations* for making the will.

What constitutes an unacceptable motivation? In general, the desire to satisfy one's "positive" feelings for another is acceptable, but the desire to be free from "negative" pressures is not.[64] In the words of a nineteenth-century English case:

> The influence to vitiate an act must amount to force and coercion destroying free agency—it must not be the influence of affection and attachment—it must not be the mere desire of gratifying the wishes of another; for that would be a very strong ground in support of a testamentary act . . . there must be proof that the act . . . was done merely for the sake of *peace*— so that the *motive* was tantamount to force or *fear*.[65]

Given this distinction, the influence of a mistress may not be undue if it involves a positive attraction, whereas the influence of the testator's wife may be undue if she causes him to act out of fear.[66] And this may occur, in the words of another nineteenth-century English case, even if "no force is either used or threatened."[67]

---

[64] The "negative" pressures on the testator need not be absolutely irresistible to constitute undue influence—"the influence is fatal to the will if it is such that the testator could not well resist." Atkinson, *Handbook*, 257.

[65] *Williams* v. *Goude*, 1 Hagg. Eccl. 577, 581 (1828) (emphasis added), cited in W.H.D. Winder, "Undue Influence and Coercion," 3 *Modern Law Review* 97, 104 (1939).

[66] Atkinson, *Handbook*, 258.

[67] *Hall* v. *Hall*, L.R. 1 P. & D. 481, 482 (1868), cited in Joseph Warren, "Fraud, Undue Influence, and Mistake in Wills," 41 *Harvard Law Review* 309, 327 (1927). Undue

Conclusions. To the extent that the law of wills provides material of interest to our inquiry, most of it lies below the surface. Other than boilerplate phrases about overborne wills and free agency, the cases (and treatises) offer little conceptual help. This is not because the decisions are typically brief. To the contrary. The frequently lengthy opinions reflect the difficulty of assessing claims about the testator's mental state, a process made even more difficult by the absence of the best source of evidence.

Interestingly, however, when one court stated that there was undue influence if a testator's will was ". . . *more* the will of another *than his own,*" it suggested, in effect, that undue influence might be understood in *comparative* terms (although there is a danger here of reading too much philosophical sophistication into what may be a judge's casual language).[68] On that view, B's will need not be entirely *his* in order not to be coerced; it need only be more *his* than *another's.* This account parallels what Robert Nozick calls the "closest relative" view of coercion. A person acts freely, says Nozick, when "no other's motives and intentions are as closely connected to [his] act" as his own, regardless of the pressures under which he acts or the limits on his alternatives.[69] We shall consider this view in more detail in Part Two.

Finding Duress and Holding Duress

In reflecting on the previous discussions, it seems that we can distinguish two questions a court might consider when faced with a coercion claim: (1) Is it more likely than not that B acted under duress? (2) Is it right to *hold* that B acted under duress? It is *not* unreasonable to think that a court might answer these questions differently. In the criminal law, for example, we seem to think that it is better for a court to hold that a guilty person is not guilty of a criminal charge than to hold that an innocent person is guilty. Yet, and this is the important point, *holding* someone to be guilty and *finding* him guilty are distinct. It is one thing for courts to adopt a *decision rule* which leads it to hold that B is not guilty because it is more unjust to convict the innocent than to acquit the guilty and quite another for those considerations to play a role in determining whether B is actually guilty.

---

influence may be exerted by threats of abandonment, litigation among the children, or criminal prosecution. See Atkinson, *Handbook,* 257, and the cases cited there.

[68] *Knudson* v. *Knudson,* 46 N.E.2d 1011 (1943) (emphasis added).

[69] *Philosophical Explanations* (Cambridge: Harvard University Press, 1981), 49.

In this chapter, I have argued, at various points, that courts have—often explicitly—justified their decisions by appealing to the *consequences* of their holding that someone acted under duress, or, as it were, on public policy grounds. We saw, for example, that the legal standards for marital duress have been motivated by a court's judgment about the relative importance of consensuality and the avoidance of bastardy. And we saw that the interests of the child and adoptive parents have led courts to place a high value on the finality and irrevocability of an adoption.

Invoking the distinction introduced above, I want to suggest that it is one thing for a court to use public policy criteria in choosing among various possible decision rules, and quite another to use them in actually adjudicating a coercion claim. It is one thing for a court to say, in effect, that it is better to err on the side of legitimacy or finality in cases of marital or adoptive duress. It is quite another thing to say that the social interest in avoiding bastardy or the welfare of the adopted child can properly motivate a *finding* of duress. True, the two-pronged theory gives the courts some room to integrate moral considerations into their adjudication of a coercion claim. The courts might, for example, use the two-pronged theory to distinguish between background circumstances and specific interpersonal threats. Here the courts would be on well-established legal ground, although we have yet to determine its philosophical firmness. But the courts sometimes appear to be making a second type of argument. Several opinions suggest that concern for reducing bastardy or ensuring the finality of adoptions has led the courts to set the standards for duress particularly high. Here the legal ground is more problematical. For even if such considerations justified a decision to *override* the voluntariness principle, it is not clear that they would be relevant to the validity of a coercion claim itself.

F I V E

BLACKMAIL AND COERCIVE
SPEECH

In most legal contexts, coercion claims have a negative function; they serve to block what would otherwise be the normal legal effect of one's act. If the coercion claim is successful, one will be returned to the *status quo ante*, where one is not bound by one's agreement, where one's right has not been waived, or where one is not liable for punishment. Put somewhat differently, coercion claims do not ordinarily serve as a basis for *independent* legal action.[1]

Extortion and blackmail appear to be exceptions to this generalization, as cases in which the very making of a coercive proposal constitutes a criminal offense. Extortion and blackmail are not identical. In the paradigm case of *extortion*, A receives property or some other benefit from B by proposing to commit a violent crime against B; extortion is, therefore, assimilable to the crime of robbery. And while it might, at first glance, be thought that the extortive threat itself is mere *speech*, that it should not be punished if unaccompanied by any other wrongful act or transaction, the criminalization of extortive threats can, without great difficulty, be assimilated to the (uncontroversial) criminalization of *attempted* robbery or assault.[2]

The criminalization of speech is more problematic if A *blackmails* B, as when A threatens to reveal damaging or embarrassing infor-

---

[1] Coercion can, although this is rare, serve as the basis of a civil wrong. "Duress as a Tort," 39 *Harvard Law Review* 108 (1925). For, in some cases, if duress could not constitute a basis for tort action, a victim of coercion might be without adequate remedy, as when A coerces B to make a contract with (an innocent) C against whom he has no cause of action, or when B is forced to forego a substantial *benefit* as a result of A's coercion. In a recent case, for example, an apparel manufacturer was awarded over $18 million for lost profits which, it claimed, had resulted from a creditor's coercive interference with decisions about changes in its management. *State National Bank of El Paso* v. *Farah Manufacturing Co., Inc.*, Court of Appeals, Eighth Supreme Judicial District, El Paso, Texas (1984).

[2] Successful extortion is considered a form of *theft* by the *Model Penal Code*, Sec. 223.4 (1980). The threat of violence is not a prerequisite of theft through extortion. One can commit theft by demanding money to reveal the whereabouts of documents that one did not take. See *Stamatiou* v. *U.S. Gypsum*, 400 F. Supp. 431 (1975).

mation.[3] For unlike the typical case of extortion, where A threatens to commit an act that is independently illegal, a blackmailer may threaten to commit an act that is, in itself, legally permissible. A may have a right to reveal information about B, A may have a right to sell the information to someone else who may reveal it, and A may have a right to sell the information directly to B. Yet A blackmails B if A *threatens* to publicize or transfer the information *unless* B buys the information from him.[4] And thus we have what Glanville Williams has called the "paradox of blackmail," a situation in which "two things that taken separately are moral and legal whites together make a moral and legal black."[5] The old saw has it that two wrongs cannot make a right. The paradox of blackmail is that two rights can make a wrong. How can that be?

The paradox of blackmail cannot be explained by supposing that while A has a legal right to do what he threatens to do, it would be morally wrong for A to do it. For A can blackmail B even if A has a moral or legal *duty* to carry out his threat, as when A threatens to reveal to the authorities that B is violating the law.[6] It might be objected that there is no paradox here because it would be wrong for A *not* to carry out his threat. But that does not resolve the paradox. It might be wrong for A not to carry out his threat, but it would not be a wrong against *B*. And it is the wrong against *B* that seems to constitute the gravamen of blackmail.[7]

Unfortunately, unlike other legal contexts I consider in this book, here the case law provides little help, for there is little case law to be

[3] A famous case of blackmail involved Senator Estes Kefauver, who was entrapped into a sexual relationship, and then blackmailed by Chicago mobsters into stopping a Senate investigation into their activities. See Mike Hepworth, *Blackmail: Publicity and Secrecy in Everyday Life* (London: Routledge and Kegan Paul, 1975), 7. Although "blackmail" once referred to extortion through physical intimidation, "blackmail" now denotes favors induced by a threat to reveal damaging or embarrassing information. James Lindgren writes that the best account of the etymology of "blackmail" is that it referred to "mail, that is, tribute or rents, exacted in crops, work, goods, or a metal baser than silver (such as copper). This distinguished blackmail or black rents from white rents, which were tribute or rents exacted in silver." See "Unraveling the Paradox of Blackmail," 84 *Columbia Law Review* 670, 675 (1984).

[4] The recognition of a right to privacy has made the criminalization of blackmail somewhat less problematic than it once seemed.

[5] "Blackmail," *Criminal Law Review* (1954), 163.

[6] A typical case is *Commonwealth* v. *Keenan*, 184 A.2d 793 (1962), in which a private investigator extracted money in exchange for not reporting information about tax evasion to the IRS.

[7] It is not just that blackmail is wrong. In the words of a former detective of Scotland Yard, "Of all the forms of crime, blackmailing is surely the most vicious, vile and villainous; it is even lower and more contemptible than cheating at cards." J. K. Ferrier, *Crooks and Crime*, cited in Hepworth, *Blackmail*, 25.

of help—"a person who pays to keep certain information quiet is not likely to step forward to orchestrate a public prosecution that of necessity reveals the very information that he wants to suppress."[8] And thus, according to one commentator, we have "a body of law that is in disarray—statutes that do not adequately describe the crime and court opinions that are poorly reasoned or just plain wrong."[9] When, for example, one court held that a blackmail statute did not apply when the defendant threatened to do what he had a legal right to do, the court failed to see that blackmail *typically* involves a threat to do what one has a right to do.[10] Fortunately, although the case law may be underdeveloped and in disarray, the theoretical problematic has occasioned a considerable scholarly literature, and it is this that I shall primarily rely upon.

Theories of Blackmail

Some libertarian writers have argued that blackmail should *not* be prohibited.[11] I shall ignore this view here. I want to see whether the arguments for the criminalization of blackmail can contribute to the development of a theory of coercion. There are, it seems, two principal types of argument for the criminalization of blackmail.[12] *Internal* arguments hold that despite the paradox of blackmail, something inherent in the blackmail relation makes it a suitable object of criminal prohibition. *External* arguments hold that blackmail should be criminal because its being criminalized has beneficial consequences.

External theories have occupied center stage, largely by default, since writers on blackmail have (often) admittedly failed to identify

---

[8] Richard Epstein, "Blackmail, Inc.," 50 *University of Chicago Law Review* 553, 561 (1983).

[9] Lindgren, "Unraveling the Paradox of Blackmail," 676.

[10] *Landry* v. *Daley*, 280 F. Supp. 938 (1968).

[11] "Blackmail would not be illegal in the free society. For blackmail is the receipt of money in exchange for the service of not publicizing certain information . . . No violence or threat of violence . . . is involved." Murray Rothbard, *Man, Economy, and State* (Princeton: D. Van Nostrand, 1962), vol. 2, 443. Also see Eric Mack, "In Defense of Blackmail," a paper delivered as commentary upon Jeffrie Murphy's "Blackmail: A Preliminary Inquiry" at the meetings of the American Philosophical Association, December 1979.

[12] On coercive speech in particular, see Kent Greenawalt, "Criminal Coercion and Freedom of Speech," 78 *Northwestern University Law Review* 1081 (1983). Also see "Coercion, Blackmail, and the Limits of Protected Speech," 131 *University of Pennsylvania Law Review* 1469 (1983). For more general discussions, see Lindgren, "Unraveling the Paradox of Blackmail"; Epstein, "Blackmail, Inc."; Robert Nozick, *Anarchy, State, and Utopia* (New York: Basic Books, 1974), 84–86; and Jeffrie Murphy, "Blackmail: A Preliminary Inquiry," 63 *Monist* 156 (1980).

the internal features of blackmail that would justify its criminalization. Certainly the fact that the blackmailer makes a *threat* is not sufficient to explain its illegality. For as we have seen in other legal contexts, there are many threats that we are entitled to make, such threats are not generally regarded as coercive, and agreements made in response to such threats are typically enforceable.[13] Indeed, and in the present context, the prospective blackmail victim might *prefer* to be the object of a blackmail threat. If the blackmailer makes his threat, the victim has the opportunity to purchase his immunity from public scandal. If blackmail laws deter such threats, but not the exposure of damaging information, the potential blackmail victim has no choice but to suffer in silence.[14] Of course, it does not follow just because one might prefer being the object of a *particular* threat that one would also prefer that such threats be *generally* allowed. But the fact that the blackmailer may have the right to carry out his threatened action and the fact that the victim might prefer to be the recipient of such threats (although not the threatened action) makes it difficult to explain why such threats are coercive and why they should be prohibited.

External Theories. Precisely for the foregoing reasons, those who advance external theories of blackmail do not typically argue that blackmail is coercive or that its putative coerciveness accounts for its criminalization. Richard Epstein, for example, says this: "Blackmail is made a crime not only because of what it is, but because of what it necessarily leads to. The popular sentiment is *wrong* to the extent that it insists that the demand for money to remain silent when there is a right to speak counts as *coercion* . . ."[15] To explore the benefits derived from criminalizing blackmail, Epstein asks us to imagine what the world would look like if blackmail were legalized, if "Blackmail, Inc." could advertise its services and threaten to market

---

[13] It is not easy to distinguish the blackmailer's proposals from other legally permissible but arguably immoral threats that characterize "hard bargaining" in a capitalist economy. See Epstein, "Blackmail, Inc.," 557. Jeffrie Murphy notes that libertarians and Marxists may both argue for the equivalence of blackmail and hard bargains. Libertarians may argue that since blackmail is equivalent to hard economic transactions, blackmail should be legal. Marxists may argue that since hard economic transactions are equivalent to blackmail, hard economic transactions should be illegal. See "Blackmail: A Preliminary Inquiry," 157–58.

[14] As Epstein suggests, the right to threaten to do what one has a right to do "is essential to the preservation of any system of liberties, for if one person does not have the right to threaten actions that he may or may not do, he has to act without giving warnings. This in turn will work to the disadvantage of the other party, who is now deprived of the choice that the threat would have otherwise given him." "Blackmail, Inc.," 558.

[15] Ibid., 566 (emphasis added).

embarrassing information. The principal undesirable consequence of blackmail, says Epstein, is that it leads to a form of *fraud* against *third parties*, namely, those who might profit from the information that the blackmailer's victim wants concealed. In the absence of this information, such persons might be deprived of a judgment against the blackmail victim (for example, a divorce), or might make decisions about the victim based on inaccurate or incomplete information.[16] And since the blackmail victim may not have sufficient funds to buy his immunity from Blackmail, Inc., the legalization of blackmail may encourage him to engage in fraud or theft in order to pay.

Other external theories have a similar consequentialist structure, but a somewhat different content. One such theory derives from the economic analysis of law. This argument claims that some social norms are typically and most efficiently enforced in the private realm, whereas others are typically and efficiently targets of public enforcement. When blackmail involves (as it sometimes does) the private enforcement of the criminal law, it interferes with the government's (efficient) monopoly of criminal law enforcement.[17] On the other hand, if the society has made a judgment *not* to enforce other (for example, sexual) norms through either the criminal or the civil law, blackmail may lead to an (inefficient) *over*enforcement of those norms.[18]

Interestingly, the difficulties in the way of developing a successful internal theory of blackmail have led two deontologically oriented philosophers to abandon their favored moral perspectives. Robert Nozick, for example, does not justify the prohibition against blackmail by appealing to the victim's rights, nor does he argue against its prohibition by appealing to the blackmailer's rights. Rather, he argues that blackmail is prohibited because it is an "unproductive exchange."[19] Whereas the buyer of a service—even at an exploitative price—is normally better off because the other person exists, the blackmailer's victim would generally be better off had the blackmailer never been born.

Jeffrie Murphy also turns to "teleological considerations of social policy" after surveying (in vain) the Kantian deontological princi-

16 Ibid., 564.
17 For a more detailed analysis of this argument, see Lindgren, "Unraveling the Paradox of Blackmail," 697–99.
18 And if we understand blackmail as a contract between the blackmailer and his victim, there are special difficulties in the way of its enforcement; the victim will be reluctant to sue the blackmailer, for fear of publicizing the very information he wants to suppress.
19 *Anarchy, State, and Utopia*, 84–86.

ples of which he is "fond."[20] Murphy argues that the prohibition against blackmail is, at its root, designed to limit incentives for the invasion of privacy. Were it not for the opportunity to trade information for money, there would be little demand for investigation into the private affairs of private citizens (although that may not be true of public figures). Blackmail is criminalized, he maintains, precisely to limit those opportunities.

Of course, even if the previous arguments correctly identify some beneficial consequences of the criminalization of blackmail, it does not follow that those effects provide the best justification of its criminalization. Epstein candidly acknowledges that his account does not explain why the blackmailer is punished while his victim goes free. Moreover, even if blackmail deprives third parties of information they *desire*, it is not clear that they have a *right* to receive it.[21] In addition, even if the argument that blackmail leads to the overenforcement or underenforcement of (different) social norms is correct, that argument does not distinguish between permissible forms of private enforcement (social stigma) and nonpermissible forms (blackmail).[22]

With respect to Nozick's argument, the fact is that blackmail is not necessarily unproductive, for without the blackmailer's service, the information that the victim wants concealed may fall into others' hands.[23] With respect to Murphy's argument, James Lindgren observes that there *is* a considerable and active legal market for investigations into private affairs, for example, by spouses, credit agencies, and employers. And even if Murphy's account explains the prohibition of *entrepreneurial* blackmail (where an investigation is undertaken precisely so that one can engage in blackmail), it does not explain the prohibition of *opportunistic* blackmail (the sale of information acquired in the course of one's normal activities).[24]

Yet the problem is not that external theories fail to capture the undesirable consequences of blackmail—for that they may do reasonably well. The problem is that they do not seem to explain *all* that is wrong with blackmail. In particular, the external arguments do not capture the intuition that there is something inherently *coercive*

[20] "Blackmail: A Preliminary Inquiry," 162.
[21] Is it important or desirable that employers know that a prospective employee is a homosexual? For a more extended analysis of Epstein's argument, see Lindgren, "Unraveling the Paradox of Blackmail," 684–87.
[22] Ibid., 668–69.
[23] Nozick recognizes this difficulty but says that to meet it would "not be worth the effort it requires." *Anarchy, State, and Utopia*, 85.
[24] "Unraveling the Paradox of Blackmail," 689–94.

about the blackmailer's threats. Perhaps that intuition is wrong; but it would be a mistake to dismiss it prematurely.

Internal Theories. And so we turn to some recent attempts to develop an internal theory of blackmail. An excellent and extremely helpful example of this genre is Kent Greenawalt's analysis of the constitutional problem raised by *State* v. *Robertson*, a case prosecuted under an Oregon "criminal coercion" statute.[25] One commits criminal coercion, under this statute, if one causes another to do something he has a legal right not to do by causing him to fear some sort of harm. Some of the listed harms are independently criminal, for example, causing physical injury or damage to property. But one may also violate this law by threatening blackmail, by proposing to "expose a secret or publicize an asserted fact, whether true or false, tending to subject some person to hatred, contempt, or ridicule . . ."[26]

Several men were convicted of having coerced their victim into performing sexual acts by threatening to send to her parents an embarrassing picture.[27] On appeal, the Oregon Supreme Court held that the statute was unconstitutional under the Oregon Constitution, because its criteria for the crime of coercion were overly broad and included constitutionally protected forms of speech. The court did not, of course, claim that the defendants' threats *were* constitutionally protected speech; it claimed that the *statute* under which those threats were criminal was constitutionally defective. And so we have an additional paradox: whereas the facts of *Robertson* serve as a paradigm of blackmail, the law under which Robertson was prosecuted shows the difficulties involved in defining the offense and justifying its prohibition.

Greenawalt wants to argue that whereas noncoercive speech has a prima facie claim to constitutional protection, coercive threats do not. To make the argument work, he must first distinguish between coercive and noncoercive speech. In that connection, Greenawalt introduces two criteria: (1) Is A's statement *action inducing*, that is, does A's statement attempt to get B to *do* something? (2) Is A's statement *situation altering*, that is, does A's statement have the effect of changing B's situation? Employing these criteria, Greenawalt distinguishes between four related types of speech: warnings, simple threats, warning threats, and manipulative threats. Greenawalt ar-

---

[25] Or. Rev. Stat. Sec. 163.275(1)(e). See Greenawalt's "Criminal Coercion and Freedom of Speech."

[26] Or. Rev. Stat. Sec. 163.275(1)(e).

[27] *State* v. *Robertson*, 642 P.2d 569 (1982).

gues that only *manipulative* threats are action inducing *and* situation altering, and that only (but not all) manipulative threats are coercive.[28] Greenawalt's distinctions are roughly as follows:

1. A *warns* B against doing X if A tells B that doing X will be harmful to B, but A does not himself propose to cause that harm—"If you don't stop speaking to your boss's wife, you're going to get fired." A's statement is action inducing but not situation altering. Although A's warning may affect B's *perception* of his environment, it does not change that environment. A's warning merely provides B with information about "external facts."[29]

2. A makes a *simple threat* when A declares that he plans to harm B—"Because you have seduced my wife, I'm going to get you someday." Simple threats are not coercive because they are not action inducing. A's threat may *frighten* B, but it does not *coerce* B, because it does not try to get B to *do* anything.[30]

3. A makes a *warning threat* when A makes an action-inducing but not situation-altering statement in which A himself threatens to bring about the harmful consequences. To use Greenawalt's example: "[Tom], disturbed by the fact that [Vanessa] is selling drugs in her apartment, decides that he will inform the police if that is necessary to get her to stop. He tells her that she had better stop or he will do so. Afraid of being arrested, she stops."[31] The general point, says Greenawalt, is that Tom is *not* making his threat just to induce Vanessa's action. Tom's threat is not a "strategic" device to alter Vanessa's behavior; it is, at least for *him*, a "natural response" to her behavior. Tom's intention to inform the police if Vanessa does not stop selling drugs is *already* a part of her environment, although she may not know this. Since a warning threat is not situation altering and since only situation-altering proposals, Greenawalt argues, lack constitutional protection, warning threats as well as warnings and simple threats, have a *prima facie* claim to such protection.[32]

4. A *manipulative threat* is both action inducing and situation altering. Consider:

[28] Greenawalt is not primarily concerned to distinguish between manipulative *threats* and manipulative *offers*. While manipulative offers are also action inducing and situation altering, they are, for the most part, typically and uncontroversially noncoercive.

[29] "Criminal Coercion and Freedom of Speech," 1096–97. Greenawalt notes that warnings fall within the literal scope of the Oregon criminal coercion statute, but argues that they are *not* coercive and therefore *should* receive constitutional protection.

[30] Ibid., 1097.

[31] Ibid., 1100. I have changed the names to facilitate comparison.

[32] Ibid., 1116.

Tim wants to make love with Vicki. Realizing that his native charm is inadequate for the task, Tim decides that success will depend on frightening Vicki. He knows that Vicki has recently had an abortion, that she cares a great deal about her parents' opinion of her, and that her parents regard abortion as a terrible wrong. Tim threatens that he will inform Vicki's parents unless she makes love with him, and she complies.[33]

Unlike a simple threat, Tim's manipulative threat is action inducing. And unlike a warning threat, Tim's threat is situation altering—if we assume that Tim would not inform Vicki's parents about the abortion in the normal course of events. Whereas (in the previous example) Tom's threat to tell the police about Vanessa's practice of selling drugs is (for Tom) a "natural response" to Vanessa's behavior, Tim's proposal to inform Vicki's parents about her abortion is (for Tim) an "unnatural response" to Vicki's situation. It is a strategic device that has been adopted solely to induce Vicki's action.

We might try to explain the distinction between warning threats and manipulative threats in a slightly different way. Tom and Tim both have an intention to execute their threats. Yet Tim also has what we might call a "metaintention" to form an intention to execute his threat—a metaintention absent in the case of Tom's warning threats.[34] Or, to put the point in still another way, it is likely that Tom would carry out his warning threat (to tell the police) even if he were not able to communicate with Vanessa; it is unlikely that Tim would carry out his manipulative threat (to tell Vicki's parents) if he were unable to communicate with Vicki.

To the best of my knowledge, the distinction between warning threats and manipulative threats has not been explicitly invoked in blackmail cases. It has, however, come to play an important role in *labor law*. An employer is not permitted to make coercive threats designed to influence the outcome of a vote on unionization. What *may* an employer say? An employer is permitted to inform ("warn") the employees of the adverse economic consequences of unionization—for example, that a major customer would stop buying its products. An employer "may even make a prediction as to the precise effects he believes unionization will have on his company . . . [that are] outside of his control."[35] An employer may also issue a

---

[33] Ibid., 1097.
[34] I owe this point to George Sher.
[35] *NLRB* v. *Gissel Packing Co.*, 395 U.S. 595 (1969).

"warning threat" of a *genuine* and *fixed* plan to close a plant upon unionization.[36] An employer may not, however, make a (manipulative) threat to close "part of a business" in response to unionization, even though it would be entitled to close the entire business for any reasons it chose, including the fact that the workers had voted to unionize.[37]

Manipulative Threats and Blackmail. The notion of a manipulative threat may narrow the field, but we must still settle what is special about the nature of a blackmail proposal. For, as we have seen, non-wrongful manipulative threats are generally not regarded as coercive.[38] It is not blackmail if A threatens to sell a product or service to C unless B pays a certain price, or threatens to sue B for damages unless B settles out of court, or threatens not to extend B's loan unless B puts up additional collateral, or threatens not to marry B unless B signs a prenuptial agreement. What is the difference between these sorts of threats and blackmail? Lindgren suggests this. In all of these cases, A threatens a consequence that is *his* to dispense— his product, his right to sue, his right to be repaid, his right to marry. On the other hand, the blackmailer's threat is typically quite different. "At the heart of blackmail . . . is the *triangular* nature of the transaction, and particularly this disjunction between the blackmailer's personal benefit and the interests of the third parties whose leverage he uses. In effect, the blackmailer attempts to gain an advantage in return for suppressing someone else's actual or potential interest."[39]

When the blackmailer threatens to embarrass his victim by releasing information, the victim is paying to avoid the loss of reputation with other persons. When the blackmailer threatens to report to the authorities that his victim has committed a crime, he is playing with the "state's chip," even if the threat of prosecution is used to secure

[36] Ibid.

[37] *Textile Workers* v. *Darlington Manufacturing Co.*, 380 U.S. 263, 268 (1965). Interestingly, while an employer would violate a prohibition against coercive speech by threatening to close the plant in response to unionization, a labor union can tell employees that if they do not join the union, they will lose their jobs if it organizes a union shop. "There can be nothing unlawful in threatening to do that which it is lawful to do." *NLRB* v. *Karp Metal Products Co.*, 134 F.2d 955 (1943).

[38] And even unambiguously coercive threats may be a legitimate means for controlling someone's behavior, and thus although coercive, should not be prohibited. Greenawalt's point is not that manipulative threats are necessarily coercive or that coerciveness is a sufficient condition of prohibition, but that manipulative threats lie outside the range of constitutionally protected freedom of expression. "Criminal Coercion and Freedom of Speech," 1099.

[39] "Unraveling the Paradox of Blackmail," 702 (emphasis added).

something to which he already has a right.[40] When the blackmailer threatens to inform a man's wife about his infidelity or an accident victim of the tortfeasor's identity, he is bargaining with legal rights that belong to a third party—"he imposes himself parasitically in an actual or potential dispute in which he lacks a sufficiently direct interest."[41]

The "triangular" argument runs counter to our ordinary and dyadic view of legal relationships. We generally think that A's relationship with B is legally suspect only if A violates a legal right of B's.[42] Precisely for this reason, it has recently been argued that coercive-speech analysis does *not* justify statutes that proscribe threats to commit acts that are neither crimes nor torts because such threats "cannot force the listener to choose between two things, to both of which the listener has a legitimate claim."[43] It has been argued that if a gangster threatens to notify the police that a tavern owner is violating the law unless the tavern owner votes for a certain candidate, "coercive speech analysis does not justify prosecution of the gangster. While the tavern owner has a right to vote his conscience . . . [he] has no right not to be charged accurately with a crime."[44]

If Lindgren is right, the gangster can, in fact, be prosecuted for blackmail. What can explain this? There are three possibilities. First, it might be argued that the prohibition of blackmail is not meant to protect *individual* rights at all. After all, blackmail is a *crime*, and crimes are said to be wrongs against the *society*.[45] This "public harm" analysis of blackmail may capture much of what is important to its criminalization, but it returns us, in part, to an "external" analysis of the offense. The question of whether blackmail is a form of *coercion* that may or may not *also* be a wrong against the society remains.

A second argument attempts to capture this coerciveness. In bar-

[40] Ibid. Although some courts have held otherwise, it is generally a crime for a creditor to accuse a debtor of a crime in order to be repaid, even if the creditor has a right to be repaid and the debtor is guilty. See 31 *American Jurisprudence*, 2d ed., *Extortion, Blackmail, and Threats*, Sec. 11, 909 (1967).

[41] "Unraveling the Paradox of Blackmail," 702. Lindgren follows Epstein in focusing on the "triangular" character of blackmail. But whereas Epstein's account focuses on the wrong to the *third* party (who is deprived of information), Lindgren focuses on the wrong to the blackmail *victim*.

[42] This includes cases where A attempts to get B to violate C's rights.

[43] "Coercion, Blackmail, and the Limits of Protected Speech," 1473.

[44] Ibid., 1473–74.

[45] Criminal cases are brought *by* the society; they involve no compensation to the victim; and if punishment involves the payment of a "debt," it is a debt paid to the society. See Lawrence C. Becker, "Criminal Attempt and the Theory of the Law of Crimes," 3 *Philosophy & Public Affairs* 262 (1974)

est outline, the argument is that there are both *simple* and *complex* rights. Consider, for example, a case in which B has committed a criminal act. Even if B has no simple right not to be punished, he has a complex right not to be punished by a person not authorized to do so. Similarly, even if one has no simple right to both X *and* Y, one may have a *complex* right not to be forced to choose *between* X and Y. The gangster may not violate the tavern owner's simple rights, for the tavern owner has no right not to be charged with a crime. Nonetheless, the tavern owner may have a complex right not to be forced to choose between being charged with a crime and voting for a specific candidate. Or perhaps he has a complex right not to be threatened with prosecution by someone not authorized to make such threats or for purposes unrelated to the administration of justice.

A third and related argument takes a slightly different tack, and, in effect, returns us to the two-pronged theory of coercion. In simplest terms, there are right and wrong ways of trying to influence the behavior of others. As Thomas Nagel observes: "There seems to be a perfectly natural conception of the distinction between fighting clean and fighting dirty. To fight dirty is to direct one's hostility or aggression not at its proper object, but at a peripheral target which may be more vulnerable."[46] Although Nagel means to apply this distinction to the rules of war, he maintains that the distinction between clean and dirty fighting is, in fact, quite general. It applies to virtually all forms of interpersonal conflict—fistfights, arguments between spouses, and elections. In each of these contexts, there are right and wrong ways of trying to win.

The point also applies to legal controversies. In contracts we saw that while A generally does not coerce B if A threatens to do something that A is entitled to do, this rule fails to hold if A uses such a threat in a way that the law considers abusive or improper—perhaps by using the threat of criminal prosecution to secure a private agreement. Consider in this context *United States* v. *Pignatelli*. Pignatelli was involved in a legal controversy and threatened to publish a book exposing the other parties as "fakers" (they claimed a title of nobility) unless they succumbed to his demands. The court said that "threats to damage another's reputation are no proper means for determining a controversy. It may be adjusted either by suit or by compromise, but . . . not . . . by using defamation as a club."[47] Similarly, it was held that a lawyer had committed black-

---

[46] "War and Massacre," 1 *Philosophy & Public Affairs* 123, 134 (1972).
[47] 125 F.2d 643 (1942).

mail when he wrote to his client's husband that if the husband did not accept the proposed property settlement, he would initiate an "embarrassing reputation-ruining divorce proceeding."[48]

Although the parallels between contractual duress and blackmail have been largely ignored in the scholarly literature, we have seen in several different legal contexts an appeal to a two-pronged theory of coercion. The two-pronged theory holds that we coerce only when our proposal is wrongful. If blackmail is a form of fighting dirty, we may say that blackmail too is coercive (assuming that a blackmail proposal also satisfies the choice prong) precisely because it is a case of fighting dirty. The *wrongness* of the blackmailer's proposal is at the center of its coerciveness.

Immoral Proposals and Immoral Actions

I do not know that the preceding analysis has convincingly shown that and how the criminalization of blackmail can be defended or explained. But whatever its success in that respect, it does serve to underline a more general point, to wit, that the "wrongness" of the blackmailer's proposal turns on (what I shall call) the *morality of proposals*, and that this is a dimension of morality which is (at least somewhat) independent of the *morality of actions*. We can see this distinction in two asymmetries. First, as we have seen in several legal contexts, it may be impermissible to propose to perform acts it would be permissible to perform. Second, in other contexts, it may be permissible to make (even credible) proposals to do what it would be impermissible to do. It may, for example, be legitimate to say to a burglar, "I'll shoot you if you take my television," even if it would be wrong to shoot him if he fails to respond to one's threat.[49]

In his famous discussion of "organic unity," G. E. Moore once argued that the "value of a [moral] whole must not be assumed to be the same as the sum of its parts."[50] We need not accept the entire corpus of Moore's argument to appreciate the force of this general point. As the discussion of blackmail vividly demonstrates, we

[48] *State* v. *Harrington*, 260 A.2d 692. In this case, the embarrassment would have been due to pictures taken of the husband in bed with a woman sent by the lawyer to get evidence about the man's adulterous proclivities.

[49] Jeffrie G. Murphy, "Consent, Coercion, and Hard Choices," 67 *Virginia Law Review* 79, 81 (1981). If nuclear deterrence can be justified, its justification may also assume that it is permissible to make a credible proposal to do what it would be wrong to do.

[50] *Principia Ethica* (Cambridge: Cambridge University Press, 1903), 28.

should not assume that the immorality of proposals can be adequately explained by the immorality of their constituent parts. I have not, of course, provided a theory of the morality of proposals. It will suffice, for present purposes, to recognize that such a theory is crucial to a fully developed theory of coercion.

SIX

CONFESSIONS AND SEARCHES

The Constitution grants several rights to suspects or defendants in criminal cases. The Fourth Amendment grants citizens the right to be free from "unreasonable searches and seizures," the Fifth Amendment states that "[n]o person . . . shall be compelled in any criminal case to be a witness against himself," the Sixth Amendment gives all criminal defendants the "right to a speedy and public trial, by an impartial jury," and the Fourteenth Amendment extends and reinforces these principles by adding that no *state* shall "deprive any person of life, liberty, or property, without due process of law." Now these constitutional rights are not technically inalienable. They can be waived, but only if the waiver is voluntary and, in particular, if it is not coerced.[1] In this chapter, I consider the way courts have adjudicated coercion claims with respect to confessions and searches, with the way coercion claims block or negate the effect of certain forms of police conduct. The next chapter considers the way courts have adjudicated coercion claims with respect to guilty pleas, with the way coercion claims block or negate the effect of certain forms of prosecutorial conduct.

Confessions

Confession may or may not be good for the soul, but it has long been crucial to the conviction of criminal defendants. John Langbein has written that early Continental criminal law was so concerned to avoid convicting the innocent that a conviction had to be based on the testimony of two eyewitnesses or a confession.[2] One eyewitness was insufficient, and circumstantial evidence was not allowed. The problem is, of course, that however well intentioned such a rule, no society can "tolerate a legal system that lacks the capacity to convict unrepentant persons who commit clandestine

---

[1] I speak loosely here. One actually waives not the right itself, but the protection secured by the right.

[2] "Torture and Plea Bargaining," *The Public Interest* (Winter 1980), 43–61.

crimes." Because the eyewitness rule was inelastic, confessions became the principal form of proof. And torture became a primary method of inducing confessions.[3]

While torture, strictly defined, has probably been rare in the United States, "giving someone the third degree" has no doubt been more common, and this has raised important questions as to just what is entailed by the notion of a voluntary confession. Interestingly, despite the Fifth Amendment's prohibition against "compelled" self-incrimination, it seems that the *voluntariness* of a confession was originally less important than its veracity. Yale Kamisar writes that whatever is *now* meant by a voluntary confession, it originally was "no more than an alternative statement of the rule that a confession was admissible so long as it was free of influences which made it 'unreliable' or 'probably untrue'."[4]

Early Cases. But that is history. And, over time, the courts came to take the voluntariness requirement more seriously. An 1897 decision on coerced confessions concerned Bram, who was accused of murder at high sea, and who was interrogated by the police after having been stripped naked.[5] When told that there was a witness to the crime, Bram blurted out that the alleged witness "could not have seen him," thereby implicating himself. He later claimed that his statements had been made under duress. The Court agreed. It argued that the rule prohibiting compulsion of incriminating testimony was "comprehensive enough" to exclude all forms of compulsion, "whether physical or moral." *Bram* serves to illustrate what I take to be an important and general feature of the confessions cases, namely, that unlike most of the legal contexts we have considered, here the Court places considerable emphasis on the *volitional quality* of the agent's act. The measure of coercion, said the Court, was to be found not in its "changing causes," but in its "resultant effect upon the *mind*."[6] Bram's statement, said the Court, could not possibly have been a "purely voluntary mental action . . .

---

[3] Ibid., 65. Langbein notes that the use of torture had nothing to do with punishment, and was, in fact, a highly rule-governed activity.

[4] "What Is an 'Involuntary' Confession?" 17 *Rutgers Law Review* 728, 742–43 (1963) (original emphasis). Thus one text on police interrogation techniques states that its recommended procedures "measure up to the *fundamental* test that not one of them is apt to induce an *innocent* person to confess." Fred Inbau and John Reid, *Criminal Interrogation and Confessions* (Baltimore: Williams and Wilkins, 1962), vii, quoted in Kamisar, 734 (emphasis added).

[5] *Bram* v. *U.S.*, 168 U.S. 532 (1897).

[6] Ibid., 547 (emphasis added).

it must necessarily have been the result of either hope or fear, or both, operating on the mind."[7]

Brown v. *Mississippi* (1935) concerned the confessions of "ignorant negroes" who had been hung from a tree by a group which included the deputy sheriff. Brown was let down, and when he continued to protest his innocence, he was strung up and let down once again. After being whipped, but still refusing to confess, he was released. After a day or two, the deputy sheriff returned, took Brown into custody, and whipped him until he "agreed to confess to such a statement as the deputy would dictate."[8] Reversing the lower court, the Supreme Court held that the confession had been coerced. So, too, in *Chambers* v. *Florida*, the Court held involuntary a confession produced by five days of interrogation, including an all-night examination, where the defendant also had to contend with the "haunting fear of mob violence . . . in an atmosphere charged with excitement and public indignation."[9]

The problem, for our purposes, is that while *Brams*, *Brown*, and *Chambers* may have reached the right conclusions, they contain little analysis of the criteria employed by the Court in deciding that the confessions had been coerced. The first extensive theoretical discussion occurs in *Ashcraft* v. *Tennessee*. In that case, the defendant confessed after being questioned for thirty-six hours "without rest or sleep" by a team of interrogators who operated in "relays."[10] In holding the confession involuntary, the Court argued that the state's action was "irreconcilable with the possession of mental freedom by a lone suspect against whom its full coercive force is brought to bear."[11]

Jackson, dissenting, conceded that a confession produced by the use of "brutality, torture, beating, and starvation . . . is prima facie involuntary," because some men are "so constituted" that they will "risk the postponed consequences of yielding to a demand for a confession in order to be rid of present or imminent physical suffering."[12] But, said Jackson, unlike violence, interrogation is not "an outlaw."

---

[7] Ibid., 562. It is not clear what a "purely voluntary mental action" would look like. Justice White's dissenting opinion stressed the importance of truthfulness rather than voluntariness: "[T]he fact that the defendant was in custody and in irons does not destroy the competency of a confession." 569.

[8] 297 U.S. 278, 281 (1935).

[9] 309 U.S. 227, 239 (1940).

[10] 322 U.S. 143, 153 (1944).

[11] Ibid.

[12] Ibid., 160.

Even a "voluntary confession" is not likely to be the product of the same motives with which one may volunteer information that does not incriminate or concern him . . . [the term] does not mean voluntary in the sense of a confession to a priest merely to rid one's soul of a sense of guilt . . . A confession is wholly and incontestably voluntary only if a guilty person gives himself up to the law and becomes his own accuser. The Court bases its decision on the premise that custody and examination of a prisoner for thirty-six hours is "inherently coercive." Of course it is. And so is custody and examination for one hour.[13]

Jackson's argument can, I think, be understood in this way. If the state's actions seriously compromise the volitional quality of a confession, it should be held involuntary. But if the state's action does not seriously compromise the volitional quality of a confession, we should employ a two-pronged theory of coercion. On that view of coercion, the confession in question was arguably not involuntary, for the following reasons: (1) the use or threat of violence produces coerced confessions in large part because violence is *wrong* (under the proposal prong); (2) arrest and interrogation are not inherently wrong and are therefore not "inherently coercive"; (3) it is virtually impossible to determine a point at which interrogation would *become* wrong and therefore coercive. Jackson concedes that there is *a* sense in which virtually *all* confessions produced by interrogation are involuntary ("so is . . . examination for one hour"), but he challenges his brethren to indicate why *this* degree of interrogation is coercive in a way that should invalidate the confession. Given that there is, in effect, no "bright line" by which to determine when interrogation is excessive, courts should hold confessions involuntary only when they have been produced by a patently suspect method or when an agent's will has been clearly overwhelmed.

The "Totality of the Circumstances" Test. In effect, the Court responded to Jackson's challenge in *Haley* v. *Ohio*. Haley, fifteen years old, confessed after questioning "through the dead of night by relays of police."[14] In holding Haley's confession involuntary, the Court foreshadowed what came to be known as the "totality of the circumstances" test. On this view, an assessment of voluntariness is based not on a single criterion, but on a reading of the entire sit-

[13] Ibid., 160, 161.
[14] 332 U.S. 596, 599 (1948).

uation, including the defendant's individual characteristics. Although a "mature" man might have been able to withstand Haley's ordeal, the Court could not "believe that a lad of tender years is a match for the police in such a contest."[15] Frankfurter (concurring) said this: "But whether a confession of a lad of fifteen is 'voluntary' and as such admissible, or 'coerced' and thus wanting in due process, is not a matter of mathematical determination. Essentially it invites psychological judgment—a psychological judgment that reflects deep, even if inarticulate, feelings of our society."[16] Frankfurter grants that there is no *clear* demarcation between voluntary and involuntary confessions; the determination of voluntariness requires "psychological judgment"—not judgment about psychology (although also that) but sensitive judgment about individual cases.[17]

Frankfurter continues this line of argument in *Watts* v. *Indiana*.[18] In holding involuntary a confession produced by "relentless police interrogation," Frankfurter says, "[T]here is torture of mind as well as body; the will is as much affected by fear as by force."[19] Now the distinction Frankfurter advances between "force" and "fear" is not quite right. When the will is affected by force, it is, after all, typically because the force already employed makes one fearful of *future* force. One who confesses after being whipped is typically motivated more by the fear that the beating will *continue* than by the beating that has *already* occurred. But this emendation actually strengthens Frankfurter's claim. For there is no reason to assume that interrogation cannot generate as much fear as physical force, in which case if physical force can render a confession involuntary, so, too, can extensive interrogation.

While the early confession cases focused on the volitional quality of the suspect's confession, strains of the two-pronged account of coercion began to appear in *Stein* v. *New York*, where the Court upheld a confession produced by extensive interrogation:

> Physical violence . . . serves no lawful purpose, invalidates confessions that otherwise would be convincing, and is universally condemned by law. When present, *there is no need to weigh*

---

[15] Ibid., 599, 600.

[16] "It would disregard standards that we cherish as part of our faith in the strength and well-being of a rational, civilized society to hold that a confession is 'voluntary' simply because the confession is the product of a sentient choice." Ibid., 603, 606.

[17] Ibid., 603.

[18] 338 U.S. 49 (1949).

[19] Ibid., 52.

or measure its effects on the will of the individual victim . . . But . . .
interrogation is not inherently coercive . . . Interrogation does
have social value in solving crime, as physical force does not
. . . Of course, these confessions were not voluntary in the
sense that petitioners wanted to make them or that they were
completely spontaneous, like a confession to a priest, a lawyer,
or a psychiatrist. But in this sense no criminal confession is voluntary.[20]

Stein is not a model of judicial clarity or consistency. First, although the claim that interrogation is not "inherently coercive" is a
plausible application of the proposal prong, the contrast between
the inherent legitimacy of interrogation and the inherent immorality of violence does not turn, at least not primarily, on their respective "social value." After all, even the use of physical violence may
produce accurate confessions and convictions that are not attaina-
ble in other ways. While such confessions may, on balance, be unacceptable, they are not necessarily without benefit to the society.
Second, while it might plausibly be argued that violence should always *invalidate* a confession under *due process* requirements, violence can hardly be said to *coerce* a confession if it has little effect on
the victim's will or choice. In my view, the Court equivocates between due process and voluntariness requirements, or, if one prefers, between voluntariness due process requirements and non-vol-
untariness due process requirements.

A similar equivocation occurs in *Leyra* v. *Denno*.[21] After a state-
employed psychiatrist had gotten the defendant to admit the crime
in private, the defendant confessed to the police. The Court held
the confessions involuntary. Minton (dissenting) objected to the
claim that the confession was involuntary "as a matter of law." The
question of coercion, he said, refers not to the legitimacy of employing the psychiatrist, but to whether his actions "continued to influence [the defendant's] mind . . ."[22] Now Minton was, I think, partly
right and partly wrong. If the Court meant to adopt some version of
the two-pronged theory of coercion, he was wrong to think that the
legitimacy of the state's action is *irrelevant* to the question of coercion. But he was right in urging the Court to distinguish between
due process and voluntariness objections to that action. For to find
that the state coerced the defendant, we must hold either that it se-

---

[20] 346 U.S. 156, 182, 184, 185, 186 (1952) (emphasis added).
[21] 347 U.S. 556 (1953).
[22] Ibid., 585, 586.

riously compromised his volition or that his choice situation was such that he had no reasonable alternative to confessing.

These excursions aside, the Court generally continued to apply a "totality of the circumstances" test for confessions, often in favor of the defendant, although sometimes not.[23] At the same time, it was not altogether clear about the precise values and interests that test was meant to protect. Consider *Spano* v. *New York*.[24] Spano, indicted for murder, confessed after prolonged interrogation. "His will was overborne by official pressure, fatigue, and sympathy falsely aroused [when] a police officer friend . . . was instructed to falsely state that because of a prior call by defendant, his job was in jeopardy, and that loss of his job would be disastrous to his children, his wife, and his unborn child."[25] In holding Spano's confession involuntary, the Court stated that society's abhorrence of involuntary confessions "does not turn alone on their inherent untrustworthiness" (only a *very* good friend would falsely confess to murder in order to preserve a friend's job) but turns, in addition, on the "deep rooted feeling that the police must obey the law while enforcing the law."[26] In effect, the Court argues that the voluntariness principle serves two purposes: it secures the accuracy of a confession and deters police misconduct. Yet *neither* of these purposes touches what I take to be the core of the voluntariness principle, namely, the protection of the autonomy of the agent.

If I am right in thinking that the Court was nominally using the voluntariness principle to in fact protect nonvoluntariness (due process) values, the Court continued to reaffirm the principle's constitutional centrality. In *Culombe* v. *Connecticut*, for example, the Court held that voluntariness is the "ultimate test" for confessions, indeed that it had been "the *only* clearly established test in Anglo-American courts for two hundred years . . ."[27] Culombe, a thirty-three-year-old "mental defective," was detained and questioned for four days. The only persons he spoke with were the police, his alleged accomplice, "of whom he was afraid," and his wife, "who by prearrangement with the police, asked him to confess." He was not informed of his right to remain silent. In holding Culombe's confession (to murder) involuntary, the Court described the inquiry into

---

[23] See *Fikes* v. *Ala.*, 352 U.S. 191 (1957); *Payne* v. *Ark.*, 356 U.S. 560 (1958); and *Crooker* v. *Cal.*, 357 U.S. 433 (1958). In *Crooker*, the Court held that the defendant's intelligence, education, and familiarity with police procedures were evidence that the confession was voluntary.

[24] 360 U.S. 315 (1959).

[25] Ibid., 323.

[26] Ibid., 320.

[27] 367 U.S. 568, 602 (1961) (emphasis added).

the voluntariness of a confession as a three-stage process: (1) one finds the "crude historical facts," the "external . . . occurrences and events surrounding the confession"; (2) one then undertakes "the imaginative recreation, largely inferential, of internal 'psychological' fact"; and (3) one applies the relevant rules of law to these psychological facts.[28]

As a general description of process, *Culombe* seems reasonably close to the mark. The Court is right to note that assessing the volitional quality of a confession requires inferential judgments about psychological facts, and that the standards for evaluating those psychological facts are matters of law (as are the standards for insanity). As the Court said: "The notion of 'voluntariness' is itself an *amphibian*. It purports at once to describe an internal psychic state and to characterize that state for legal purposes."[29] That is fine as far as it goes. But the Court did not say, as I think it should have, that while voluntariness, as a legal construct, may capture some of the factors that might invalidate a confession, it need not capture them all.

Confessions and Informed Consent. A further problem with the Court's theory of coerced confessions emerges in *Haynes* v. *Washington*.[30] Haynes confessed to robbery sixteen hours after he had been arrested, during which time he was refused permission to call his wife or an attorney. Did the simple denial of Haynes's request for an attorney compromise the voluntariness of his confession? The majority of the Court held that it had. A dissenting opinion said this: "[I]n light of petitioner's age, intelligence and experience with the police, in light of the comparative absence of any coercive circumstances, and in light of the fact that petitioner never, from time of his arrest, evidenced a will to deny his guilt . . . his written confession was not involuntary."[31] Now if the dissenting view is slightly recast, both views may be right. It can be argued, after all, that although Haynes's plea was not coerced, it was less than fully voluntary. For despite the Court's tendency to equate voluntary and noncoerced confessions, they are not identical. Just as a contract is voidable for both duress and *fraud*, by volitional and *cognitive* defects, the same may be true for confessions. A confession to a policeman posing as a priest, for example, would not be coerced, but it is arguably less than fully voluntary.[32]

[28] Ibid., 603.
[29] Ibid., 605 (emphasis added).
[30] 373 U.S. 503 (1963).
[31] Ibid., 525.
[32] Kamisar wrongly concludes that this case could *not* be brought under the rubric of voluntariness. See "What is an 'Involuntary' Confession?" 747.

How *important* is the cognitive dimension of a confession? That depends upon what we take a confession to be. If a confession is understood as the intentional relinquishment or abandonment of a *known* right or privilege, then the Court can consistently hold that the absence of an attorney affected the voluntariness of Haynes's confession, even if it grants that it did not affect Haynes's *volition*.[33] A suspect might incriminate himself simply because he does not know that he has a right to remain silent. Even if he is not coerced into waiving his Fifth Amendment right, he might not give *informed* consent to such a waiver.

Enter *Miranda* v. *Arizona*.[34] Miranda, twenty-three, was indigent, had completed only half of ninth grade, and had been diagnosed as mentally ill. Miranda was arrested in connection with a rape and kidnapping and taken to the police station. The victim picked Miranda out of a lineup, and two officers then took him into a separate room for interrogation. Miranda gave a detailed oral confession and then wrote and and signed a brief statement admitting and describing the crime. It appears that all this was accomplished in two hours and without any physical force.

In reversing Miranda's conviction, the Court conceded that his self-incriminating statements had not been produced by "overt physical coercion or patent psychological ploys." The problem, said the Court, was that the officers did not "afford appropriate safeguards at the outset of interrogation to insure that the statements were truly the product of free choice": "An individual swept from familiar surroundings into police custody, surrounded by antagonistic forces, and subjected to the techniques of persuasion . . . cannot be otherwise than under compulsion to speak."[35] Despite the Court's reference to the *compulsion* under which Miranda confessed, the rule that suspects must be apprised of their rights is, I think, more concerned to protect the *cognitive* dimension of the suspect's choices than his *volition*. Indeed, the Court implies that the presence of counsel is primarily *evidentiary*. It is not that statements made without counsel or without a Miranda warning are *necessarily* uninformed or "the product of compulsion." Rather, the presence of counsel is a useful prophylactic to ensure that they are not com-

---

[33] *Johnson* v. *Zerbst*, 304 U.S. 458 (1938), which involved the waiver of the right to counsel. Whether the absence of an attorney *did* affect Haynes's cognition is another matter.

[34] 384 U.S. 436 (1966). *Miranda* was actually one of several related cases that the Court decided.

[35] Ibid., 457, 461.

pelled or uninformed. But however it is understood, *Miranda* clearly goes beyond the "totality of the circumstances" test with which the Court had previously worked.

And not all members of the Court were happy. According to the dissenters, *Miranda* constituted an illegitimate extension of the voluntariness principle. The new rules, they said, are "not designed to guard against police brutality or other unmistakably banned forms of coercion . . . [but] to negate all pressures . . . and ultimately to discourage any confession at all. The aim in short is toward 'voluntariness' in a utopian sense . . . voluntariness with a vengeance."[36] The dissenters advanced both conceptual and policy objections to the majority's view. First, from a conceptual perspective, they argued that the Court set the standards for voluntariness too high. It is certainly appropriate, they said, to pay "close attention to the individual's state of mind and capacity for effective choice."[37] Protecting suspects from "undue pressure" is indeed a design of the Constitution. On the other hand, they maintained, it is not the design of the Constitution to ensure "spontaneous confessions."[38] That is to demand too much. Second, from a policy perspective, the dissenters argued that the majority paid too little attention to "countervailing" values—in particular, to "society's interest in the general security."[39]

In my view, both sides are partially right and partially wrong. Both sides are wrong because neither the majority nor the dissenters squarely confront the potential conflict between the voluntariness principle and society's interest in security. The majority simply ignores the issue, while the dissenters interpret voluntariness in a way that would sharply reduce the potential conflict. Both sides are also right. The majority is right to hold, in effect, that we cannot pack all legitimate social interests into the voluntariness principle, that the criteria of voluntariness cannot be entirely defined by considerations of security. And the dissenters are right to note that a strict interpretation of the voluntariness principle may have genuine costs (although the actual criminogenic effects of the *Miranda* rule are far from clear).[40]

---

[36] Justice Harlan (Justices Stewart and White concurring), Ibid., 505.

[37] Ibid., 507.

[38] Ibid., 515.

[39] Justice White dissenting, ibid., 537. White bitterly chastised his colleagues for ignoring the "unknown number of cases" in which *Miranda* will put "a killer, a rapist" back on the streets, and sarcastically added that "there is . . . this saving factor: the next victims are uncertain, unnamed and unrepresented in this case." 542.

[40] The expansion of the use of involuntariness claims as a basis for invalidating

Searches

There is an important asymmetry between confessions and searches. A constitutionally valid confession must be (held) voluntary, however that requirement is interpreted. By contrast, the police may be "warranted" to conduct a nonconsensual search. Even so, it is often more convenient (or otherwise desirable) for the police to conduct a "consent" search, and the Supreme Court must decide when such consent meets the appropriate constitutional standards.

Consider *Bumper* v. *North Carolina*. The defendant's grandmother allowed the police to search her house after one of them claimed to have a search warrant.[41] The grandmother did not ask to see the warrant—"I just give them a free will to look because I felt like the boy wasn't guilty."[42] At a hearing on a motion to suppress evidence found by the police, the state relied on the grandmother's consent to justify the search.[43] The Court ruled the search unconstitutional: "When a law enforcement officer claims authority to search a home under a warrant, he announces in effect that the occupant has no right to resist the search. The situation is instinct with coercion—albeit colorably lawful coercion. Where there is coercion there cannot be consent."[44] Black (dissenting) argued that the grandmother had voluntarily consented to the search, as evidenced by her statement that she "wanted the officers to search her house—to prove to them that she had nothing to hide."[45]

It is not clear whether the two sides differ with respect to the *actual* voluntariness of the grandmother's consent or with respect to the *burden of proof*. The majority seems to maintain that, as a matter

---

confessions appears to have peaked. The Court has since refused to hold involuntary a confession made after the police had misrepresented statements made by the suspect's confederate. *Frazier* v. *Cupp*, 394 U.S. 731 (1969). In a more recent case, while the suspect was being taken to headquarters in a police car, the officers remarked that it would be "too bad if a handicapped girl found the weapon and hurt herself." *R.I.* v. *Innis*, 446 U.S. 291 (1980). The suspect, affected by the remark, directed the officers to the spot where he had thrown the weapon. Although the suspect had been apprised of his right to remain silent and had requested a lawyer, the Court ruled that his statement was admissible because he had not been interrogated, because no *question* had been addressed to him. Justices Brennan and Marshall dissented on the grounds that the police conduct was likely to produce a response from the suspect.

[41] 391 U.S. 543 (1968).

[42] Ibid., 566, cited in Black's dissenting opinion.

[43] Although the Supreme Court was later told that the officers had had a warrant, nothing was said about the conditions under which the alleged warrant had been issued.

[44] Ibid., 550.

[45] Ibid., 556.

of fact, the situation was "instinct with coercion," while Black argues that the consent was freely given. On the other hand, the majority also says that "a prosecutor . . . has the *burden of proving* that the consent was, in fact, freely and voluntarily given" and that this cannot be *established* by "showing no more than acquiescence to a claim of lawful authority."[46] Thus the majority could accept Black's claim that the grandmother's consent *was* (probably) voluntary, but still insist that the state did not satisfactorily show or ensure that it was.

Upon what theory of coercion was the Court relying? *Bumper* seems either to reject a two-pronged theory of coercion, or to fail to apply it in a manner analogous to contractual duress. For the Court seems to say that even if the officers had had a valid warrant to search the house, this would have *no* bearing on the voluntariness of the grandmother's consent—there would still have been "colorably lawful coercion." Perhaps they decided wrongly, or perhaps the two-pronged theory was not adopted because the consent to a search was thought to be better handled as a case of nonvolitional coercion. But that is mere speculation.

The question of coercion aside, *Bumper* also fails to indicate whether a valid waiver of a constitutional right must be voluntary and *knowing*. But in *Schenckloth* v. *Bustamonte*, the Supreme Court unambiguously *rejected* the more demanding standard it had adopted in *Miranda*.[47] An officer stopped a vehicle with a defective headlight. The driver had no license. Alcala, a passenger, said that the car belonged to his brother. The officer asked Alcala for permission to search the car. Alcala consented and even assisted in the search, which resulted in the discovery of three stolen checks. The constitutionality of the search was upheld by the California courts and reversed by the federal court of appeals.[48]

In reversing the court of appeals, the Supreme Court noted a distinction between the theories of voluntariness held by the lower courts. The California courts understood voluntariness as "a question of fact to be determined from the totality of all the circumstances . . . [in which] the state of a defendant's knowledge is only one factor to be taken into account . . ."[49] The (federal) court of ap-

[46] Ibid., 550.

[47] 412 U.S. 218 (1973). See Wayne R. LaFave, *Search and Seizure: A Treatise on the Fourth Amendment*, vol. 2 (St. Paul: West, 1978), 613. LaFave's multivolume work contains a long and helpful discussion of "consent searches" as well as a detailed treatment of virtually all the important issues raised by the Fourth Amendment.

[48] 448 F.2d 669 (1971).

[49] 412 U.S. 218, 223.

peals, on the other hand, viewed a consent search as one which placed the state "under an obligation to demonstrate not only that the consent had been uncoerced, but that it had been given with an understanding that it could be freely and effectively withheld."[50]

In choosing between these two views, the Court turned to its Fifth Amendment decisions for assistance. Although the Court (on safe ground, I suppose) held that the self-incrimination decisions did not yield a "talismanic definition of 'voluntariness,' mechanically applicable to the host of situations where the question has arisen," the Court described the thrust of the decisions as follows:

> In determining whether a defendant's will was overborne in a particular case, the Court has assessed the totality of all the surrounding circumstances—both the characteristics of the accused and the details of the interrogation . . . In all of these cases, the Court determined the factual circumstances surrounding the confession, assessed the psychological impact on the accused, and evaluated the legal significance of how the accused reacted.[51]

In adopting a "totality of the circumstances" test, the Court conceded that knowledge of one's constitutional right to refuse consent is "*one* factor to be taken into account," but held that it is not a "*sine qua non* of effective consent."[52]

There are two questions which might be asked about *Schenckloth*: (1) Is it sound constitutional law? (2) Does it reflect a sound theory of coercion? As an exercise in constitutional law, the Court's account of pre-*Miranda* thinking is unexceptionable. Nonetheless, the Court does not indicate why *Miranda* should *not* be applied to searches, why explicit knowledge of one's rights is not a necessary condition of a valid consent search. Perhaps the Court believes that the criteria for voluntary confessions are distinguishable from the criteria for voluntary consent to searches. But the Court neither explains why this should be nor seems sensitive to the need to do so.

I do not think that *Schenckloth* does, in fact, reflect a principled distinction between the criteria for voluntary searches and the criteria for voluntary confessions. Given that the majority echoes the sentiments expressed in the *Miranda* dissent, *Schenckloth* more likely reflects a belief that *Miranda* was decided incorrectly: "As with police questioning, two competing concerns must be accommodated

[50] Ibid., 221.
[51] Ibid., 224, 226.
[52] Ibid., 227 (emphasis added).

in determining the meaning of a 'voluntary' consent—the legitimate need for such searches and the equally important requirement of assuring the absence of coercion."[53] There are at least two difficulties with this argument. First, as Marshall (dissenting) notes, the Court entirely ignores the cognitive dimension of consent and wrongly equates the absence of coercion with (full or informed) voluntariness. Second, it is not clear that society's legitimate need for searches can or should be accommodated "in determining the meaning of a 'voluntary' consent." Not only does society provide for nonconsensual searches, but however important society's need for searches, it arguably has nothing to do with the voluntariness of consent.

I suggested above that the two-pronged theory of coercion did not figure prominently in "search and seizure" decisions. Something like it, however, has surfaced in several recent cases. A Drug Enforcement Administration (DEA) agent stopped McCaleb in an airport because he met their "drug courier profile."[54] The agent told McCaleb that he wanted to search his bag and that he could refuse to consent, but that he would then be detained until a warrant was obtained. McCaleb hesitated, and then unlocked the suitcase. The Court noted that McCaleb had been read his *Miranda* rights, and that several additional factors (education, intelligence, no prolonged questioning) contributed to the voluntariness of McCaleb's consent. On the other hand, the Court held that among the factors militating *against* the voluntariness of the consent was that McCaleb had been subject to an "unconstitutional stop," suggesting that the *unconstitutionality* or wrongness of the stop is relevant to its coerciveness.[55]

In a similar case, the putative constitutionality of the government's action generated the opposite conclusion. Mendenhall, a black woman, was stopped in Detroit Metropolitan Airport by two white male DEA agents who believed that she, too, fit the "drug courier profile."[56] She was asked to accompany the agents to the DEA office for further questioning, where she was asked to consent to a search of her person and handbag. After being told she could refuse the search, she said "go ahead." The Supreme Court held that Mendenhall's consent had not been given under duress be-

[53] Ibid.
[54] *U.S.* v. *McCaleb*, 552 F.2d 717 (1977).
[55] Ibid., 721.
[56] *U.S.* v. *Mendenhall*, 446 U.S. 544 (1980).

cause, unlike in *McCaleb*, the search had not been "the fruit of . . . an unconstitutional detention."[57]

Conclusion

It appears that coercion claims have been understood differently with respect to confessions and searches. With respect to searches, the Court has recently adopted something close to the two-pronged theory we have encountered in other legal contexts. With respect to confessions, the Court comes closer to the account of coercion we observed in the law of wills. If I am right, wills and confessions share two related characteristics which distinguish them from the other legal contexts we have considered. First, in both contexts, the adjudication of coercion claims unambiguously stresses the psychological or volitional dimensions of consent. Second, in both contexts consent is fundamentally unilateral. In a bilateral agreement, B usually expects to gain something from succumbing to A's pressure, even if, as in the paradigmatic gunman case, it requires him to sacrifice one of his rights (his money) in order to save another (his life). If B gains something significant by his decision, it is plausible to presuppose that its volitional quality meets the requirements of valid consent. On the other hand, one arguably expects to gain nothing of enduring (nonmoral) value by succumbing to "undue influence" in making a will or by waiving one's Fifth Amendment rights. Although it may be in the short-term interest of the one interrogated to confess (to stop the interrogation), it is typically no more in his long-term interest than a decision to refuse life-saving surgery because the pain is too much to bear.[58] For this reason, it is not surprising that the Court should pay close attention to the volitional quality of a confession.

Given this similarity between wills and confessions, it is perhaps also not surprising that the standards of voluntariness employed in the law of wills have been used to attack the Court's position on

[57] Ibid., 550. In response to the argument that she "would not voluntarily have consented to a search that was likely to disclose the narcotics," the Court responded that "the question is not whether [she] acted in her ultimate self-interest, but whether she acted voluntarily." A state court upheld the validity of a consent search (of a car), noting that "a threat to do what the officer had a legal right to do cannot constitute duress in the setting of this case." *State* v. *Paschal*, 241 S.E.2d 92, 94 (1978).

[58] Alan Donagan has argued that although the legal right not to incriminate oneself has a moral basis, it is not a *moral* right, that it may be *morally* obligatory to confess to one's crime. See "The Right Not to Incriminate Oneself," 1 *Social Philosophy and Policy* 137, 147 (1984).

confessions. In arguing that the courts have been (or were) insufficiently sensitive to the voluntariness of confessions, Arthur Sutherland asks us to imagine that potential and worthy beneficiaries of a well-to-do testatrix believe that her intended beneficiary will make "base use of her property." They capture her, place her in a room, "keep her secluded there for hours while they make insistent demands, weary her with contradictions of her assertions," and get her to change her will. Sutherland asks: "Would any judge of probate accept the will so procured as the 'voluntary' act of the testatrix?"[59]

The answer to Sutherland's (rhetorical) question is obvious. Its import is not. It may be true, as he notes, that "we . . . let a man sign away his life under circumstances in which we would not recognize his conveyance of a sub-divided lot."[60] And it may be that "no consensual dealing in any other field of law—no signature of a deed, no execution of a contract . . . would stand in any court when made under the circumstances of the confession . . ."[61] Yet, even if this is strictly correct, it is not clear what follows.

Suppose that less "external" pressure is needed to invalidate a will than to invalidate a confession. What would that show? It *might* show that the courts have manipulated the criteria for voluntary confessions in order to accommodate society's interests in obtaining valid confessions (there is no comparable interest in validating wills). But there is an alternative and less cynical explanation. Suppose that we apply the "totality of the circumstances" test in both settings. It seems plausible to suppose that the paradigmatic suspect may have more strength of mind than the paradigmatic testatrix. In addition, and more important, the testatrix's motives for *not* capitulating to the pressure are, by comparison, weak, whereas the suspect's motives for not confessing are relatively strong. Because a criminal suspect arguably has a lot to *lose* by succumbing, he can be expected to withstand considerable pressure. What *appear* to be different standards of voluntariness may only reflect Frankfurter's observation that determination of voluntariness requires "psychological judgment," that a multitude of factors must be taken into account.

On closer inspection, Sutherland's criticism of the way the voluntariness test has been applied to confessions reflects a deeper

[59] "Crime and Confession," 79 *Harvard Law Review* 21, 37 (1965).
[60] Ibid.
[61] Ibid.

aversion to the notion of "voluntariness" itself, an aversion that is shared by other commentators. What the Court describes in *Culombe* as an "amphibian," Kamisar describes as "little more than a fiction designed to beautify certain . . . interrogation techniques . . ."[62] What Frankfurter concedes is "not a matter of mathematical determination," Monrad Paulsen describes as "absolutely useless."[63] What do the critics recommend? Simply put, some would abandon the concept of voluntariness. "The real reasons for excluding confessions have long been obscured by traditional language," says Kamisar. The time has come to abandon the "Indians-attacking-the-covered-wagon tactics" and adopt a "more direct approach."[64]

What would a direct approach entail? Kamisar and Paulsen suggest that "due process" objections to confessions actually involve two distinct issues: (1) the reliability or veracity of a confession; (2) the propriety of the police techniques employed. We might say that confessions made under conditions which are likely (*how* likely is another question) to produce a false confession should not be permitted. A confession would also be invalid if obtained by methods which themselves offend due process.[65] And while the methods that "offend due process" would have to be specified, they need not involve coercion. It is settled constitutional doctrine, for example, that "a confession is involuntary if induced by any direct or implied promise, however slight, of reward or immunity."[66] While there is no reason to think a confession is *involuntary* or *coerced* just because it is induced by a "slight" promise or reward, it is not implausible to prohibit the use of such techniques on due process grounds.

But this would show only that due process objections should not be *restricted* to considerations of coercion or voluntariness. It would *not* show that we can or should do without that "amphibious" term. I suspect that the voluntariness principle captures important underlying values which the "reliability" and "proper technique" tests do

[62] "What is an 'Involuntary' Confession?" 745.

[63] "The Fourteenth Amendment and the Third Degree," 6 *Stanford Law Review* 411, 430 (1954).

[64] "What is an 'Involuntary' Confession?" 759. We should avoid the "dissonance of argument about voluntariness," says Paulsen, and define the criteria for invalid confessions without regard to such an unhelpful notion. "The Fourteenth Amendment and the Third Degree," 437.

[65] Paulsen, "The Fourteenth Amendment and the Third Degree," 429.

[66] "Annotation, Admissibility of Pretrial Confession in Criminal Cases," *Supreme Court Reports*, 4 L.Ed.2d 1833 (1959).

not, that there is independent moral value in ensuring that a confession is voluntary—however that difficult notion is ultimately understood. If, as the critics suggest, the notion of voluntariness were to be abandoned, I suspect that the problems which haunt its specification would only reappear under another heading.

SEVEN

PLEA BARGAINING

A defendant can waive his right to a trial by jury by pleading guilty—if the guilty plea is not coerced.[1] The problem is this. A guilty plea is typically the product of a plea bargaining process in which the state offers the defendant a choice between (1) standing trial and risking a (relatively) severe sentence and (2) pleading guilty and accepting a certain but (relatively) lenient sentence. It is at least *plausible* to argue that the structure of this choice situation coerces the defendant into pleading guilty.[2]

Here the stakes are particularly large. In most legal contexts, a successful coercion claim will invalidate a specific transaction or act. We can say that *a* contract is void for duress without holding *all* contracts void for duress. It can be argued, however, that plea bargaining is not just coercive under abnormally stressful conditions, but that coercion is the *norm*. And if the *standard* negotiated guilty plea violates the constitutional requirement of voluntariness, then we must either override the voluntariness principle in the name of other objectives or conclude that plea bargaining is unconstitutional and must be prohibited.

The Practice of Plea Bargaining

Some maintain that, like the poor, plea bargaining has always been with us. Others point to a (golden?) era in which a high proportion

---

[1] This chapter relies heavily on my "Freedom, Morality, Plea Bargaining, and the Supreme Court," 8 *Philosophy & Public Affairs* 203 (1979). The application of the voluntariness principle to guilty pleas is accepted in all the relevant cases and is even enshrined in statute. The Federal Rules of Criminal Procedure, for example, state that a court should not accept a guilty plea "without . . . determining that the plea is made voluntarily with understanding of the nature of the charge and the consequences of the plea." Rule 11 (1975). A typical Supreme Court statement appears in *Machibroda* v. *U.S.*: "A guilty plea, if induced by promises or threats which deprive it of the character of a voluntary act, is void." 368 U.S. 487, 493 (1962).

[2] See, for example, Kenneth Kipnis, "Criminal Justice and the Negotiated Plea," 86 *Ethics* 93 (1976). I have discussed Kipnis's argument in "The Prosecutor and the Gunman," 89 *Ethics* 269 (1979).

of criminal convictions were obtained by jury trials.[3] But whatever was once the case, trials in criminal cases are now the exception, not the rule. Although there are variations among jurisdictions and types of crime, one statistic stands out—approximately 90 percent of convictions result from guilty pleas.[4]

Even in the absence of any special incentives, a defendant might plead guilty to avoid the embarrassment or costs of a public trial, to get things over with as quickly as possible, or because he simply thinks it the right thing to do. But most guilty pleas result from a plea bargaining process in which defendants plead guilty because the *expected penalty* from a guilty plea is considerably less than the expected penalty from a trial. A defendant's expected penalty is a function of its *severity* and its *probability*. If a defendant expects to receive a 6-month sentence if he pleads guilty, then the expected penalty is (1.0 times 6 months) 6 months. If he believes there is a 75 percent chance that he will be convicted at trial and expects to receive a 4-year sentence if convicted, then the expected penalty is (.75 times 4 years) 3 years.[5] We may refer to the difference between the two expected penalties as the defendant's *sentence-differential*.[6]

Sentence-differentials may be created by *explicit* or *tacit* plea bargaining. In *explicit* plea bargaining, a prosecutor may propose to accept a guilty plea to a lesser included charge, or to drop additional charges in return for a plea of guilty to a specific charge, or to recommend a specific sentence in return for a guilty plea, or to bring additional charges if the defendant does not plead guilty to the original charge. Although different prosecutors may prefer different

[3] Albert W. Alschuler, "Plea Bargaining and Its History," 79 *Columbia Law Review* 1 (1979).

[4] If one includes indictments which result in dismissals, significantly less than 10 percent of criminal cases are resolved in a trial. See Milton Heumann, *Plea Bargaining* (Chicago: University of Chicago Press, 1977). For other general discussions, see James E. Bond, *Plea Bargaining and Guilty Pleas* (New York: Clark Boardman, 1975); Donald J. Newman, *Conviction: The Determination of Guilt and Innocence without Trial* (Boston: Little, Brown, 1966); Arthur Rossett and Donald Cressey, *Justice by Consent* (Philadelphia: J. B. Lippincott, 1976). Also see several excellent articles by Albert Alschuler: "The Prosecutor's Role in Plea Bargaining," 36 *University of Chicago Law Review* 50 (1968); "The Trial Judge's Role in Plea Bargaining," 76 *Columbia Law Review* 1059 (1976); "The Defense Attorney's Role in Plea Bargaining," 84 *Yale Law Journal* 1179 (1975).

[5] The psychological impact of one's expected sentence may not be a direct function of the actual expected penalty if, for example, certainty is weighted more heavily than severity.

[6] See Albert Alschuler, "The Prosecutor's Role in Plea Bargaining," 50. In the case just described, the sentence-differential would favor pleading guilty even if there were only a 25 percent chance of conviction (6 months versus [.25 times 4 years] 1 year).

techniques, virtually all come to adopt some method of generating a sentence-differential that makes it attractive for a defendant to plead guilty. (There will, of course, be some cases in which prosecutors refuse to bargain.)[7]

A defendant's sentence-differential may be based on a *tacit* understanding that he will be treated less severely if he pleads guilty. The pattern of a judge's sentences may indicate that he typically assigns stiffer sentences to those who are convicted at trial. There are several reasons why this might occur. Some judges believe that a defendant who pleads guilty is thereby demonstrating repentance and is on the road to rehabilitation. Some judges respond to what they believe is a defendant's perjury in the course of his trial. Some judges simply believe that it is wrong for a defendant to take a case to trial when he does not have a reasonable defense.[8] But whatever its cause, the result is the same. Defendants may have a well-founded expectation that they will be treated more leniently if they plead guilty.

The practice of offering incentives to defendants would not properly be described as plea *bargaining* unless the defendant had something to offer the state. Defendants have, in essence, two things to offer—quiescence and assurance of conviction. The most common explanation of the state's interest in plea bargaining focuses on the need to reduce the load on the prosecutorial and judicial systems. If the defendant pleads guilty, the state need not support the defendant while he awaits trial in jail, the prosecutor need not prepare the case for trial or appear in court, the state need not track down witnesses or compel them to appear, police need not take time off to testify, juries need not be called or paid, judges need not preside over trials, courts and offices need not be built and staffed. Others argue that system overload is less important than the state's desire

---

[7] I am assuming, of course, that the prosecutor has a good-faith belief that the defendant is guilty of the offense. Defense attorneys will typically try to get a "good deal" for their clients, but they, too, understand that the point of the process is to get the defendant to plead guilty. Douglas Maynard taped the following conversation between between a prosecutor and a defense attorney about a case in which the defendant (Delaney) allegedly "tore up a bar." Defense attorney: "Okay is there an offer in Delaney?" Prosecutor: "Yeah, plead to mal mish [Malicious Mischief] and, modest fine and uh restitution." Defense attorney: "Okay, fifty dollars." Prosecutor: "Right." See "The Structure of Discourse in Misdemeanor Plea Bargaining," 18 *Law and Society Review* 75, 81 (1984).

[8] As one judge crudely stated, "He takes some of my time—I take some of his." See Alschuler, "The Trial Judge's Role in Plea Bargaining," 1089. Also see "The Influence of the Defendant's Plea on Judicial Determination of Sentence," 66 *Yale Law Journal* 204 (1956).

to guarantee a conviction. A prosecutor could, after all, be confident of a defendant's *factual* guilt yet be less confident that he will be *found* guilty at trial.[9] A prosecutor might well prefer a guaranteed conviction that carries a relatively lenient punishment to the possibility that the defendant will be acquitted and receive no punishment at all. From the judge's perspective, a guilty plea virtually guarantees that the conviction will not be successfully appealed, and rare is a magistrate who likes to see his decisions overturned.[10]

Whatever the best explanation of its current role, plea bargaining is now a ubiquitous and integral part of our criminal justice system. At the same time, it is widely and vigorously criticized. It is, for example, argued that (1) plea bargaining leads to excessively lenient punishments, thus compromising the retributive, deterrent, and incapacitative effects of punishment; (2) plea bargaining leads to unjust punishments which depend more on the defendant's willingness to waive his right to trial than on appropriate sentencing criteria; (3) the leniency of plea bargaining is illusory, as prosecutors overcharge defendants, and then reduce the charge to what would have been appropriate; (4) plea bargaining hides and perpetuates violations of defendants' rights and creates sentence-differentials so great that even innocent defendants plead guilty.[11] But whatever the merits of these criticisms, and I believe that many have substantial merit, they are, it seems, distinct from the claim that plea bargaining coerces. And that is the argument with which I am principally concerned.

The Coercion Claim

Albert Alschuler suggests that the "civilized solution" would be to eliminate plea bargaining, and that if we "deny the coercive character of the system . . . we magnify its injustice as we delude our-

---

[9] There may be gaps in the evidence, the evidence may be procedurally tainted (e.g., by an illegal search), witnesses may be unavailable or uncooperative. Moreover, there is no guarantee that a jury will convict even when the evidence clearly justifies a conviction. Heumann describes the case of a prosecutor who refused to bargain and was extremely confident that the defendant would be convicted at trial. In the course of the trial, his confidence was confirmed by the defense attorney's last-ditch effort to reach a deal. But to everyone's surprise, the jury acquitted. See *Plea Bargaining*, 111–12.

[10] Ibid., 144ff.

[11] We need not agree on what *are* appropriate grounds for sentencing to agree that the defendant's willingness to waive his right to trial is *not* an appropriate basis for sentencing.

selves."[12] But to assert that plea bargaining is coercive is to beg the question. True, plea bargaining presents a situation in which a defendant is required to choose between two starkly presented options, both of which leave him badly off. For this reason, the coercion claim may look stronger here than in other contexts. Nonetheless, we have seen that even very great pressure and legally recognizable coercion are quite distinct things in *many* legal contexts. Perhaps we "delude ourselves" in *all* of them. But, if not, then it must be shown that plea bargaining is coercive in a way that other pressures are not. Assertions aside, what kind of *arguments* can be advanced in defense of the claim that plea bargaining coerces?

Arguments based on nonvolitional coercion clearly will not do. If plea bargaining typically compromised the volitional quality of guilty pleas, there would be little controversy. But the decision to waive one's right to trial is patently *not* involuntary in *that* sense. Nor is it regarded that way by its critics.[13] Quite the opposite. A bargained guilty plea is almost always an intelligent and eminently rational choice in the defendant's choice situation. The question is whether that choice *situation* is coercive and not whether the defendant's "will" has been impaired.

The Analogy with Contracts. A second line of argument compares plea bargaining to *contracts* and maintains that the conditions which render a contract void for duress are to be found in the standard plea bargain. Kenneth Kipnis has argued that a defendant's decision to accept a plea bargain is analogous to the victim's decision to turn over his money in the gunman example—"Your money or your life." Just as the contract between a gunman and his victim is void on grounds of duress, so is the agreement between the defendant and the prosecutor—"the same considerations that will drive reasonable people to give in to the gunman compel one to accept the prosecutor's offer."[14]

Would an appeal to the principles of contractual duress support the claim that plea bargaining coerces? It is possible, but unlikely. We have seen that contract law employs a two-pronged theory of duress. Suppose we grant that the defendant's choice situation meets the *choice* prong. Like the gunman's victim, the defendant

---

[12] "The Defense Attorney's Role in Plea Bargaining," 1298.

[13] Defendants typically have ample time to make their decisions, have the advice of counsel, and are not subjected to face-to-face pressure by the prosecutor (although they may be under such pressure from their attorneys).

[14] "Criminal Justice and the Negotiated Plea," 99.

has no reasonable alternative but to plead guilty. Does the prosecutor's proposal meet the *proposal* prong? It is at least doubtful that it does. The gunman's proposal is wrong, after all, because he has no right to do what he threatens to do, namely, to kill his victim. To use Vinit Haksar's terminology, the gunman's "declared unilateral plan" (what he says he will do if his proposal is not accepted) would violate the victim's rights.[15] But even ignoring the obvious move that the prosecutor is offering leniency and not threatening severity, the prosecutor has the right (and arguably the duty) to carry out his declared unilateral plan. Whatever else we may want to say about the prosecutor, he is *not* a gunman.[16]

Of course, it does not suffice to say that the prosecutor is not a gunman. We have seen, in several contexts, that the moral criteria for applying the proposal prong are not exhausted by the moral status of the proposer's declared unilateral plan. A contract may be made under duress if one proposes to exercise one's right in a way or for purposes that the law considers improper. Similar considerations underlie the prohibition of blackmail. And it is possible that some such considerations pertain to plea bargaining. Even so, it is clear that the principles of contractual duress do not, in a straightforward way, support the claim that plea bargaining is coercive.

The Constitutional Analogy. A third line of argument for the coercion claim stresses the *constitutional* dimension of the right to trial. It argues that a consistent application of the relevant principles developed in Supreme Court decisions on confessions and Fifth Amendment privileges would require the Court to hold that bargained guilty pleas are coerced.

Consider first the analogy with confessions. In the previous chapter we saw that the coerciveness of a confession turns on volition. But in plea bargaining, unlike confessions produced by extensive interrogation, the defendant is not typically threatened in "face-to-face encounters," has "competent counsel and full opportunity" to weigh the merits of the alternatives, and does not make "an impulsive and improper response to a seeming but unreal advantage."[17] There is another and crucial disanalogy between confessions and plea bargaining. As I suggested in the previous chapter, the discontinuation of interrogation procedures aside, the accused

[15] See "Coercive Proposals," 4 *Political Theory* 65, 76 (1976).

[16] I have developed this argument in more detail in "The Prosecutor and the Gunman."

[17] *Brady* v. *U.S.*, 397 U.S. 742, 754 (1970).

does (or should) not lose anything by refusing to confess.[18] By contrast, bargained guilty pleas are normally decidedly in the defendant's interest. For this reason, too, the analogy with confessions is not likely to support the claim that plea bargaining coerces.

More closely analogous to plea bargaining is the deliberate waiver of one's Fifth Amendment right not to be compelled to *testify* against oneself. Consider *Garrity* v. *New Jersey*.[19] Garrity, a police officer, was asked to testify in connection with an investigation into traffic ticket fixing. He was told that his testimony could be used against him in a criminal proceeding and that he had the right to remain silent, but that if he did not testify, he would be subject to removal from office. Garrity testified, and his testimony was subsequently used to convict him in a criminal action. Garrity appealed, claiming that his testimony had been coerced. The Supreme Court *agreed*: "the option to lose [one's] means of livelihood or to pay the penalty of self-incrimination is the *antithesis of a free choice . . .* the statements were infected by the coercion inherent in this scheme of questioning and cannot be sustained as voluntary . . ."[20] In a companion case, the Court went on to hold that the penalties which can render testimony involuntary are not "restricted to fine or imprisonment," but include "the imposition of *any* sanction which makes the assertion of the Fifth Amendment privilege 'costly.' "[21]

Justice Harlan strongly dissented:

> The majority is apparently engaged in the delicate task of riding two unruly horses at once: it is presumably arguing that [Garrity's] statements were *involuntary as a matter of fact . . .* and *inadmissible as a matter of law*, on the premise that they were products of an impermissible condition imposed on the constitutional privilege. These are very different contentions and require separate replies . . .[22]

Harlan noted that Garrity had been informed of his rights, reminded that information might be used against him, and not placed in "imminent danger" or subjected to "physical deprivation." Given all this, said Harlan, "there is no basis for saying that any of these statements were made involuntarily."[23]

---

[18] I am ignoring any psychic benefits the accused might get from confessing.

[19] 385 U.S. 493 (1967).

[20] Ibid., 497, 498 (emphasis added).

[21] *Spevack* v. *Klein*, 385 U.S. 511, 515 (1967) (emphasis added). This case involved the threat of disbarment.

[22] 385 U.S. 493, 501 (emphasis added).

[23] Ibid., 506.

Harlan argues, in effect, that the majority's view rests on a category mistake. Voluntariness, says Harlan, is a "matter of fact"—a fact about one's volition. The majority would have been on firm *conceptual* ground had it argued that the state was not entitled to burden Garrity's exercise of his right (although Harlan thought the state was entitled to do so), but, said Harlan, the majority was simply wrong to hold that Garrity's testimony had been coerced.

It must be said that the Court did not adequately explain the account of coercion on which its decision was based. Nonetheless, contra Harlan, voluntariness in the law is not typically a "matter of fact." *Garrity* can, at least in principle, be defended on the same two-pronged theory of coercion that is utilized across an entire spectrum of legal contexts. The Court could be understood as saying this: (1) Garrity's situation meets the choice prong of duress; (2) the state's "impermissible burden" on Garrity's right not to testify is relevant to the morality of the state's proposal (the proposal prong); (3) therefore, the "impermissible burden" *is* relevant to whether Garrity acted under duress. If this is the sort of argument the Court means to make, the question is precisely whether the state was within its rights in framing Garrity's options in the way it did. While the Court may have been wrong to hold that both prongs were met, its account of coercion is certainly coherent and by no means unique.

Let us suppose *Garrity* was rightly decided. What follows? It has been argued that even on a "narrow reading" of *Garrity*, a good-faith application of *stare decisis* would entail that bargained guilty pleas are unconstitutional.[24] If it is impermissible to induce someone to waive his right not to *testify against himself* by threatening to *fire* him, it must surely be impermissible to induce someone to waive his right to a *jury trial* by threatening a *severe punishment*. The Court need not strike new ground to find bargained guilty pleas involuntary or unconstitutional. It need only be consistent with its own Fifth Amendment decisions.

A Brief Constitutional History

What has the Court said? Plea bargaining, as it is currently understood, does not have a long constitutional history, although, according to Alschuler, it would not have been viewed with favor

---

[24] "The Unconstitutionality of Plea Bargaining," 83 *Harvard Law Review* 1387, 1400 (1970).

throughout the nineteenth and early twentieth centuries.[25] Indeed, but for a (perhaps tactical) decision by the solicitor general in *Shelton* v. *United States*, plea bargaining might have been ruled unconstitutional.[26] Paul Shelton claimed that his guilty plea had been coerced because it had been induced by a promise of leniency. His claim was accepted by a panel of the United States Court of Appeals for the Fifth Circuit.[27] Justice Tuttle, cognizant of the "very considerable implications this decision will have on the administration of justice," offered a strong dissent. Tuttle maintained that he would reject as coerced a guilty plea entered in response to promises to discontinue improper harassment, and such a plea might also be invalid if "the defendant was not fully aware of the consequences of his plea."[28] But, he said,

> a plea of guilty entered by one fully aware of the direct consequences, including the actual value of any commitments made to him by the court, prosecutor, or his own counsel, must stand unless induced by threats (or promises to discontinue improper harassment), misrepresentation . . . , or perhaps by promises that are by their nature improper as having no proper relationship to the prosecutor's business (e.g. bribes).[29]

In a rehearing of *Shelton* by the *en banc* court of appeals, Tuttle's view prevailed.[30] Shelton then appealed to the Supreme Court, which resolved the case in a *per curiam* opinion: "Upon . . . confession of error by the Solicitor General that the plea of guilty may have been improperly obtained, the judgment of the . . . Court of Appeals . . . is reversed . . ."[31] Why did the solicitor general admit to (an unspecified) error? Alschuler speculates that he feared that the Supreme Court would rule plea bargaining unconstitutional, and he did not want to give them that opportunity.[32]

United States v. *Jackson* set the stage for the Court's first major plea

---

[25] "Plea Bargaining and Its History."
[26] 356 U.S. 26 (1958).
[27] *Shelton* v. *U.S.*, 242 F.2d 101 (1957).
[28] Ibid., 113.
[29] Ibid., 115.
[30] 246 F.2d 571 (1957).
[31] *Shelton* v. *U.S.*, 356 U.S. 26 (1958).
[32] "Plea Bargaining and Its History," 37. In the decade following *Shelton*, the Supreme Court apparently focused on confessions rather than guilty pleas and passed up other opportunities to consider the constitutionality of plea bargaining. It appears, says Alschuler, that the Court decided to treat police rather than prosecutors "as the principal villains of the criminal process," although "the pressures for self-incrimination were ordinarily far greater at the courthouse than at the stationhouse."

bargaining decision.[33] The Federal Kidnapping Act provided for the execution of those convicted "if the verdict of the jury shall so recommend."[34] By implication, execution was not permitted if conviction resulted from a guilty plea. Jackson did not plead guilty, and was convicted. On appeal, a United States district court held this section of the act unconstitutional because it discouraged the free exercise of the Sixth Amendment right to a trial by jury. The Supreme Court affirmed, holding that the sentence-differential constituted "an impermissible burden upon the exercise of a constitutional right."[35]

Brady v. *United States* involved the same statute. Like Jackson, Brady had a choice between a jury trial with the risk of execution and pleading guilty. He originally pleaded not guilty, but changed his plea after learning that a codefendant had confessed and might testify against him. His plea was accepted after he assured the trial court that it was voluntary. Brady then appealed, claiming that under *Jackson*, his plea was involuntary and invalid. The Supreme Court accepted Brady's claim that his plea was principally motivated by his fear of execution (ignoring the role of his codefendant). At the same time, it held that it was not "unconstitutional for the State to extend a benefit to a defendant for waiving the right to a jury trial."[36] Moreover, said the Court, "*Jackson* ruled neither that all pleas of guilty encouraged by the fear of a possible death sentence are involuntary nor that such encouraged pleas are invalid whether involuntary or not."[37]

In a companion case, the Court came to the same conclusion with respect to a nonfederal crime.[38] Parker, a fifteen-year-old black male, was charged with first-degree burglary, then a capital offense in North Carolina. He pled guilty under a statute which allowed a defendant to avoid the possibility of execution by pleading guilty and was given the mandatory sentence of life imprisonment. Although Parker stated to the trial court that he tendered the plea "freely without any fear or compulsion," he subsequently claimed that his plea had been coerced. The Supreme Court disagreed.

In an important dissent to *Brady* and *Parker*, Justice Brennan argued that the statutory imposition of a higher penalty for a defend-

[33] 390 U.S. 570 (1968).
[34] 18 U.S.C. Sec. 1201(a).
[35] 390 U.S. 570, 572.
[36] Ibid., 753.
[37] *Brady* v. *U.S.*, 397 U.S. 742, 747 (1970).
[38] *Parker* v. *N.C.*, 397 U.S. 790 (1970).

131

ant who asserts his right to a jury trial is coercive and unconstitutional. Although Brennan did not make clear the theory on which that claim was based, he distinguished a *statutory* sentence-differential from the "give and take negotiation common in plea bargaining . . ."[39] Thus, even on Brennan's view, normal plea bargaining does not compromise the voluntariness of guilty pleas.

The Court's approval of plea bargaining was reinforced in *North Carolina* v. *Alford*.[40] Alford was indicted for murder under a North Carolina statute which provided for the death sentence unless the jury recommended life imprisonment. Life imprisonment was mandatory upon a plea of guilty. Alford pleaded guilty to second-degree murder, but *simultaneously* claimed that he was *innocent*: "I just pleaded guilty because they said if I didn't they would gas me for it . . . I'm not guilty but I plead guilty." The trial court heard additional testimony supporting the allegation of guilt and accepted the plea. The court of appeals reversed Alford's conviction, holding that a guilty plea was involuntary if its "principal motivation was fear of the death penalty under the unconstitutional statutory framework." The Supreme Court reversed and reinstated the conviction. The Court said: "The standard was and remains whether the plea represents a voluntary and intelligent choice among the alternative courses of action open to the defendant . . . [but] an individual . . . may voluntarily, knowingly, and understandingly consent to the imposition of a prison sentence even if he is unwilling or unable to admit his participation in the acts constituting the crime."[41] And thus an "Alford plea," a guilty plea accompanied by a protestation of innocence, has become an accepted feature of the plea bargaining process.

Santobello v. *New York* raised a different issue, but carried even further the Court's general approval of plea bargaining.[42] Santobello agreed to plead guilty to a gambling offense in exchange for the prosecutor's promise to make no sentence recommendation. By the time his case came to trial, a new prosecutor was in control, and citing Santobello's prior record, recommended the maximum sentence of one year in prison. The judge sentenced Santobello to one year, but claimed that the prosecutor's recommendation had not influenced his decision. Santobello appealed. In a ringing endorsement of plea bargaining, the Court held that one who pleads guilty

[39] Ibid., 799.
[40] 400 U.S. 25 (1970).
[41] Ibid., 29, 30, 31.
[42] 404 U.S. 257 (1970).

in exchange for a promise has a constitutional right to relief if the promise is broken. Extolling its many virtues, Chief Justice Burger proclaimed that plea bargaining is "an essential component of the administration of justice. Properly administered, it is to be encouraged."[43]

In *Bordenkircher* v. *Hayes*, the Supreme Court extended even further the use of sentence-differentials to encourage guilty pleas.[44] Hayes, who had previously been convicted of two felonies (although not imprisoned), was indicted for forgery. The prosecutor offered to recommend a sentence of five years if Hayes agreed to plead guilty, but stated that if Hayes did not "save the court the inconvenience and necessity of a trial," he would seek an *additional* indictment under the Kentucky Habitual Criminal Act (applicable to those convicted of three felonies), conviction under which would result in a mandatory sentence of life imprisonment. Hayes refused to plead guilty and was convicted at trial. True to his word, the prosecutor obtained an additional indictment and conviction under the Habitual Criminal Act, and Hayes was sentenced to life imprisonment.

Hayes's conviction was reversed by the United States court of appeals. In reinstating the conviction (by a five-four decision), the Supreme Court held, in effect, that there is no significant distinction between offering a more lenient punishment than permitted under an original charge and threatening a more severe punishment than permitted under the original charge—*if* the more severe punishment is otherwise legally permissible.[45]

The Supreme Court's Theory of Coercion

The Court has defended two positions. On *constitutional* grounds, the Court has held that bargained guilty pleas are typically voluntary; on *policy* grounds, the Court has held that plea bargaining is

[43] Ibid., 260. For a superb discussion of the issues raised in this case, see Peter Westen and David Westin, "A Constitutional Law of Remedies for Broken Plea Bargains," 66 *California Law Review* 471 (1978).

[44] 434 U.S. 358 (1978).

[45] Blackmun (dissenting) argued that there *is* a significant distinction between offers of leniency and threats of additional severity, but he, too, indirectly reinforced the view that plea bargaining is at least normally consistent with the constitutional requirement of voluntariness. Ibid., 367, 378. In a separate dissent, Justice Powell argued that the prosecutor's offer of five years in prison for forging an $88.30 check "hardly could be characterized as . . . generous" and that the threat to penalize Hayes's exercise of his right to trial with a punishment of "unique severity" violated his constitutional right to due process. Ibid., 369.

an essential and desirable feature of our criminal justice system. Given the Court's less indulgent position on self-incrimination, it is not implausible to suggest that its policy preferences have motivated its constitutional reasoning.[46] But the question is not whether the Court was motivated by policy considerations, but whether the Court could *justify* its claim that plea bargaining is compatible with the voluntariness principle.

Although the Court has not explicitly attempted to square its self-incrimination and plea bargaining decisions, *could* it do so? Not if coercion is a matter of volition. The Court cannot believe that the pressures on Garrity's volition were greater than those on the volition of Brady or Alford. But if the Court is relying on a two-pronged theory of coercion, it could maintain something like this: (1) the choice prong is met in both *Garrity* and *Alford*; (2) whereas *Garrity* meets the proposal prong of coercion, *Alford* does not, because the state was not entitled to propose that Garrity would lose his job if he refused to testify, but the state was entitled to propose that Alford could be executed if he did not plead guilty; (3) therefore, Garrity's testimony was coerced, but Alford's guilty plea was not.

The Court, then, *could* rest its decisions on a two-pronged theory of coercion. And there is evidence that it has implicitly done so. *Hayes*, for example, says that ". . . acceptance of the basic legitimacy of plea bargaining necessarily implies rejection of any notion that a guilty plea is *involuntary in a constitutional sense* . . ."[47] Here the Court implies that although bargained guilty pleas may be coercive in *some* sense—the choice prong may be met—such pleas are not wrong in the moral or constitutional sense required by the proposal prong. This reconstruction of the Court's view also helps to explain an otherwise peculiar assertion in *Brady*, to wit, that "*Jackson* ruled neither that all pleas of guilty encouraged by the fear of a possible death sentence are involuntary *nor that such encouraged pleas are invalid whether involuntary or not.*"[48] If the Court is committed to the voluntariness principle, it *cannot* claim that a guilty plea can be both involuntary and constitutional. The Court no doubt meant to say (or should have) that even if (under the choice prong) the defendant has no reasonable alternative but to plead guilty, a guilty

[46] As one commentator puts it, because the Court was unwilling to abolish what it itself describes as an "essential component" of the criminal justice system, it rationalized its constitutional analysis by "redefining the concept of voluntariness." Bond, *Plea Bargaining and Guilty Pleas*, 96.

[47] 434 U.S. 358, 363 (emphasis added).

[48] 397 U.S. 742, 747.

plea need not be coerced as a matter of law (under the proposal prong).

Interestingly, even those opinions which reject the Court's roseate view of plea bargaining also rely on a two-pronged theory. When the court of appeals argued that Alford's plea was involuntary because "its principal motivation was fear of the death penalty under the *unconstitutional* statutory framework," it implicitly conceded that Alford's fear of the death penalty was *not* sufficient to establish the involuntariness of his plea. The *unconstitutionality* of the statutory framework was also necessary to support the coercion claim. Brennan's dissent in *Parker* suggests that his disagreement with the majority was moral, not empirical or conceptual: "the legal concept of 'voluntariness' has not been narrowly confined but refers to a surrender of constitutional rights influenced by considerations that the government cannot properly introduce. The critical question that divides the Court is what constitutes an *impermissible* factor . . ."[49]

Applying the Two-Pronged Theory

I have argued that the Court's position is neither inconsistent nor incoherent. Is it *defensible*? It is one thing to assert that *Alford* can, in principle, be distinguished from *Garrity* and quite another to produce plausible moral arguments that support the distinction. How has the Court defended its view?

Basic to the Court's position is its understanding of the defendant's choice situation. Recall the gunman analogy. The gunman's proposal is wrong (in part) because he has created the victim's coercive choice situation. We evaluate the victim's choices by comparing them with his choices *prior* to the gunman's proposal. The victim must now waive one right (his money) in order to preserve another (his life), whereas he previously had both his money and his life. Kipnis argues that the defendant's situation should be similarly understood, that the state forces him to choose between "adverse consequences that *it* imposes."[50] And to respond by arguing that the sentence-differential occurs only *after* being charged, says Kipnis, is to ignore "the good reasons there are for the presumption of innocence in dispositive criminal proceedings."[51]

The Court implicitly rejects this line of argument. It seems to be

[49] 397 U.S. 790, 794 (emphasis added).
[50] "Criminal Justice and the Negotiated Plea," 100 (emphasis added).
[51] Ibid.

saying something like this. The presumption of innocence is a *procedural* principle. It requires that a defendant shall not be punished until duly convicted. The presumption of innocence does not require a *substantive* belief that the defendant is innocent, nor does it require that his treatment should be predicated on such a belief. After all, if we believed a defendant was innocent, we would hardly be justified in charging him, holding him in jail, requiring bail, or placing him on trial. We should not, of course, assume that a defendant is guilty just because he has been accused. It would be a mistake to assume that the defendant has brought his dilemma upon himself. But if the charge is made in good faith and justified by the evidence, we are entitled to understand the defendant's situation as subsequent to accusation, as one in which trial is warranted.[52]

The point is, then, that unlike the gunman's victim, who is required to sacrifice one right to preserve another, the criminal defendant is not required to waive his right to a trial in order to preserve his right to freedom, because he has no right to be free without an adjudication of his case. Applying this argument to the cases at hand, the Court could say that whereas the threat of being fired was a *new* element in Garrity's situation, the threat of execution was already part of Alford's environment. At the times the respective proposals were made, Garrity had (by hypothesis) a right to his job, but Alford had no right to his freedom from trial.

The point can be put this way. We ordinarily say that threats to make a person worse off are coercive whereas offers to make him better off are not. Yet to characterize a proposal as an offer or a threat, we need a "baseline" from which to evaluate the proposal— a view of the person's present situation, a view of his status quo. If the defendant's baseline is understood as *prior* to accusation, the prosecutor's proposal is a threat. If the defendant's baseline is understood as *subsequent* to accusation, the prosecutor's proposal is an offer, and offers do not coerce.[53]

Which is the better account of the defendant's baseline? One thing is clear; baselines do not come to us prelabeled. We must de-

[52] As Joseph Goldstein puts it: ". . . the statutorily authorized sentence is not something especially dreamed up by the prosecutor to force the particular accused to plead guilty. It is part of any accused's reality in the plea bargain setting . . ." See "For Harold Lasswell: Some Reflections on Human Dignity, Entrapment, Informed Consent, and the Plea Bargain," 84 *Yale Law Journal* 683, 699 (1975).

[53] See Howard Abrams, "Systemic Coercion: Unconstitutional Conditions in the Criminal Law," 72 *Journal of Criminal Law and Criminology* 128 (1981). Also see Conrad Brunk, "The Problem of Voluntariness and Coercion in the Negotiated Plea," 13 *Law and Society Review* 527 (1979).

cide how a defendant's baseline is best *understood*, and no particular account of that baseline has an obvious claim to our assent. But there is an alternative to arguing about which baseline provides the best picture of the defendant's "actual" status quo. The defendant's baseline could be defined by the options that the state has a *right* to exercise. On this view, if the state proposes to impose *less* punishment than it is otherwise *entitled* to do, the state is making an offer, and offers do not coerce. Call this a *rights-based baseline analysis*.

I think that something like this rights-based baseline analysis has been crucial to several plea bargaining decisions. In *Brady*, the Court notes that the state encourages guilty pleas "at every important step in the criminal process," as when a defendant concludes that a "trial is not worth the agony and expense to [him] and his family."[54] And in an offhand comparison which deserves much more attention than it has received, the Court goes on to say that such guilty pleas are "no more *improperly compelled* than is the decision by a defendant at the close of the State's evidence at trial that he must take the stand or face certain conviction."[55] Compelled, yes; improperly and therefore illegally compelled, no. As the Court correctly observes, *no one* (seriously) argues that a defendant who chooses to take the stand in his defense is coerced into doing so, even if he is under great psychic pressure, and even if he has no reasonable alternative to testifying if he is to have any chance of acquittal. For the defendant is not coerced when the prosecutor is exercising his rights (or, in this case, his duty).

This rights-based baseline analysis also helps to explain the Court's decision in *Hayes*. There the Court noted that the habitual-criminal charge had been justified by the evidence, that the prosecutor had had ". . . the evidence at the time of the original indictment," and that the prosecutor had apprised Hayes of his intentions.[56] If Hayes's baseline is defined by what the prosecutor is entitled to do (rather than what he has already done), the Court can reject as irrelevant the distinction between proposing a more lenient punishment (as in *Brady* or *Alford*) and proposing a more severe punishment (as in *Hayes*): "As a practical matter . . . this case would be no different if the grand jury had indicted Hayes as a recidivist from the outset and the prosecutor had offered to drop that charge as part of the plea bargain."[57]

The Court's view is that a prosecutor's threat to exercise legiti-

[54] 397 U.S. 742, 750.
[55] Ibid.
[56] 434 U.S. 358, 360.
[57] Ibid.

mate options is not immoral and therefore does not coerce. Then what was the problem in *Jackson*—where the Federal Kidnapping Act allowed for a more severe penalty upon conviction after trial? The answer may be this. In several constitutional contexts, the Court has held that a practice may be unconstitutional if it has a "chilling effect" on the exercise of constitutional rights.[58] In *Jackson*, the Court said this:

> Congress' objectives . . . cannot be pursued by means that *needlessly* chill the exercise of basic constitutional rights . . . The question is not whether the chilling effect is "incidental" rather than intentional, [but] whether that effect is *unnecessary and therefore excessive* . . . A procedure need not be inherently coercive in order that it be held to impose an impermissible burden upon the assertion of a constitutional right.[59]

The distinction drawn here between "inherent coercion" and an "unconstitutional chilling effect" or "impermissible burden" is, I think, roughly equivalent to the distinction between nonvolitional coercion and coercion on a two-pronged theory. Although the Federal Kidnapping Act does not produce nonvolitional guilty pleas, the "needlessness" and "excessiveness" of the "chilling effect" are relevant to the application of the proposal prong. In this case, the chilling effect *was* needless and excessive because, according to the Court, the government's alleged purpose could have been accomplished by a different procedure—for example, by letting a special jury set the sentence even if conviction resulted from a guilty plea.[60]

In contrast to the chilling effect of the statutory procedure contained in the Federal Kidnapping Act, the chilling effect of "ordinary" plea bargaining has been held by the Court to be neither needless nor excessive. It is not needless because the alternatives would be to (1) stipulate a single invariable penalty for each offense, or (2) place the sentencing decision in an authority having no knowledge of how the conviction was obtained, or (3) forbid either prosecutors or judges or both from accepting pleas to selected,

[58] In *N.C. v. Pearce*, for example, the Court was concerned about the chilling effect on a prisoner's right to appeal his conviction if he could be given a longer sentence upon retrial after a successful appeal than he received after his original trial. 395 U.S. 711 (1969).

[59] 390 U.S. 570, 581, 582 (emphasis added). The Court accepted the government's claim that the act's controversial section had the legitimate purpose of avoiding "the more drastic alternative of mandatory capital punishment in every case," but held that its intent was irrelevant.

[60] 390 U.S. 570, 584.

lesser, or reduced charges.[61] By hypothesis, these are unacceptable alternatives, in large part because they would greatly reduce the tendency of defendants to plead guilty. And that is a consequence the state cannot afford.[62] The Court has also maintained that the chilling effect of plea bargaining is not excessive—at least if it does not encourage too many innocent defendants to plead guilty. For to require a defendant to stand trial because his rights would otherwise be compromised would be, said the Court, "an exercise in arid logic [and would] render those constitutional guarantees counterproductive and put in jeopardy the very human values they were meant to preserve."[63]

Immoral Plea Bargaining

What, according to the Court, would make plea bargaining wrong and hence coercive? What may the state *not* do to encourage defendants to waive their right to trial? Prosecutorial conduct that overbears the will of a defendant, so that he does not understand or cannot act in his own interests, would not be permissible, although this would be an instance of nonvolitional coercion. In addition, the Court has held that the prosecutor's conduct must be appropriate in other ways. In *Brady*, quoting Justice Tuttle's dissent in *Shelton*, the Court said:

> A plea of guilty entered by one fully aware of the direct consequences . . . must stand unless induced by threats (or promises to discontinue *improper* harassment), misrepresentation (including unfilled or unfulfillable promises), or perhaps by promises that are by their nature improper as having no proper relationship to the prosecutor's business (e.g. bribes).[64]

Here the Court invokes ideas about the moral prong that we found in examining contract law and blackmail. The "levers" a prosecutor uses to induce guilty pleas must be both independently legitimate *and* substantively related to the business at hand.[65] While it is not

---

[61] *Brady* v. *U.S.*, 397 U.S. 742, 753.

[62] "If every criminal charge were subjected to a full-scale trial, the States and the Federal Government would need to multiply by many times the number of judges and court facilities." *Santobello* v. *N.Y.*, 404 U.S. 257, 260 (1970).

[63] *N.C.* v. *Alford*, 400 U.S. 25, 39.

[64] 397 U.S. 742, 750 (emphasis added).

[65] Recall that B's contract may be invalid if made in response to A's threat to exercise a right that has no proper relationship to the substance of the contract (e.g., to press criminal charges against B). See p. 43.

clear just what this principle would entail, it does imply that prosecutors cannot overcharge defendants to induce them to plead guilty—for that is not the point of the charging process.

It is important to note that the Court's defense of plea bargaining on policy grounds, however sound, is arguably irrelevant to the application of the proposal prong. The Court has held that because plea bargaining serves the society's interests, it is not immoral. But, as I have argued in previous chapters, it can be maintained that these "external" moral concerns are not the sort of moral concerns which the proposal prong is meant to capture. Let me be clear: I am not arguing that plea bargaining *is* immoral in the way required by the proposal prong; I am arguing that the social interests served by plea bargaining may be irrelevant to its morality or immorality under the proposal prong, and hence to its coerciveness.

Innocent Defendants. Let us assume that there has been no overcharging, no threat of improper penalties, and that the prosecutor has a good-faith belief that the defendant is guilty. The Court has held that there are additional limits on the terms that may be offered to a defendant.[66] The principal limit is suggested in *Brady*: "We would have serious doubts about this case if the encouragement of guilty pleas by offers of leniency *substantially increased* the likelihood that defendants . . . would falsely condemn themselves. But our view is to the contrary . . ."[67] The Court's view is that the chilling effect of plea bargaining would be excessive, unconstitutional, and therefore coercive if it encouraged too many innocent defendants to plead guilty.

Is this a problem? Certainly the fact that plea bargaining unintentionally convicts *some* innocent defendants is not, in itself, a decisive objection against it. Any known system of criminal justice will do that.[68] The question is whether plea bargaining "substantially increases" the likelihood of conviction of the innocent or (what is not quite the same) raises it to an unacceptable level. Some believe that it must. One argument goes like this. Assume that the prosecutor believes a group of defendants to be guilty, but some of the defendants are actually innocent. It is at least plausible to suppose that (1) the evidence against innocent defendants is generally weaker than the evidence against guilty defendants; (2) the differences between the sentences offered to defendants will be negatively correlated with the strength of the evidence; (3) therefore, innocent defend-

[66] *Bordenkircher* v. *Hayes*, 434 U.S. 357, 365.
[67] 397 U.S. 742, 753 (emphasis added).
[68] See my "Punishing the Innocent—Unintentionally," 20 *Inquiry* 45 (1977).

ants will (unintentionally) be offered better deals than guilty defendants; (4) therefore, innocent defendants will be under greater
pressure to plead guilty than guilty defendants.[69] Now despite its
initial plausibility, this argument is seriously flawed. If we suppose
that (1) and (2) are true, it does follow that the difference between
the *actual* punishments received by innocent defendants convicted
at trial and innocent defendants who plead guilty will exceed the
difference between the punishments received by guilty defendants
convicted at trial and guilty defendants who plead guilty. At the
same time, it does *not* follow that innocent defendants face greater
sentence-differentials, because, *ex hypothesi*, innocent defendants
have a greater probability of being acquitted at trial.[70]

But even if innocent defendants have no *more* incentive to plead
guilty than guilty defendants, plea bargaining might still lead to a
higher probability of conviction of the innocent than would occur if
all defendants were to go to trial. Is that a ground for concern? Perhaps, but it is arguably *not* a concern for the *innocent defendant*. For
even if an innocent defendant is more likely to be convicted under
plea bargaining than if he stands trial, it does not follow that it is in
his interest to require him to stand trial. His factual innocence does
not, after all, guarantee that he will be *found* innocent, and he might
rationally prefer a sure but relatively lenient punishment to one that
is less probable but more severe.[71] Thus even if Alford was innocent
(that appears unlikely), his decision to plead guilty may have made
the best of a bad situation. If Alford had gone to trial, he might have

[69] Alschuler, "The Prosecutor's Role in Plea Bargaining," 60. In addition, a legally
innocent defendant can falsely plead guilty because he mistakenly believes himself
to be guilty, as when one pleads guilty to murder but is actually guilty only of man-
slaughter. And to the extent that plea bargaining screens out potentially valid insanity pleas, it also arguably convicts innocent persons. See Abraham Goldstein, *The Insanity Defense* (New Haven: Yale University Press, 1967), 171.

[70] Compare the sentence-differentials offered to I (innocent) and G (guilty) who
would both receive a 5-year sentence if convicted at trial. Because the case against I
is relatively weak, the prosecutor offers a 1-year sentence if I pleads guilty. Because
the case against G is relatively strong, the prosecutor offers a 2-year sentence if G
pleads guilty. It would seem that I's sentence-differential is 4 years, and G's is only
3. But that is false. For, by hypothesis, I also stands a greater probability of being acquitted at trial. If I's probability of conviction is (let us say) 50 percent, whereas G's
probability of conviction is (let us say) 90 percent, I's true sentence-differential is ([.50
times 5 years] minus 1 year) 1.5 years and G's sentence-differential is ([.90 times 5
years] minus 2 years) 2.5 years. I has a *lower* sentence-differential.

[71] Imagine a system which was concerned to prevent innocent people from being
convicted of traffic offenses and required all those given traffic tickets to appear in
court. Would innocent defendants regard such a system as being in their interests? I
doubt it.

141

been convicted and then executed. Would that have been more just (assuming his innocence) than his life sentence?

It might be objected at this point that if it is in the interests of the defendant to allow him to waive his right to trial in exchange for the benefit of a lower sentence, then we should also allow defendants to waive their right to *counsel* in exchange for still *lower* sentences or other benefits. And, the argument goes, if we are not prepared to do the latter, why should we do the former?[72] There is, however, a crucial disanalogy between the right to counsel and the right to trial. Without counsel, a defendant cannot make an *informed* judgment about the costs and benefits of waiving other constitutional rights. In that sense, the presence of counsel is a *precondition* of voluntariness in a way not true of the right to stand trial.

The outcome, then, is this. If the only objective served by a constitutional right is to protect the *individual*, it can be argued that we should let the defendant decide whether he wishes to stand trial or accept the prosecutor's offer.[73] On this view, there is no reason to be overly concerned about the possibility that innocent defendants might plead guilty. It can be argued, however, that constitutional rights serve not only the individual's interests but *society's* interests as well. Perhaps it is *we* who do not want innocent defendants pleading guilty because *we* have a stake in the accuracy of the criminal justice system. That may be. But if that is the moral basis of our concern with the punishment of the innocent, it is not clear that the punishment of the innocent has anything to do with the *voluntariness* principle. It is a real concern, to be sure, but it is arguably irrelevant to the question of coercion.

Conclusion

Critics of plea bargaining are right to point to the very great pressures it places on defendants to waive their right to trial. But the critics of plea bargaining have been too quick to assume that the severity and efficacy of those pressures establish that plea bargaining is coercive or violates the constitutional requirement of voluntariness. If we examine other bodies of law, we find that even *very* great pressures do not establish duress—at least not legally recognizable duress.

Nonetheless, plea bargaining may still be morally indefensible. It

[72] See Alschuler, "The Defense Attorney's Role in Plea Bargaining," 1278.

[73] "We would let *him* decide how much a trial by jury was worth *to him*." Westen and Westin, "A Constitutional Law of Remedies for Broken Plea Bargains," 490.

may convict too many innocent persons. Its utilitarian benefits to the society may be less than is often supposed. And it may be seriously unjust to fix sentences on the basis of factors unrelated to criminal desert and, in particular, on the basis of the defendant's willingness to waive his constitutional rights.

There is much more that could be said about this. As Alschuler suggests, a full-scale jurisprudential assessment of plea bargaining not only requires a consideration of the concept of voluntariness but also demands an examination of "the reasons for prohibiting a variety of *consensual* arrangements in other legal contexts."[74] But that is precisely the point. As I have observed in previous chapters, there may be good reasons for prohibiting some uncontroversially voluntary agreements or not enforcing their terms. So, too, with plea bargaining. The Supreme Court's claim that bargained guilty pleas are not coerced may, then, be much more defensible than its critics suppose. On the other hand, the Court's enthusiastic moral endorsement of plea bargaining may be less defensible than the Court supposes.

[74] "The Trial Judge's Role in Plea Bargaining," 1152.

EIGHT

DURESS AND NECESSITY
AS DEFENSES IN THE
CRIMINAL LAW

In Anglo-American criminal law, an act that would ordinarily constitute a punishable offense can be *justified* or *excused* under one of several accepted conditions, for example, self-defense, necessity, duress, or insanity. Although a great deal of theoretical ink has been spilled attempting to define the precise contours and underlying basis (or bases) of these technical legal defenses, they are, in a sense, "but extensions of homely, routine apologies for causing harm."[1] "I had to do it," "I didn't mean to do it"—these are everyday claims. Their mundane analogues notwithstanding, the most famous cases of duress and necessity are anything but commonplace. Here we encounter murder, treason, prison escape, shipwrecks, and cannibalism.

Consider what is perhaps the best-known exemplar of this genre—*Regina* v. *Dudley and Stephens*.[2] On July 5, 1884, the crew of a yacht, the *Migonette*, consisting of three adult seamen (Captain Dudley, mates Stephens and Brooks) and a boy of seventeen (Parker) had to abandon ship and took to an open boat. They subsisted for twelve days on small rations. On the eighteenth day, one thousand miles from land and having been without food and water for several days, Stephens and Dudley suggested to Brooks that Parker, who was in a helpless condition, be sacrificed. Brooks rejected the idea. On the twentieth day, having been without food and water for eight days (it was believed that drinking seawater was fatal), Stephens and Dudley killed Parker, and the three fed on his

---

[1] George Fletcher, "The Individualization of Excusing Conditions," 47 *Southern California Law Review* 1269 (1974).

[2] 14 Q.B. 273 (1884). For a full-scale treatment of the history of the case, see A. W. Brian Simpson, *Cannibalism and the Common Law* (Chicago: University of Chicago Press, 1984). This case is also the basis of the most famous allegory in modern jurisprudence. See Lon Fuller, "The Case of the Speluncean Explorers," 62 *Harvard Law Review* 616 (1949).

body for four days. Then they were rescued by a passing ship. Dudley and Stephens made no effort to conceal the events, thinking that they merited sympathy if not admiration. Perhaps they did, but they were also tried for murder.

In setting the case for trial, the court adopted an unusual division of labor. The jury was charged to find a very limited set of facts, while the court would render the actual verdict. Following its instructions, the jury found that "there was no appreciable chance of saving life except by killing some one for the others to eat." Despite the jury's finding, the court rejected the claim of necessity, or, more accurately, denied that a genuine situation of *necessary murder* could ever exist. The notion that circumstances, however harsh, could justify or excuse murder was "at once dangerous, immoral, and opposed to all legal principles and analogy."[3] Dudley and Stephens were convicted and sentenced to death. The Crown commuted the sentence to six months' imprisonment.

If, as Justice Holmes said, "Great cases like hard cases make bad law,"[4] the law of necessity and duress should be downright awful. And that is a not uncommon view. James Fitzjames Stephen once remarked, "[H]ardly any branch of the law . . . is more meagre or less satisfactory than the law on this subject."[5] Although I doubt that Stephen's claim was based on a rigorous comparative analysis, the case law does, in fact, seem quite thin.[6] Fortunately, the dearth of theoretically interesting case law is complemented by a wealth of jurisprudential discussion. For whatever their practical import, which may be small, the various defenses to a criminal charge go to the heart of the underlying rationale of the criminal law. Culpability, retribution, deterrence—all the crucial concepts of punishment and responsibility—come to the fore.[7]

Here I am less concerned to use the defense of duress to probe the aims of the criminal law than to see what it can contribute to the development of a theory of coercion. And it does, I think, make a significant contribution. To see the contribution, it will be best to

[3] 14 Q.B. 273, 275, 281. See Jerome Hall, *General Principles of Criminal Law* (New York: Bobbs-Merrill, 1960), 430ff.

[4] *Northern Securities Co.* v. *U.S.*, 193 U.S. 197 (1904).

[5] *A History of the Criminal Law of England* (1883), 105.

[6] It is not clear why this is so. Perhaps the facts of the more dramatic cases overwhelm discussion of the underlying legal principles, or perhaps genuine situations of necessity and duress rarely arise, and when they do arise, are screened out by a decision not to prosecute. See Walter H. Hitchler, "Duress as a Defense in Criminal Cases," 4 *Virginia Law Review* 519 (1917).

[7] The best example is the insanity plea, for despite its rarity as a defense in criminal cases, it continues to give rise to extensive theoretical discussion and popular debate.

broaden the analysis somewhat. Even though the law has traditionally distinguished between duress and necessity, they have always
been closely linked, and a consideration of necessity will serve to
deepen our understanding of duress.

Some Traditional Views

Necessity and Duress. The demarcation between necessity and duress has never been entirely clear, in part because it has traditionally
reflected two different distinctions, which may or may not pull in
the same direction. One distinction refers to the *cause* of the defendant's situation, that is, whether it is caused by *nature* or another *person.* The second and more important distinction refers to the moral
force of the defense. Roughly stated, a defense to a criminal charge
can be understood either as a *justification* which challenges the alleged wrongfulness of the act, as in cases of self-defense or "justifiable homicide," or as an *excuse* which "concedes that the act is
wrongful, but seeks to avoid the [moral] attribution of the act to the
actor," as in the claim that one killed accidentally or while under a
psychotic delusion.[8] Although the law has not always been consistent on this matter, "necessity" has generally referred to choice situations imposed by nature (for example, destroying a dike to protect more valuable property from flooding), whereas "duress" has
typically referred to choice situations imposed by personal threats.[9]
And whereas necessity has generally been understood as a justification, duress has generally been regarded as an excuse.

English courts invoked the principle of necessity as early as 1551,
when it was held that "a man may break the words of the law, and
yet not break the law itself . . . where the words of them are broken
to avoid greater inconvenience, or through necessity, or by compulsion."[10] Thus when a prisoner departed to escape a fire, it was
held that the necessity to save his life "excuseth the felony."[11] Interestingly, the early view was that both necessity and duress were excuses rooted in a defect of volition. Francis Bacon, for example, says
this: "The law chargeth no man with default where the act is compulsory and not voluntary, and where there is not a consent and
election; and, therefore, if either there has been an impossibility for

---

[8] George Fletcher, *Rethinking Criminal Law* (Boston: Little, Brown, 1978), 759.

[9] *U.S.* v. *Bailey*, 444 U.S. 394, 409 (1980).

[10] *Reninger* v. *Fagossa*, 1 Plowd. 1, 75 Eng. Rep. 1 (1551). Cited in Edward Arnolds
and Norman Garland, "The Defense of Necessity in Criminal Law: The Right to
Choose the Lesser Evil," 65 *Journal of Criminal Law and Criminology* 289 (1974).

[11] 1 Hale P.C. 611 (1736), cited in *People* v. *Lovercamp*, 118 Cal. Rptr. 110, 112 (1975).

a man to do otherwise, or so great a perturbation of the judgement and reason as in presumption of law man's nature cannot overcome, such necessity carrieth a privilege in itself."[12] Blackstone's *Commentaries on the Laws of England* takes a similar view. All of the pleas which "protect the committer of a forbidden act" involve "the want or defect of *will*."[13] In cases of compulsion and necessity, a "man is urged to do that which his judgment disapproves; and which . . . his will (if left to itself) would reject." And since punishment should be applied only for the "abuse of free will," it is "highly just and equitable that a man should be excused for those actions, which are done through unavoidable force and compulsion."[14]

With respect to duress, Blackstone distinguishes two types: (1) duress of imprisonment, where a man "actually loses his liberty," and (2) duress *per minas*, where "the hardship is only threatened and impending."[15] While Blackstone was willing to allow that the *threat* of harm (as well as its actual infliction) can excuse, he argued for two important limitations. First, the duress *per minas* that will excuse a crime is *only* for "fear of loss of life . . . or limb." A fear of battery is no duress, nor are threats to one's property, because, says Blackstone, in these cases "a man may have satisfaction by recovering equivalent damages: but no suitable atonement can be made for the loss of life or limb."[16] Second, duress *never* applies to a charge of *murder*, because, says Blackstone, one "ought rather to die himself than escape by the murder of an innocent."[17]

In addition to these two forms of duress, Blackstone also allows for a necessity defense. Somewhat surprisingly, however, he writes that one should be excused when from "reason and reflection," one commits a criminal act because it is the "least pernicious" of "two evils." He does not characterize necessity as a justification. It is not that one voluntarily chooses to do the *right* thing in choosing the lesser evil; even when one acts from "reason and reflection," the point, says Blackstone, is that one's will is not "freely active."[18]

[12] *The Elements of the Common Laws of England* (London, 1630), in *Works*, vol. XIII, ed. Montague (London, 1831), 131.

[13] (1765), Bk. IV, sec. 21.

[14] Ibid., sec. 27.

[15] Ibid., bk. I, chap. 1.

[16] Ibid.

[17] Ibid., sec. 30.

[18] Ibid., sec. 28. As with duress, Blackstone places limitations on the use of a "lesser evil" defense. It does not apply to cases of economic necessity. Excusing the starving man for stealing a loaf of bread would put property under a "strange inse-

Deontological and Utilitarian Defenses. We can better understand the attempt to define and distinguish necessity and duress if we briefly explore the way these defenses might themselves be justified or explained. It will be useful, in this connection, to invoke the traditional contrast between deontological and utilitarian theories. Roughly speaking, a deontologist will argue that a person should be acquitted when and because it would be unjust to punish him, either because he does nothing wrong or because he should not be held responsible for his act. The utilitarian will argue that a person should be acquitted just in case conviction of the defendant would promote less overall social utility than acquittal.

Some minor deviations aside, Blackstone's emphasis on the defendant's freedom of will exemplifies the deontological approach.[19] The idea is that it is unjust to punish those who do not will the acts they are "compelled" to perform. Hobbes, on the other hand, offers a distinctly utilitarian explanation of duress. Consider, he says, a man threatened with death if he fails to kill another: "If a man by the terrour of present death, be compelled to doe a fact against the Law, he is totally Excused; because no Law can oblige a man to abandon his own preservation. And supposing such a Law were obligatory; yet a man would reason thus, If I doe it not, I die presently; if I doe it, I die afterwards; therefore by doing it, there is time of life gained."[20] Because punishment would not have a deterrent effect on such a person, and because deterrence is the only legitimate aim of punishment, there should be no punishment.

In one of the more famous examples of his utilitarianism at work, Jeremy Bentham developed a similar argument. Bentham's argument is this. Punishment is inherently evil (because painful). It ought never be applied where it is not efficacious, where it does not produce a compensating benefit by actually reducing crime or "mischief." If we consider the way the threat of punishment actually works, we see that not only is punishment "necessarily inefficacious" with respect to acts which are "absolutely involuntary," as when a man's hand "is pushed against some object which his will disposes him NOT to touch," it is also inefficacious in those cases of necessity and duress where the expected harm from choosing to

curity." Moreover, since English law provides for the poor, it is "impossible that the most needy stranger should ever be reduced to the necessity of thieving . . ." Ibid.

[19] If duress and necessity are both rooted in a defect of volition, it is not clear why the threat of battery should not excuse a crime or why duress should not be a defense to murder. If one's will is overcome, one's will is overcome.

[20] *Leviathan*, chap. 27.

commit a crime is less than the expected harm from choosing not to commit a crime. And this is true whether the expected harm results from natural events or from the "intentional and conscious agency of MAN."[21] It is not that it is *unjust* to punish those acting under necessity or duress. On Bentham's view, there is no independent concept of justice. Rather, it is *pointless* to punish those who act under duress, for it will and can have no effect on their actions.[22]

It is a philosophical commonplace that utilitarian footings are extremely unstable: the consequences may go the other way. As Hart points out, even if Bentham is right in claiming that threats of legal punishment have no effect on those actually under duress (and that is by no means self-evident), "the actual *infliction* of punishment on those persons, may secure a higher measure of conformity to law on the part of *other* persons than is secured by the admission of excusing conditions."[23] And even if the threat of punishment is inefficacious once a person is *in* a situation of necessity or duress, it may serve to keep him out of that situation in the first place. As Lord Macaulay argued on behalf of his recommendations for the Indian Penal Code, even if a starving man may not be deterred by the threat of punishment, the threat may "keep him from being in a starving state."[24] And although Macaulay concedes that it would be "useless cruelty to punish acts done under the fear of death, or even of evils less than death," for the reasons noted above and also because he thinks it difficult to define genuine cases of necessity in advance, he argues that utilitarian considerations tell against the explicit adoption of a duress defense. It would, he argues, be "in the highest degree pernicious to enact that no act done under the fear even of instant death should be an offence."[25] For better or worse, these utilitarian arguments against duress and necessity have not

---

[21] *An Introduction to the Principles of Morals and Legislation*, (1823), chap. XIII.

[22] Bentham explains all of the standard defenses (e.g., infancy, insanity, intoxication) in this way.

[23] *Punishment and Responsibility* (Oxford: Oxford University Press, 1968), 19.

[24] "Notes on the Indian Penal Code" (1837), in *Miscellaneous Works of Lord Macaulay*, ed. Trevelyan, vol IV (New York: Harper, 1899), 210. Similarly, even if the threat of punishment for driving while intoxicated is ineffective with respect to those already drunk, it may keep people from getting drunk (or driving while drunk).

[25] Lest the reader get the wrong impression, I should note that the English did not confine their opposition to necessity and duress defenses to their colonies. James Fitzjames Stephen, for example, advanced a similar argument for his own country: "Criminal law is itself a system of compulsion on the widest scale. It is a collection of threats of injury to life, liberty, and property if people do commit crimes. Are such threats to be withdrawn as soon as they are encountered by opposing threats? . . . Surely it is at the moment when temptation to crime is strongest that the law should speak most clearly and emphatically to the contrary." *History of the Criminal Law*, 107.

held sway in India or in Anglo-American law. Whatever their ultimate philosophical motivation, necessity and duress have come to be accepted defenses to a criminal charge, even if they are only rarely invoked with success.

Necessity

While there is still considerable dispute as to whether duress is best understood as a justification or an excuse, there is much less debate about necessity. Under the heading "Justification Generally: Choice of Evils," The *Model Penal Code* (MPC), whose provision has been adopted in several states, says this: "Conduct which the actor believes to be necessary to avoid a harm or evil to himself or to another is *justifiable*, provided that . . . the harm or evil sought to be avoided by such conduct is greater than that sought to be prevented by the law defining the offense charged."[26] Under this provision, the defendant need not disclaim responsibility for his act or claim that his will was overborne. Rather, he claims that he was justified in breaking the law because the anticipated harm of disobedience was less than the anticipated harm of obedience.[27]

If the MPC's account of necessity is explicitly justificatory, its approach to justification is also explicitly impartial and utilitarian. One cannot—under this provision—*justify* acting on behalf of a special responsibility to another person (for example, one's spouse), nor may one place greater weight on one's own interests than on the interests of others (although the law may permit such reasons as part of a duress defense).

Not surprisingly, however, despite the specific wording of this provision, one *cannot* successfully justify disobeying the law whenever the utility of disobedience exceeds the utility of obedience. Greater utility is necessary but not sufficient. In adjudicating necessity claims, courts have generally employed three criteria: (1) the defendant must be trying to avoid a *significant* and *imminent* harm; (2) disobedience must be the *only* way to avoid the harm; (3) the form of disobedience must be *proportionate* to the harm avoided.[28] These criteria sharply reduce the potential scope of the necessity defense and, in particular, have been used to block its use in "politi-

[26] Sec. 3.02, Proposed Official Draft (1962) (emphasis added).

[27] Despite the historical association between necessity and "natural" causes, this provision of the MPC contains no such limitations. One can break the law to protect oneself from arson as well as from lightning. See P. R. Glazebrook, "The Necessity Plea in English Criminal Law," 30 *Cambridge Law Journal* 87, 88 (1972).

[28] See Arnolds and Garland, "The Defense of Necessity in Criminal Law: The Right to Choose the Lesser Evil," 294.

cal" cases, as when Dorsey unsuccessfully argued that the dangers of nuclear power justified his trespass at the Seabrook (New Hampshire) Nuclear Power Plant.[29]

Courts have also sometimes barred a necessity defense in cases where the defendant's act was, by all accounts, clearly and objectively the lesser evil, where disobedience was the only way to avoid a significant and imminent harm.[30] Green, who had been subject to a series of homosexual rapes by his fellow inmates, unsuccessfully sought help from the prison authorities. On the day of his departure, four convicts told him that he would be raped that evening. Although he could have told the authorities, he had reason to fear being killed for "snitching."[31] He fled. He was captured and then charged with escape. When his necessity defense was not allowed, he was convicted and sentenced to an additional three years.

Why was Green's necessity defense not allowed? Simply put, Green lost not so much because the court decided that Green himself had acted wrongly, but because the court was averse to establishing a precedent that would encourage other maltreated prisoners to go over the wall. *Green* exemplifies a tendency for courts to interweave two distinct questions in adjudicating necessity claims: (1) Did the defendant do the right thing? (2) Would it be right to acquit the defendant?[32] And while this conflation is arguably unfair to the individual defendant, it also flows quite readily from the utilitarian basis of the necessity defense. It is a commonplace, after all, that just because an individual *act* would maximize utility, it does not follow that a general *practice* of allowing (and therefore encouraging) similar acts would also maximize utility; there are often good utilitarian reasons to adopt some version of "rule utilitarianism" over "act-utilitarian" principles.[33] If necessity is rooted in considerations of social utility, it is arguable that the crucial question for the

---

[29] *State* v. *Dorsey*, 395 A.2d 855 (1978). Not only had the legislature decided that nuclear power was *not* a harm, said the court, but Dorsey had "other lawful means of protesting nuclear power." 857.

[30] Actually, neither the MPC nor the case law seems to require the defendant's act to be *objectively* the lesser evil. A demonstrably *reasonable*, even if mistaken, *belief* that one is choosing the lesser evil seems sufficient. When a driver involved in a two-car collision failed to stop and render aid to the injured driver of the other car, he claimed that his passenger had been injured and needed immediate treatment. *Woods* v. *State*, 121 S.W.2d 604 (1938). Although the occupants of the other car may have been in more urgent need of help, the court allowed the necessity defense. For a different view, see *Butterfield* v. *State*, 317 S.W.2d 943 (1958).

[31] *State* v. *Green*, 470 S.W.2d 565 (1971). See George Fletcher, "The Individualization of Excusing Conditions," 1285.

[32] George Fletcher, "The Individualization of Excusing Conditions," 1285.

[33] See R. M. Hare, *Moral Thinking* (Oxford: Clarendon Press, 1981). I ignore the difficulties in defining what counts as a "similar" act.

law is not whether the defendant's *act* maximizes utility, but whether it would maximize utility to adopt a *rule* under which the defendant would be acquitted. In many moral contexts, the preference for a rule-utilitarian solution seems to generate intuitively attractive results, as when it strengthens the obligation to keep a promise when breaking a promise would appear to promote greater utility. Here, by contrast, it seems less attractive, as it might very well work against the use of a necessity defense where intuitive morality seems to favor it.

Given the utilitarian motivation of the necessity defense, the problem for the courts (or legislatures) is to develop criteria which successfully steer a course between over- and undercompliance with the law. We do not want to encourage slavish obedience to the letter of the law, particularly when violations would yield greater social utility. *Ceteris paribus*, we want citizens faced with a genuine case of necessity to choose the lesser of two evils.[34] On the other hand, whether a necessity defense will actually maximize social utility will depend on the extent to which citizens will make correct judgments about those situations. If people are inclined to overestimate the conditions under which they are justified in breaking the law, we may prefer that they obey even when, in an individual case, it would promote more utility to disobey.

Now a priori, there is no reason to fear that ordinary citizens will systematically "take advantage" of a suitably constructed necessity defense. They are not particularly attentive to the nuances of the criminal law, and general compliance is not likely to be undermined by the defense. But unlike ordinary citizens, prisoners are sophisticated and attentive students of the criminal law. They are likely to know precisely what kinds of behavior the law does and does not permit. Thus it is possible that even a suitably constructed necessity defense would lead to a pattern of prisoner behavior that does not maximize utility.

Duress

Under "Duress," the *Model Penal Code* says this: "It is an affirmative defense that the actor engaged in the conduct charged to constitute an offense because he was coerced to do so by the use of, or a threat to use, unlawful force against his person or the person of another, which a person of reasonable firmness in his situation would have

[34] See Meir Dan-Cohen, "Decision Rules and Conduct Rules: On Acoustic Separation in Criminal Law," 97 *Harvard Law Review* 625 (1984).

been unable to resist . . ."[35] Several features of this account are worth noting. First, although the MPC distinguishes duress from a lesser-evil defense (for which it makes separate provision), it does not explicitly classify duress as an excuse *or* a justification.[36] Instead, it employs the more neutral term "defense." Second, while the MPC nominally employs a two-pronged account of duress (coercion must result from "*unlawful* force"), here, unlike in the other legal contexts we have considered, it is not clear what work the proposal prong is meant to do. After all, it seems likely that there could not be a lawful threat which forces someone to commit an (otherwise) illegal act that did not simultaneously remove the act's illegality. Third, and perhaps most significantly, while the MPC's account of duress appears to place substantial weight on the volitional quality of the defendant's act, it does so in an importantly attenuated sense. For the criterion is not whether the actual defendant was unable to resist the pressure, but whether a person of "reasonable firmness" would have been unable to resist.

The MPC aside, what do the *cases* suggest about the way duress is understood in the criminal law? Unfortunately, we know little about cases in which a duress defense was successful at trial. For unlike in the civil law, in which either party may appeal, in criminal law the double jeopardy rule prevents the prosecution from appealing a successful duress defense, and trial courts do not write opinions. We know more of cases in which it was alleged that the trial court improperly *excluded* a duress defense. When, for example, a defendant allegedly assisted in a robbery under a threat of death, the appellate court ruled that he was entitled to have the jury consider his claim of duress.[37]

As a general rule, it seems more difficult to establish criminal duress than civil duress. This difference is explicitly acknowledged in *McCoy* v. *State*:

It must be obvious to the deliberate judgment of every reflecting mind that *much less freedom of will* is requisite to render a per-

---

[35] Sec. 2.09

[36] "When the conduct of the actor would otherwise be justifiable under Section 3.02 [Justification], this Section does not preclude such defense."

[37] *White* v. *State*, 203 S.W.2d 222 (1947). On the other hand, when a defendant charged with bigamy alleged that a mob, intent on enforcing the community's mores, had demanded that he marry a young girl with whom he was suspected of having sexual relations, it was held that no instruction on duress was required because the alleged threats had occurred the night before the wedding ceremony, and there had been no "immediate personal constraint" at the time of the bigamous marriage. *Burton* v. *State*, 101 S.W. 266 (1907). Also see Hall, *General Principles of Criminal Law*, 441.

son responsible for crime than to bind him by a sale or other contract. To overcome the will, so far as to render it incapable of contracting a civil obligation, is a mere trifle compared with reducing it to that degree of slavery and submission which will exempt from punishment.[38]

The distinction between civil and criminal duress is confirmed in another case in which, once again, the law proves that we do not have to invent bizarre cases, that real ones will suffice. Patterson had been convicted of embezzlement and borrowed money from Osler to make good the shortage.[39] Osler then told Patterson to embezzle from his present employer, and threatened to expose his previous conviction if he did not. Patterson claimed that the second embezzlement had been performed under duress, but the trial court did not permit the defense to be presented to the jury. The supreme court of Oregon affirmed: Patterson had not acted under duress because Patterson's second crime had its origin in his own "voluntary shortcoming." It was he who "began the digression from the path of rectitude."[40] Of special and present interest, although the court rejected Patterson's claim of duress as a defense to the *criminal* charge, it added that Osler's threat might have been relevant to a claim of *contractual* duress, to whether the money Patterson gave Osler was a "gift or a loan."[41]

The previous cases are, in a way, exceptions to a general pattern of judicial reticence. Courts typically dismiss duress claims without much comment.[42] One famous exception is the case of "Tokyo Rose." When Ms. D'Aquino argued that her treasonous activities had been performed under duress, the trial court held that duress requires that "one must have acted under the apprehension of *im-*

---

[38] 49 S.E. 768, 769 (1887) (emphasis added). McCoy was convicted of murder after a key witness retracted earlier testimony that he did not know the identity of the killer. The witness said that his earlier (allegedly false) testimony had been made under duress, and in charging the jury, the trial court used a definition of duress derived from contract law.

[39] *State* v. *Patterson*, 241 P.2d 977 (1925).

[40] Ibid , 978

[41] Ibid.

[42] When a federal bank employee misappropriated funds by knowingly cashing her daughter's bad checks because her daughter had allegedly threatened to commit suicide if the checks were not cashed, the court ruled there had been no duress, but offered no explanation. *U.S.* v. *Stevison*, 471 F.2d 143 (1974). When Atencio failed to appear for trial because a "contract" had allegedly been put out on his life, the court ruled there had been no duress because he could have turned himself in to the authorities. *U.S.* v. *Atencio*, 586 U.S. 744 (1978).

mediate and impending death or of serious and immediate bodily harm."[43]
A fear of injury to property or remote bodily harm is not sufficient.
Nor is a mere order to commit treason, because "there is nothing in
the mere relationship of the parties that justifies or excuses obedience to such commands."[44] In upholding the trial court's view, the
circuit court added this:

> We think that the citizen owing allegiance to the United States
> must manifest a determination to resist commands and orders
> until such time as he is faced with the alternative of immediate
> injury or death. Were any other rule to be applied, traitors in
> the enemy country would by that fact alone be shielded from
> any requirement of resistance. The person claiming the defense
> of coercion and duress must be a person whose resistance has
> brought him to the last ditch.[45]

Duress and Murder. If a threat of imminent death or bodily harm is
required for a duress defense to treason (or other crimes), many
cases follow Blackstone in completely barring duress as a defense to
murder. In a recent case, for example, the defendant claimed that
his family had been threatened with murder, but the court held that
the coercion defense is simply not available for a case of homicide,
although the reason for the exclusion is not entirely clear.[46]

Barring a duress defense to murder is at least a *plausible* move if
duress is best understood as a *justification*. For it can be argued that
it is not justifiable to intentionally kill another innocent person just
to save one's own life. If, on the other hand, duress is understood
as an *excuse*, one which turns on the volitional quality of the defendant's actions, it is not obvious why the exclusion should hold.[47] No
such exclusion applies in German law, and it has recently come under attack in two important British cases. In *Lynch* v. *Director of Public Prosecutions*, the defendant claimed that he had been ordered by
three members of the Irish Republican Army to drive a car to a place

---

[43] *D'Aquino* v. *U.S.*, 192 F.2d 338, 357 (1951) (emphasis added).
[44] Ibid.
[45] Ibid., 359.
[46] *Cawthon* v. *State*, 382 So.2d 796 (1980). Some cases which state that the duress
defense is unavailable as a matter of *law* in cases of murder go on to discuss whether
there is, in fact, a reasonable claim of duress. This suggests that the principle is not
completely accepted. The MPC does not specifically endorse such an exclusion. One
court did try to explain the distinction between treason and murder. See *State* v. *Nar-
gashian*, 58 A.2d 953, 954 (1941).
[47] See Fletcher, "The Individualization of Excusing Conditions," 1289. Also see
"Duress, Murder, and Criminal Responsibility," 96 *Law Quarterly Review* 208 (1980).

where they then shot and killed a policeman.[48] He was charged with murder as an aider and abettor. A (3-2) majority of the House of Lords held that the defense of duress *was* available. Arguing with the majority, Lord Wilberforce said this: "I find no convincing reason, on principle, why, if a defence of duress in the criminal law exists at all, it should be absolutely excluded in murder charges whatever the nature of the charge; hard to establish, yes, in cases of direct killing so hard that perhaps it will never be proved: but in other cases to be judged, strictly indeed, on the totality of facts . . ."[49]

Lynch notwithstanding, in *Abbott* v. *Regina*, the House of Lords held that a murderer could not argue duress as a defense.[50] It would take too much space to describe the sordid situation in which Abbott came to participate in the stabbing and live burial of a young woman under the orders of a man who was subsequently hanged for murder himself. The court attempted to distinguish *Abbott* from *Lynch* on the grounds that Abbott was a direct participant in murder, whereas Lynch was not. Does this justify barring a duress defense to murder? Wilberforce, now in the minority, said no. Consider, he said, a case of attempted murder. If the attempt fails, "no one can doubt that our law would today allow duress to be pleaded to a charge . . . of wounding with intent." Yet, he noted, should the victim die after the conclusion of a first trial in which the duress plea was successful, "the accused when faced with a murder charge would be bereft of any such defence": "It is not the mere lack of logic that troubles one. It is when one stops to consider why duress is *ever* permitted as a defence even to charges of great gravity that the lack of any moral reason justifying its *automatic* exclusion in such cases as the present becomes so baffling—and so important."[51]

Now Wilberforce's argument may show somewhat less than he thinks. For better or worse, the way a person is treated (in the law and elsewhere) often depends on "moral luck."[52] Consider, for example, a case of assault with the intent to injure but not to kill. If the victim dies because the ambulance is delayed, the defendant may be tried for (some form of) homicide. If the victim lives, the defendant may be tried only for assault and battery. All the same, as Wil-

[48] A.C. 633 (1975).
[49] Ibid., 680–81.
[50] A.C. 755 (1975).
[51] Ibid., 772–73 (original emphasis).
[52] See Bernard Williams, *Moral Luck* (Cambridge: Cambridge University Press, 1981).

berforce rightly observes, it is at least not clear why there should be an automatic exclusion of a duress defense to murder or on what theory that exclusion is based.

A Recent Development. While American courts once seemed to employ the single standard of a threat of imminent death or bodily harm for duress as a defense to *any* crime (except murder), a different approach has been advanced in a recent case. Joseph Toscano, a chiropractor, was convicted of conspiring to obtain money by false pretenses in a scheme to defraud insurance companies.[53] Toscano alleged that he had participated only after having been threatened by the organizer of the scheme, Leonardo, whom he had briefly met when Leonardo was an inmate at a prison where Toscano served as a guard. Although Toscano had attempted to avoid any relationship with Leonardo, the latter had allegedly made this not-so-veiled threat: "Remember, you just moved into a place that has a very dark entrance and you leave there with your wife . . . You and your wife are going to jump at shadows . . ."[54] The trial court refused to charge the jury on the defense of duress because there had been no threat of present, imminent, and immediate death or serious bodily harm.

The supreme court of New Jersey acknowledged that the trial court's position was consistent with "precedents which may have had their origin in the proclivities of a 'tougher minded age,' or [in] judicial fears of perjury and fabrication of baseless defenses."[55] But, said the court, given that there were no applicable New Jersey statutes, it had to be guided "only by common law principles which conform to the principles of our criminal justice system and reflect contemporary notions of justice and fairness," and went on to proclaim the following rule: "Henceforth, duress shall be a defense to a crime other than murder if the defendant engaged in conduct because he was coerced to do so by the use of, or threat to use, unlawful force against his person or the person of another, which a person of reasonable firmness in his situation would have been unable to resist."[56] While hesitant to discourage citizens from making heroic efforts to resist coercive threats, the court was "not persuaded that capitulation to unlawful demands is excusable only when there is a

---

[53] *State* v. *Toscano*, 378 A.2d 755 (1977).

[54] Ibid., 758.

[55] Ibid., 762. The cited phrase is from *R.I. Recreation Center* v. *Aetna Casualty and Surety Co.*, 177 F.2d 603, 605 (1949).

[56] Ibid., 765.

'gun at the head' of the defendant."[57] Instead, the court proposed that the jury should be charged to balance the gravity and imminence of the threatened harm (along with the possibilities for escape, resistance, or seeking official help) against the seriousness of the crime.

Two Special Situations

Our effort to understand duress as a defense in the criminal law will be enhanced by attending to two special legal contexts in which duress or necessity defenses have generally been advanced without much success.

Intimidated Witnesses. In a footnote to his opinion in *Piemonte* v. *United States*, Justice Frankfurter remarked that fear is not and cannot be a legal excuse for refusing to testify in a criminal case.[58] Despite its origins in this minor obiter dictum, this view seems to have become a general rule of law: duress is simply not available as a defense to contempt of court. In one case, a woman was threatened with contempt of (a state) court for refusing to testify about a homicide that she had witnessed. She told the judge "that she was in fear of her life and the lives of her children."[59] Although she was offered protection and relocation, she claimed that the gang involved would find her anyway. It is not clear whether her fears were justified, but it appears that it would not have mattered. Fear, said the court, "is not a valid reason for not testifying. If it's a valid reason then we might as well close the doors."[60]

This is not an isolated judicial anecdote. One study found *no* reported federal decisions in which duress had been successfully used as a defense by an allegedly intimidated witness. Indeed, no less than six of the eight circuit courts have held a duress defense unavailable to putatively intimidated witnesses as a matter of *law*.[61] Yet despite the refusal to accept claims of duress, one government study claims that prosecution witnesses account for nearly ten percent of the victims of murders attributed to organized crime. In-

[57] Ibid., 764.
[58] 367 U.S. 556, 557 (1961).
[59] *People* v. *Carradine*, 287 N.E.2d 670 (1972).
[60] Ibid., 672.
[61] "The Dilemma of the Intimidated Witness in Federal Organized Crime Prosecutions," 50 *Fordham Law Review* 582 (1982). One circuit court has given conflicting signals, and one has indicated that a duress defense is available as a matter of law, but denied it on the facts of the case. The status of a duress defense for intimidated witnesses in the fifty *state* courts is not clear.

deed, the government's "witness protection program" is evidence that the government itself regards retaliation as a genuine phenomenon. Some intimidated witnesses, then, face a genuine dilemma without the potential relief of a duress defense. They can risk retaliation or find themselves in contempt of court.

Prison Escapes. Prison escapes present a difficult case for the traditional distinction between necessity and duress. Unlike the typical case of necessity, prison escape is rarely prompted by a natural event. Unlike in the typical case of duress, no one demands that the prisoner escape. Rather, the typical claim is that the actions of prison authorities or other inmates have made prison life intolerable.[62] Yet despite the arguable reasonableness of at least some such claims, they have generally been treated as legally unacceptable. Unsanitary conditions, a fear of being shot, guard brutality, inadequate medical treatment—one have protected the escapee from conviction and additional punishment.[63]

Consider, in particular, the problem of homosexual rape. *People* v. *Noble* said this:

> The problem of homosexuality in the prison is serious and perplexing, and never more so than in a case such as this where such activity is forced upon a young man against his will. However, the answer to the problem is not the judicial sanctioning of escapes. While we have no reason to doubt the sincerity of this defendant, it is easy to visualize a rash of escapes, all rationalized by unverifiable tales of sexual assault.[64]

It is not clear what the court intends to say here. It could be arguing that threats of homosexual attack *never* justify or excuse prison escape. Or, as seems more likely, the court might be making a special and forward-looking epistemological point, to wit, that while the courts could verify Mr. *Noble's* claim of duress, to find for Noble would create a situation in which the courts would not be able to separate genuine cases of homosexual attack from "unverifiable tales of sexual assault." In any case, *Noble* follows a long line of precedents which hold that threats of homosexual attack neither justify nor excuse a prison escape.

[62] See "Prison Escape and Defenses Based on Conditions: A Theory of Social Preference," 67 *California Law Review* 1183 (1979), and David Dolinko, "Intolerable Conditions as a Defense to Prison Escape," 26 *UCLA Law Review* 1126 (1979). I am ignoring cases in which inmates simply want to regain their freedom.

[63] Excellent discussions of the history of the case law can be found in *People* v. *Lovercamp*, 118 Cal. Rptr. 110 (1975), and *U.S.* v. *Bailey*, 585 F.2d 1087 (1978).

[64] 170 N.W.2d 916, 918 (1969).

There has been some movement in the other direction. Lovercamp and Wynashe had been inmates of the California Rehabilitation Center for two and a half months, during which time they were allegedly threatened by a group of lesbian inmates—"the exact expression was 'fuck or fight.' "[65] They complained to the authorities, but nothing was done. On the day of the escape, they were approached by ten or fifteen inmates and offered the stated alternative. They fought and were told that they "would see the group again."[66] Fearing for their lives, Lovercamp and Wynashe left and were promptly recaptured. Guided by precedents which barred a necessity defense for prison escape, the trial court rejected an offer of proof for the defendant's claims. Lovercamp and Wynashe were convicted.

The California Court of Appeal reversed, although the court was deliberately cautious about breaking new ground.[67] *Lovercamp* allows a prisoner to plead necessity if (1) faced with a specific threat of imminent death, forcible sexual attack, or bodily injury *and* (2) there is no time for a complaint to the authorities or there is a history of futile complaints *and* (3) there is no opportunity to resort to the courts *and* (4) "the prisoner immediately reports to the proper authorities when he has attained a position of safety . . ."[68]

The United States Supreme Court, in *United States* v. *Bailey*, has adopted a similar principle with respect to escape from federal prison: "in order to be entitled to an instruction on duress or necessity . . . an escapee must first offer evidence justifying his continued absence from custody as well as his initial departure, and . . . *an indispensable element of such an offer is testimony of a bona fide effort to surrender or return to custody as soon as the claimed duress or necessity had lost its coercive force."*[69] It is, perhaps, not surprising that few, if any, escapees have turned themselves in under the *Lovercamp/Bailey* criteria. But are the criteria reasonable? It could, after all, be objected that the rule requiring an escapee to surrender immediately is unreasonable because it requires him to risk return to the environment

[65] *People* v. *Lovercamp*, 118 Cal. Rptr. 110, 111 (1975).
[66] Ibid.
[67] "Before *Lovercamp* becomes a household word in prison circles and we are exposed to the spectacle of hordes of prisoners leaping over the walls screaming 'rape,' we hasten to add that the defense of necessity to an escape charge is extremely limited in its application." Ibid., 115.
[68] Ibid. Because the defendants were promptly apprehended, it is impossible to say whether they would have turned themselves in. The court was prepared to allow the jury to decide that question upon retrial.
[69] 444 U.S. 394, 412, 413 (1980) (emphasis added).

that created the original problem.[70] Whatever might be said about the merits of the rules, the general view seems to be that surrender is required if the duress defense is to be allowed.

Conclusion. It is not my intention to argue in favor of any particular rule with respect to intimidated witnesses or prison escapes. The society's interest in encouraging witnesses to testify and limiting prison escape is real. In addition, because both cases may present special epistemological problems, society may have to choose between permitting numerous false claims and excluding (perhaps) a smaller number of genuine claims. For these reasons, considerations of social utility might support severe limitations on the use of a duress defense.

Yet we must also squarely confront the moral shortcomings of such a policy. The principle that it is especially wrong to convict the innocent is, after all, a cornerstone of our criminal justice system. Blackstone himself said, "It is better that ten guilty persons escape than one innocent suffer."[71] If we assume, as seems reasonable, that a defendant who has a valid duress defense is innocent of the crime, then despite some recent modifications in the law, Blackstone's principle does not seem to apply in the context of witness intimidation and prison escape.

The Theory of Duress as a Defense

If we stand back from the cases and special situations, does the previous analysis contribute to the development of a *theory* of coercion? I think so. We can, for example, learn from the comparison between civil and criminal duress. Here we find at least two important differences in emphasis. First, although the criminal law nominally invokes a two-pronged account of duress, unlike civil duress, in which the morality of A's proposal seems to be the crucial factor, criminal duress places *little* weight on the moral criteria of the *proposal prong.* Since it is unlawful to coerce (or induce) someone to do something unlawful, there is no potential "lawfulness" of the coercion to distinguish cases of duress from cases where there is no duress.[72]

---

[70] Justice Blackmun (dissenting in *Bailey*) was sympathetic to the objection: "it seems too much to demand that respondents, in order to preserve their legal defenses, return forthwith to the hell that . . . compelled their leaving in the first instance." Ibid., 420.

[71] *Commentaries*, bk. IV, sec. 27.

[72] I suppose the provision does bar claiming that one committed one crime (e.g., eluding a police officer) under duress because one had reason to fear legal punish-

If the moral criteria of the proposal prong do not carry much weight, the *choice prong* has become thoroughly moralized. Recall the court's opinion in *McCoy*. In refusing to allow a duress defense, the court held that "much less freedom of will is requisite to render a person responsible for crime than to bind him by a sale or other contract."[73] While the court's language suggests that duress turns on the volitional quality of the defendant's act (his "freedom of will"), the real issue, it seems, is not the amount of pressure on the defendant, but whether the defendant should be held responsible for his act. And that is clearly a moral matter.

Two- and Three-Party Cases. Let us probe this issue a bit further. *Why* is less pressure sufficient to excuse in the civil law than in the criminal law? The complete answer to this question is no doubt complex, but part of the story seems to lie in the different structures of two- and three-party cases and correlative notions about the ascription of responsibility. One difference may be this. If, as in the typical two-party civil case, A gets B to *agree* to do X by wrongly applying pressure to B, a rule that excuses B from the agreement shifts the burden back to the wrongdoer (A) himself. If, as in the typical three-party case of criminal duress, A wrongly exerts pressure on B to commit a crime against C, a rule that excuses B shifts the harm to an innocent third party (C).

Given this, the law's standards for duress may reflect the moral view that it is worse for B to harm an innocent C than to harm a guilty A, and therefore that less pressure is necessary to shift the wrong back to a guilty A than to shift it to an innocent C. That this seems to capture part of the story is confirmed by a feature of contract law we noted above. When A coerces B to contract with an innocent C, the law is, in fact, *less* willing to invalidate the contract than when A coerces B to contract with A, for the former situation is structurally akin to the typical criminal case.[74] By contrast, self-defense is more akin to bilateral contractual relations, and here B is typically permitted to injure a wrongful A in response to a threat that would *not* excuse B from injuring an innocent C.

A second difference is this. Some special cases aside, the resolution of most *civil* disputes seems to assume what we might call the

---

ment for a different crime (e.g., a burglary). Similarly, if one *abandons* a criminal act "out of fear that the police must be coming," one cannot claim moral or legal credit for one's act. See *State* v. *Woods*, 357 N.E.2d 1059 (1976), and Fletcher, *Rethinking Criminal Law*, 190.

[73] 49 S.E. 768, 769 (1887).

[74] See pp. 47–48.

conservation of responsibility. On this principle, the total responsibility for an act cannot exceed 100 percent (it could be less). If A is responsible for coercing B into signing a contract, B is not responsible for the contract.[75] They cannot both be responsible. By way of contrast, *criminal* responsibility is not conserved in this way. Here there is plenty of responsibility to go around. Consider, for example, a ("contract killing") case in which A pays B to kill C. A cannot claim that he is not responsible because B acted voluntarily; B cannot claim that he is not responsible because A paid him to commit the act. Both are responsible. Both are punishable. And as with inducements, so too with coercion. A's liability for pressuring B into harming C does not *necessarily* remove B's responsibility for what he has done. Before B's claim of duress will be granted, we need to be assured that it would not be just to punish *B*. That it might also be just to punish *A* will not resolve that question.[76]

Volition and Normativity. Although I think it transparent that the application of the choice prong rests on moral criteria, its normativity has been concealed by two features of the legal debate: the language of voluntariness and the argument for an "objective" standard of criminal duress. Consider first the issue of voluntariness. It is often said that a criminal offense requires *actus reus* and *mens rea*: *actus reus* requires that there be a criminal act; *mens rea* requires that the defendant have a "guilty mind," that (in the required sense—it is not necessary to get this too precise) he *intend* to commit the crime.[77] Cases of automatism and physical force (where A pushes B's knife-holding hand down on C's throat) are said to negate *actus reus*. It is not just that there has been an *unintentional* act; there has been no *act* at all.[78] On the other hand, cases of ignorance, mistake,

[75] If A injures B and B sues A in tort, either A or B will be assigned responsibility for the harm (under a principle of "contributory negligence") or they will share responsibility (under a principle of "comparative negligence"). In either case, the total responsibility cannot add up to more than 100 percent. There are exceptions to the principle of conservation. For a philosophical discussion, see Judith Jarvis Thomson, "Remarks on Causation and Liability," 13 *Philosophy & Public Affairs* 101 (1984).

[76] Just why the civil and the criminal law employ different accounts of the conservation of responsibility is an interesting question. Part of the explanation may be this. In the civil law, A compensates B for the *harm* to B, and (punitive damages aside) there cannot be more than 100 percent compensation. The criminal law punishes persons for the *wrongness* or *public* harm of an act, and that is somewhat independent of the amount of harm to a specific victim.

[77] See Hyman Gross, *A Theory of Criminal Justice* (New York: Oxford University Press, 1979), 91ff.

[78] George Fletcher, *Rethinking Criminal Law*, 802. Compare the joke in the movie *Beverly Hills Cop* (Paramount Pictures, 1984) in which Eddie Murphy is arrested for

and insanity are said to involve *mens rea*. Here, there has been an act; the question is whether the act can be morally attributed to the agent in view of the defects in the agent's volition.

Now it is uncontroversial that one acts (or is moved) involuntarily when there is no *actus reus* and that whether there is *actus reus* is, more or less, a straightforward empirical question. Of course— rightly or wrongly—we also use the *language* of voluntariness to talk about cases of *mens rea* and ordinary (constrained-volition) coercion.[79] Since the first (*actus reus*) form of involuntariness is primarily physical or empirical, it is not unreasonable to suppose that all contexts in which we use the notion of voluntariness are also empirical.[80] But as we have seen, no empirical inquiries, at least none of a reasonably straightforward sort, can answer the question whether the defendant *should* have yielded to the pressure. The law of criminal duress (in its present form) may or may not give the right answer to that question, but that is the question it is designed to answer.

Objective and Subjective. It is sometimes said that the law employs an "objective" test of criminal duress. If this is so, and I think there *is* a sense in which it is so, does that weaken my claim that the choice prong is *moralized*? I think not. The problem here is that "objective" typically takes its meaning from one of several contrasting terms. And the danger is that the sense (or senses) in which a test for duress is properly regarded as objective will be confused with a sense (or senses) in which it is not.

"Objective" can mean, among other things, (1) external as opposed to phenomenological or internal; (2) empirical as opposed to normative; or (3) standardized as opposed to individualized. Consider this analogy. In determining whether a suit fits a given man, we do not ask whether it fits the "average man." Fit is individualized to the characteristics of the wearer. No size fits all. In *that* sense, proper fit is subjective. At the same time, proper fit is *not* purely phenomenological. Someone may *think* his suit fits well, but it does not follow that it *does*. "Feeling comfortable" may be a *necessary* condition of proper fit, but it is not sufficient. In *that* sense, proper fit is

---

disturbing the peace after having been thrown through a glass window by a group of thugs.

[79] Several commentators suggest that we speak of an *involuntary act* when there is no act at all, and reserve the term *not voluntary* "for those occasions when the actor is not responsible for what he does because of factors affecting choice." Hyman Gross, *A Theory of Criminal Justice*, 141. Martin Wasik makes a similar suggestion in "Duress and Criminal Responsibility," *Criminal Law Review* 453, 454 (1977).

[80] Fletcher, *Rethinking Criminal Law*, 494.

objective. Proper fit is also decidedly normative. It requires the application of aesthetic criteria. So putting aside the arguably unhelpful "objective" for a moment, we can say that proper fit is individualized, external, and normative.

Now the general characteristic of an "objective" test of duress is that it posits a *standard* (nonindividualized) test by which to adjudicate the claims of an individual defendant. One asks whether "the reasonably steadfast man" (or some analogue) would yield to the pressure. Part of the case for a standardized test rests on the eminently sensible rejection of the view that an agent acts under duress merely because he thinks he does. But the real issue is not whether the test for duress is purely internal (it is not subjective in *that* sense), but whether it should take account of the *characteristics* of individual defendants. And that remains an open question. There are plausible arguments both ways. On behalf of a *standardized* test, it may be argued that it is simply too difficult to adjust a finding of duress to a defendant's individual characteristics. It may also be argued that those who are less able to resist coercive pressure are responsible for their character and should therefore be held to a higher standard than they are now capable of meeting. On behalf of an individualized test, it has been argued that a standardized test for duress "penalizes those of less than average understanding or judgment," and that the proper question is not what a "person of reasonable firmness" would do, but what it would be reasonable to expect this person (given all his characteristics) to do.[81]

Fortunately, it is not necessary to settle the controversy here. For the general and important point is that whether we decide for a standardized *or* an individualized test for duress, we do so principally because one or the other is thought to be more consistent with the *normative* point of duress claims.

Justification or Excuse?

Suppose I am right in arguing that the point of the choice prong is fundamentally normative. It is still not entirely clear what the normative force of the duress defense amounts to. Although duress is traditionally understood as an *excuse*, some contemporary scholars

---

[81] See K.J.M. Smith, "Duress—The Role of the Reasonably Steadfast Man," 98 *Law Quarterly Review* 347 (1982). We saw that in adjudicating the voluntariness of confessions, courts explicitly take account of individual differences. *Ceteris paribus*, there is no reason that the law of criminal duress should employ a different standard.

and cases have tended to emphasize its justificatory dimensions.[82] In the words of one text, "the rationale for the defense of duress is that, for reasons of social policy, it is better that the defendant . . . choose to do the lesser evil."[83] In *United States* v. *Bailey*, Justice Wilkey says this: "the rationale for the defense is that . . . conduct which violates the literal language of the criminal law is *excused or justified* because [the defendant] has thereby avoided a harm of greater magnitude. Thus the defense of duress rests on the *social utility* of a defendant's actions . . ."[84] On this view, one should be acquitted for aiding an armed robbery at the point of a gun, because one promotes greater social utility by acquiescing than by risking one's life; one should not be acquitted for aiding in a homicide, because it is "not necessarily better" that one kill another than that one be killed.[85]

There are at least two related problems with this account. First, it lacks the right intuitive feel. If one should be acquitted for aiding the armed robbery, it does not seem to be because, or at least not primarily because, acquiescing promotes greater *social* utility. Second, it does not seem right to limit the defense of duress to cases in which one's action *does*, in fact, maximize social utility.

While these considerations suggest that we should preserve the distinction between duress and necessity, there are also reasons to think that duress is better understood as a justification than as an excuse. The traditional view that duress is not a defense to homicide and that one's life (or body) must be in danger certainly suggests that "the defense of duress is available only to those who protect an interest (namely life) that is greater than the harm caused . . ."[86] And even if we reject those special limitations on the duress defense, it seems to depend on *some* sort of balancing of interests— even if not a radically impartial balancing. Although a successful duress defense may not require that the harm averted by a criminal act be *greater* than the harm caused, it may require that the harm averted be *not significantly less*:

> if an actor kills in order to avoid mutilation of his body . . . his conduct could not be justified on the ground that he furthers

[82] Kent Greenawalt argues that there is no important distinction between justification and excuse. See "The Perplexing Borders of Justification and Excuse," 84 *Columbia Law Review* 1897 (1984).

[83] Wayne R. LaFave and Auston W. Scott, *Handbook on Criminal Law* (St. Paul: West, 1972), 374.

[84] 585 F.2d 1087, 1111 (1978) (dissenting opinion).

[85] Ibid.

[86] Fletcher, "The Individualization of Excusing Conditions," 1288–89.

the greater good. Nonetheless, he may have a perfectly sound claim of duress . . . Yet if the gap between the harm done and the benefit accrued becomes too great, the act is . . . inexcusable. For example, if the actor has to blow up a whole city in order to avoid the breaking of his finger, we might appropriately expect him to endure the harm . . .[87]

Agent-Neutral and Agent-Relative Justification. The effort to understand the moral point of duress claims may be impeded by the assumption that if duress is not a social-utility justification, it is not a justification at all, and instead must be an excuse. But that assumption is at least too quick and probably false. To see this more clearly, let us employ Thomas Nagel's distinction between *agent-neutral* and *agent-relative* reasons for actions. "If a reason can be given a general form which does *not* include an essential reference to the person to whom it applies," Nagel writes, "it is an *agent-neutral* reason . . . If, on the other hand, the general form of a reason *does* include an essential reference to the person to whom it applies, it is an *agent-relative* reason."[88] To illustrate: the reason which we all have to save two lives rather than one is an agent-neutral reason; but if someone does something because it is in the interest of him or his wife, he acts for an agent-relative reason.

Nagel argues that there are *two* types of agent-relative reasons. *Autonomy* reasons stem from the "desires, projects, commitments, and personal ties of the individual agent." They give a person reason to act in "pursuit of ends that are his own."[89] *Deontology* reasons stem "from the claims of others not to be maltreated in certain ways."[90] They give a person reason not to maltreat others because it is *he* who would perform the acts of maltreatment. Agent-relative reasons can be both less and more demanding than agent-neutral reasons. Autonomy reasons permit us to place greater weight on our own (or our loved ones') interests than on the interests of others, thus widening the scope of permissible action.[91] They would explain, for example, why one seems justified in failing to risk one's life in order to save the lives of two strangers. Deontolog-

[87] Fletcher, *Rethinking Criminal Law*, 803–4.

[88] Thomas Nagel, "The Limits of Objectivity," in *Tanner Lectures on Human Values*, vol. I (Salt Lake City: University of Utah Press, 1980), 102 (original emphasis). Also see Derek Parfit, *Reasons and Persons* (New York: Oxford University Press, 1984), 27, and Kent Greenawalt, "Conflicts of Law and Morality—Institutions of Amelioration," 67 *Virginia Law Review* 177, 190 (1981).

[89] Nagel, "The Limits of Objectivity," 120.

[90] Ibid.

[91] There are limits. Even if one is entitled to place *greater* weight on one's own interests than the interests of others, one cannot assign them *infinite* weight.

ical reasons tend to narrow the scope of permissible action. They explain, for example, why it would be wrong for one to kill an innocent person in order to save a greater number of lives.

I suggest this. We can understand a criminal act performed under duress as one that we have agent-relative but not agent-neutral reasons to perform. Unlike necessity, which is agent-neutral, duress is agent-relative. Like necessity, duress is a justification, not an excuse. Understanding duress in this way has two important advantages: it is consistent with the justificatory dimensions of duress we have encountered, and it is also consistent with the view that there is an important distinction between duress and necessity.

Even if this is roughly correct, it might be objected that there is another reason for thinking that duress is better understood as an excuse, a reason which turns on the different effects of justification and excuse on the rights of second and third parties. To excuse a wrongful actor does not typically affect the rights of other persons to resist or assist him. Although an insane person may be excused for his crime, one does not have the right to assist him, and one has the right to resist. On the other hand, a valid justification seems to affect "a matrix of legal relationships." When B is *justified* in doing X, others may acquire a right to assist him, and it is even possible that the victim has no right to resist.[92]

But the previous point, even if sound, does no damage to duress as an agent-relative justification. As Nagel points out, one may have agent-relative reason to perform an act that others lack agent-neutral reason to help us perform, and one may have agent-relative reason not to perform an act that others have no reason to prevent.[93] Suppose, for example, that A is torturing B and threatens to continue doing so unless B provides some important information. If B provides the information, A will use it to harm two innocent persons. Now suppose, further, that B *wants* to succumb to A's coercion, but cannot do so. B needs C's help to recall this information. Whereas B might have agent-relative reason to give A the information if he could recall it on his own, C may have neither agent-relative nor agent-neutral reason to help B do so.

In arguing that duress is best understood as an agent-relative justification, I have not, of course, suggested that *all* legal excuses are most accurately understood in that way. Insanity is an excuse, but it is no kind of justification. So, too, perhaps for cases of nonvoli-

---

[92] Fletcher, *Rethinking Criminal Law*, 762. Thus if one is justified in destroying a dike to avert a greater disaster, others have a right to help.

[93] "The Limits of Objectivity," 126.

tional duress. But if I am right in believing that duress is ordinarily best understood as an agent-relative justification, we will then reencounter what I have called the voluntariness problem. If duress is a justification rather than an excuse, it is arguable that B need not deny his responsibility for his actions or claim that he acted involuntarily. Whether we can maintain the view that duress is a justification and simultaneously claim that duress compromises the voluntariness of acts is a question I consider in Chapter 16.

NINE

COERCION AND THE LAW:
CONCLUSION

Although we have covered a good deal of ground, we have not covered it all. Coercion claims arise in several legal contexts we have not begun to consider. When, for example, a trial judge stated that it was the jury's "duty" to reach a verdict, it was held, on appeal, that he had coerced the jury, and the verdict was set aside.[1] When a defendant claimed that he stopped his crime in midstream, the court held that to abandon a criminal attempt "out of fear that the police might be coming cannot reasonably be considered voluntary," and therefore does not bar prosecution.[2]

Or consider the crime of rape. A man commits rape only when he has sexual relations with a woman "forcibly and against her will."[3] What sort of coercion is necessary for sexual relations to constitute rape? One case held that a woman is not coerced unless she has put up the "utmost resistance."[4] Another case held that if a woman consents *at all*, even if the consent is "reluctantly given, and although there may be some force used to obtain her consent, the offense cannot be rape."[5] Yet, the criteria for rape have undergone considerable change, and may undergo even more. Pressure that was once insufficient to establish rape will do so now or may do so in the future.

Coercion claims can arise even in *international* law. It appears, for example, that if a soldier surrenders and is taken prisoner of war, he cannot argue that he acquires no obligations to his captors be-

[1] *Decker* v. *Schumacher*, 19 N.W.2d 466. Jurors were once regarded as prisoners of the court and kept together until they had agreed upon a verdict. We now believe that a verdict must be arrived at freely. See *People* v. *Sheldon*, 50 N.E. 840 (1898).

[2] *State* v. *Woods*, 357 N.E.2d 1059, 1064 (1976). Also see George Fletcher, *Rethinking Criminal Law* (Boston: Little, Brown, 1978), 190.

[3] *Black's Law Dictionary*, 4th ed. (St. Paul: West, 1951). See Susan Estrich, "Rape," 95 *Yale Law Journal* 1087 (1986).

[4] *State* v. *Cottengim*, 12 S.W.2d 53, 57.

[5] *Welch* v. *State*, 198 S.E. 810, 811.

cause he surrenders under duress.[6] And whereas coercion applied to the *representative* of a state will invalidate a treaty, the coercion "imposed by the victor [state] upon the vanquished [state]" will not.[7]

Although I do not doubt that a consideration of these and other legal contexts would expand our understanding of the *law*, I do not think it would add much to our understanding of *coercion*. So let us now take stock. What can we say, in a general way, about the adjudication of coercion claims?

1. *Nonvolitional coercion.* While coercion that undermines an agent's capacity to make rational choices will almost always constitute legally recognizable coercion, we have encountered only two legal contexts in which coercion is fundamentally or frequently a problem of volition: wills and confessions.[8] We also saw that wills and confessions share three other important and related similarities. First, in both cases, we have reason to be especially concerned about the agent's mental capacities, whether, as in wills, such concern focuses on internal (mental) impairments or, as in confessions, on external factors, such as prolonged interrogation. Second, in both contexts, the agent arguably gains nothing of *enduring* value by succumbing to pressure, and thus there is some reason to doubt that the agent's choice reflects his underlying preferences. Third, in both contexts, the question whether an agent's will is overborne is treated—more or less—as a question of *fact*, one to which the law generally adopts an "individualized" or "totality of the circumstances" approach.

2. *Constrained volition.* In most legal contexts, a coercion claim involves an agent who is confronted with unwanted alternatives and makes an arguably rational choice among them—a choice which he may regret having to make (because of his circumstances) but which he will not regret having made (under the circumstances). In adjudicating such cases, judges often *refer* to "overborne wills," and will *say* that such coercion renders the agent's action "involuntary." But even if the use of those locutions can ultimately be defended, deci-

---

[6] See Michael Walzer's "Prisoners of War: Does the Fight Continue after the Battle?" in his *Obligations* (Cambridge: Harvard University Press, 1970). For a more extended discussion of this question, see Chapter 13.

[7] L. Oppenheim, *International Law*, 8th ed., vol. I (London: Longmans, Green, 1955), 891. Also see "Draft Convention on the Law of Treaties," 29 *American Journal of International Law*, Supp. (1935), Article 32, Duress.

[8] Nonvolitional coercion may not constitute legally recognizable coercion if B is responsible for being in a position in which he cannot exercise volition.

sions under circumstances of constrained volition are not involuntary in the *same way* as in cases of nonvolition.

3. *The two-pronged theory.* In contexts of constrained volition, the law employs what I have called a two-pronged theory of coercion, although it is not invoked by the courts in these terms. On the two-pronged theory, A coerces B to do X if and only if (1) A's proposal creates a choice situation for B such that B has no reasonable alternative but to do X and (2) it is *wrong* for A to make such a proposal to B. I have referred to (1) as the *choice prong* and to (2) as the *proposal prong*. The specific criteria used to apply the two-pronged theory vary according to legal context. Moreover, within each legal context, the criteria have changed over time, and may differ from court to court. Nevertheless, the basic *structure* of the two-pronged theory has, I think, remained remarkably stable.

3a. *The choice prong.* With the exception of duress as a criminal defense, the law pays relatively little attention to the choice prong. The requisite criteria are not spelled out in great detail. We can say this much: In determining what counts as a *reasonable* alternative, the law adopts a *contextual* and *moralized* approach. The law will concede that A's threat leaves B no reasonable alternative but to *contract* to do X while denying that a similar threat leaves B no reasonable alternative but to commit a crime.

3b. *The proposal prong.* A acts wrongly for the purposes of the proposal prong if A proposes to do something that is independently illegal. It is ordinarily not coercion if A proposes to do what he has an independent legal right to do, so long as the right is not abused or used for purposes that the law considers illegitimate.

4. *Coercion and responsibility.* Let us try to place the law's theory of coercion in a more general context. A case involving a coercion claim can be said to involve two questions: (a) a *coercion question*—has B been coerced? (b) a *responsibility question*—should B be held responsible for the normal legal effects of his act? We could understand the law's approach to these questions in two ways. On one model of judicial reasoning, judges first answer the coercion question, and that answer determines their answer to the responsibility question.[9] On a second, or *bottom-line*, model, judges first answer the responsibility question, and that answer determines their answer to the coercion question. The bottom-line model might be better understood as a judicial form of "reflective equilibrium," in

[9] I prefer not to refer to this model as *deductive* because that term suggests that the criteria are (more or less) self-applying.

172

which the principles that generate the legal conclusion and the legal conclusion itself are revised in the light of each other until they are brought into a reasonable degree of harmony.[10] The bottom-line or reflective equilibrium model is emphatically not another name for (what is often called) *judicial realism*. It does not imply that judicial decisions represent a judge's political or ideological preferences, which are then merely rationalized by his decision. The judge may arrive at the bottom line through rigorous moral reasoning.

Given this distinction, I suggest a general observation about the law's approach to coercion. *Within* a well-developed body of law (for example, contracts, torts, or plea bargaining), judicial reasoning typically follows the first model: judges use the accepted principles to answer the coercion question, and the answer to that question determines the answer to the responsibility question. On the other hand, the *development* of the principles that are to govern a body of law typically follows the bottom-line model. Given a generic situation in which B acts under considerable pressure (for example, contracts made while in financial straits or plea bargaining), the law's answer to the responsibility question will help shape its answer to the coercion question. If the courts believe that someone should (or should not) be held responsible for the normal legal effects of his act, they will develop criteria for coercion which permit a negative (or positive) answer to the coercion question.

Now I am not suggesting that the law's answer to the responsibility question is *entirely* independent of the sorts of considerations that might motivate an "independent" answer to the coercion question, although it is not clear what an independent answer would look like. Courts are motivated to answer the responsibility question precisely because they believe that certain sorts of coercive pressures *ought* to remove or mitigate responsibility. Nonetheless, I do mean to stress that the ultimate question for a court is whether someone will be *held responsible* for the normal legal effects of his act, and the courts must always determine whether the *degree* or *type* of pressure is of the sort that should negate the agent's responsibility.

If this is roughly correct, there is a comprehensive and radical sense in which the law adopts a moralized or normative approach to coercion. It is not that the proposal prong introduces a moral dimension into what is otherwise essentially an empirical inquiry; *both* prongs are thoroughly moralized, and each gives legal expression to and allows a more sophisticated development of the law's

[10] Rawls, *A Theory of Justice* (Cambridge: Harvard University Press, 1971), 20ff.

concern with the what is irreducibly a moral question—the ascription of responsibility.

5. *Responsibility: internal and external considerations.* In considering various bodies of law, I have observed that judges respond to both *internal* and *external* moral considerations. By internal considerations, I mean any factors intrinsic to B's choice situation and the interests of parties directly affected by B's actions. By external considerations, I mean the indirect effects of *holding* B responsible (or not responsible) for his act. The internal question asks whether, on balance, it is right or just to hold B responsible for his act. The external question asks whether, on balance, it is in the interests of the society to hold B responsible.

In adjudicating coercion claims, the courts rely primarily on the sorts of internal moral considerations captured by the choice and proposal prongs. Nonetheless, we have seen that the courts can be acutely sensitive to external considerations. Courts will often grant that B acted under considerable and wrongful pressure, but (sometimes candidly) say that they cannot *hold* that B was coerced because doing so would have undesirable consequences. Rather than say that B *has* been coerced, but that, for reasons of public policy, B should be held responsible nonetheless, the courts have generally attempted to pack those social interests into their account of coercion.

I think it is at least doubtful that this appeal to external considerations can be defended within the framework of a theory of coercion. I believe that our concern with coercion is motivated by considerations of *justice* and *rights*. We want to know whether it is right or fair to hold a person responsible for the normal legal effects of his act. If this is correct, then the law is unfaithful to the moral basis of its concern with coercion when it allows external moral considerations to motivate its adjudication of coercion claims.

I am not, of course, arguing that considerations of social utility have no place in social *legislation* or, of more immediate relevance, in deciding what to do in the face of a plausible coercion claim.[11] Consider the role of "moral fault." Although moral fault is ordinarily a prerequisite for ascriptions of legal responsibility, for reasons of social utility we may adopt *strict liability* laws that can hold someone responsible who is (by everyone's admission) *not* at fault. For similar reasons, it may sometimes be wise to hold accountable those

[11] It can, of course, be argued that considerations of social utility should play little role in *judicial* decisions. See, for example, Ronald Dworkin, *Taking Rights Seriously* (Cambridge: Harvard University Press, 1977).

who are coerced. Even so, it would not follow that these considerations should be incorporated *within* the structure of the law's account of coercion. It is one thing to override the principle that coercion nullifies the ascription of responsibility and another to say that one is *not coerced* whenever—for whatever reason—it seems best to hold one legally responsible or to refuse to undo the normal legal effects of one's act.

PART TWO

PHILOSOPHY

T E N

THE LANGUAGE OF COERCION

From Law to Philosophy

I have argued that, in most legal contexts, the law adopts a two-pronged theory of coercion and that both prongs are moralized. Let us assume that this account is roughly correct. It is not clear what this shows. That the law adopts a particular theory of coercion settles nothing, in and of itself. The law is interested in a special (although not unique) set of problems, and there is no reason to assume that its interests are coextensive with all the interesting questions about coercion, or that its account of coercion is philosophically defensible.

Indeed, it may be objected that what I took to be a virtue of the law's approach to coercion is a distinct philosophical *liability*. The objection may go something like this. Precisely because a court's account of coercion must be compatible with what it takes to be an acceptable result, it will be driven to adopt an account of coercion that allows it to reach the desired conclusion. When contract law says, for example, that "threats cannot constitute duress unless they are wrongful, even though they exert such pressure as to preclude the exercise of free judgment," we are entitled to feel somewhat puzzled.[1] For here the law is saying, in effect, "there is duress, but we do not *count* it as duress." Thus despite its omnipresence in the law, it may be thought that a moralized theory of coercion is largely a mere judicial rationalization.

This line of objection can take a more political form. The law's approach to coercion, it may be said, is inherently *conservative*. Judges tend to presuppose and accept a set of background institutions (such as private property) *within* which questions of coercion arise, but which cannot, in themselves, be said to coerce. Or, it might be said, judges are loath to reach (and could not enforce) decisions that would prove politically unacceptable or cause major economic upheaval. Indeed, from a jurisprudential viewpoint, it might be main-

[1] *Restatement of Contracts* (St. Paul: West, 1932), Sec. 492.

179

tained that judges must and perhaps *should* be conservative, that the whole point of the principle of *stare decisis* and the incremental process of case law is to place severe constraints on judicial decision making.

To push this point just a bit further, suppose that a new philosophical analysis of coercion convincingly demonstrates that once we *really* understand what it means to say that "A coerces B to do X," we will see that most employment contracts in a modern capitalist society are coerced. Suppose, further, that in response to a suit for breach of contract, an employee claims that since his choice was to work or starve, he signed his employment contract under duress and should not, therefore, be bound by its terms. In support of his client's position, the employee's attorney relies on the new philosophical analysis. A court is unlikely to say, "Since we now understand what coercion *really* means, and since coerced contracts are not binding, we find for the employee." If, as is more likely, the court will tailor its account of coercion to uphold the contract, why should a philosopher take seriously what the court has to say? Indeed, even if, as on some political theories, a court's reasoning *ought* to be restrained by its institutional role (because radical change in a society's basic institutions is a job for democratically elected representatives), that would merely strengthen the claim that attention to adjudicative law is apt to lead the philosopher astray, not closer to the truth.

Of course, even if the previous line of objection were sound, the project of Part One would still be of considerable value. The various legal contexts clearly raise important *questions* about coercion and would continue to provide a set of realistic situations which an adequate theory of coercion would have to be prepared to handle. On the other hand, we would not be entitled to assume that the law provides anything like the right *answers* to these questions. If we are to evaluate the law's theory of coercion, we cannot attend only to the law itself. We must consider, in a direct way, whether that theory is philosophically defensible.

If we shift our focus from law to philosophy, what do we find? Although contemporary Anglo-American philosophy is less interested in questions of language than some of its critics suppose, many philosophical analyses of coercion take their task to be the specification of the necessary and sufficient conditions for the linguistic truth of a coercion claim. The philosopher will posit a set of hypothetical cases and ask: Is it proper to say "A coerces B to do X" or "A is threatening B," and so on? Or would we say, instead, "A is making an *offer*, not a threat," or "A may be *exploiting* B, but A is not coercing B," and so on?[2]

In my view, this strategy has not proved particularly helpful. I believe that attempts to identify a precise set of necessary and sufficient conditions for the truth of coercion claims are not likely to succeed, in large part because our linguistic intuitions are, themselves, unclear and controversial. In addition, and of more importance, I believe that very *little* of genuine moral or political significance ultimately turns on what we *say* about coercion—on whether, for example, there is some *plausible* sense in which workers are "coerced" into accepting capitalist wage offers or prisoners have "no choice" but to participate in experiments. To defend this view, and to set the stage for the analysis that follows, I must first attend to what I take to be a crucial defect of the philosophical literature on coercion—an insufficient sensitivity to the contextual character of coercion claims.

Coercion and Contextualism

There is an old joke about three men discussing a question with a rabbi. After listening to the first man, the rabbi says, "You're right." The second man disagrees, and the rabbi says, "*You're* right." To this, the third man says, "But, Rabbi, they can't *both* be right." And the rabbi responds, "You're right, too."

Harry Frankfurt begins his important article "Coercion and Moral Responsibility" with the following observation: "The courts may refuse to admit in evidence, on the grounds that it was coerced, a confession which the police have obtained from a prisoner by threatening to beat him. But the prisoner's accomplices, who are compromised by his confession, are less likely to agree that he was genuinely coerced into confessing."[3] Can the courts *and* the prisoner's accomplices both be right? Not if we assume that, barring

[2] See, for example, David Zimmerman, "Coercive Wage Offers," 10 *Philosophy & Public Affairs* 121 (1981); G. A. Cohen, "Capitalism, Freedom, and the Proletariat," in *The Idea of Freedom*, ed. Alan Ryan (New York: Oxford University Press, 1979); Joel Feinberg, "Noncoercive Exploitation," in *Paternalism*, ed. Rolf Sartorius (Minneapolis: University of Minnesota Press, 1983). Robert Nozick develops his conceptual analysis of coercion in "Coercion," in *Philosophy, Science and Method*, ed. Sidney Morgenbesser et al. (New York: St. Martin's, 1969), and then applies it to a set of political problems in *Anarchy, State, and Utopia* (New York: Basic Books, 1974).

[3] In *Essays on Freedom of Action*, ed. Ted Honderich (London: Routledge and Kegan Paul, 1973), 65.

some metaphorical uses of the term, the truth conditions of a coercion claim are always the same. But if, as I believe, the truth conditions of a coercion claim can vary with context, then the courts and the prisoner's accomplices may both be right.[4] About coercion, the rabbi (and the third man) would be wrong.

Contextualism. Many English words are technically ambiguous: they have more than one literal meaning. To confuse those meanings within the context of an argument is to commit the *fallacy of equivocation*.[5] A standard example is this:

(1) 1a. The end of life is happiness.
1b. Death is the end of life.
1c. Death is happiness.

The problem, of course, is that because "end" means "goal" in (1a) and "termination" in (1b), (1c) does not follow from (1a) and (1b).[6]

Because the meaning of most ambiguous terms is fixed by their context, we rarely commit the fallacy of equivocation. Ambiguity becomes a bit more problematic when we use "relative" or "contextual" terms. It is not easy to define this notion precisely. Copi says that relative terms such as "tall" have different meanings in different contexts.[7] It might, however, be better to say that "tall" always has the same *meaning*—above average height—but that its standards are relative to the type of object being described, for example, a building, a tree, or a man.

"Cold" is another contextual term. While "cold" always refers to a temperature that is less than some baseline standard, the relevant baseline may vary, depending on whether we are discussing food, the human body, or an automobile engine.[8] Indeed, even in describing air temperature, "cold" is relative to location and date. Given locational and seasonal norms, it is false to describe a January temperature of 35° F. in Vermont as cold. But if a visitor from Miami says, "It's cold up here," while the weather bureau describes it as "mild," we understand the sense in which both are correct. The

[4] Frankfurt explicitly acknowledges that although he is attempting to develop an account of coercion which defines the conditions for the exclusion of moral responsibility, other accounts of coercion do not have that aim. Ibid., 85.

[5] For a general discussion, see Irving Copi, *Introduction to Logic*, 5th ed. (New York: Macmillan, 1978), 110ff.

[6] I have borrowed this example, with some alterations, from Copi, ibid., 110.

[7] Ibid., 111.

[8] "Cold" can, of course, also be equivocal, for there are senses of "cold" that have nothing to do with temperature.

general point is that a descriptive claim (for example, "It's cold") which employs a contextual term is true if and only if the underlying facts (for example, the air temperature) are consistent with the *point* of the claim—for example, to describe the air temperature from a Floridian perspective. And the point of the claim can vary.

Moral Contextualism. We often make moral arguments by appealing to and extending the use of words. We try to convince others that the moral principles to which they are committed have implications which they do not acknowledge. It is possible that genuine moral progress can be made in this way. Some advocates of slavery may have altered their views by being shown that they were committed to certain principles about the treatment of human beings and that they could not deny that slaves were, in fact, human beings. Nonetheless, what appears to be a simple linguistic move— the extension of a contextual term to cases not previously covered by the word—generally involves a more controversial and substantive moral argument. And it is the substantive moral argument that does the work. Consider

(2) 2a. Killing is wrong.
    2b. Capital punishment is killing.
    2c. Capital punishment is wrong.

The problem, of course, is that it is not clear what "killing" in (2a) refers to. If (2a) refers to *all* killing, (2b) and (2c) are true. A proponent of capital punishment could argue, however, that although he agrees with (2a), "killing" is ambiguous, and that in the version of (2a) which he accepts, "killing" refers only to the *unjustified* killing of *innocent* people. On this view, neither killing in self-defense nor capital punishment constitutes killing in the sense implied by (2a), and thus even if (2b) is true under *one* description of killing, it is *not* true under the description of killing implied by the preferred version of (2a). Capital punishment may be wrong, of course, but the argument that capital punishment is wrong must be made on *moral* grounds. It will not be made by appeals to the word "killing."[9]

The equivocation on "killing" is rather obvious, and it is not, therefore, likely to mislead. Some equivocations are more subtle. Consider the following, which, roughly speaking, formalizes an argument made in Locke's *Second Treatise of Government*.

---

[9] Put somewhat differently, whatever we *call* capital punishment, it is not obvious that there is no important moral distinction between the execution of a person duly convicted of a serious crime and the nonjustifiable killing of an innocent person.

(3) 3a. One is obligated to obey the laws if one consents to do so.

3b. One who benefits from living in a society gives his consent.

3c. One who benefits from living in a society has an obligation to obey its laws.[10]

There are various forms of consent—some weak, some strong. The strength of the "consent" required by a particular "consent claim" is fixed by its context. It may be true, as in (3a), that one who consents to do X acquires a (prima facie) obligation to do X, but the truth of (3a) may require that the consent be of a particular *form* or *strength*. Not just *any* consent is sufficient to establish even a prima facie obligation to obey the law. Thus even if (3b) is true given a sufficiently *weak* notion of consent, its truth may not be sufficient to establish (3c).[11]

Coercion as Contextual

Normative Force and Truth Conditions. I now want to argue, in some detail, that coercion claims are emphatically and technically contextual. To deepen and broaden our understanding of this point, I shall describe several contexts in which we use the family of coercion terms, although the categories are neither exhaustive nor mutually exclusive. The list is designed to show two things. First, in each context, the coercion claim has a certain point. In some, the point is mainly *descriptive*. In others, the point is primarily *normative*—that A is acting wrongly, that B is not responsible for his action, and so forth. Call this the *normative* or *moral force* of a coercion claim. To illustrate: the normative (legal) force of a coercion claim in a contract case is that the contract is voidable; the normative force of a coercion claim in a criminal trial is that the defendant is not guilty.

Second, a coercion claim with a given descriptive or normative force will have certain correlative *truth conditions*. Roughly speaking, the truth conditions of a coercion claim are what must be the case for the coercion claim to be valid or acceptable. (I do not want to put much weight on the term "truth.") In some cases, the truth conditions will be (more or less) factual. In other cases, the truth

---

[10] As Locke puts it, "every man that hath any possession or enjoyment of any part of the dominions of any government doth thereby give his tacit consent . . ." *Second Treatise of Government*, chap. 8.

[11] It may be that those who remain in a society or benefit from living in a society acquire an obligation to obey the society's laws for reasons *independent* of consent.

conditions will include normative judgments. To illustrate: the truth conditions of a claim of contractual duress are those contained in the choice and proposal prongs of the two-pronged theory.

Coercion Contexts. In assembling the following list of coercion contexts, I deliberately include situations in which we would not normally use the *word* "coercion," but would, instead, prefer a related expression, for example, "B was forced to do X," "B had no choice but to do X," or "B did X involuntarily." Once again, I do not deny that the linguistic differences may reflect distinctions of moral importance. Nonetheless, if we were to attend only to contexts in which "coercion" is at home, there is a substantial risk that we would beg important philosophical questions. For that reason, I continue to cast my net widely. We may still make such linguistic distinctions later, should it prove desirable to do so (although I shall argue that it is not desirable to do so).

1. As I noted in Part One, we sometimes use coercion claims to describe cases in which the agent's actions or movements are non-volitional. The typical normative force of such coercion claims is that the agent is not legally or morally responsible for his action.[12]

2. We sometimes use coercion claims in legal and moral contexts to describe cases of constrained volition. Such claims are meant to cancel the normal legal and moral effects of one's act—to deny one's obligation to keep a promise, to cancel the effects of the waiver of a right, or to absolve one of moral or legal responsibility for one's immoral act. There is, however, at least one important difference between the way coercion claims work in legal contexts and the way they work in moral contexts. The law generally makes *binary* judgments: a court will hold that B was (or was not) coerced and therefore is not (or is) responsible.[13] Moral discourse allows for finer-grained distinctions. If A applies coercive pressure to B, a judge cannot say, "B has some but not much legal obligation to perform on his contract," but *we* can say that B has a weaker moral obligation than he otherwise would.[14]

3. A coercion claim can *explain* or *justify* to others (or to ourselves) what might otherwise be a puzzling or criticizable action. The normative force of such claims is that certain background conditions

[12] I ignore the possibility that the agent is responsible for placing himself in a position where his actions will become nonvolitional.

[13] There are, of course, some legal contexts in which one's responsibility may be partially "mitigated."

[14] For an interesting analysis of this difference, see Brian Barry, "And Who Is My Neighbor?" 88 *Yale Law Journal* 629 (1979), a review of Charles Fried, *Right and Wrong* (Cambridge: Harvard University Press, 1977).

have created a situation in which B has only one *prudent* or *reasonable* choice. B may want others to understand that this is so, that he is not stupid, irrational, or cowardly. A football coach may defend his decision not to punt on fourth down by saying, "We were behind, it was late in the game, and we had to go for it." The seller of a house might say, "We were moving in a few weeks, so I was forced to lower the price." A mugger's victim might say, "He had a knife, so I had no choice but to give him my wallet." Here, as in many contexts, one can make a perfectly plausible coercion claim without any expectation that it will nullify one's responsibility for one's actions.[15]

4. A coercion claim may convey the *spirit* in which one acts—in particular, that one is not *happy* about one's action, that one acts reluctantly. A college professor might say "I was forced into signing the loyalty oath" to indicate that he would have preferred not to do so, but that it was a condition of employment. Voters frequently make such claims about their choice of candidates.

5. We can use coercion claims to draw attention to a person's very limited options, or to express the view that more options should be made available. We may say that "she was forced to become a prostitute" to stress the absence of welfare support or other, decent job opportunities, or that the poor are "forced" to join the military because they have few civilian career opportunities. We may also use coercion claims to describe cases in which a previously available option is no longer available: "I used to be able to cut through the yard, but now I'm forced to go around."

6. A frequently invoked and important type of coercion claim captures the fact that the state has required some behavior as a matter of *law*. Whereas coercion claims often indicate moral disapproval, this is not so here, where we may want only to distinguish between actions undertaken in response to legal prohibitions and those that are not or to distinguish between legal processes which involve punishment and those that do not (as in the distinction between coercion, regulation, and taxation).[16] We may say, "Wearing a seat belt is compulsory in New York" and "Australia has compulsory

[15] Indeed, one may take *pride* in seeing that there is only one prudent decision, particularly when others are not similarly astute.

[16] One might say that characterizing the law as coercive is not completely neutral, for we would not identify the use of legal prohibitions in this way unless we thought there was some moral significance in doing so. I think that is true. But this does not entail that we make moral judgments of approval and disapproval in characterizing the use of the law as coercive.

voting," while approving of the former and disapproving of the latter. Although the truth conditions of coercion claims are often quite problematic, here they are quite straightforward. A statute or court order will generally do.[17]

7. Analogously, a coercion claim may signify the use of nonlegal penalties or requirements. We may say "This university compels its students to take a foreign language" to point out that completion of foreign language courses is a degree requirement. Similarly, we might say "That child was forced into playing the violin" to note that he did so in response to parental pressure rather than because he wanted to.

8. We sometimes use coercion claims to emphasize the efficacy or unfairness of informal pressures that do not involve specific penalties. We may say, for example, "Students at that university are virtually compelled to join a fraternity," or "Socialization forces women into adopting traditional life styles."[18] It has, in this vein, been argued that athletes who use steroids to improve their strength are, in effect, coercing other athletes into doing so as well.[19] These sorts of coercion claims have moral force: they are often intended to signify that there are good moral reasons for changing the relevant background situation. But even when that is so, they do not necessarily serve to bar or mitigate individual responsibility.

9. Analogously, inducements are sometimes described as coercive, particularly when they are thought to be inappropriate or so great as to make refusal completely irrational.[20] When the federal government threatens to withhold state highway funds if a state does not raise its drinking age to twenty-one, it may be said that it is "forcing" (or "blackmailing") the states into compliance. Or suppose, for example, that a mandatory national health insurance plan had premiums for nonsmokers which were 50 percent lower than

[17] Interestingly, it does *not* follow just because the state coerces its citizens (in this sense) that citizens have "no choice" (in the prudential sense) but to comply with the law, if, for example, the legal penalties are slight or rarely applied.

[18] See George Sher, "Our Preferences, Ourselves," 12 *Philosophy & Public Affairs* 34 (1983).

[19] See Thomas H. Murray, "The Coercive Power of Drugs in Sports," 13 *Hastings Center Report* 24 (August 1983). Also see Robert Simon, *Sports and Social Values* (Englewood Cliffs, N.J.: Prentice-Hall, 1985), 66ff.

[20] Thus when I inquired of the local synagogue as to the Hebrew School tuition for nonmembers, I was told: "It's so much more for nonmembers that it will pay you to become a member." When I remarked, "That's a rather coercive price structure, isn't it?" the response was, "Yes."

the premiums for smokers. One might say that the government was coercing citizens into not smoking.[21] Indeed, even small incentives may be described as coercive if we want to contrast actions undertaken in response to incentives with those undertaken in the absence of incentives. Richard Titmuss, for example, argues that to pay people for giving blood makes such donations less than fully voluntary.[22]

10. We sometimes use a noncoercion claim to note that a certain *form* of pressure was *absent*, even though we know that the action was performed under (sometimes very great) pressure. Thus we may say that a suspect turns himself in "voluntarily," although he may do so only because he fears being brought in involuntarily, or that the Japanese imposed "voluntary import quotas," although, had they not done so, Congress would have imposed quotas for them.

11. Although coercion claims frequently serve to negate moral *blame*, they can also nullify the ascription of moral (or legal) *credit*.[23] Of the philistine who is attending an opera, we may say, "Don't be misled, his wife forced him to go." Credit-denying coercion claims perplex some philosophers. Because it is generally wrong to make coercive threats (and we sometimes call them coercive only if they are wrong), some conclude that legitimate threats cannot be coercive.[24] Suppose, for example, that A finds B assaulting his wife and threatens to shoot B if he does not stop. Cheyney Ryan claims that because A is not acting wrongly, it is "absurd" to say that A has coerced B into not raping his wife.[25] But it is *not* absurd. In cases where B ceases a wrong act, it is often important to know whether or not B acts in response to a proposal to harm him if he does not.[26]

---

[21] This would not settle the moral issue. Even if we thought the incentives were sufficient to constitute coercion, we might see it as a form of *justified* paternalistic coercion. See Daniel Wikler, "Persuasion and Coercion for Health: Ethical Issues in Government Efforts to Change Life Styles," in *Paternalism*, ed. Sartorius.

[22] For Titmuss, the only *truly* voluntary system of blood donation is one in which there are *no* incentives to give blood, that is, no cash payments, no special provisions for oneself or one's family (e.g., free blood for a year), and so forth. See *The Gift Relationship* (New York: Random House, 1971), chap. 5.

[23] See Daniel Lyons, "Welcome Threats and Coercive Offers," 50 *Philosophy* 425, 427 (1975).

[24] That this is false can be seen with respect to the law, where we often speak of legitimate coercion.

[25] "The Normative Concept of Coercion," 89 *Mind* 481, 483 (1980).

[26] As I noted in Chapter 9, one can, for example, be convicted of an attempted crime if one was coerced into abandoning the attempt, but not if one voluntarily did so.

Conclusion

What does all this show? It does *not* show that coercion claims are meaningless or that we can make them in any way we want.[27] It does show, first, that there is no reason to think that coercion claims have only one sort of moral force. We might, of course, *stipulate* that "coercion" refers only to those claims which serve to bar the ascription of responsibility, but we would then need other expressions to make coercion claims (broadly speaking) with different moral force.[28] Unlike the family of "homicide expressions," which in our language contains the distinction between "murder" and "killing," each of which has different moral force, the family of coercion words contains no comparable linguistic placemarks. I suppose that we could try to introduce such distinctions. But rather than create an artificial linguistic precision, it seems best simply to remain sensitive to the contextual character of coercion claims.

Second, I hope to have shown that coercion claims do not have one set of *truth conditions*. In some cases, informal pressures are sufficient to coerce; in other cases, only those pressures sufficient to negate responsibility are coercive. Once again, we could *stipulate* that "coercion" always involves specific and serious threats, but then we would need to know whether other pressures could have comparable moral force—whether, for example, such pressures could invalidate an agreement. Whatever their advantages for analytic purposes (and I think these are negligible), such linguistic stipulations would settle nothing of substantive moral importance.

Third, and joining the two previous points, a coercion claim with a specific moral force may have specific correlative truth conditions. Just as "X is a murder" has different moral force than "X is a killing," it also has different truth conditions. "X is a murder" must be

[27] As H.L.A. Hart and A. Honore have noted, "It is fatally easy and has become increasingly common to make the transition from the exhilarating discovery that complex words like 'cause' cannot be simply defined and have no 'one true meaning' to the mistaken conclusion that they have no meaning worth bothering about at all, but are used as a mere disguise for arbitrary decision or judicial policy." See *Causation in the Law* (Oxford: Clarendon Press, 1959), 3.

[28] Harry Frankfurt says this: "Phrases like 'did it freely' are actually used somewhat equivocally: at times they connote that the agent did what he did willingly, and at times they connote his moral responsibility for doing it. If we must have an established and univocal philosophical usage for 'free action', we must decide whether it is preferable to satisfy the one requirement or to satisfy the other. So far as I can see, there is little to choose between these alternatives." "Three Concepts of Free Action," 49 *Proceedings of the Aristotelian Society*, Supplementary Volume 113 (1975).

supported by more and different sorts of facts—for example, that the killing is not in self-defense. As with "killing," so, too, with coercion. A claim that A coerces B in a way that nullifies B's responsibility must be supported by different underlying facts than a claim which signifies only that B's background conditions should be changed.

Consider Frankfurt's example once again, this time in syllogistic form.

(4) 4a. Coerced confessions are not valid.
    4b. A coerced B into confessing.
    4c. B's confession is not valid.

(5) 5a. Agents are not responsible for acts they are coerced into performing.
    5b. A coerced B into confessing.
    5c. B is not responsible for confessing.

What can we say about these arguments? First, we can say that (4) and (5) have different normative force. Second, we can say that (4) and (5) may have different truth conditions. The facts sufficient to support (4b) may *not* establish the truth of (5b).

The point might be put this way. It may be claimed that coercion claims have identical truth conditions. Call this the *equivalence thesis*. With respect to any two coercion claims, the equivalence thesis may or may not be true. With respect to (4) and (5), I believe that the equivalence thesis is false.

Is the equivalence thesis a problem? Consider this analogy. Derek Parfit has noted that, in one sense, all of a person's relatives are equally his relatives. On this use of "relative," a person's cousins are as much his relatives as his children are. Although there is a point to this claim, it is not, as Parfit points out, a "deep truth." And although it is technically misleading, it rarely, in fact, misleads.[29]

It may also be true that all forms of coercion are equally forms of coercion. Nonetheless, with respect to coercion, this claim does not represent a deep truth. Does it *mislead*? Here I believe that it does. The problem, I think, is that philosophers have typically developed their analyses of coercion claims because of an interest in specific substantive moral and political questions. At the same time, the conceptual or linguistic analyses are often based on contexts in which coercion claims have a normative force and, therefore, truth conditions that are distinct from those of coercion claims in the con-

---

[29] *Reasons and Persons* (New York: Oxford University Press, 1984), 315.

texts that motivated the analysis in the first place. Many philosophical analyses proceed as if the equivalence thesis were true generally, as if it were possible and desirable to identify a single set of necessary and sufficient truth conditions for all coercion claims. I have, of course, only asserted that this is so. I hope to show that it is so—and that it is important to see that it is so—in what follows.

E L E V E N

NO CHOICE

It is frequently said, particularly by those who advocate empirical theories of coercion, that the crux of coercion is that there are some choice situations in which B has "no choice" but to do what A proposes. In other cases, B supposedly does have a choice. In this chapter I shall argue that there is something to this notion, but that it is of little help to a theory of coercion. In my view, the core of coercion lies elsewhere. It will, however, be useful to see what is and is not entailed in the argument that some situations involve no choice.

Suppose that B has a choice between X and Y and that X is more attractive (given B's preferences).[1] Such a choice situation may arise in several ways, but I shall ignore those differences here.[2] For the present question is this: are there any identifiable and intrinsic features of B's choice situation that make it plausible to say that B has no choice? And, if so, would anything of moral significance flow from that fact?

At first glance, there are two ways in which choice situations differ. In some choice situations the alternatives are more widely separated than in others. Whether B has a choice might be a function of the *distance* between the alternatives. In some choice situations the alternatives are more attractive to B than in others. Whether B has a choice might be a function of their *valence*.

Distance

Consider choices made within a game. In chess, a player may be "forced" by the rules to make a given move, as when his king is in check and there is only one move that will get the king out of check.[3] Similarly, a (college) basketball coach has no choice but to replace a

---

[1] Except where noted, I shall assume that a choice's attractiveness is defined in terms of the agent's preferences.

[2] It may arise, for example, from natural events, or from the unintentional acts of others, or from intentional proposals.

[3] For an interesting discussion of "forced moves," see Daniel Dennett, *Elbow Room* (Cambridge: MIT Press, 1984), 71.

player who has acquired five fouls. So, in the original "Hobson's choice," if one wanted one of Hobson's horses, one took the one closest to the door.[4] Relatively few choices are forced in this way. More interesting are situations in which there are several "legal" moves, but, as Daniel Dennett puts it, "only one non-idiotic, non-'suicidal' move." (Of course a move may be "idiotic" yet not "suicidal.") In these cases, the decision is forced not by the rules of the game, but by the "dictates of reason." Thus a chess player may plausibly say, "I had no choice but to exchange queens," and a coach may say, "I had to take him out—he had three fouls after ten minutes of the first half."

As a general rule, we say that B has no choice only when X is markedly superior to Y.[5] But why should that be? Suppose C, a chess player, is able to calculate the probability that he will win a game given a particular move. Suppose that in Game 1 he must choose between H and J and that in Game 2 he must choose between K and L, and that the probabilities of winning, given these moves, are as represented in Figure 1. C's choice between K and L is not importantly different from his choice between H and J.[6] For given the goal of winning, C will always prefer the maximizing strategy.[7]

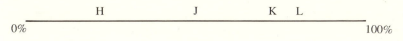

Figure 1.

Still, there seems to be *something* to the notion that C has a choice between K and L but not between H and J. The explanation may be this. The probabilities of winning associated with various moves do not present themselves already ranked. In (what I shall call) the *pre-*

[4] Hobson was an English liveryman.

[5] Or we might say that the extent to which B has a choice is a function of the distance between X and Y. Thus David Zimmerman writes that A can coerce B into doing X only if the utility of B's doing X and not suffering the threatened consequences is *"considerably* greater" than the utility of his not doing X and suffering them. "Coercive Wage Offers," 10 *Philosophy & Public Affairs* 121, 124 (1981) (original emphasis).

[6] If, over the course of 200 games, C faces 100 choices comparable to the choice between H and J and 100 choices comparable to the choice between K and L, we would expect C to choose each J over each H *and* each L over each K. It would be no more reasonable to choose a K over an L than to choose an H over a J.

[7] This is not *quite* correct. C may sometimes choose an inferior strategy to explore a new line from which he might learn; he might decide that the lower probability of winning a particular game is compensated by what it might add to his ability to win future games.

deliberation stage, it may be obvious that J is superior to H (even if the absolute distance is unclear), but it may not be obvious that L is superior to K. Unlike the ranking of H and J, the ranking of L and K comes only in the *postdeliberation* stage. Once C concludes that L is superior to K, C has no reasonable choice. But coming *to* that conclusion requires C to engage in considerable analysis and deliberation. It is deliberation, not choice, that is affected by the distance between alternatives.

It might be thought that the propensity to deliberate is negatively correlated with the predeliberation distance between alternatives.[8] This is only partially correct. Just as it may be obvious that one alternative is superior, it may be equally obvious that the distance is so small (or the stakes so low), that it's "six of one, half dozen of the other." This is, after all, a recurrent claim about the choice between political candidates—tweedledum and tweedledee.[9] This suggests, then, that deliberation requires enough potential distance to make a choice worthwhile, but not so much as to make it unnecessary.

When choices can be accurately arrayed on a single continuum, there will be a uniquely superior alternative (ties excluded). But many—indeed, most—choices cannot be represented in that way. Consider an investment decision. If B must choose between a savings account which pays 5 percent and one which pays 6 percent, where both are equally safe, B has no reasonable choice but to elect the account with the higher yield. Suppose, however, that B is choosing between investments which vary according to yield and safety, as represented in Figure 2. Although (b) is clearly superior to (a), because it ranks higher on *both* axes, in no other pairing is one alternative clearly preferable. To choose between (b), (c), and (d), B may engage in two forms of deliberation. First, B may reflect on his own preferences about safety and yield. For up to this point, he may not have given this much thought. Second, B may want to evaluate his preferences. Given that it is not irrational to weigh yield more

---

[8] At least if one thinks there is a reasonable chance that the difference between X and Y will be great enough to make worthwhile the decision costs involved in identifying that difference. A chess player may believe that there is a difference between X and Y, but think that identifying it would not be worth the time and energy required.

[9] Of course, voting is an atypical choice situation in at least two ways. First, there is a sense in which one's individual vote does not make much difference to the outcome, so the sense that one should not bother to vote may have less to do with the distance between the candidates than with the efficacy of one's act. Second, unlike choice situations in which we clearly must make a choice, here we have the illusion that there is a third option (abstention) which makes choice unnecessary.

heavily than safety (or vice versa), B must determine how much weight it makes *sense* to ascribe to each factor.

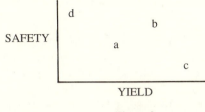

Figure 2.

The trade-off between dimensions may become so extreme as to transform a nominally multidimensional choice into one that is, in effect, *uni*dimensional. It might be unreasonable to prefer (d) to (b) because (b)'s edge in yield is considerable while (d)'s edge in safety is minute. The general point is that just as moderate predeliberation distance between two alternatives in one dimension creates the need for deliberation and choice, the preservation of a multidimensional space also allows for the exercise of our deliberative capacities.

Choosing Choice

Would a rational B prefer to be confronted with alternatives one of which is uniquely superior? Or would B prefer to have to deliberate, to make a choice? Our attitudes toward deliberation and choosing are, I think, complex. If, on the one hand, we want to minimize our decision costs (time, anxiety, the acquisition of information), we may prefer choice situations in which deliberation is unnecessary. In addition, if B wants to maximize his postdecision preference satisfaction, he will prefer to have a clearly superior alternative. For the greater the distance between alternatives, the less likely is it that B will make a mistake.

At the same time, I believe that we also get satisfaction from the process of making the right choice, from the process of choosing itself. Why might this be? This is no doubt a complicated story and admits of explanations on different levels. For developmental reasons, it is probably a good thing that we enjoy deliberation.[10] We

---

[10] As Dennett observes, while this tendency to get satisfaction from choosing is "perhaps a genetically encouraged or even strongly hard-wired part of our charac-

might also offer a Millian explanation. Choosing, says Mill, involves our deepest and most personal characteristics—our capacity for judgment, our intelligence, our values. Choosing—even when it results in wrong choices—is a morally valuable expression of our autonomy.

> He who lets the world, or his own portion of it, choose his plan of life for him, has no need of any other faculty than the ape-like one of imitation. He who chooses his plan for himself, employs all his faculties. He must use observation to see, reasoning and judgment to foresee, activity to gather materials for decision, discrimination to decide, and when he has decided, firmness and self-control to hold to his deliberate decision.[11]

I suggest this. When the distance between alternatives is such that one choice is *obviously* correct, it is *as if*, in Mill's words, the "world" had chosen for us. Such decisions are *my* decisions to a lesser extent than decisions that do not involve an obvious choice. Obvious choices may still be "dictated by reason," but it is *anyone*'s reason, and not especially *mine*. There is a choice, but there is no (complex process of) choosing.

Now this is not completely right. B may see that X is the clearly superior choice because he is especially astute. The expert chess player not only makes the superior move when the distance between alternative moves is small, he sees that a move is obviously correct when this is by no means obvious to others. If, by training or study, B brings himself to the point where a predeliberation choice is obvious (and hence requires no deliberation), this is not well described as a case in which the world is choosing for him. Or B may regard a choice as obvious because it reflects his character. B may, for example, always pay his legally required taxes *without* deliberating. He does not weigh his obligation against the likelihood that he could save money and get away with it. He would regard it as a moral defect to give that choice "a moment's thought." B feels that he has no choice, but it is he who has decided that he has no choice. Thus these cases are, I think, not really exceptions to the rule that we prefer choice situations in which we are, in some way, directly connected with our choices.

Now if, as I have argued, we can make sense of the claim that B

---

ters, it is also dictated by reason." *Elbow Room*, 72. We are more likely to choose correctly if we develop our ability to analyze, deliberate, and choose. If our choices are too easy, we will make more mistakes when we have difficult decisions to make.

[11] *On Liberty*, chap. 3.

has "no choice" by focusing on the distance between alternatives, what will be the moral force of this claim? For our purposes, not much. The tendency for certain choice situations to engage our deliberative capacities may be of considerable moral interest—as it was for Mill—but it has no immediate or obvious bearing on coercion and responsibility.[12] If B accepts an offer that is (nonironically) too good to refuse—a comparable job at a much higher salary—he is not entitled to be released from its terms (should an even better offer come along) on the grounds that he had no reasonable choice but to accept it. If B agrees to an amputation of his leg in order to avoid certain death, he cannot later sue for battery, on the grounds that his consent was not valid because he had no choice. If B's car is disabled on a deserted road, and A offers to help for a *non*exorbitant price, B cannot refuse to pay because he had no reasonable choice. Having no choice—as measured in distance—does not, in itself, nullify or even mitigate our responsibility for the normal moral or legal effects of our acts.

Valence

Perhaps the emphasis on distance misses the point. Perhaps it is the desirability of the alternatives that counts. Dennett says this:

> One is always somewhat desperate when faced with an opportunity in which there is obviously only one rational thing to do. Sometimes we are put in such binds by other agents: "I made him an offer he couldn't refuse." Sometimes Nature impersonally fences us in so that our very survival depends on our managing to follow a very particular (and foreseeable) trajectory . . . We rightly dread such confining circumstances, where our (sane) options are reduced to one.[13]

It is not clear what Dennett means. On one reading, we dread *any* circumstance in which there is—as measured in distance—a uniquely superior alternative. On a different reading, we dread only circumstances in which all alternatives, including the uniquely superior alternative, are distasteful, or perhaps in which there is only one alternative that we find acceptable.

---

[12] Even when there is only one rational choice, we have to *make* the rational choice, and as Frankfurt suggests, ". . . a person may well be praiseworthy for having made a plainly reasonable choice." "Coercion and Moral Responsibility," 77.

[13] *Elbow Room*, 71–72.

There may be *something* to *both* readings. I argued above that, *ceteris paribus*, we typically prefer choice situations which engage our capacity for choosing. Some vestige of that (meta)preference may remain even when both alternatives are quite attractive, although it would, I think, be *silly* to say that we "dread" such situations.[14] But if, as I have argued, the tendency of a choice situation to engage our deliberative capacities is of little moral relevance, the question remains whether the *valence*, attractiveness, or acceptability of the alternatives is of moral significance, and, if so, in what way.

Scaling Alternatives. Suppose that alternatives can be arrayed on a unidimensional continuum. There are two ways in which such a ranking might be made. Just as we can measure temperature on a scale whose baseline is defined as "absolute zero," all temperatures having a positive valence, we could rank alternatives relative to a baseline which is defined by the worst alternative (for example, death), all other alternatives being (more or less) attractive. Call this a K-scale, after Lord Kelvin (see Figure 3).

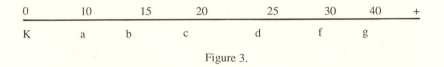

Figure 3.

We can also measure temperature on a scale in which temperatures have negative or positive valence relative to a baseline such as the freezing point of water. Similarly, we can rank alternatives with valences which are positive or negative relative to some sort of baseline, threshold, or zero point. Call this a Z-scale (see Figure 4). One thing is clear. If the ranking of B's alternatives is to be of any moral relevance, we must assume *some* sort of Z-scale. A K-scale presents all choice situations as questions of distance, and we have already seen that distance, in and of itself, has little moral significance.

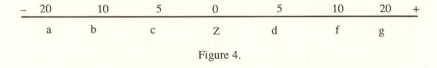

Figure 4.

[14] Some vestige of that (meta)preference may remain too even when all of one's choices are awful, as when the State of Utah permits those to be executed to choose between being hanged and being shot.

Psychological Acceptability. There are various ways in which a Z-scale can be understood. We could understand Z as the threshold between those alternatives which B "likes" or finds "acceptable" and those B "dislikes" or finds "unacceptable."[15] Suppose, for example, that B is choosing among items on a menu. Although B has strong likes and dislikes, he prefers all items to continued hunger (a). Consider three possible menus, in which the alternatives are ranked in accordance with Figure 4:

Menu 1: (f) or (g)
Menu 2: (c) or (d)
Menu 3: (a = not eating), (b), or (c)

Now there is no doubt but that *absolute* valence matters to B. B will be *happier* with Menu 1 than with Menu 2 and happier with Menu 2 than with Menu 3. But are the differences between the menus relevant to whether B has "a choice"? They might certainly affect the way B *feels*. If B ever feels that he has a choice, he does so with Menu 1, for there B gets to choose between two items which he likes. With Menu 2, B might complain, "There's only one thing I like, so I guess I have no choice." Interestingly, that complaint might be even more intense with Menu 3, where B has the proverbial Hobson's choice (between evils), even if, as seems plausible, it can be said that since all choices are *below* his acceptability threshold, there is as much (or as little) choice as with Menu 1.

But would any of this be of moral significance? It depends. If B has reason to expect that he will get to choose among at least two "acceptable" items, then his expectation is not fulfilled with Menu 2 or Menu 3. If B can legitimately expect only one acceptable item, Menu 2 but not Menu 3 gives him that choice. But suppose that B's only *legitimate* expectation is to "eat what's put in front of him or go hungry." B may *feel* he has no choice—but so what? Or, to alter the example, suppose that the market price is higher than what B regards as an "acceptable price" for an apartment. He considers any-

---

[15] Economists may argue that it is *irrational* to make much of threshold points, that the absolute difference in expected utility is the only thing that should matter. On this view, whether an investor has a profit or a loss in a stock is irrelevant to any investment decision (tax considerations aside). In deciding whether to sell a stock in which he has a loss, the important question is whether there is a superior alternative for his funds. But whatever its rationality, the fact is that we do systematically frame decisions in terms of baselines or thresholds. See Amos Tversky and Daniel Kahneman, "The Framing of Decisions and the Psychology of Choice," 211 *Science* 453 (January 1981).

thing more than $500 per month unacceptable, but because there are no (decent) units at that price, B signs a lease for $600. I take it that B's acceptability threshold is without much moral force, that it has no bearing on the validity of B's lease.[16]

If this is correct, then the moral relevance of the fact that B has no choices which he regards as acceptable depends entirely on the *independent* moral importance of Z. By itself, such valence has little moral force. There may, for example, be good moral reasons to cater to the dietary preferences of vegetarians or Orthodox Jews, because those dietary preferences reflect personal commitments that we should respect. But in the absence of such reasons, we need not be concerned that others find no or only one dish acceptable, that they feel they do not have any choice.

Actually, that may be too strong. As I argued in the previous chapter, coercion claims can have *different* moral force. That people may not have alternatives which they find acceptable may be of *some* moral interest. It may be a better world if people have a range of alternatives they find acceptable. And, in some contexts, it may be more important than that. We may, for example, deplore the conditions that lead many poor persons to regard military service as the only "acceptable" career alternative, and think that it is of considerable moral importance to change those conditions. Nonetheless, even if the poor have "no choice," in that sense, but to enlist, it does *not* follow, nor is it generally claimed—even by those who make this sort of "no choice" argument—that the poor are not bound by the agreements they make with the military.

Moral Acceptability. I have argued that in some contexts and for some purposes, Z can be set in terms of B's likes and dislikes, by what B finds acceptable. In other contexts, Z can be set by independent normative criteria. Let us return, briefly, to the law. Recall Mr. Kaplan, whose wife threatened to release embarrassing information if he did not agree to a property settlement.[17] He claimed that he had done so under duress, because the alternative had been to endure considerable ridicule. Now if Mr. Kaplan is seeking our sympathy, we may (or may not) agree that enduring the embarrassment was unacceptable. But if the point is that he should not be held to the terms of the property settlement, it is arguable that he

[16] As Fried notes, "any consumer facing a perfectly competitive market for some necessity . . . has no real choice but to pay the market price . . . and the producers have no real choice but to accept that price." *Contract as Promise* (Cambridge: Harvard University Press, 1981), 104.

[17] See p. 32.

did have an acceptable alternative—to endure the embarrassment and fight it out. For moral and legal purposes, *his* view of the situation is unimportant.

Or recall *Austin* v. *Loral*.[18] When Loral gave in to Austin's demand, the court held that it had done so under duress because the alternative—to sue for breach of contract—would not have provided an adequate remedy. Loral acted under duress not because Loral regarded that alternative as unacceptable, but because, on independent grounds, it was an alternative Loral was under no obligation to accept.

Conclusion

Robert Nozick has argued that when other persons' actions place limits on one's alternatives, "whether this makes one's resulting action non-voluntary depends upon whether these others had the right to act as they did."[19] Some find this absurd. Michael Taylor writes that Nozick's account of coercion is "an arbitrary and bizarre stipulative definition." After all, says Taylor, the "effects on the individual's choice conditions are the same whether the others act within their rights or not."[20] Nozick's view may be wrong, of course, but it is neither arbitrary nor bizarre. In effect, his view captures the theory of coercion that characterizes virtually the entire corpus of American law.

But the point is not to defend Nozick. Rather, the point is this. If the argument of this chapter is on the right track, there are no structural features of an individual's "choice conditions" which are of much moral interest. We can make *sense* of "no choice" in a way that turns on the *distance* between alternatives or by reference to B's *preferences*, but these accounts have little moral relevance. We can also make sense of "no choice" in a way that does have important moral significance, but that view of "no choice" is not based on structural or empirical features of B's choice situation. To the contrary, it requires precisely the sorts of normative judgments that "no choice" arguments were meant to avoid.

[18] See p. 27.

[19] *Anarchy, State, and Utopia* (New York: Basic Books, 1974), 262.

[20] Michael Taylor, *Community, Anarchy, and Liberty* (Cambridge: Cambridge University Press, 1982), 99.

TWELVE

COERCIVE PROPOSALS: I

I argued in the previous chapter that little of normative significance can be read off structural features of B's choice situation. Perhaps the key to coercion is not in the choice situation itself, but in its genesis, in the sorts of proposals that create B's choice conditions. The dominant philosophical view about coercion is to be found along these lines. That view maintains that threats coerce whereas offers do not. In this chapter I shall argue that this view, properly understood, is correct and that despite appearances to the contrary, it is consistent with the two-pronged theory of coercion we found in the law. In subsequent chapters, I shall consider, among other things, the claim that (exploitative) offers can coerce and the claim that one can be coerced by circumstantial pressure as well as by specific proposals.

The problem may by set up in various ways, but for our purposes the distinctions between them are relatively unimportant. The generic situation is that A attempts to get B to do X (which can be a nonaction) in the following way: A proposes that (1) if B does X, A will bring about or allow to happen a certain state of affairs (S), and (2) if B does not do X, A will bring about or allow to happen another state of affairs (T). Coercive proposals are typically *bi*conditional because of the conjunction of (1) and (2).[1] A might make a simple *conditional* proposal to bring about S if B does X, leaving open what he will do if B does not do X (he might bring about S anyway). But it will simplify matters if we focus on biconditionals.

Getting a complete and precise account of the necessary and sufficient conditions of coercive proposals is a complicated business. As Harry Frankfurt points out, whether A is "actually making a threat or an offer depends in part on his motives, intentions, and beliefs. Considerations of the same kinds are also relevant in interpreting the subsequent response of the person to whom the threat

[1] See Vinit Haksar, "Coercive Proposals," 4 *Political Theory* 65 (1976).

or offer is made."[2] We may say, for example, that B cannot be coerced unless he does X *because* of A's proposal, that B cannot be coerced unless A's proposal is *credible*, that A cannot threaten B unless A *intends* that his proposal will get B to do X, and so on. The possibility of *tacit* or nonverbal proposals introduces additional difficulties.[3]

It will be best to ignore these complications. Following Frankfurt, I shall generally assume that all the necessary conditions relating to A's and B's beliefs, intentions, and motives are satisfied.[4] I shall assume that all proposals are credible and clear (whether verbal or not), and that everyone involved "has sufficient reason to believe that the proposals in question will be carried out if their conditions are fulfilled."[5] I shall also assume that B's actions are based on a *reasonable* (although not necessarily correct) judgment about the consequences of various courses of action. In other words, I shall assume that A's proposal does *not* distort B's judgment.[6]

I shall generally make two further assumptions. First, I shall assume that A's proposals are successful in getting B to do X. After all, A's threat does not *coerce* B to do X if B decides that it is better to suffer the threatened consequences. Second, I shall assume that B is, in some sense, entitled to succumb to A's proposal. For if B has adequate remedies for being made (temporarily) worse off, or if we think that B should resist A's threat, then even if B is motivated by A's threat to do X, we may want to deny that B is truly coerced. All

[2] "Coercion and Moral Responsibility," in *Essays on Freedom of Action*, ed. Ted Honderich (London: Routledge and Kegan Paul, 1973), 66.

[3] As Nozick points out, it may be clear that if B does X, A will bring about S and that if B does Y (or not-X), A will bring about T—although nothing may be said. See "Coercion," in *Philosophy, Science and Method*, ed. Sidney Morgenbesser et al. (New York: St. Martins, 1969), 444.

[4] Joseph Raz provides perhaps the best account of the *necessary* conditions of a coercive proposal. Raz says that "[A] coerces [B] into not doing [Y] only if (1) [A] communicates to [B] that he intends to bring about or have brought about some consequence, [T] if [B] does [Y]. (2) [A] makes this communication intending [B] to believe that he does so in order to get [B] not to do [Y]. (3) That [T] will happen is, for [B], a reason of great weight for not doing [Y]. (4) [B] believes that it is likely that [A] will bring about [T] if [B] does [Y] and that [Y] will leave him worse off, having done [Y], than if he did not do [Y] and [A] did not bring about [T]. (5) [B] does not do [Y]. (6) Part of [B's] reason for not doing [Y] is to avoid (or to lessen) the likelihood of [T] by making it less likely that [A] will bring it about" (letters changed). See "Liberalism, Autonomy, and the Politics of Neutral Concern," in *Midwest Studies in Philosophy*, vol. VII, ed. Peter French et al. (Minneapolis: University of Minnesota Press, 1982), 108.

[5] Frankfurt, "Coercion and Moral Responsibility," 66.

[6] To use J. P. Day's terminology, I shall assume that A's proposal does not "intimidate" or "entice" B to do X. See "Threats, Offers, Law, Opinion, and Liberty," 14 *American Philosophical Quarterly* 257, 262 (1977).

the same, there is no reason to deny that A can make a coercive *proposal* that does not or should not *coerce*.[7] In this and the following two chapters, I concentrate on the nature of such proposals. In Chapter 15, I shall consider the question of when coercive proposals actually *coerce*.[8]

Threats and Offers

When are proposals coercive? The intuitive answer is that threats are coercive whereas offers are not, that threats limit freedom, whereas offers enhance it, that one acts involuntarily in response to a threat, whereas one voluntarily accepts an offer, that the recipient of an offer can decline to accept it, whereas the recipient of a threat cannot.[9] It is important to see that the distinction between threats and offers is *not* a function of the *distance* between the options or their *efficacy* in securing the desired response. In the case of an offer, the distance between X and Y may be *very* great, whereas the consequences of ignoring a threat may be only slightly worse than the alternative.[10] And it may be no less irrational to refuse an offer than not to succumb to a threat.

The crux of the distinction between threats and offers is quite simple: A *threatens* B by proposing to make B *worse* off relative to some baseline; A makes an *offer* to B by proposing to make B *better* off relative to some baseline. More precisely, A makes a threat when, if B does *not* accept A's proposal, B will be worse off than in the relevant baseline position. A makes an offer when, if B does *not* accept A's proposal, he will be *no* worse off than in the relevant baseline position. A's proposal may, of course, include both a threat and an offer (what Michael Taylor calls a "throffer"): "If you do X, I'll give you a large reward; if you don't do X, I'll kill you."[11] On my account, a "throffer" is a threat, for if B does not accept A's proposal he will be worse off than in the relevant baseline position.

It should be emphasized that the distinction between *better* and

[7] See Peter Westen, " 'Freedom' and 'Coercion'—Virtue Words and Vice Words," 85 *Duke Law Journal* 541, 562 (1985).

[8] See H. J. McCloskey, "Coercion: Its Nature and Significance," 18 *Southern Journal of Philosophy* 335, 344 (1980).

[9] Frankfurt, "Coercion and Moral Responsibility," 67. Of course, the recipient of a threat might say, "You can't threaten me, go ahead!"

[10] Thus the old joke in which one person says, "If you don't do what I ask, I'll never speak to you again," to which the other responds, "Is that a promise or a threat?"

[11] *Commmunity, Anarchy, and Liberty* (Cambridge: Cambridge University Press, 1982), 12.

worse off always requires *some* baseline. To say "better off" is always to say "better off than ———." Without some benchmark, there would be better and worse alternatives, but no better and worse *off*.

Now the distinction between better and worse off works easily for the normal range of cases. When A proposes to give B a salary higher than the adequate salary he is now receiving, A is making what might be an attractive offer. If A proposes to give B a lower salary than the adequate salary he is now receiving, A is making an *unattractive* offer, but it is an offer nonetheless, for B is no worse off if he refuses A's offer. If, on the other hand, A proposes to kill B if B does not give A his money, A is making a threat. For if B does not accept A's proposal, he will be worse off than in his baseline situation, in which he keeps both his life and his money.

The previous cases are simple because, in each case, B's baseline—the account of B's situation against which A's proposal counts as making B better or worse off—is quite straightforward. Things are not always so straightforward. Consider what appears to be a relatively minor complication, yet reveals a principle of some importance. In defining B's baseline, we do *not* take a high-speed snapshot of B's present state of affairs. As a first approximation, we may say that B's baseline includes the normal and predictable consequences of his present position.[12] We understand B's present situation in the way we understand debts and assets. If B takes on a debt, he is worse off because he *now* has a stream of *future liabilities*.[13] On the other hand, if B is given a (nonredeemable) bond, he is now better off, because he *now* has a stream of *future income*. Similarly, if B is sentenced to ten years in prison, his baseline includes a future behind bars. On the other hand, if B stands to get an award for his accomplishments, his baseline situation is one that will get better (whether or not he knows this).[14]

It follows that if, in the normal course of events, B's situation would become worse, and A prevents B's situation from becoming worse, A is making B better off.[15] Similarly, if, in the normal course

[12] As Westen puts it, "The question is not whether the proposal conditionally promises to leave a recipient worse off than he *is*, or worse off than he *has been*, but whether it conditionally promises to leave him worse off than he otherwise *will be*." " 'Freedom' and 'Coercion'," 579.

[13] I ignore the uses to which he puts the borrowed money.

[14] See Theodore Benditt, "Threats and Offers," 58 *The Personalist* 382 (1977).

[15] Harry Frankfurt notes that B may be in a situation where things do not get worse, but just remain bad. In such cases, a person's condition becomes worse because he endures a bad thing longer, for example, a chronic illness. Frankfurt also notes that there are situations (such as illness) in which we cannot stop a situation

of events, B's situation would become better, and A prevents B's situation from becoming better, A is making B worse off. And it follows that if A proposes to prevent B's situation from becoming worse, as it would in the normal course of events, A is making an *offer*, as when A proposes to cancel B's debt in exchange for a favor, or to commute B's sentence if B makes a public apology for his crime.[16] On the other hand, if A proposes to prevent B's situation from improving, as it would in the normal course of events, A is making a *threat*, as when A proposes to take B's bond or to prevent B from receiving his award unless B pays him $500.

When we say that A makes a threat (or an offer) by proposing to make B worse off (or better off), B's baseline ordinarily includes the normal course of events *without* A's proposed intervention. It can be argued, however, that threats and offers are intertranslatable, because we can always redefine B's baseline so as to *include* A's proposed intervention. On this view, we could say that the gunman is offering one's life in exchange for one's money, or that A is offering not to take B's bond, and so forth. Similarly, we could say that the employer is threatening not to give B a higher salary unless B accepts his job, or that A is threatening not to cancel B's debt unless A is done a favor, or that A is threatening not to commute B's sentence unless B makes a public apology. It is true, of course, that we could say all of these things, for we can *say* anything we want. But while threats and offers may admit of such intertranslations when there are competing and plausible interpretations of B's baseline,[17] in these cases such a switch would be quite perverse. For in each of them we have a relatively unproblematic account of B's situation, and it is one that excludes A's intervention.

Moral and Nonmoral Baselines

In his seminal article "Coercion," Robert Nozick shows that fixing B's baseline is not always so unproblematic. He begins in the traditional way. He maintains that if A's proposal makes the consequences of B's not doing X worse than they would be "in the normal and expected course of events, [A's] proposal is a threat; if it makes

---

from becoming worse except by also making it better. See "Necessity and Desire," 45 *Philosophy and Phenomenological Research* 1, 6 (1984).

[16] To avoid complications, I assume that A's "price" for providing these benefits is not unreasonable.

[17] As, for example, it seems equally plausible to say that gas stations charge more for using a credit card and to say that they charge less for paying cash.

the consequences [of B's doing X] better, it is an offer." Nozick then says this: "The term 'expected' is meant to shift between or straddle *predicted* and *morally required*."[18] Adopting Feinberg's useful terminology, let us call these the "statistical test" and the "moral test" of B's baseline.[19]

Consider one of Nozick's examples (which I condense).

> *The Drowning Case.* A comes upon B, who is drowning. A proposes to rescue B if B agrees to pay him $10,000. A and B both know that there are no other potential rescuers.[20]

Under the statistical test, whether A is making an offer or a threat will depend on what is "normal" in their society. That may vary. In some societies, it may be likely that A will rescue B; in other societies, not. Under the moral test, whether A is making an offer or a threat will depend on whether A is morally required to rescue B. If he is, then B's baseline *includes* A's beneficial intervention, and A's proposal is a threat. If he is not, then A's proposal is an offer.[21]

The contrast between a moral and a statistical test for B's baseline, is, I think, better understood in terms of a broader contrast between moral and nonmoral baselines. The reason is this. A "statistical" or "objective" test for B's baseline is only one nonmoral way to think of B's situation. It will sometimes be useful to think of B's baseline as it is seen by B (or perhaps by A). Call this a *phenomenological* test. It may, for example, be neither statistically likely nor morally required that A rescue B without compensation. Nonetheless, B may *believe* that A is morally required to rescue him or may mistakenly *expect* A to do so. In either case, A's proposal may *feel* like a threat rather than an offer. The phenomenological test captures that feeling.

To elucidate the notion of a moral test, consider two similar cases in which the moral test gives different results.

> *The Private Physician Case.* B asks A, a private physician, to treat his illness. A says that he will treat B's illness if and only if B gives him $100 (a fair price).[22]

---

[18] "Coercion," 447.

[19] Joel Feinberg, *Harm to Self* (New York: Oxford University Press, 1986), 219. I want to thank Joel Feinberg for making this material available to me when it was in manuscript form.

[20] "Coercion," 449–50.

[21] See Feinberg, *Harm to Others* (Oxford: Oxford University Press, 1984), 142.

[22] See Martin Gunderson, "Threats and Coercion," 9 *Canadian Journal of Philosophy* 247, 256 (1979), for a similar example.

The Public Physician Case. B asks A, a physician, to treat his illness. A is employed by the National Health Plan, and is legally required to treat all patients without cost. A says that he will treat B's illness if and only if B gives him $100.

Under the moral test, A is making an offer in the Private Physician Case, because A does not have an obligation to treat B's illness free of charge. A is making a threat in the Public Physician Case, because A does have an obligation to treat B's illness free of charge.

B's moral baseline is not necessarily static. It can be changed by transactions with A. If A (B's parent) says, "I'll give you $5 per week if you keep your room clean," A is making an offer. But if A says, "I'll give you an allowance of $5 per week for one year," with no *quid pro quo* demanded, but subsequently proposes to give B his allowance only if B cleans his room, A's proposal is a threat.[23]

To say that there are moral and nonmoral tests for fixing B's baseline is not, of course, to deny that there are connections between them. One hopes that moral standards influence behavior, that B can statistically expect A's help when it is morally required. In addition, moral beliefs are phenomenologically important. As Mill suggests, "It makes a vast difference both in our feelings and in our conduct toward [another] whether he displeases us in things in which we think we have a right . . . or in things in which we know that we have not."[24] Moreover, although this is a complicated matter, A's moral obligations may be somewhat dependent on the statistical norms of his society.

Indeed, precisely because there is no necessary divergence between the results of the statistical and moral tests in the previous cases, they do not elucidate the problems that arise when the results of the tests differ. To bring these problems into sharper relief, Nozick presents the following case.

The Slave Case. A beats B, his slave, each morning for reasons unconnected with B's behavior. A proposes not to beat B the next morning if and only if B does X.[25]

Under the statistical and phenomenological tests, A is making an offer. B expects to be beaten each morning, and relative to that expectation, A is proposing to make B better off. Under the moral test,

[23] See Feinberg, *Harm to Self,* 219.
[24] *On Liberty,* chap. 4.
[25] "Coercion," 450.

A is making a threat. For A is morally required not to beat B any morning (indeed, not to have B as a slave), and relative to that baseline, A is proposing to make B worse off. The dual baseline can be represented diagramatically as in Figure 5, where N = B's nonmoral (statistical or phenomenological) baseline; M = B's morally required baseline, that is, where B would be if A did what he is morally required to do; and X = B's location if he does X.

_	N		X	M		+

Figure 5.

Setting B's baseline under the nonmoral and moral tests is, of course, often more complicated than the previous cases suggest. Consider

> *The Drug Case.* A is B's normal supplier of illegal drugs for $20 per day. One day, A proposes to B that he will supply B's drugs if and only if B beats up C.[26]

Nozick maintains that under the statistical test for B's baseline, A is making a threat, but that under the moral test, A is making an offer. Why? Because A is not morally required to supply drugs for money (and may be morally required not to supply drugs at all). Now the moral situation may be murkier than Nozick suggests.[27] But let us assume, for the sake of argument, that Nozick is right, and that under the moral test, A is making B an (immoral) *offer*. Diagramatically, the Drug Case can be represented as in Figure 6.

_	M		X	N		+

Figure 6.

Harry Frankfurt argues that Nozick's account of the Drug Case is unsatisfactory because it cannot distinguish between a *threat* and a *less attractive offer*. If a butcher raises his price for meat, we do not say that he is threatening his customers; he is merely making a poorer offer. Why not say that the drug dealer, like the butcher, is

---

[26] Ibid.

[27] Even if the drug relationship is immoral from an external perspective, it is arguable that *within* that relationship, A is morally required to continue to supply B with drugs, perhaps at no more than the market price.

merely demanding a higher (immoral) price, one that now includes B's beating up C? Nozick cannot make this distinction, says Frankfurt, because his "normalcy" baseline refers to the previous transactions, and so he must treat the butcher and drug cases alike.[28]

I do not think that is Nozick's view, and in any case, neither the statistical nor the phenomenological test need be understood in that way. For both tests, properly understood, are based on a reasonably rich and complex account of the *future*. In the ordinary capitalist marketplace, each transaction is regarded as (somewhat) discrete. Although one may expect, as a matter of statistical probabilities, to be charged something close to the previous price, one's expectations also incorporate the capitalist ideology that sellers will charge "what the market will bear."[29] Drug-selling relationships may or may not be understood in that way. If they are, the drug seller is making a poorer offer. But it is possible that the buyer has a reasonable expectation that the seller will continue to sell drugs at the previous price or at least at the going market price, and relative to that expectation, Nozick's drug seller is making a threat.[30]

Of course, even in a capitalist economy, a buyer-seller relationship may generate specific expectations about future transactions.

> *The Produce Case* (my example). A, a large university food service, has purchased all of its produce from B, a produce wholesaler. A now accounts for 50 percent of B's sales. A tells B that it will take its business elsewhere unless B cuts his price by 20 percent.

A's proposal may be a threat under both the statistical and the phenomenological test. A's proposal may, for example, be quite uncommon business practice, and even were that not so, B might experience A's proposal that way. On the other hand, if we assume that capitalist transactions are not immoral, then under the moral test for B's baseline, A is making a poorer offer, because B has no right to expect A's future business at the previous price.

The previous point can be extended to noncommercial transactions.

---

[28] "Coercion and Moral Responsibility," 69.

[29] On this view, the butcher no more threatens the buyer with a higher price than the buyer threatens the butcher by proposing not to buy at the higher price.

[30] Frankfurt notes that if there were an oversupply of drugs, we might regard A's proposal as merely an unattractive offer. We might say that, but we might also regard it as an *ineffective threat*, for A *intends* to get B to beat up C by proposing to make B worse off. He simply does not succeed. But I do not think that much turns on which way we describe it.

The Dating Case (my example). Each week, A calls B and asks her for a date. They have grown fond of each other, but they have not had sexual intercourse. After three months, A tells B that unless she has sexual intercourse with him, he will stop dating her.

Under a statistical or phenomenological test, B may or may not regard A's proposal as a threat. That would depend upon the history of their relationship and B's expectations. And while a complete moral account of the situation would be complex, it is clear that B has no *right* that A continue to date her and do so on her preferred terms. Relative to that moral baseline, A's proposal is an offer.

Let me summarize, in barest form, the argument of the chapter to this point. I have identified two nonmoral tests and a moral test for B's baseline. Each test allows us to describe some proposals as offers and others as threats. Sometimes tne results of these tests converge. Sometimes they diverge.

A *Right Answer?*

I suggested above that the preanalytic or intuitive way of distinguishing between coercive and noncoercive proposals is to assume that threats are coercive whereas offers are not. I think the intuition is basically sound. Relative to one's baseline, a threat reduces one's available options whereas an offer increases them. At the same time, we have seen that there are at least three plausible tests of B's baseline, all of which can be used to characterize A's proposal as an offer or a threat. This helps to explain why intuitions about the coerciveness of proposals are ambiguous or conflicting. Feinberg maintains, for example, that the "pre-analytic" or "common sense" judgment about the Slave Case is that A is making an *offer*—which confirms the power of the statistical test.[31] But we are also tempted to regard A's proposal as a threat, and that is explained by the role of the moral test.

If there are at least three *plausible* tests for B's baseline, which is the right one? Is the slave the recipient of an offer or a threat? Is he coerced or is he not? Call this the *coercion question*. Nozick maintains that in the Slave Case A's proposal is coercive because the moral test takes precedence over the statistical test. Does it always? Nozick thinks not. For Nozick maintains that in the Drug Case, where *ex hypothesi* A is making an offer under the moral test, A is making a

[31] *Harm to Self*, 223.

211

threat. Here, the statistical test has precedence over the moral test. What explains the distinction between the cases? Why does the moral test take precedence in the Slave Case whereas the statistical test takes precedence in the Drug Case? Nozick's view (or conjecture) is that when the result of the moral and statistical tests diverge, the *proper* baseline is the one that B *prefers*.[32] This is Nozick's answer to the coercion question. Other writers give different answers. But virtually all writers on coercion seem to accept the more general proposition that there is, at least in principle, *a* right (or single best) answer to the coercion question.[33]

I disagree. I believe that there are right answers to the various *independent* tests for B's baseline, but I do not believe that there is or must be *a* best answer to the choice *between* the various tests. In summary form, my argument is this: (1) There is no single right answer to the coercion question when the results of the nonmoral and moral tests diverge. Each test supports a defensible or plausible coercion claim. (2) The moral force of an answer to the coercion question will depend upon the test used in setting B's baseline, and the required baseline will be determined by the moral force the coercion claim is meant to support. In other words, even if (1) is true, there *is* a right answer to the coercion question, *given* that a coercion claim is meant to have a *particular* moral force, such as to bar or mitigate the ascription of responsibility. (3) The moral test for B's baseline allows us to understand the motivation for the two-pronged theory of coercion found in the law.

My argument for (1) is simple. Without some compelling reason for maintaining that we are required to adopt either a moral, a statistical, or a phenomenological baseline from which to make the distinction between coercive and noncoercive proposals, we need not assume that only one of these baselines is legitimate or that there must be a principle for determining which test takes precedence when their results diverge. As I argued in Chapter 10, coercion claims are contextual. They have variable descriptive and normative force. Given that, I do not see any general theoretical motivation for saying that there is or must be a unique and proper way for setting B's baseline.

[32] "Coercion," 451.

[33] Haksar offers "my solution to the problem of distinguishing coercive proposals from non-coercive proposals." "Coercive Proposals," 67. Lyons attempts to define the "sufficient conditions for A's offer counting as clearly coercive," in "Welcome Threats and Coercive Offers," 50 *Philosophy* 425, 427 (1975). Feinberg says, "The correct criterion of normal expectance is a statistical test . . ." *Harm to Self*, 227–28.

As for (2), consider two cases in which the results of the moral and statistical (or phenomenological) tests diverge. Nozick's Slave Case may be represented as in Figure 7. Because X is superior to N, we understand why B may experience A's proposal as an offer, why B might even feel grateful. Yet when the results of the statistical and moral tests diverge, the fact that B may legitimately *feel* grateful (or threatened) may not have significant moral force. Even if B experiences A's proposal as an offer, this certainly does not mean that B would be *bound* by his agreement to do X—as is generally the case with offers.[34] Although it is perfectly reasonable, for some purposes, to say that A is making an offer to B, for most interesting moral purposes—at least with respect to the ascription of responsibility—A is making a threat.

–	N		X	M	+

Figure 7.

Or consider a case introduced by Daniel Lyons.

The Uncle's Contribution. A ordinarily gives a school a large annual contribution. The school has traditionally refused to admit women. A tells B, the school's dean, that he will make this year's contribution if and only if the school changes its policies. The dean promises to do so, and A gives his usual contribution.[35]

This is, I think, a tricky case because one's intuitions about the school's obligation to admit women may be affected by a belief that the school's traditional policy is inherently wrong and that it might be obligated to admit women even apart from its promise to do so. But assume, *arguendo*, that single-sex schools are not wrong. Lyons argues that A has threatened B, although he thinks it somewhat a puzzle that if B promises to start admitting women in response to A's threat, B will be *bound* by the agreement. But it is not a puzzle. A's proposal is a *threat* under the statistical test because A would ordinarily have given the money without the *quid pro quo*. Yet B would

---

[34] Or suppose that doing X would be (otherwise) immoral. One is ordinarily not excused for immoral acts performed in response to (even immoral) *offers*, but one may be excused for immoral acts performed in response to *threats*. If B does X in response to A's proposal, B may not be (fully) to blame for doing X because relative to M, he is coerced into doing X.

[35] "Welcome Threats and Coercive Offers," 429.

be bound by an agreement to admit women, because under the moral test, A is not bound to give anything at all, and thus his proposal is an *offer*. For moral purposes, it is not that B is bound *despite* being coerced; B is not coerced at all.

Multiple Baselines and the Two-Pronged Theory

I have argued for claims (1) and (2). I now want to argue that the multiple baseline account of coercion allows us to understand the motivation for the two-pronged theory of coercion we found in the law. Consider first two contemporary philosophical analyses of coercion. To explain the distinction between coercive and noncoercive threats, Vinit Haksar says that we should look at A's "declared unilateral plan," that is, what A will do if B does not do X.[36] A does not make a coercive threat, says Haksar, unless A's declared unilateral plan is *immoral* or would be a violation of A's "moral duty." Morally permissible threats are still threats, but they are not coercive threats.[37] Martin Gunderson makes a similar claim. A coerces B into doing X, he says, only if A has a "prima facie duty" not to bring X about (or allow X to happen).[38] We need this criterion, says Gunderson, to explain the distinction between these sorts of cases:

> *The Stock Market Case.* A realizes that B is about to lose a large sum in the stock market. A tells B that he will help B avoid the loss if and only if B gives him 15 percent of the amount he would have lost.

> *The Ambulance Case.* A comes upon an auto wreck and an injured B on a desolate stretch of road. A tells B that he will call an ambulance if and only if B gives him $100.[39]

Gunderson argues that A makes an offer to B in the Stock Market Case, because A has no obligation to help B avoid a stock market loss, but threatens B in the Ambulance Case, because A does have an obligation to secure an ambulance.

Although Haksar and Gunderson use slightly different terminology, both offer very close philosophical analogues to the two-pronged theory of coercion we found in the law. The problem is that the moral criteria they (and the law) use to make the distinction be-

[36] "Coercive Proposals," 67.
[37] Joseph Raz makes a similar point, namely, that A coerces B only if "P's actions . . . are prima facie wrong." "Liberalism . . . ," 108.
[38] "Threats and Coercion," 257.
[39] Ibid., 258.

tween coercive and noncoercive proposals seem entirely unmotivated. Both Haksar and Gunderson understand that some moral test is necessary if they are to account for their intuitions about the hypothetical cases. But they do not explain why the moral test seems to work.

The answer should now be clear. Although Haksar and Gunderson abandon the "better off"/"worse off" terminology in terms of which we usually distinguish between coercive and noncoercive proposals, their views are readily assimilable to such a framework. Relative to B's baseline as set by the moral test, what Haksar calls a *moral* (that is, morally permissible) *threat* can be redescribed as an *offer* to make B *better off*. And relative to B's moral baseline, A is proposing to make B *better off* in Gunderson's Stock Market Case, and *worse off* in his Ambulance Case.

As we have seen, the law has long held a similar view, namely, that A's proposal is not coercive if A threatens to do what A has a right to do. We are now in a better position to understand why, despite appearances, the two-pronged theory is not merely a judicial rationalization. Simply put, the proposal prong captures B's moral baseline, which in turn allows us to translate morally permissible threats into offers. A moral threat does not constitute legally recognizable duress because relative to B's moral baseline, A's *moral* threat is actually an *offer*. And offers do not coerce.

Consider some examples. Sony told B.I.C. that unless the latter agreed to new terms, Sony would terminate their relationship.[40] The court held that the new contract had not been made under duress because Sony had had a right to terminate the contract. Thus if we establish B.I.C.'s baseline by the *moral* test, Sony was offering to make B.I.C. better off, albeit on inferior terms.

Or recall our discussion of the right to sue. When the IRS threatened to take DuPuy to court, and DuPuy settled in response, it was held that the government had not coerced DuPuy's settlement.[41] Assuming that the government had the right to sue DuPuy, it was proposing to do *less* than it had the right to do, and relative to that baseline, it was actually making DuPuy an offer.

Or recall the discussion of marriage. The law once held that if B marries A because A threatens to prosecute B for seduction, the marriage is not made under duress.[42] If, in such cases, we set B's baseline by what A has a *right* to do—and if we accept the (Victo-

[40] *Business Incentives Co. Inc.* v. *Sony Corp.*, 397 F. Supp. 63 (1975).
[41] *DuPuy* v. *U.S.*, 35 F.2d 990 (1929). See p. 24.
[42] *Ingle* v. *Ingle*, 38 A. 953 (1897). See p. 75.

rian) view that it is morally permissible for A to propose prosecution—A is, in effect, making a genuine offer *not* to prosecute B if B will marry her.

The Supreme Court's position on plea bargaining is a simple extension of this general point of view. Recall *Bordenkircher* v. *Hayes*, where the prosecutor said that if Hayes did not plead guilty to forgery and accept a five-year sentence, he would seek an additional indictment under the Habitual Criminal Act. The Supreme Court said that the prosecutor had made a constitutionally permissible *threat*.[43] But if we define Hayes's baseline by what the prosecutor was permitted to do (by what I referred to in Chapter 8 as a "rights-based baseline analysis"), which *ex hypothesi* included prosecuting Hayes under the Habitual Criminal Act, the prosecutor's proposal of a five-year sentence for forgery was an offer. A nongenerous offer, perhaps, but an offer nonetheless.

The moral test may also explain why interrogation need not invalidate a confession. If we assume that the state is permitted, within certain limits, to interrogate suspects, the state's proposal to continue such interrogation (within those limits) if the suspect does not confess is not a proposal to make the suspect worse off than he is entitled to be. The state's proposal can be reformulated as an offer not to continue (legitimate) interrogation if the suspect confesses.

If this is all correct, we must consider a further question. If what can be described as a *moral threat* can *also* be described as an *offer* in which the baseline is set by the moral test, why do we (*and* the law) typically refer to morally permissible *threats*? Would it not be simpler to restate everything in terms of the moral baseline and preserve the equivalence between threats and coercion, offers and noncoercion? The answer is, I think, that while it might be simpler, linguistic simplicity is a limited virtue. The traditional terminology, in which we speak of moral threats, derives from and captures important dimensions of our experience. And not all our experience is moral experience. We often and, I think, appropriately define our situations in terms of where we (think we) are, and not in terms of where we have a right to be.

To see this more clearly, let us consider some of the legal cases once again. Prior to the prosecutor's proposal, Hayes was not in prison. If Hayes now faces a five-year sentence for forgery (not even having thought of the possibility of being prosecuted under the Habitual Criminal Act), it is not surprising that he should experience

[43] *Bordenkircher* v. *Hayes*, 434 U.S. 358 (1978). See p. 133.

the prosecutor's proposal as a threat. If Sony and B.I.C. have had an ongoing contractual relationship for some years, it is not surprising that B.I.C. should think that Sony's proposal would make it worse off. The same holds for DuPuy's reaction to the government's proposal to sue him and for the reluctant bridegroom facing prosecution for seduction.

The result is this. If the distinction between moral and immoral threats (and offers) *can* be restated in terms of the familiar better off/worse off distinction, that will explain why moral threats do not coerce and immoral threats do. It will also show that the law's two-pronged account of coercion is not a judicial rationalization, but instead reflects a plausible and, I think, philosophically defensible point of view. If it explains all of this adequately, that should be sufficient. It is neither necessary nor desirable to alter our ordinary discourse.[44]

Setting the Moral Baseline

I have argued that B's moral baseline does most of the important work in distinguishing between coercive and noncoercive proposals in cases which involve the ascription of responsibility. But how do we *set* B's moral baseline? In my view, a full answer to this question would require nothing less than a complete moral and political theory, and thus I shall invoke the customary disclaimer that this is beyond the scope of my project.

I can, however make some general remarks. First, A's proposal can be immoral in a variety of ways without proposing to move B below his moral baseline. Generally speaking, the moral baseline approach rests on a theory of *rights*. To set B's moral baseline, we need to know what A is morally *required* to do for B (or not do to B). Whether these moral requirements are *ultimately* grounded in a deontological or consequentialist theory, the structure of coercion discourse presupposes that A and B have certain obligations and rights which establish a background against which A's proposals are understood. A theory which denied that B has any rights

[44] As Ronald Dworkin puts it, albeit in another context, "once the semantic sting is drawn, we need not worry so much about the right answer to the question . . . Or rather we should worry about this in a different, more substantive way. For our language and idiom are rich enough to allow a great deal of discrimination and choice in the words we pick to say what we want to say, and our choice will therefore depend on the question we are trying to answer, our audience, and the context in which we speak." *Law's Empire* (Cambridge: Harvard University Press, 1985), 103.

would, I think, also have to deny any fundamental moral importance to coercion.

Now in some contexts, such as punishment, it may prove easier to think of B's moral baseline in terms of the requirements of *justice* rather than rights, although I do not think that much turns on this distinction. If the state proposes that B do X (plead guilty, testify against another, and so forth) in exchange for more lenient treatment than B would otherwise receive, it is important to know whether the baseline punishment is just. In a recent case, for example, a couple was convicted of causing the death of their daughter by criminal neglect. The judge proposed the following alternative sentences: two and a half years in prison or one and a half years in prison *if* they agreed to sterilization.[45] This proposal may, of course, be morally objectionable on a variety of grounds. Whether it was a *coercive* proposal, however, depends on whether two and a half years in prison is an unjust sentence for the offense. If it is not, the judge's proposal was a noncoercive offer.

In this connection, it may be observed that the moral baseline approach permits us to distinguish between B's rights against other *individuals* and B's rights against the *society* or the *state*. Suppose, for example, that a political theory gives B a right to be provided with adequate medical care. This right might be fulfilled through a practice of socialized medicine in which B has a right to be treated without fee by a publicly employed physician or through a scheme of national insurance, which provides B with the means to pay a private physician. In the latter case, B's moral baseline with respect to the *society* includes his right to medical care, but his moral baseline with respect to a *private physician* does not. If a private physician says that he will treat B only if paid, he is making an *offer*, not a threat. But if a government official says that he will give B his medical payment only if he receives a kickback, that proposal is coercive.

Second, and of capital importance, the moral baseline approach to coercion is fundamentally *neutral* with respect to the *content* of B's rights or the criteria for just treatment. Whether, for example, A's proposal is an offer or a threat in the Drowning Case depends on whether B has a right to be rescued. If B has such a right, A's proposal is a threat. If not, it is an offer. Either view can be accommodated. Similarly, if, in the case mentioned above, two and a half years is a just punishment, the proposal was an offer; if it is an excessive punishment, the proposal was a threat. Here, too, either

45 CBS Evening News, March 26, 1986.

view can be accommodated. Similarly, we saw that a recurring question in tort law is whether an employee voluntarily assumes job-related risks of injury. While not strictly dispositive of the answer to this question, a major consideration is whether A has a right to offer the job to B on any terms he wishes.[46] If A does have such a right, his proposal is not coercive; if he does not, it may be coercive. Once again, either view can be accommodated.

Third, and related to the previous points, the moral baseline approach allows us to distinguish—to the extent that we want to—between B's background conditions for which A is not responsible and rights-violating threats to B's welfare which are specifically attributable to A, or in slightly different terms, between coercive proposals and hard bargaining. Thus when LaBeach signed an agreement with Beatrice Foods Corporation because he was under pressure to repay a personal loan, it was held that this was part of LaBeach's background situation for which Beatrice had not been responsible, and hence the agreement had not been made under duress.[47]

The previous point might be put in a different and more general way. A liberal society is one in which individual rights and liberties play a fundamental role in defining just relationships. Such rights and liberties do not define the requirements of desirable (as opposed to permissible) social interaction. As Rawls has observed, the principles of justice do *not* represent a *social ideal*.[48] One can, of course, conceive of a regime in which agreements would be set aside if substantively unfair or objectionable on other grounds, but that would also be a regime in which rights and liberties played a smaller role. Perhaps such a regime is preferable. But, in any event, it is not the case that such a regime would have adopted a different conception of coercion. Rather, it seems more accurate to say that the absence of coercion would play a smaller role in defining permissible transactions.

There are additional complexities to establishing B's moral baseline, in part because we need a theory of the morality of *proposals*, as well as a theory of independent rights. And as I suggested in Chapter 5, this is philosophically underdeveloped territory. And it is territory on which I am not prepared to chart much new ground. I can say this. As our discussion of the law suggests, there are reasons for thinking that it is sometimes seriously wrong (rights-violating) for

[46] See p. 60.
[47] 461 F. Supp. 152 (1978). See p. 28.
[48] *A Theory of Justice* (Cambridge: Harvard University Press, 1971), 9.

A to threaten to do what it would not be *independently* wrong (or, more accurately, rights-violating) for A to do. We saw, for example, that contract law does not approve the use of (even otherwise justifiable) threats of criminal prosecution for securing private agreements. The idea seems to be that it is wrong to secure our ends by using other people's bargaining chips and that it is wrong to assert our rights to gain advantages with which those rights have no intrinsic connection and which they are not designed to serve. Similar considerations may motivate the criminalization of blackmail.

We may see this more clearly by attempting to merge the moral baseline analysis with the distinction between warning threats and manipulative threats.[49] Recall one of Greenawalt's cases (which I condense and then alter to produce a second case).

> *The Moralistic Informer*. A is disturbed that B is selling drugs, and decides to inform the police if B does not stop. A tells B of his plan, and B stops.[50]

> *The Greedy Informer*. A knows that B is selling drugs. A is not disturbed by this practice, but tells B that he will inform the police unless B pays him $500.

The Moralistic Informer and the Greedy Informer are both proposing to inform on B if B does not perform some act. There is this difference.[51] The Moralistic Informer elicits B's action by telling B about his *preexisting* plan, one which is included in B's baseline (even if B does not know this). A's *warning threat* is therefore translatable into a *noncoercive offer* not to tell the police if B stops. The Greedy Informer, on the other hand, elicits B's action by *developing* a plan through which he can motivate B to pay him off. In addition, whereas the action demanded by the Moralistic Informer is arguably germane to the point of the threat, this is not so with respect to the Greedy Informer. For these reasons, the Greedy Informer's plan should *not* be included in B's moral baseline, and therefore his (*manipulative*) proposal is properly understood as a coercive threat.[52]

At the outset of this book, I suggested that an entire political the-

---

[49] See p. 97.

[50] See p. 97.

[51] I ignore the difference in their *aims*.

[52] We saw, for example, that when Zigler used his threat not to execute a lease for the buyer of Hochman's business unless Hochman paid Zigler $3,500, the court held, in effect, that Zigler had wrongly devised his threat just for this purpose. *Hochman* v. *Zigler*, 50 A.2d 97 (1946). See pp. 25–26.

220

ory may rest on a theory of coercion. At one level, I continue to think that is true. Here I have argued that a theory of coercion rests on a moral and political theory—in particular, on a theory which allows us to set moral baselines. This view, I suspect, is the more important of the two.

THIRTEEN

COERCIVE PROPOSALS: II

Some say that tennis is all in the follow-through. Or is it the foot-work (or the grip, or the knees)? Actually, in tennis, it may not all be in anything. But I have argued, in effect, that the coerciveness of proposals is all in the baseline. And relative to that baseline, only threats are coercive. Some disagree. They argue that offers as well as threats can coerce. In this chapter I consider several versions of that claim.

Unreasonable Incentives

It is sometimes said that moderately attractive offers are not coer-cive, but that *extremely* attractive offers are different. As Virginia Held puts it, "An unreasonable incentive to accept a good might be no less coercive than an unreasonable incentive to avoid an evil."[1] What might this mean? The first possibility is this. A might present B with an incentive that makes X so attractive that it would be irra-tional for B to turn it down. For example, A might offer B a job at three times the salary he is now receiving. But as I argued in Chap-ter 11, although we may plausibly say that the distance between the alternatives is such that B has "no choice," the claim would be vir-tually without moral force. There is little of moral interest to be gained by referring to genuine and generous offers as coercive.[2]

There is a second, more plausible, account of Held's view, one which is suggested by her reference to unreasonable incentives as cases of "seduction." Say that A makes an *inducive* offer when B is psychologically capable of rejecting A's offer and that A makes a *se-ductive* offer when B is unable to resist A's proposal.[3] Psychological

---

[1] "Coercion and Coercive Offers" in *Nomos XIV: Coercion*, ed. J. Roland Pennock and John Chapman (New York: Aldine-Atherton, 1972), 58.

[2] I ignore the sorts of offers which are "too good to refuse" made famous in *The Godfather*.

[3] See Bernard Gert, "Coercion and Freedom," in *Nomos XIV: Coercion*, ed. Pennock and Chapman. Note that B's inability to resist A's proposal is distinguishable both from A's intention and from the proposal's actual effects on B's interests. A may not

seduction has been brought to the fore by several recent and important analyses of self-control (what Thomas Schelling calls "ego-nomics"), in connection with the difficulties many persons experience controlling behavior that they prospectively or retrospectively prefer not to engage in but tend to engage in nonetheless—for example, smoking, drinking, or overeating.[4]

Although the previous examples of psychological seduction need not involve a response to proposals, they could arise in that way. Just as B might prefer not to be seduced by his own preferences, B might also prefer that A not make him an offer because B knows that he will be unable to resist. B may, for example, prefer that A not offer him a cigarette precisely because he knows he will accept. B might not want to receive seductive monetary offers because he knows, in advance, that he will find such offers difficult to reject and that accepting such offers will change his character or life in ways he will later regret (a theme of the TV show "The Millionaire").[5]

It is, I believe, our concern with psychological seduction—not coercion—that explains our uneasiness about some of the informed consent situations discussed in Chapter 3. Consider

> *The Prison Experiment.* A, a cancer researcher, proposes that if B, a prison inmate, takes part in A's cancer research project, B's sentence will be reduced and B will be moved to a cell with an innerspring mattress and color TV.[6]

Assuming that B's baseline situation has not been made worse (or unjustifiably bad) just to render him more receptive to such proposals, then A's proposal is an offer. It might be a *seductive* offer. If B is

---

be aware of B's ability to resist his proposal, and thus A may unintentionally seduce B's agreement. In addition, A's seductive proposal may or may not be contrary to B's long-term preferences.

[4] See Thomas Schelling, "The Intimate Contest for Self-Command," in his *Choice and Consequence* (Cambridge: Harvard University Press, 1984), and Jon Elster, *Ulysses and the Sirens* (New York: Cambridge University Press, 1979). Precisely because we may know that we are vulnerable to psychological seduction, we may search for ways to constrain our own behavior, for example, flushing cigarettes down the toilet, asking a friend not to let us drink, or placing the alarm clock on the other side of the room. The problem of self-control is largely but not exclusively one of seduction or temptation. Fears, pain, and phobias also present such problems.

[5] One who is, in fact, quite capable of spurning what he regards as immoral offers might prefer not to have to reject them. A professor might not want to be offered a bribe to change a student's grade not because he thinks he will succumb, but because he does not want to have to fight his temptation to succumb.

[6] John Kleinig, "The Ethics of Consent," *Canadian Journal of Philosophy*, Supplementary Volume 8 (1982), 101.

not able to fully weigh the costs and benefits of the proposal because his present condition makes the short-term benefits seem unduly attractive (compared to the risks), the distortion of his judgment compromises the (full) voluntariness of his agreement.[7]

For these reasons, Held may be right to say that "A person unable to spurn an offer may act as *unwillingly* as a person unable to resist a threat . . ." But it does not follow that such offers are *coercive*.[8] I have, at several points, argued that coerciveness is not a necessary condition of acting involuntarily.[9] We have seen, for example, that cognitive defects can compromise the voluntariness of one's consent, even in the absence of external pressure.[10] For Held's claim to go through, we would need an argument that seductive offers are *coercive*, and that has not been provided.

Of course, even if seduction is not coercive, it might have comparable moral force. Although fraud is not coercion, it can invalidate agreements. Do (psychological) seduction and coercion have comparable moral force? It is not clear. It certainly does not follow that just because B acts involuntarily in response to A's seductive offer B is not responsible for his actions. While this is a complex matter, we *can* be responsible for our involuntary acts (for example, what we do while drunk), especially when we might have but did not take prior action to control our involuntary responses. In the absence of an argument or special reasons to the contrary (for example, that A makes his seductive offer to deliberately take advantage of B's inability to resist his proposal), we should, I think, assume that B is responsible for acts he performs in response to A's seductive offers.

I have, of course, been using "seduction" in a special—psychological—sense. The claim that offers do not coerce is said not to apply to (the standard) instances of *sexual* seduction.[11] Rosemary Tong

---

[7] In acknowledging this possibility, we must be careful. We should not assume that B is psychologically seduced simply because we disagree with B's preferences. As Feinberg points out, even when we do not think much of another's reasons, "we may still have to concede that he is making a perfectly genuine voluntary choice . . . albeit an unreasonable one by our standards." "Autonomy, Sovereignty, and Privacy: Moral Ideals in the Constitution?" 58 *Notre Dame Law Review* 445, 465 (1983).

[8] "Coercion and Coercive Offers," 58 (emphasis added).

[9] Indeed, as I have observed, it can be argued that being coerced is not a *sufficient* condition of acting involuntarily—in a technical sense.

[10] For example, as in a contract induced by fraud, or less than fully *informed* consent to a medical procedure, or a confession produced by ignorance of one's Fifth Amendment rights.

[11] It is certainly not self-evident that recipients of sexually seductive offers are psychologically seduced, that they are typically unable to resist such proposals.

writes that "like sexual threats, sexual offers are coercive. It is just that the bitter pill of coercion is coated with a sugary promise . . ."[12] Consider this case:

> *The Seducing Chairman.* A, a department chairman, offers B, a mediocre graduate student, an assistantship which she does not deserve if and only if she goes to bed with him. Preferring the assistantship to not going to bed with A, B does so.[13]

Tong maintains that A coerces B because it "is not clear that she would have freely chosen to move from the pre-offer to the post-offer stage."[14] Perhaps a rational B would *not* want to receive such an offer, because it would get her to do something she would later regret (even if she got the assistantship). But, and as we have seen, a proposal is not coercive just because its recipient would prefer not to receive it. And assuming that B would *not* be made worse off if she spurned A's offer than if there had been no offer at all, there is no reason to regard A's proposal as *coercive*.

It may, however, be objected that I have misrepresented the way in which sexual seduction usually occurs. A typically does *not* only offer to improve B's situation, but *also* threatens to harm B if she spurns his proposal. I do not deny that sexually seductive proposals often contain (implicit or explicit) threats or that if they do contain such threats, such proposals are coercive. But that does not weaken my argument. To the contrary. That Tong supports her claim that sexual seduction is coercive by arguing that such proposals typically include a threat serves, I think, to reinforce my claim that they would not be coercive in the absence of a threat.

Exploitation

What of exploitative offers? Haksar argues that exploitative offers are not *threats*, but that they are coercive, because they "involve an attempt to take an unfair advantage of the recipient's vulnerability."[15] Frankfurt writes that a proposal "acquires the character of a threat" when one has another in one's power and demands "an exploitative price."[16] And Feinberg has argued that if A exploits his su-

---

[12] *Women, Sex, and the Law* (Totowa, N.J.: Rowman and Allanheld, 1984), 68.

[13] See Michael Bayles, "Coercive Offers and Public Benefits," 55 *The Personalist* 242 (1974).

[14] *Women, Sex, and the Law*, 69.

[15] "Coercive Proposals," 4 *Political Theory* 65, 69, (1976).

[16] "Coercion and Moral Responsibility," in *Essays on Freedom of Action*, ed. Ted Honderich (London: Routledge and Kegan Paul, 1973), 71–72.

perior power over B by manipulating B's options so that B accepts his offer or suffers an "unacceptable" consequence, then A's offer is coercive.[17]

Are these arguments correct? Do exploitative offers coerce? It is important to set up the problem correctly. While exploitation and coercion often go hand in hand, they have fundamentally different foci. As Feinberg has noted, to determine whether A's proposal is *coercive* we look primarily to its effect on *B's options*. To determine whether A's proposal is *exploitative*, we look to its effect on *A's interests*.[18] A's proposal can, of course, be exploitative *and* coercive, as when A benefits himself at B's expense by making a *threat*. But to see the difference between coercion and exploitation, note that A's proposal can be coercive and *non*exploitative, as when A (paternalistically) coerces B to do something that is in B's interest but does not benefit A. And A's proposal can be exploitative and noncoercive, as when A charges a "scalper's price" for a ticket to a rock concert.[19]

The question, then, is not whether exploitative *proposals* can coerce—for they surely can—but whether exploitative *offers* can coerce. To answer this question, we need to do more than identify the foci of exploitation, we need to identify its central characteristics. Unfortunately, this is quite difficult. Inequality of bargaining *power*, for example, is certainly not the key. A may have the *capacity* to exploit B, but treat B fairly nonetheless. It seems, then, that we need an independent criterion of exploitation. Yet it is hard to provide such a criterion without appealing to the highly problematic notion of a "just price," a standard of value which is independent of market considerations.[20]

Despite the difficulties in the way of defining exploitation, the intuition that "prices" (broadly construed) can be unfair is too strong not to be taken seriously. So let us adopt a different strategy, and put the problem this way: How might exploitation arise? Exploitation might arise from *market imperfections*. A may exploit B because

[17] "Noncoercive Exploitation," in *Paternalism*, ed. Rolf Sartorius (Minneapolis: University of Minnesota Press, 1983), 208–9.

[18] "Noncoercive Exploitation," 202.

[19] Ibid. These are my examples, not Feinberg's.

[20] I ignore *systemic* or *technical* accounts of exploitation, although I do not want to deny that some such account is possible. It is, I should say, this type of exploitation upon which Marxist critics of capitalism focus their energies. See, for example, John Roemer, "Should Marxists Be Interested in Exploitation?" 14 *Philosophy & Public Affairs* 30 (1985). Roemer argues, in fact, that a systemic account of exploitation does *not* define exploitation relationally, that it "refers to the relationship between a person and society as a whole." 31.

B lacks information, negotiating skills, time, mobility, or the like. For these sorts of reasons, A is able to get a better price than he would receive under more perfect market conditions. Exploitation may also arise when B has needs for which the market or the society does not provide—as in Jeffrie Murphy's example of the offer to sell a baseball autographed by Babe Ruth to the parent of a leukemia victim for an exorbitant price.[21] Although there may be no "going rate" for autographed baseballs, we know this form of exploitation, like pornography, when we see it.

Because it is more common, let us consider exploitation that arises from market imperfection. There are two ways to understand how a price can be unfair. On the first account, A exploits B if A is paid much more (or pays less) than the normal price for X. Call this the *normal price* account.[22] On the second account, A exploits B only if A's gain from the agreement is much greater than B's. Call this the *comparative* account.[23]

Consider two examples.

The Stingy Employer. A proposes that B work for him at a salary of $30,000. A values B's labor at $40,000 and would usually pay that wage, but he knows that B is now earning $29,000, that B is willing to switch jobs for the extra $1,000, and that B hates to haggle. B accepts A's offer of $30,000.

The Greedy Mechanic. B's car is disabled and needs a new fan belt. A ordinarily charges $10, but seeing that B needs it desperately and knowing that there are no readily available alternative sources, he charges $50.

We can represent the situations in a matrix which contrasts A's and B's utility gains from the agreements, as in Figure 8 (the absolute numbers are unimportant). The Stingy Employer exploits B under *both* accounts: A is paying less than the normal price for B's services, and A is getting the lion's share of the surplus benefit generated by B's employment. The Greedy Mechanic, on the other hand, exploits B under the normal price account, but *not* under the comparative account. For B is actually getting *more* utility from the agreement than

---

[21] "Blackmail: A Preliminary Inquiry," 63 *Monist* 156, 160 (1980).

[22] A's normal price must be adjusted for special inconveniences or costs incurred in delivering the good or service to B. If A normally charges $25 for some service, but gets up in the middle of the night to help B, a price of $50 would not necessarily be abnormal.

[23] We assume that A and B are both better off, otherwise the agreement would not have occurred.

A. And that is of capital importance. That we are inclined to regard the Greedy Mechanic as exploitative suggests that the normal price account must be closer to the truth. This view is also confirmed by our general experience. When, because of abnormal conditions, a buyer gets unusually high utility from a purchase, we typically expect the seller to be satisfied with his normal gain. B may feel, as they say, "ripped off" by an unusually high price, even if he gains more utility from the transaction than A.

THE STINGY EMPLOYER

	A	B
AGREEMENT	10	1
NO AGREEMENT	0	0

THE GREEDY MECHANIC

	A	B
AGREEMENT	10	20
NO AGREEMENT	0	0

Figure 8.

But if, as the previous examples suggest, it is A's gain that defines the exploitativeness of an agreement, it is hard to see why exploitative *offers* should be regarded as coercive. If, counter to fact, the Stingy Employer would usually *not* pay more than $30,000 for B's services, B would clearly not be coerced into accepting A's offer. Why, then, should the fact that the Stingy Employer would be willing to pay more make a difference? B's choice would be identical in both cases.

We could, of course, *define* B's moral baseline so as to include the principle that A is required not to exploit B, in which case A's exploitative offers would be coercive. But such a move is vulnerable to two objections. First, by absorbing exploitation into the moral baseline, it yields the result that exploitative offers are coercive only by tautology. Second, it is not clear that such a move can be comfortably accommodated within the normative framework that motivates a theory of coercion. For as I argued in the previous chapter, our concern with coercion is fundamentally motivated by the principle that individuals have *rights* which they can choose to exercise in their interactions with each other. A view which defines acceptable transactions in terms of the values exchanged allows less room for the exercise of such rights. Perhaps such a justice-oriented view is correct. But, if so, it would not follow that exploitative offers coerce. Rather, it would follow that the absence of coercion is less important to the validity of agreements than it first appeared.

Exploitation + Unacceptability = Coercion?

There is more that can (and will) be said about the relationship between exploitation and coercion, but I want to consider first another version of the argument that exploitative offers can coerce. Some writers on coercion are particularly disturbed by the following sort of case, which I borrow from Feinberg.

> *The Lecherous Millionaire.* B's child will die unless she receives expensive surgery for which the state will not pay. A, a millionaire, proposes to pay for the surgery if B will agree to become his mistress.[24]

I assume that A's proposal is an *offer* under either the moral or the statistical test for B's baseline: B does not expect A to pay for her child's surgery, and A is not morally required to do so. Feinberg agrees. But, he says, A's proposal is a *"coercive* offer" because it "manipulates [B]'s options in such a way that [B] has 'no choice' but to comply or else suffer an unacceptable alternative."[25] In matrix form, the case may be represented as in Figure 9, where any point below 0 represents an unacceptable situation, and where, let us say, − 10 represents a point of desperate need.

---

[24] "Noncoercive Exploitation," 208. Theodore Benditt develops a similar example in "Threats and Offers," 58 *The Personalist* 382, 384 (1977). And Harry Frankfurt develops an example involving a butcher and his customer which shares the essential features of the Lecherous Millionaire in "Coercion and Moral Responsibility," 71ff.

[25] "Noncoercive Exploitation," 208 (my emphasis).

THE LECHEROUS MILLIONAIRE

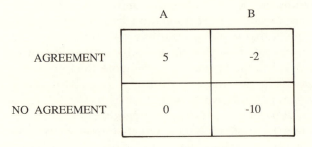

	A	B
AGREEMENT	5	-2
NO AGREEMENT	0	-10

Figure 9.

In what does the putative coerciveness of A's proposal consist? Feinberg says that the Lecherous Millionaire "manipulates" B's options to his benefit. That is true. But it is also true that A manipulates B's options to his benefit whenever A makes a standard offer which B finds attractive, for example, when A offers B three times his present salary to change jobs. "Manipulation," then, does little moral work. Indeed, here the appeal to manipulation can cut both ways. For suppose that B (manipulatively) proposes to become the Lecherous Millionaire's mistress if he will help her daughter. We would, I assume, want to deny both that A is coerced by B's proposal and that B's proposal is a case of self-coercion.

If this is right, then Feinberg regards A's offer as coercive, not because it is manipulative, but because it combines an exploitative price and the absence of an acceptable alternative.[26] Now I have already argued that an exploitative price is not, by itself, coercive. Does the absence of an acceptable alternative make the difference? In one sense, clearly not. The fact that B has no acceptable *alternative* to accepting A's proposal is, I take it, of no great importance if accepting A's proposal is itself a reasonably attractive option. Assume that it is not attractive. Is the absence of an acceptable alternative sufficient to support a coercion claim? On one view, it is irrelevant to a coercion claim. On another view, it is relevant, but when it is relevant, exploitation adds nothing of importance.

To see why this is so, let us consider the Honest Mechanic, who charges the normal price ($10) for the fan belt that B desperately

[26] Something like this combination seems to occur in *Caivano* v. *Brill*, where, in the midst of the depression, Brill took advantage of Caivano's unemployed status and got him to agree to a kickback arrangement. See p. 25.

needs. If the fact that B has "no acceptable alternative" (because he desperately needs the fan belt) were sufficient to render A's proposal coercive, the Honest Mechanic's proposal would be coercive. But, if anything, that seems to show that the absence of this sort of "acceptable alternative" does *not* establish coercion—at least not in any interesting way. On the other hand, as I argued in Chapter 11, the absence of an acceptable alternative *can* support a coercion claim that bars the ascription of responsibility—if there are *independent* moral reasons for thinking that it is A's responsibility to provide B with an alternative B regards as acceptable. But this does not help Feinberg's view, since, *ex hypothesi*, the Lecherous Millionaire has no such obligation. Moreover, when A does have an obligation to provide B with an acceptable alternative, A's obligation may have little to do with avoiding exploitation. It is his *independent* obligation that does the moral work.

Less hypothetically, consider an exploitative labor agreement. B is unemployed and desperately needs a job. A, an entrepreneur, could start a business which might employ B, but he might also invest or spend his money in other ways. Now whatever we might want to say about the generalized economic pressures on B, it seems fair to say that *A* does not coerce B if he decides not to start the business, even though A's decision not to start a business "reduces the options available to any prospective employee."[27] But if A does not coerce B if A is not *able* to offer B a job because he does not start a business, it arguably is not coercive, in any important sense, for A to offer B a position that A creates, even though, when offered it, B has no acceptable alternative but to accept.

I should stress, once again, that I do not deny that there is something *wrong* with exploitation. I do not deny even that exploitation can serve as a ground for invalidating agreements. There may be some agreements that are *so* exploitative that they should not be allowed to occur, even though they are arguably in the interests of all concerned. The present and narrower point is this. If (1) an exploitative price and (2) the absence of an acceptable alternative do not independently render A's proposal coercive, it is not clear why or how the *synthesis* of (1) and (2) does so. It is, of course, possible that the union of (1) and (2) could create a coercive "organic whole" which cannot be explained by the coerciveness of either component. But in the absence of an *argument* to that effect, and no such

[27] Richard Epstein, "A Common Law for Labor Relations: A Critique of the New Deal Labor Legislation," 92 *Yale Law Journal* 1357, 1372 (1983).

argument has been produced, it seems more sensible to say that while the Lecherous Millionaire's proposal may be unseemly, it is not coercive. And it is *not* coercive, because it *expands* rather than reduces B's options relative to B's moral baseline.

Feinberg grants much of this. He acknowledges that the Lecherous Millionaire's proposal is "freedom enhancing," but argues, nonetheless, that it should be described as a "coercive offer."[28] Is the notion of a "freedom-enhancing coercive offer" self-contradictory or even paradoxical? Feinberg thinks not.

> It is a coherent description simply because it is a fact that one person can effectively force another person to do what he wants by manipulating his options in such a way as to render alternative choices ineligible and, in so doing, quite incidentally enlarge his freedom in general. This fact of life seems paradoxical only when there is uncritical acceptance of the dogma that coercion *must* have the immediate effect of restricting freedom on balance.[29]

What Feinberg calls his "compatibilist solution" gives rise to the following question: if freedom-enhancing coercive offers do not restrict freedom (by definition), what is gained by calling them *coercive*? Interestingly, on Feinberg's *own* account, not much. Feinberg explicitly accepts what I have claimed, to wit, that it is the moral force of a coercion claim that is of ultimate importance.[30] And while Feinberg wants to *call* such offers coercive, he admits that their putative coerciveness has limited moral significance. Feinberg says, for example, that the Lecherous Millionaire coerces B to become his mistress, but denies that the Lecherous Millionaire commits rape. It is not *that* kind of coercion. Moreover, says Feinberg, "when A merely exploits circumstances that he finds ready-made, then frequently, though not always, B's consent . . . remains valid."[31] It is not *that* kind of coercion, either. There may, of course, be rhetorical advantages to describing such proposals as coercive, but B's moral baseline does the real moral work, and for such purposes, Feinberg

[28] *Harm to Self* (New York: Oxford University Press, 1986), 233.

[29] Ibid. (original emphasis).

[30] He notes that the "purely conceptual question is inherently murky . . . and that the important thing . . . is to determine what sorts of influence do invalidate consent, not deciding what word to apply . . ." Ibid., 246–48.

[31] Ibid., 244. It would seem, then, that Feinberg might agree with the decision in *Hackley* v. *Headley* (as opposed to *Caivano*), where it was held that although Hackley had taken "unjust advantage" of Headley's situation, Headley had not been coerced. See p. 24. Indeed, on Feinberg's view, *Caivano* was decided wrongly.

seems to grant that freedom-enhancing exploitative offers do not coerce.

Hard Choices

Yet the previous argument both overstates the point and cuts against the general view I have defended, namely, that coercion claims are contextual, that they can have different sorts of moral force. There *is* a point—indeed, there may be several points—to describing some freedom-enhancing exploitative offers as coercive.

One point is this. Sometimes one faces a choice situation in which rejecting a proposal means remaining in dire straits, but accepting the proposal is also unpalatable. Call this a *hard choice*. Hard choices are importantly different from other choices. They have a particularly severe constraining effect. There is, as Joseph Raz suggests, a sense in which people do not act autonomously when they are struggling to maintain the "minimum conditions of a worthwhile life."[32] Now the relation between hard choices and autonomy is, I think, more complex than this. Although the *scope* of our hard choice options is limited by their unattractiveness, the choice *among* those options may be of especial *importance*. In the latter sense, making a hard choice may constitute an important and positive assertion of our autonomy. Nonetheless, just as the prospect of hanging is said to focus the mind, (very) hard choices produce too much focus and not enough scope. For that reason we can, I think, plausibly use the family of coercion terms to describe hard choice situations.

Hard Choices and Justice. Hard choices are not all morally equivalent. Some hard choices are alterable, others not. Some alterable hard choices should be altered, others not. The woman who must choose between death and a mastectomy deserves our sympathy, but her hard choice is simply a regrettable fact. We *could*, on the other hand, eliminate the prisoner's hard choice between remaining in prison and participating in a medical experiment by granting an immediate parole, but here it is arguable that we *should* not eliminate his hard choice, at least not in this way.

As opposed to the previous cases, there are situations in which society can and should remove (or mitigate) hard choices. Whereas Jeffrie Murphy rightly notes that the grimness of our alternatives is

---

[32] "The more one's choices are dictated by personal needs, the less autonomous one becomes." "Liberalism, Autonomy, and the Politics of Neutral Concern," in *Midwest Studies in Philosophy*, vol. VII, ed. Peter French et al. (Minneapolis: University of Minnesota Press, 1982), 112.

often nothing more than "a sad fact about the human condition rather than any unjust disadvantage brought on by the wrongful actions of others," it is a non sequitur to suppose that the *effects* of such disadvantages must and should be borne solely by their recipients.[33] Suppose B must choose between death and an expensive and potentially debilitating medical procedure. He has two hard choices: whether to undergo the procedure on medical grounds, and whether to jeopardize his family's financial security. Although we can do nothing to remove B's hard medical choice, it may be thought that a just society should mitigate such financial dilemmas by socializing the monetary burdens of medical care.[34] By referring to such choices as coercive, we may signify that there is a strong, if rebuttable, case for their amelioration.

There are two points that must be made about this view. First, to reemphasize a point we have made, not all hard choices are rooted in social injustice. Illness, accident, and the like may present dilemmas which no set of feasible social arrangements can entirely preclude. Even if, with Rawls, we seek a conception of justice that leaves aside "those aspects of the social world that seem arbitrary from a moral point of view,"[35] there may be important arguably arbitrary aspects—"sad facts"—of one's world that cannot be avoided. Put somewhat differently, hard choices which do not arise from injustice are not coercive in any important moral sense.

The second point is this. Even if a hard choice is rooted in social injustice and therefore supports a plausible coercion claim, the moral force of the coercion claim is not self-evident. By referring to hard choices as coercive, we may signal that there is a (rebuttable) case for the mitigation of B's background conditions. That is one sort of moral force. At the same time, the coerciveness of hard choices does *not* necessarily bar the ascription of responsibility for the normal moral and legal effects of acts. That is a different sort of moral force and requires a different sort of argument.

Hard Choices and Agreements

Let us pursue the previous point in more detail. Assume that B finds it rational to accept A's proposal because B's background cir-

---

[33] "Consent, Coercion, and Hard Choices," 67 *Virginia Law Review* 79, 82 (1981).

[34] A similar point can be made about the victims of natural disasters. Perhaps the victims of hurricanes should bear all the burdens and hard choices such events cause, but it is also arguable that the costs should be shared by the fortunate as well as the unfortunate, so that the "hard choices" of those affected by such events are at least minimized if not altogether eliminated.

[35] *A Theory of Justice* (Cambridge: Harvard University Press, 1971), 15.

cumstances are less than fully just. In a world in "strict compliance" with the principles of justice, B would not have to make such a choice, but B's world is in only "partial compliance" with the principles of justice.[36] The question is this: what is the moral effect of these conditions on the validity of B's agreement?

Suppose, for example, that B is in need of medical care and that A proposes to provide such care for a fee. B accepts A's proposal. Suppose further that a just society would defray B's costs, but that B's society is not just. Given this, there may be no way to mitigate B's responsibility without shifting the burden to A, who has not done anything wrongful. Thus Feinberg argues that B has an obligation to pay A, even if the society should have paid for him.[37]

Or suppose that in response to A's offer, B surrendered her child to A for adoption because her personal and economic circumstances were particularly difficult. Suppose, further, that her situation has changed for the better and she now wants the child back. Suppose, finally, that society *should* have arranged things so that she did not face such a choice in the first place. Here we can ask two questions: (1) Is B's surrender coerced? (2) Should the child be returned to the biological mother? (Or, in other terms, who is to bear the burden of B's earlier unjust dilemma?) With respect to (1), we have two options: we can say that the initial surrender was not coerced, despite the background injustice, and that the child therefore should stay with its new parents; or we can say that the initial surrender was coerced, and that there is at least a prima facie case for returning the child to the biological mother. With respect to (2), we can say what we like, although I suspect the answer will turn, in large part, on the interests of *all* the parties involved. But whatever we want to *say* about the original choice situation, no waving of hands about coercion can alter the choice that must be made here. Solomon notwithstanding, the child is indivisible and will either stay with the adoptive parents or be returned to the biological mother.

Or consider the problem faced by the soldier who surrenders and is taken prisoner of war. Is such a soldier morally bound to give up fighting his captors in return for benevolent quarantine?[38] Or can he argue that because he has been wrongly placed in this dilemma (I assume there would be no war in a world in strict compliance with the principles of justice), he has surrendered under duress, and is therefore not bound to keep his agreement?

[36] These are Rawls's terms. See ibid., 8–9.
[37] *Harm to Self*, 197.
[38] Michael Walzer, "Prisoners of War: Does the Fight Continue after the Battle?" in *Obligations* (Cambridge: Harvard University Press, 1970), 150.

There are two alternatives. We can think that such surrenders are made under duress and are not binding, in which case the capturing side may prefer to execute captured soldiers or hold them as slaves.[39] Or we can think that despite their origins in unjust conditions, it is better to think of such surrenders as not coerced and therefore as binding. Once again, whatever we want to say about coercion, one fact stands out: given the choice between benevolent quarantine, slavery, and death, a potential POW would probably *not* prospectively prefer a practice which would release him from his obligation to cease fighting because his surrender was made under stressful and unjust conditions. For then he would not be granted the opportunity to surrender in the first place.

Let us push the analysis a bit further. In the medical care, adoption, and POW cases just described, it is arguable that even if B faces a hard choice because of background injustices, A has not taken unfair advantage of B's circumstances. Would exploitation make a difference? Is there, in the end, something to Feinberg's notion that a hard choice *and* exploitation combine to make a coercive whole?

Consider, once again, the case of the Lecherous Millionaire. Assume that a just society would have altered B's background situation so that she did not face such a choice. Assume further that A is not morally *required* to help B, but that A makes an exploitative proposal which B accepts. Feinberg argues that while such *proposals* should *not* be *prohibited*, such *agreements* should *not* be *enforced*. Is this view correct?

Consider the problem this way. What would happen if B's agreement with the Lecherous Millionaire were unenforceable? There are two possibilities. If the Lecherous Millionaire does not know that the agreement is unenforceable, the agreement may occur, B's child be saved, and B then be released from her part of the agreement. Perhaps that is a good result.[40] On the other hand, if A *knows* that the agreement would be unenforceable, the agreement will not occur. Is that a good result? Certainly B may not think that it is. For her child now dies. To the extent that such predictable unenforceability deters such agreements from being made, there is, at least from B's perspective, no significant distinction between prohibiting such agreements and not enforcing their terms.

The sorts of proposals for which the case of the Lecherous Mil-

<hr>

[39] Indeed, Rawls argues that because a treaty to hold prisoners as slaves is less unjust than a practice of putting soldiers to death, it may be a defensible practice under nonideal conditions. *A Theory of Justice*, 248.

[40] I ignore the possibility that such a result is unfair to A.

lionaire serves as a model raise several interesting questions about coercion, circumstantial pressure, and the like. It can, however, be argued that the most important question is this: given B's unfortunate circumstances, what do we want B to be able to do? If we want to enable B to improve her position, then A must be permitted to exploit B and B must be allowed to let herself be exploited. From B's perspective, the only thing worse than an exploitative agreement would be no agreement at all. And if we want to allow such agreements and simultaneously retain our commitment to the voluntariness principle, then we must also assume that *these* sorts of exploitative agreements are *not coerced*, at least not in the sense that would invalidate the agreement.

Would that be a hedging? If we want to say, for example, that the POW's or the mistress's consent is not given under duress because it is in *their* interest that the agreements be upheld, have we not, in effect, allowed the truth of a coercion claim to be determined by *consequentialist* considerations? Would we not be making the same sort of external or policy argument which I criticized when discussing the law?[41] I do not think so. The reason is this. In arguing (in Part One) that "external" or policy considerations should have little bearing on the validity of a coercion claim, I meant principally to contrast the effects of a decision on the parties involved with the effects of a decision—as a precedent—on other members of the society. I argued, for example, that even if holding that B had been coerced into escaping from prison would have bad consequences (inside and outside of prisons), this has little bearing on the validity of the coercion claim itself. On the other hand, it seems prima facie odd to think that B is coerced by a proposal that *B* would like to receive or by an agreement that B would like to make.

The point can be put in a different way. I have argued that to assess the validity of a coercion claim, we must assume *some* conception of B's baseline or background situation. I have also suggested that for some moral purposes—for example, the amelioration of B's background conditions—we may want to assume that B's baseline is determined by what would be the case if the arrangements were just. On the other hand, it is possible that for other moral purposes, and, in particular, for coercion claims whose moral force is to invalidate an agreement, we should assume a *different* set of background

[41] See pp. 174–75. I wish to acknowledge an anonymous reader of the manuscript for bringing this question to my attention.

conditions, namely, the background conditions that B would (hypothetically) prefer us to assume.

We would, of course, need to *justify* the adoption of (something like) this procedure for setting B's moral baseline, but it is important to stress that it does not follow that all moral bets are off simply because the world is not just. To set B's moral baseline, we need a moral theory for a world which is in only partial compliance with the principles of justice. And assuming that such a theory could be properly grounded and that it yields something like the moral baseline that B would—under the circumstances—prospectively prefer us to adopt, it would not be hedging for us to say that the POW's or the mistress's consent is not given under duress.

If this is basically right, we must confront an additional question: should we *ever* preclude B from improving his situation by limiting the sorts of agreements that we will enforce? The answer must be yes. For even with straightforward coercion, as in the paradigmatic gunman example, there will be some cases in which B would be better off if he were able to make a binding agreement with A. Precisely because the gunman knows that his victim cannot be bound by an agreement (say, to pay him $1,000), he may not give him the opportunity to buy his life. But we would *not* want to say that, for this reason alone, such agreements must always be binding. On the other hand, if B would prefer that A make a freedom-enhancing proposal, given a plausible understanding of B's present situation, and if, at least prospectively, B would prefer to be bound by his agreement, it is arguable that there should be at least a reasonably strong presumption that the agreement is not coerced and ought to be enforced.

Usury. I suggested above that, at least under extreme conditions, the presumption that noncoercive agreements should be enforced might be overridden by considerations of exploitation. What would justify such an overriding? To focus our inquiry, let us consider the justification of usury laws (which specify a ceiling on allowable interest rates) as a model for the more general theoretical problem.[42] To set up the problem, let us make the following assumptions: (1) there are two classes of potential borrowers—Good Risks (GRs) and Bad Risks (BRs); (2) lenders find it profitable to lend to GRs at rates within the legal limits; (3) lenders find it unprofitable to lend to BRs within the legal limits; (4) lenders are under no obligation to lend money to BRs at unprofitable rates; (5) there is no monopoly on

---

[42] Seven states allow any agreed rate. All the others have some restrictions.

lending.[43] Given these assumptions, usury laws will inevitably prevent mutually beneficial and noncoercive transactions between lenders and BRs. Can that be justified?

One justification might be this. A prohibition against usurious loans may be thought of as a "second-best device for preventing certain forms of deception and duress that cannot be attacked more directly."[44] If there are categories of loans in which duress is difficult to detect and enforce, a general prohibition of such loans will protect a class of (potential) borrowers, even though it occasionally works against individuals. And that would be nothing new or extraordinary in social life.[45]

Let us assume, however, that we can determine which usurious loans are not coerced. Could we then justify prohibiting such loans or not enforcing their terms? There are at least three possible justifications. The first appeals to a principle of paternalism. It argues that we should prevent BRs from doing something that will not serve their long-term interests because they tend to overestimate the benefits and underestimate the costs of such loans. On this view, (most) BRs are better off not borrowing at all, and usury laws protect them from their own errors of judgment.[46]

A second argument maintains that while lenders would find it profitable to lend to GRs at a "normal" rate, market imperfections allow them to charge higher rates. If we prohibit usurious loans, the

[43] Feinberg argues that the moneylender has the needy borrower "over the barrel." *Harm to Self*, 264. But assuming that there is no monopoly in lending, no individual lender has BRs over a barrel. If A's rates are too high, BR can try elsewhere. As Mill argued, "If he cannot borrow at the interest paid by other people it must be because he cannot give such good security: and competition will limit the extra demand to a fair equivalent for the risk of his proving insolvent." *Principles of Political Economy*, bk. V, chap. X, sec. 2.

[44] Anthony Kronman, "Paternalism and the Law of Contracts," 92 *Yale Law Journal* 763, 777 (1983).

[45] The requirement that landlords provide a nondisclaimable warranty of habitability may prevent a prospective tenant from making a beneficial contract (the lower price might be worth the risk of an uninhabitable dwelling), but landlord-tenant relations are so fraught with possibilities of exploitation, fraud, and duress that the class of tenants may be better off.

[46] On closer inspection, this argument suggests that usurious interest rates are not necessarily exploitative. Although the lender is charging a "high" *rate*, he is not receiving an exorbitant *profit*—given the risks inherent in lending to BRs. A slightly different ("moralistic") version of this argument claims that we should not be free to enter into agreements (such as contracts for self-enslavement) that specifically compromise our autonomy (as opposed to our interests) or that are so fundamentally immoral (e.g., prostitution) that they should not be enforced—even if both parties would prefer otherwise. See G. Dworkin, "Paternalism," 56 *The Monist* 64 (1972). Also see Feinberg, "Autonomy, Sovereignty, and Privacy," and Arthur Kuflik, "The Inalienability of Autonomy," 13 *Philosophy & Public Affairs* 271 (1984).

same transactions will occur at a nonexploitative level. Usury laws leave some GRs (those who would otherwise be charged a higher rate) better off, but they leave BRs worse off, for they prevent BRs from borrowing at all.[47]

A third, more political, argument claims that the very fact that BRs might benefit from borrowing at exploitative rates is a poignant indication that something is fundamentally wrong about their background situation. And while it is true that these particular BRs might be better off if lenders could charge usurious rates, allowing them to do so would postpone social efforts to rectify the background situation of future BRs.

I am inclined to think that the second argument holds the greatest promise. The first argument rests on dubious empirical claims. It is, for example, far from clear that BRs do tend to make erroneous judgments and that *they* (as a class) are better off as a result of usury legislation. Moreover, even if that were the case, such legislation would be vulnerable to the well-known—but nonetheless important—charge that such paternalism is at least presumptively unacceptable because it violates one's freedom.[48] I shall ignore the third argument. Although it may ultimately be sound or of considerable importance, its validity turns on moral and empirical considerations about political change and revolution which would take us far afield.

By contrast, the second argument is eminently plausible. Usury laws may compensate for market imperfections and allow many GRs to borrow money at lower rates than they would be able to secure without such laws. If so, usury laws will offer GRs protection from exploitation. At the same time, it should be noted that they will do so at the expense of BRs. The trade-off between the interests of GRs and BRs might serve to justify such laws, but we must recognize that we are, in fact, choosing to protect one group from exploitation by preventing others from making noncoercive and mu-

---

[47] It is, I think, this argument from market imperfections that lies behind much "unconscionability law," such as restrictions on "contracts of adhesion." A contract of adhesion is a "form contract" in which the buyer is said not to have the ability and knowledge to bargain over the specific terms. Contracts in which a seller disclaims liability for defects in the product, particularly when such disclaimers are in fine print, are examples.

[48] Even if some forms of legal paternalism are justifiable, usury laws cannot be justified solely on the grounds that they have beneficial effects. I do not know what Mill would say about the Lecherous Millionaire, but he does not regard incurring a burdensome debt as analogous to slavery. He says that a person "must be presumed to be a sufficient guardian of his pecuniary interests . . ." *Principles of Political Economy*, bk. V, chap. X, sec. 2.

tually beneficial transactions.[49] To what extent this justification of the prohibition of mutually beneficial exploitative agreements can be extended to other contexts (for example, labor agreements) is an open question. I am inclined to think that at least some extension is possible.

[49] Nozick refers to this as a choice "among suboptimal patterns," where in order to prevent some people from coming to harm we render someone else unfree to perform a particular act. "Coercion," in *Philosophy, Science and Method*, ed. Sidney Morgenbesser et al. (New York: St. Martin's, 1969), 457.

MORALITY, INTENTIONALITY,
AND FREEDOM

I have argued that only threats are coercive and that the distinction between threats and offers is rooted in a moral account of one's baseline. There is more work to be done. Although all threats are coercive, not all threats coerce—at least in the sense that they nullify the normal moral and legal effects of one's acts. A (relatively) complete theory of coercion should indicate what further conditions are necessary if A's coercive proposal is to genuinely coerce B. I shall take up that task in the next chapter.

But before proceeding further down what some maintain is an erroneous path, I want to take up two related objections to the account of coercion that I have been developing: (1) that a *moralized* account of coercion is fundamentally misconceived, and (2) that the emphasis on *coercion* as a constraint on freedom is, in itself, a serious error. The objections are related in this way. Both objections maintain, albeit in different ways, that a moralized account of coercion places arbitrary or improper limitations on the way freedom is said to be constrained.

Although these challenges to a moralized theory of coercion must stand or fall on their own philosophical merits, they are often associated with a *political* claim, to wit, that the adoption of a moralized account of coercion or the emphasis on deliberate restraints has pro-capitalist or conservative consequences, that such a theory conceals the manifold ways in which capitalism effectively limits individual freedom. In what follows, I hope to see what there is (and is not) to these views.

Objections to a Moralized Theory

I have argued for an account of coercive proposals which is rooted in a moral account of B's baseline. I have not denied that there are other sorts of plausible coercion claims (some of which are not moralized), but I have maintained that those coercion claims will not bar or mitigate the ascription of responsibility. In that sense, I have claimed that coercion is "an essentially moral concept."[1] On my view, the truth of a coercion claim does not rest only on facts of an ordinary sort.[2]

Before considering the objections to a moralized theory of coercion, it is important to review the way in which this account is and is not moralized. First, a moralized theory of coercion does have empirical or descriptive requirements. Nothing in my argument denies that morality is supervenient on facts. Second, as we have seen, A's proposal is coercive only if A acts wrongly in particular ways. To say that A makes a coercive proposal to B *only* if A proposes to move B below his moral baseline is *not* to say that A coerces B just in case A acts wrongly.[3] On my view, coercion claims do not serve as mere linguistic placeholders for general moral disapproval of the relevant proposals.

All the same, there are still several reasons for thinking that a nonmoral theory of coercion would be more attractive—if it were true. First, there is the *circularity* problem. A coercion claim often works as a premise in the following sort of moral argument:

(1) It is wrong to make coercive proposals.
(2) A makes a coercive proposal to B.
(3) Therefore, A acts wrongly.

Now if A's proposal is coercive (as in [2]) only if it is already wrong, as a moralized theory seems to maintain, it is hard to see how we can say without lapsing into circularity that A acts wrongly (as in [3]) *because* A makes a coercive proposal.

Even if the circularity objection can be avoided (as I think it can), we encounter a second difficulty, which might be called the *triviality* objection. It might be argued that on a moralized theory of coercion, the "preanalytic" sense of coercion—the view that coercion has to do with the amount of *pressure* on B—is relatively unimportant. On a moralized theory, we can say whether A's proposal is coercive once B's moral baseline has been set. But once B's moral baseline

---

[1] David Zimmerman, "Coercive Wage Offers," 10 *Philosophy & Public Affairs* 121, 122 (1981).

[2] See p. 7.

[3] In criticizing Frank Knight's moralized theory of coercion, Gerald Dworkin says this: "If some kind of moral evaluation goes into decisions about the application of 'coercion', it will be more subtle and complex than the judgment that what is happening is wrong . . ." See "Compulsion and Moral Concepts," 78 *Ethics* 227, 229 (1968).

has been set, all the interesting theoretical work will have already been done: "the only real issue would be over [the] prior rights and wrongs."[4]

Third, it is said that a moralized theory does not "link up in the right way with the underlying idea that coercion undermines freedom . . ."[5] Even if a moralized theory can explain why it is wrong for A to make his proposal or why B should not be bound by his agreement, it does not give the *kind* of explanation that a theory of *coercion* should give. It does not explain why a proposal to move B below his moral baseline interferes with B's *freedom* or renders B's action *involuntary*.

A fourth objection maintains that a moralized theory gives wrong or misleading answers to important questions about putatively coercive situations. It has been argued that a moralized theory ignores or denies important facts about B's choice situation, that it fails to see that B can be forced to do something even if A is acting within his rights.[6] It has also been argued that if A coerces B only if A acts wrongly, it would seem that *justified* coercion must be impossible, despite the frequency and obvious sensibleness with which we discuss the justification of coercion.[7]

Rather than assess these objections in serial fashion, I shall begin by considering two of the more prominent arguments against a moralized theory. In the section that follows, I shall consider David Zimmerman's analysis of coercive wage offers, which is, I believe, the most sustained and sensitive attempt to develop a nonmoral account of coercion. In the subsequent section, I shall consider G. A. Cohen's critique of Nozick's moralized theory. I shall then reconsider the objections I have noted above.

Zimmerman's Alternative

In advancing his account of "coercive wage offers," Zimmerman's intention is not primarily to show (what I have denied) that *offers* as well as threats can coerce. His primary intent is to provide a *non-*

---

[4] Zimmerman, "Coercive Wage Offers," 122.

[5] Ibid., 123.

[6] See G. A. Cohen, "Robert Nozick and Wilt Chamberlain: How Patterns Preserve Liberty," in *Justice and Economic Distribution*, ed. John Arthur and William Shaw (Englewood Cliffs, N.J.: Prentice-Hall, 1978). Also see Cohen's "Capitalism, Freedom, and the Proletariat," in *The Idea of Freedom.* ed. Alan Ryan (New York: Oxford University Press, 1979).

[7] See, for example, Jon Elster, "Exploitation, Freedom, and Justice," in *Nomos XXVI: Marxism*, ed. J. Roland Pennock and John Chapman (New York: New York University Press, 1983), 285.

moral account of coercive proposals—whether threats *or* offers. Zimmerman argues that A coerces B whenever B's options in the postproposal situation are worse than they would be in some relevant baseline situation.[8] On his view, threats are coercive because B would prefer his actual or statistical preproposal situation to his postproposal situation. Yet, persuaded by the force of Nozick's Slave Case, Zimmerman wants to explain how A's proposal can also be a coercive *offer*, and for the reasons noted above, he wants to do so without resorting to a moralized baseline.

Can that be done? Zimmerman argues (to condense his argument somewhat) that A makes a coercive offer to B under the following conditions: (C-1) B prefers the postproposal situation to the actual preproposal situation; (C-2) B would prefer an alternative preproposal situation to his postproposal situation; (C-3) B's preferred preproposal situation is technologically and historically *feasible*; and (C-4) A *actively prevents* B from being in the preproposal situation which B would prefer.[9]

These conditions work in this way. (C-1) defines A's proposal as an offer. The remaining conditions define (what I shall call) the *Zimmerman Baseline* in terms of which A's offer is allegedly *coercive*. (C-2) captures the potential coerciveness of A's offer; (C-3) blocks our saying that *all* offers are potentially coercive because there are an infinite number of logically possible preproposal situations that B might prefer; and (C-4) determines just which of B's preferred feasible alternative preproposal situations are relevant to the coerciveness of A's proposal.

The Zimmerman Baseline represents the slave owner's proposal as coercive because the slave would prefer the preproposal situation of not being a slave to the slave owner's offer, this preferred preproposal situation is historically and technologically feasible, and the preferred alternative is one which the slave owner actively prevents. Although the slave owner's proposal is also coercive under a moral baseline, Zimmerman claims two advantages for his approach: first, since it specifies only one baseline, there are advantages of "explanatory simplicity"; second, the "prevention" condition explains the slave owner's proposal as wrong because it limits the slave's *freedom* and not simply because it is otherwise unjust or violates his rights.

Having shown how his baseline works in the Slave Case, Zim-

---

[8] "Coercive Wage Offers," 124.
[9] Ibid., 132ff.

merman then applies this account to capitalist wage offers. He asks us to consider this case (which I condense).

> *The Kidnapping Case.* A kidnaps B and takes B to an island where A and C are the only employers. After stranding B on the beach, A and C offer B comparably low wages for terrible jobs, an employment situation inferior to B's prior situation on the mainland.[10]

Zimmerman says that A's and C's proposals are *offers* because A and C propose to make B better off than he is in his actual postkidnapped preproposal situation. Zimmerman also claims that while both offers would *exploit* B's vulnerable position, only A makes a coercive proposal, because it is A and not C who prevents B from being in his preferred preproposal situation (on the mainland). Whether capitalist wage offers are coercive similarly depends on whether capitalists actively prevent workers from being in a superior preproposal situation—and that, says Zimmerman, is a complicated question. Its answer would require an adequate analysis of capitalism and a satisfactory account of the distinction between *preventing* and *not providing* B's preferred preproposal situation.[11]

Zimmerman's Theory Evaluated. Zimmerman's theory does not deliver on all of its promises. First, it is not obvious that Zimmerman's theory is, in fact, simpler than the moral baseline approach. Contrary to his claim, Zimmerman does not rely on only one baseline. A's proposal is an *offer*, after all, because it is measured against B's actual preproposal baseline, but it is a *coercive* offer because it is measured against the Zimmerman Baseline.[12]

There is another difficulty. A's proposal might be coercive even if B *prefers* the postproposal situation to the preproposal situation that A prevents. For even if the employment situation on Zimmerman's island were *superior* to B's opportunities on the mainland, it is arguable that B would still be coerced by A's proposal, or more accurately, that it is the *kidnapping* that is coercive, and that casts its moral shadow over A's subsequent actions. If this is so, then (C-2) is not a necessary condition of coercion.

---

[10] Ibid., 135.

[11] Ibid., 144.

[12] In any case, theoretical simplicity may be overrated. As Bernard Williams has noted, while it is generally "a good idea to make the minimal assumption . . . this is not necessarily the same as an assumption of the minimum. The most effective set of assumptions need not be the shortest." See *Ethics and the Limits of Philosophy* (London: Fontana, 1985), 105–6.

Moreover, while (C-4) may attempt to capture something important about coercion, it is not clear that "prevention" is the right way to put the point, or from what vantage point the alleged prevention occurs. Suppose that A has died or has moved to a remote spot on Zimmerman Island. If prevention is a forward-looking notion, it may be C and not A who now actively prevents B from returning to the mainland. Given this, if Zimmerman wants to say that C is coercing B, the kidnapping is irrelevant. If, on the other hand, (C-4) is meant to begin with the past—with the kidnapping that has the effect of preventing alternatives in the future—it is not clear that "prevention" is the most felicitous way to capture this view.

There is a fourth and perhaps more important problem. Given the centrality of the prevention condition, a *great* deal turns on the distinction between preventing and not providing an alternative. If we assume that at least *some* acts of omission are properly regarded as acts of prevention, it is doubtful that we can identify those omissions without appealing to normative criteria. On one view, A's act of omission prevents something from occurring only if A has an independent obligation to ensure that it occurs. Otherwise, A merely does not provide it. But if something like this criterion is necessary to determine which acts of omission are also acts of prevention, Zimmerman's claim to have offered a nonmoral account of coercive offers is undercut.[13]

Comparing the Zimmerman and Moralized Theories. These criticisms do not show that Zimmerman's *basic* strategy is wrong. Explanatory simplicity is, after all, a limited virtue, and it is possible that some of my objections can be met or finessed. The more basic question is whether Zimmerman's approach is more promising than its (straightforwardly) moralized competitor.

Although it will come as no surprise that I think the moral baseline strategy is superior on this score, I think there is much less to the difference than meets the eye. Although Zimmerman speaks of coercive offers, he also implicitly concedes that only threats coerce. A's proposal is an offer because it proposes to make B better off with respect to his (preproposal) baseline. But it is, on Zimmerman's ac-

---

[13] Larry Alexander argues that it may be impossible to give a nonmoral account of the distinction between preventing and not providing in "Zimmerman on Coercive Wage Offers," 12 *Philosophy & Public Affairs* 160 (1983). Zimmerman replies that it is possible to give a nonmoral account, but that it does require more work than he may have previously thought. See "More on Coercive Wage Offers: A Reply to Alexander," 12 *Philosophy & Public Affairs* 165 (1983).

count, a *coercive* offer only because it proposes to make B *worse* off with respect to the Zimmerman Baseline. Moreover, Zimmerman and I both argue *against* the view that coercion is a function of structural features of B's choice situation. It can be argued, after all, that from B's perspective on Zimmerman Island, the choice situations created by A's and C's proposals are virtually identical. Yet Zimmerman maintains that A's proposal is coercive, whereas B's is not. According to Feinberg the failure to see that both proposals create identical choice situations is a defect in Zimmerman's theory.[14] I regard it as a virtue.

Yet despite these affinities, there are differences which tell against Zimmerman's theory. First, Zimmerman's theory fails to explain how "Drowning Case" offers can plausibly be described as coercive. For if A does nothing, A does not actively prevent B from attaining his preferred preproposal situation. One could, I suppose, say that A prevents B's rescue by omitting to rescue him, but that claim presupposes a moralized account of the distinction between preventing and not providing an alternative, in which case Zimmerman's claim to have provided a nonmoral theory would be undercut.

Zimmerman chooses to handle the Drowning Case in a different way. His view is that A is *exploiting* but *not coercing* B, but he then insists that exploitation may be just as wrong as coercion, and that commitments made to exploiters "are often (always?) as void as those made under duress."[15] There are three problems here. First, as I noted above, Zimmerman's view fails to capture the possibility that A is, in fact, making a genuinely coercive proposal. Second, it is simply not true that exploitative agreements are typically as void as those made under duress, unless we tautologically define an agreement as exploitative only if it is so exploitative as to render it void. Third, if, as Zimmerman claims, it is wrong to coerce because coercion limits *freedom*, there is at least one wrong-making characteristic that is lacking in cases of noncoercive exploitation but present in cases of coercive exploitation. On Zimmerman's own terms, noncoercive exploitation is not as wrong as coercive exploitation.

But the major difficulty with Zimmerman's theory is *not* that it fails to explain the coerciveness of some (Drowning Case) propos-

---

[14] *Harm to Self* (New York: Oxford University Press, 1986), 243–44. Actually, B may not perceive the proposals as identical. Given that A and not C caused his condition, B may be angrier at A than at C.
[15] "Coercive Wage Offers," 134.

als, but that it fails to explain the *non*coerciveness of proposals that are threats on a nonmoral baseline, but offers on a moral baseline. To see the problem, let us recall our discussion of plea bargaining. It would seem that Zimmerman must argue that plea bargaining is coercive, because the prosecutor actively prevents the defendant from attaining his preferred preproposal situation. But while plea bargaining *may* be coercive, it is at least not obviously so, given a certain—moralized—understanding of the defendant's *present* baseline.[16] And whether we decide to describe the prosecutor's proposal as an offer or a threat, it is certainly not clear that bargained guilty pleas are invalid. Distinguishing coercive from noncoercive proposals is often difficult because determining the right view of B's *present* (preproposal) baseline may be problematic. A moralized theory provides a plausible solution to this problem. Zimmerman's theory does not even begin to respond to these difficulties.

Or consider the sort of problem raised by a standard contract law case, for example, *B.I.C.* v. *Sony*.[17] Recall that B.I.C. had a contract with Sony which was terminable by either party. Sony told B.I.C. that it would terminate the relationship unless B.I.C. agreed to new terms. The court ruled that the new contract between Sony (S) and B.I.C. (B) had not been made under duress and that the agreement was binding. On a moralized theory, the court's argument looks like this:

M1. S makes a morally permissible threat (if threat is defined nonmorally).

M2. S does not coerce B (because the morally permissible threat can be restated as an offer on a moral baseline).

M3. B acts voluntarily (because S's proposal is an offer).

M4. B's agreement is binding.

Zimmerman argues, in effect, that a moralized theory does not explain how the *morality* of S's threat in (M1) leaves the voluntariness of B's action in (M3) intact. If threats are coercive and coercion limits freedom, B's freedom should be limited in (M3). And, it is argued, the moralized theory does not show how that conclusion can be avoided. Now that is not quite true. I have argued that, on a mor-

---

[16] Zimmerman recognizes that plea bargaining poses a problem for his theory, and argues that the prevention condition may have to include reference to the proposer's intentions. Ibid., 137–38. Perhaps it does. But all this makes the claim to have produced a nonmoral theory look less clear.

[17] 397 F. Supp. 63 (1975). See p. 41

alized theory, morally permissible threats can be recast as offers, and offers do not restrict one's freedom. Nonetheless, I think it fair to say that I have not (yet) provided a sustained defense of the view that one acts voluntarily when responding to morally permissible threats. And if such an argument cannot be provided, that will be a point in Zimmerman's favor.

But coercion not only limits freedom, it also has moral force. Although Zimmerman's theory claims to explain coercion without appeal to a moralized baseline, it offers relatively little guidance with respect to the move from coercion to voluntariness to bindingness (or responsibility). How would Zimmerman want to handle *B.I.C. v. Sony*? Let us assume that S is making a threat because B would prefer its preproposal situation to the postproposal situation. Given this, Zimmerman might make one of the following arguments:

(Version A)
Z1a. S makes a morally permissible threat.
Z2a. S coerces B.
Z3a. B acts involuntarily.
Z4a. B's agreement is not binding.

(Version B)
Z1b. S makes a morally permissible threat.
Z2b. S coerces B.
Z3b. B acts involuntarily.
Z4b. B's agreement is binding.

(Version C)
Z1c. S makes a morally permissible threat.
Z2c. S coerces B.
Z3c. B acts voluntarily.
Z4c. B's agreement is binding.

If Zimmerman wants to say that B acts *involuntarily* in response to S's morally permissible threat (as in [Z3a] and [Z3b]), he has two alternatives. He could swallow the view that B's agreement is *not* binding (Z4a), but then the argument would no longer be consistent with our most basic moral intuitions, not to mention the entire corpus of American law. Or Zimmerman could say that B's agreement *is* binding (Z4b), but then he would have to explain how we can get from B's involuntary action (Z3b) to a binding agreement (Z4b). On the other hand, if Zimmerman wants to say that B acts *voluntarily* in response to S's morally permissible threat (Z3c), he must explain how we get from coercion (Z2c) to a voluntary action (Z3c). Thus even if Zimmerman's theory gives us a plausible account of coercive proposals, it cannot explain the way in which coercion, voluntariness, and bindingness are related.

Cohen and Nozick

In two important articles, G. A. Cohen has argued against Nozick's version of a moralized theory of coercion. Cohen argues that a moralized theory is false on its face and that it conceals the ways in which capitalism not only restricts economic liberty, but may even force workers into selling their labor.[18]

Cohen begins this way. Assume that B lives in a non–welfare state capitalist society and owns only his own labor power. B has two alternatives: to work or to starve. Cohen points out that on Nozick's moralized theory, B is "forced to choose between working and starving only if . . . the actions bringing about the restrictions on his alternatives were illegitimate . . ."[19] On Nozick's moralized theory, B accepts employment *voluntarily* if B's situation is the result of others' exercising their (legal or moral) rights. Cohen's explication of Nozick's position is basically correct.[20] In advancing something quite close to the law's two-pronged theory of coercion, Nozick says: "Whether a person's actions are voluntary depends on what it is that limits his alternatives. If facts of nature do so, the actions are voluntary. Other people's actions place limits on one's available opportunities. Whether this makes one's resulting action non-voluntary depends upon whether these others had the *right to act as they did*."[21]

But, says Cohen, not only is Nozick's position false, it is *obviously* false. Most of Cohen's criticism is accomplished through this example:

> farmer F owns a tract of land across which villager V has a right of way . . . if F erects an insurmountable fence around the land, V is forced to use another route . . . since F . . . acted illegitimately . . . [F]armer G, whose similar tract is regularly traversed by villager W, not as of right, but by dint of G's tolerant

[18] See "Robert Nozick and Wilt Chamberlain: How Patterns Preserve Liberty" (hereafter referred to as "Wilt Chamberlain") and "Capitalism, Freedom, and the Proletariat" (hereafter referred to as "Capitalism").

[19] "Wilt Chamberlain," 259.

[20] Actually, Nozick speaks of "coercion" rather than (the arguably less precise) "force," but nothing turns on this.

[21] *Anarchy, State, and Utopia* (New York: Basic Books, 1974), 262 (my emphasis).

nature . . . erects an insurmountable fence around his land for reasons which . . . justify him in doing so.[22]

Cohen's point is this. Although V and W now face similar obstacles, a moralized theory holds (1) that since F acted illegitimately, V is forced to use another route and (2) that since G acted legitimately, W is not forced to use another route. Since it is obvious, says Cohen, that "W is no less forced to change his route than V," it follows that a moralized theory is false.[23] Q.E.D.

But is it so obvious that W is forced to change his route? Yes and no. Yes, it is obvious that there is a descriptive sense in which both V and W are equally forced to use another route. In what sense, then, can we say that W is *not* forced to use another route? Consider my extension of Cohen's story.

> F proposes to sell V a key to a gate that will allow V to traverse F's tract. Because the value of traversing the tract exceeds the cost of the key, V buys the key from F. G makes an identical proposal to W, who buys his key from G.

Suppose that V and W now claim that they made their payments under duress, because, as Cohen says, F's and G's actions forced them to choose between making the payments and what they regard as an unacceptable alternative, that is, not being able to traverse the tracts of land. I assume that whereas V can recover his payment, even Cohen would grant that W cannot.

How could Cohen reach that conclusion? He could say that W cannot recover even though he was forced to pay. But, at least with respect to the sense of "force" that has the relevant moral implications, we are, in fact, more inclined to say that W voluntarily paid for the right of way (whereas V did not). But I do not want to quibble about words. The point is that whatever locutions we want to use here, there is an important distinction between the bindingness of W's agreement and that of V's agreement.

What is going on here? Why should Nozick want to deny that there is a sense in which W is forced to go around the tract of land or pay for the right of way? And why should Cohen want to deny that there is another sense in which W is not forced to pay? I am inclined to think that their errors can be traced to a common difficulty. Both Nozick and Cohen assume (or at least there are passages which can be *read* as if they assumed) different versions of the "right

[22] "Wilt Chamberlain," 259.
[23] Ibid.

answer" thesis. Nozick can be read as arguing that the moralized account of coercion exhausts the field, and that there is no important sense in which W is forced to go around the fence. Although, as Cohen observes, that is obviously false, a moralized theory of coercion need hardly deny that such justified "forcings" have the effect of constraining actions or behavior. On the other hand, Cohen is wrong to assume that a nonmoral account of coercion (or forcing) can do the requisite moral work. Cohen can treat all forcings as coercive if he prefers, but then he will need another principle to distinguish the coercion or forcing that invalidates agreements from the coercion or forcing that does not. And, I suggest, even Cohen would need a moralized theory to make *that* sort of distinction.

Once we see that a moralized theory is not mistaken in the way Cohen asserts, the structure of his political argument is undercut. The political argument must be made in a different way if it is to have its desired force. Consider Cohen's argument that capitalism restricts liberty. Cohen argues that private property restricts liberty because the very fact that A owns property P places limits on B's freedom to use P, and thus "The sentence 'free enterprise constitutes economic liberty' is demonstrably false."[24] Now it is true that a practice which assigns A a property right in P places limits on the freedom of others to buy, sell, and otherwise use P. And perhaps some defenders of capitalism, wishing to appropriate the rhetorical advantages of defending "freedom," are actually blinded to that fact. But does a serious defender of capitalism need to deny that capitalism restricts freedom in that way? I do not think so. Advocates of capitalism need not deny that A's property rights restrict B's freedom to do what he wants or to satisfy his preferences. They need only argue that property rights define one's moral baseline, and that relative to that *baseline*, capitalist offers do not coerce, restrict one's options, or reduce one's freedom.[25] True, capitalism must *defend* its view of the rights that define one's baseline, but whatever the ultimate status of such justifications, Western political

---

[24] "Capitalism," 12. It has similarly been argued by others that a libertarian theory necessarily and nonconsensually restricts liberty because A's right not to be assaulted limits B's freedom to assault A. See, for example, Hugh LaFolette, "Why Libertarianism Is Mistaken," in *Justice and Economic Distribution*, ed. Arthur and Shaw, 197.

[25] As Richard Epstein notes: "The baseline for forced exchanges is individual entitlement to personal autonomy, not individual preferences regardless of their content." *Takings* (Cambridge: Harvard University Press, 1985), 333.

thought does not lack for theories which attempt to do precisely that.

It might be said, at this point, that I have misrepresented the argument that "left-wing" critics of capitalism are likely to endorse, that the claim that capitalism coerces need not be based on the rejection of a moralized theory of coercion.[26] The objection may go something like this. The circumstances in which the proletarian (B) must work for the capitalist (A) or starve are the result of a historical process by which the workers, as a class, were robbed of their communal rights to property by the capitalists as a class. The contract between worker and capitalist is coerced, then, not because of the "objective" circumstances, but because of the wrongful nature of A's past actions or the past actions of A's class. The claim that capitalism coerces is rooted not in a nonmoral theory of coercion, but in a moral theory which is tied to a certain historical vision.

This objection deserves to be taken seriously. Among other things, it raises a number of very important questions: What is the moral relevance of wrongful actions that occurred well in the past? Is a Marxist vision of the history of capitalism correct? Can the actions of (previous or other) members of one's *class* affect the status of one's agreements? I shall not even try to answer these questions here. Nonetheless, there are several points that can be made. First, the Marxist critique of capitalism vividly demonstrates what I have already claimed, namely, that regardless of the general theory of justice we adopt, we will still need a partial compliance theory for setting B's moral baseline for a world that is less than fully just (or "moral"—if, as some suggest, Marxism is not concerned with justice).[27] Determining what we are morally required to do when our background circumstances are not what they should be is a problem for *any* moral theory—Marxist or otherwise. Second, even if the best (Marxist or non-Marxist) theory of B's moral baseline does *not* yield the conclusion that employment contracts in a capitalist society are *invalid*, that theory might give considerable support to coercion claims whose moral force is to argue for a change in B's background circumstances.

Third, and most central to the argument under discussion, if I have captured the sort of argument that left-wing critics of capitalism really intend to make, not only can we put aside one entire line of criticism of a moralized theory of coercion, we can have greater

---

[26] I want to thank an anonymous reader of the manuscript for raising this question.

[27] See, for example, Allen Wood, "The Marxian Critique of Justice," 1 *Philosophy & Public Affairs* 244 (1972).

confidence that the basic structure of that theory is correct. For as I have argued, a moralized theory can accommodate many different views about the content of morality. Perhaps B's baseline should include A's exclusive right to use his private property as he sees fit. Perhaps not. As I have argued, a moralized theory is, for example, perfectly compatible with the view that A's proposal in Nozick's Drowning Case is coercive.[28] If the relationship between employers and employees should be similarly understood, then (some) capitalist practices *do* force workers to sell their labor power in the relevant moral sense. The general and important point is that a moralized theory of coercion does *not* assume any particular system of property rights. It does not specify B's moral baseline. That is the job of moral theory.[29]

While a moralized theory of coercion does not preclude anticapitalist conclusions of the kind Cohen advocates, it does make it more difficult to show that behavioral forcings have radical political consequences. But that is, I think, as it should be. Critics of capitalism must do more than show that there is *some* sense in which capitalism restricts freedom. They must show that these sorts of restrictions have the moral force they attribute to them. If such arguments can be produced, then so much the worse for capitalism. If they cannot, then the claim that capitalism limits freedom should be regarded as less important than its advocates assume.

Objections to a Moralized Theory Reconsidered

I have argued that politically inspired critiques of a moralized theory of coercion lose much of their (philosophical) power if we understand that coercion claims can have different moral force. This also explains how justified coercion is possible. As I argued in Chapter 10, there is a standard sort of coercion claim which allows us to say that A coerces B into doing X just in case A proposes to punish B if B does not do X. Justified coercion is possible because the truth conditions of the coercion claim embedded in "The state is justified in coercing citizens to pay taxes" are not identical with the truth conditions of the coercion claim embedded in "B's agreement is not binding because A coerced B."

---

[28] See p. 218.

[29] Cohen seems to recognize this point: "a moralized definition does not by itself deliver this conclusion . . . The marriage of liberty and private property requires not only a moralized definition of liberty but also a moral endorsement of private property." "Capitalism," 12.

Why is this so? One reason is this. In most coercion contexts, B's action would change his moral or legal status—were it not for the coercion. He would, for example, be obligated to do something he was otherwise not obligated to do. By contrast, the state's coercive threats typically give B prudential reasons to do what he is morally obligated to do in any case (not kill, not steal, pay his taxes, and so forth). Because the coercion does not change B's moral status, whether the state is exercising coercion is not problematic. Put slightly differently, the moral considerations that (help) determine whether someone is coerced (in the sorts of responsibility-affecting contexts on which I have focused) are importantly distinct from the sorts of moral considerations that figure in the justification of state coercion. In any case, the claim that some (state) coercion is justified does no damage to the moralized theory of coercion that I advance.[30]

There is another objection to a moralized theory which I shall briefly consider. What might be called a "dialectical" objection to a moralized account of coercion stems from a broader critique of the use of moralized concepts. It is claimed that we can intelligently disagree about the morality of the use of coercion only if we start from a morally neutral account of coercion itself.[31] This argument does not assert that moralized concepts are "false" or that nonmoral concepts are "true." For concepts are neither true nor false. Rather, the argument asserts that coercion (or freedom) *can* be defined in nonmoral terms, and that there are analytical and argumentative advantages in doing so.[32]

While I am generally quite skeptical of stipulative or "constructive" definitions of crucial concepts, I am not concerned to defend ordinary language. My principal response to the objection is this. First, there is no a priori reason to believe that fruitful moral discourse requires that we begin with nonmoral concepts. Second, there is no evidence (broadly construed) that moral discourse which rests on nonmoral accounts of crucial concepts is, in fact, more fruitful than moral discourse which rests on moralized accounts of those concepts (establishing this would, of course, require a controversial metric of moral fruitfulness).[33]

---

[30] I thank David Zimmerman for pressing me on this point.

[31] "An agreed descriptive language is a prerequisite for a fruitful discussion of normative issues." Felix Oppenheim, " 'Constraints on Freedom' as a Descriptive Concept," 95 *Ethics* 305, 309 (1985), a critique of David Miller's "Constraints on Freedom," 94 *Ethics* 66 (1983). Also see Oppenheim's very helpful *Dimensions of Freedom* (New York: St. Martin's, 1961), 211.

[32] See Oppenheim, *Dimensions of Freedom*, 5–6.

[33] Indeed, it is surprising that Oppenheim should think that conceptual analysis

Still, I have not answered all the objections to a moralized theory that I introduced above. Recall the *circularity* objection. If A's proposal is coercive only *if* it is wrong, can we also say, without circularity, that A acts wrongly *because* he makes a coercive proposal to B? Perhaps not. But even if this special sort of coercion argument is circular (and that is not clear), the coercion arguments in which I have been interested do not have this particular form. Consider the following sort of argument.

(1) Coerced agreements are not binding.
(2) A makes a coercive proposal only if A acts wrongly (in the requisite way).
(3) Because A acts wrongly (in the requisite way), A makes a coercive proposal.
(4) A coerces B (by whatever further conditions are necessary if A's coercive proposal is to coerce B).
(5) B is not bound by his agreement.

There is no circularity in this argument if the moral judgment expressed in (5) is not *identical* to that identified in (2) and presupposed in (3) and (4). And they are not identical.[34] For (5) expresses a judgment about what we should do in the *light* of B's moral baseline as determined by (2) *and* further facts contained in (3) and (4).

If the circularity objection can be defused, is there not still something to the *triviality* objection? Even if the moral judgment identified in (2) and presupposed in (3) is not *identical* to the moral judgment made in (5), is it not also true that once the criteria for (2) have been settled and applied in (3), (5) adds little of moral interest? Not entirely. For as we shall see in the following chapter, the move from (3) to (5) is by no means automatic. (5) also presupposes (4), which rests on different moral criteria than those applied in (3).

All the same, there is, I think, a sense in which the triviality objection is essentially *right*. For by the time we have settled (3), we are at least well down the road to our argument for (5). Is this a cause for concern? I do not think so. The reason is this. Lurking beneath

should be evaluated by its contribution to fruitful moral discourse, since he also argues that basic moral principles cannot be rationally defended. He calls this "moral noncognitivism." See *Moral Principles in Political Philosophy* (New York: Random House, 1976). On his own metaethical theory, it is not clear what "fruitful normative discourse" would look like.

[34] As Charles Fried suggests: "It is always neater if a moral conclusion can be made to turn directly on non-moral criteria, for when the moral depends on the moral there is always the danger of a vicious circle . . . But if a moral criterion is deeper, more general, or at any rate independent of the moral issue it determines, there is no circularity at all." *Contract as Promise* (Cambridge: Harvard University Press, 1981), 97.

most conceptual analyses of coercion is, I think, the hope that by getting clear about the *concept* of coercion, we shall be in a position to resolve *substantive* moral, legal, and political problems. And if the conceptual analysis were to yield a nonmoral account of coercion, we would be able to go from nonmoral premises to (important) moral conclusions. It would, of course, be nice to make progress on substantive moral problems in ways that do not, themselves, require substantive moral arguments. Yet to set up the motivation for the analysis of coercion in this way is to make this hope seem implausible from the outset. There is simply no reason to think that we can generate interesting moral conclusions from some combination of careful conceptual analysis and rigorous empirical investigation.

Now it may be objected that I have overstated the case. Assuming that we accept a basic moral principle, we can sometimes go fairly directly from an empirical claim to a moral conclusion. Consider:

(1) X is killing.
(2) Therefore, it is wrong to X.

It is generally noncontroversial whether X is killing, so identifying X as killing is often sufficient to establish that X is wrong. The attentive reader will, of course, quickly object that it is not always uncontroversial whether X is the *sort* of killing that it is *wrong* to commit. Is killing in self-defense included? Is killing in a (just) war? Is capital punishment? No analysis of the concept of killing along with even a complete account of the relevant facts will establish whether a nonstandard killing is the sort of act it is wrong to commit. That is a job—it *has* to be a job—for moral analysis.

So, too, for coercion. Perhaps there *can* be a nonmoral account of coercion. It might be possible to define coercion so that all proposals of a readily identifiable type would be classified as coercive. But it is a bit far-fetched to think that such a definition could tell us much about plea bargaining, contracts, experimentation with prisoners, capitalism, and the like. Interesting and difficult moral questions will always be answered by moral argument.

Constraints on Freedom

Assuming that I have adequately defended a moralized account of coercive proposals, the question remains whether the focus on coercion is, in itself, a fundamental mistake. It may be argued that the important task is to identify the conditions under which one's *freedom* is constrained and not to determine whether one is coerced.

The critic may, for example, concede that "A constraint is not 'coercive' unless it is brought to bear on an agent X *by another agent*."[35] But, it may be argued, not being coerced is not equivalent to being free, and the emphasis on coercion understates the way in which nonintentional or circumstantial forces can constitute deprivations of freedom.[36] On this view, we should be interested not just in coercion, but also in the following sorts of questions: Does capitalism ("free enterprise") really promote more freedom than socialism? Does libertarianism really maximize liberty?[37] Does inequality limit freedom? Or is it equality? Or advertising? Or socialization?

Now it may be thought that the answers to *these* sorts of questions must rest, to a large extent, on a satisfactory account of the concept of *freedom*. I disagree, for reasons that parallel my view of coercion. The point is not to show that a plausible freedom claim can be made or defended. The point is to determine its moral force. We can see this more clearly by briefly considering some of the debates that have arisen among writers on freedom.

Negative and Positive Freedom. Contemporary discussions of freedom often and properly start with Sir Isaiah Berlin's well-known distinction between "negative" and "positive" liberty.[38] Negative liberty, which has its roots in the Hobbesian individualist tradition, is the absence of *external* or *social* constraints.[39] Positive liberty, which has its roots in the Platonic, Rousseauian, and Hegelian traditions, is a form of "self-mastery." One is negatively free just in case no other person (intentionally) interferes with one's opportunities for action. One is positively free only if one's rational, true, or

[35] Peter Westen, " 'Freedom' and "Coercion'," 85 *Duke Law Journal* 541, 560 (1985).

[36] Nozick points out a more technical sense in which being coerced is neither a necessary nor a sufficient condition of unfreedom. If A is prepared to punish B if B does X, and (knowing this or not) B does X, then B was unfree to do X, although he was not coerced. If A makes a bluffing but apparently credible threat to punish B should B do X, and B does not do X, then B is coerced into not doing X, although he is free to do X. See "Coercion," in *Philosophy, Science and Method*, ed. Sidney Morgenbesser et al. (New York: St. Martin's, 1969), 440.

[37] Some critics have argued against libertarianism by claiming that it is false on its own terms. It is not. Most versions of libertarianism are better understood not in terms of the *maximization* of liberty, but as *negative rights* theories, or what Nozick calls "side constraint" theories. Such theories posit certain rights that cannot be violated even if violating them would promote more liberty or rights (assuming there could be a metric of liberty and rights). If so, libertarianism cannot be condemned, on its *own terms*, for failing to maximize liberty, for it does not or need not claim to do so.

[38] See *Two Concepts of Liberty*, reprinted with some answers to his critics in *Four Essays on Liberty* (Oxford: Oxford University Press, 1969).

[39] Hobbes says this: "Liberty, or freedom, signifieth, properly, the absence of . . . external impediment of motion . . ." *Leviathan*, chap. 21.

autonomous self is in control and perhaps only if one also has the requisite resources and abilities to fulfill one's plans or desires.[40]

The political uses of this distinction go both ways. Berlin champions negative freedom because he fears regimes will justify repression in the name of positive freedom—"forcing people to be free." Others argue that negative freedom represents a seriously impoverished ideal. Wheeling out some heavy rhetorical artillery, one author has recently juxtaposed the "broader and richer" Marxist notion of (positive) freedom with the "bourgeois . . . political, individual, and negative notion."[41] And who could want *that*?

Fortunately, the disputes among contending notions of freedom can be recast and (somewhat) defused. As Gerald MacCallum has argued, political or social freedom can be understood in terms of a "triadic relation" in which B (an agent) is (or is not) constrained by A (some obstacle) with respect to X (some action).[42] On this view, the dispute over contending concepts of freedom can be reformulated into this question: what should *count* as a constraint? There are several ways to categorize the possible constraints. One typology looks like this:[43]

	PSYCHOLOGICAL	EXTERNAL
NATURAL	(a)	(b)
INTENTIONAL	(c)	(d)
UNINTENTIONAL	(e)	(f)

Posing the issue this way places only minimal limits on what *might* count as a constraint on freedom. In principle, (a)–(f) could all qual-

[40] There are many different accounts of what negative and positive liberty entail. Some accounts of negative liberty focus on interference with actions, although I think Berlin is right to focus on *opportunities* for action. One's negative freedom is restricted if an opportunity is foreclosed, even if one has no desire to exercise that opportunity. Some accounts of positive liberty focus on one's *psychological* capacities, whereas others include economic and social resources. See, for example, Charles Taylor, "What's Wrong with Negative Liberty?" in *The Idea of Freedom*, ed. Alan Ryan.

[41] George Brenkert, *Marx's Ethics of Freedom* (London: Routledge and Kegan Paul, 1983), 87.

[42] See "Negative and Positive Freedom," 76 *Philosophical Review* 321 (1967). I discuss some of these issues in "Social Theory and the Assessment of Social Freedom," 7 *Polity* 334 (1975). I leave aside the question whether statements about metaphysical freedom can be recast in this way.

[43] Joel Feinberg distinguishes four categories of constraints: internal positive constraints, such as headaches and obsessions; internal negative constraints, such as ignorance and weakness; external positive constraints, such as barred windows; and external negative constraints, such as poverty. See *Social Philosophy* (Englewood Cliffs, N.J.: Prentice-Hall, 1973), 13. My categorization is closer to that advanced by Jon Elster in *Sour Grapes* (New York: Cambridge University Press, 1983), 126.

ify. Given the range of possible constraints, the advocate of positive freedom has nothing to fear from this view. He can assert what the defender of negative freedom would deny, for example, that (e) and (f) should count as constraints on freedom.

There is, nonetheless, at least one essential limit on the sorts of factors that can count as constraints on freedom: the structure of freedom discourse always presupposes *some* distinction between the *agent* who is constrained and the *constraint* itself. There is a radical sense in which constraints are always *conceptually* external, even if they operate within the person. We can, for example, speak of addiction as an internal or psychological *constraint*, but only because we can posit a purified conception of the agent that is distinguishable from the "empirical" conception that includes the addiction.[44] We can think of a person as constrained by his compulsion because, but only because, we can also imagine him without it. We can push such purified conceptions of the self pretty far. But there are limits. And the primary limit is that there must be some plausible independent conception of the person whose freedom from constraint is at issue.[45] Those who argue, for example, that socialization limits freedom would do well to remember that not *everything* about a person or his condition can be said to limit his freedom without devouring the self who is capable of being constrained and whose freedom is to be valued.

Freedom and Ability. Questions as to what can count as a constraint frequently surface in attempts to distinguish *freedom* from *ability*. Jon Elster suggests that we distinguish between B's "formal freedom" and B's "real ability" to do X.[46] B has the formal freedom to do X unless obstacles have been deliberately created for the purpose of preventing B from doing X. B has the real ability to do X just in case B will do X if B desires to do X.

Should inabilities count as constraints on freedom? There are two possibilities. If we think of a person as including whatever abilities and resources he happens to have, his inabilities do not limit his freedom, particularly if there is no external impediment to his acquiring those abilities. On this view, B may be *unable* to play backgammon or travel to Europe but be *free* to do both things. It is, on

---

[44] Brenkert says that the "bourgeois" or "negative" notion of freedom must deny that such constraints are genuine. That is false. See *Marx's Ethics of Freedom*, 221.

[45] "To be," wrote Santayana, "is to be something in particular." Cited in Joel Feinberg, *Social Philosophy*, 9. Original reference not given.

[46] *Sour Grapes*, 126.

the other hand, certainly possible to think of these inabilities as constraints, in which case they do interfere with B's freedom.[47]

Does it matter which view we choose? Rhetorically, perhaps; philosophically, no. If we distinguish freedom from ability, we will need to determine whether we have moral reason to be concerned about B's inabilities just as we care about his freedom. On the other hand, even if we think of inability as a form of unfreedom, we will need to determine whether the moral force of unfreedom qua inability is equivalent to, let us say, the moral force of unfreedom qua deliberate constraint (or coercion). The same moral questions arise, or at least can arise, on both conceptual views.

Unintentional Constraints. The same point can be made about the unintended effects of social acts. I might be prevented from proceeding through an intersection by a policeman, or another driver might intentionally or negligently block my way. These seem to be constraints on my freedom. On the other hand, a steady stream of traffic could have an identical effect on my action. Simply by engaging in their normal activity, other drivers might sharply curtail what I can do.[48]

Do such circumstances coerce or limit freedom? David Miller suggests this: (1) only intentional acts coerce; (2) unintentional but negligent acts do not coerce, but they do limit freedom; (3) unintentional and nonnegligent acts do not coerce or limit freedom.[49] To illustrate: A coerces B into not moving his car if he proposes to punish B should B move it; A does not coerce B but does limit B's freedom of movement if A unintentionally but negligently blocks B's way, for example, by leaving his car in B's driveway; A neither coerces B nor limits B's freedom if A blocks B's movement by waiting to move safely into a stream of traffic.

Is this view correct? On the one hand, whatever we want to *say* about these cases, there seems to be something to the distinction Miller advances. On the other hand, whether we want to say that unintentional and nonnegligent acts reduce one's *freedom* is largely a matter of linguistic preference and has no obvious moral significance. If, for example, we choose not to describe unintentional and nonnegligent constraints as limitations on freedom, we will still need to know what to make of such cases. Can such constraints af-

[47] This view is defended by Larry Preston in "Freedom, Markets, and Voluntary Exchange," 78 *American Political Science Review* 959 (1984).

[48] See Mark Fowler, "Coercion and Practical Reason," 8 *Social Theory and Practice* 329, 334 (1982).

[49] "Constraints on Freedom."

fect one's responsibilities? Can one justifiably complain about such constraints? And so on. No linguistic view about the proper referents of freedom can answer these questions.

Natural Constraints. Writers on freedom generally maintain that nature does not limit freedom.[50] On this view, the fact that I cannot jump twenty feet in the air or fly is not a constraint on my *freedom*, nor is my inability to become pregnant. This view does not, of course, deny that nature inhibits or prevents certain *actions* or states of affairs, nor need it deny that natural forces can create choice situations which parallel those inflicted by deliberate threats. The question is what to make of such natural limitations or forcings. Some prefer to speak of constraints on "freedom" only in the context of restrictions caused by human beings; others prefer an account which includes the facts of nature. But the important question is not what we call these restrictions, but whether natural restrictions have any moral force. Can I, for example, legitimately *complain* about natural limitations, and, if so, what would follow from such complaints? Can I be relieved of responsibility for my acts because of natural obstacles or events? These are the important sorts of questions. And these are the questions that must be answered—on any view of the concept of freedom.

Coercion, Intentionality, and Freedom

Let us conclude this chapter by posing a question in general terms: are intentional constraints importantly different from nonintentional constraints? At first glance, there seems to be at least something psychologically special about deliberate and intentional constraints. Just as we have different *psychological* responses to murder and accidental death, we do, I think, feel differently when coerced by another person than when compelled by "circumstances."[51]

---

[50] A typical statement is Feinberg's: "I can lament . . . that I cannot give birth to a baby . . . but to characterize . . . natural limitations as restrictions on my freedom would be to base lament on a platitude." *Social Philosophy*, 8. Nozick says this: "Whether a person's actions are voluntary depends on what it is that limits his alternatives. If facts of nature do so, the actions are voluntary." *Anarchy, State, and Utopia*, 262.

[51] As Dennett suggests, "It is one thing to be born and live on Elba, and another to be put and kept on Elba by *someone*." *Elbow Room* (Cambridge: MIT Press, 1984), 8. Or, as Fried puts it, "it hurts more and in a different way to be consumed by the state than to be consumed by a tiger." "Is Liberty Possible?" in *Tanner Lectures on Human Values* (Salt Lake City: University of Utah Press, 1982), 96.

Even Marx sees fit to distinguish the "direct coercion" of slavery and feudalism from the "dull compulsion of economic relations."[52]

But psychology aside, is there, in a general way, anything philosophically *special* about coercion? We have seen, for example, that the law tends to make a sharp distinction between specific interpersonal threats and general economic pressures. And while this distinction may be less important than the partisans of capitalism seem to believe, it is also likely, as Richard Epstein observes, that great circumstantial pressure notwithstanding, even radical critics of capitalism would consider it "a meaningful choice to refuse employment altogether; no one would count it the loss of a meaningless choice if employers were given the right to conscript employees into service."[53] Or, as Elster suggests, it is, in itself, a "good thing not to be subject to another person's will . . ."[54] If Epstein and Elster are right, and I believe they are, the question is not whether there are *any* important differences between circumstantial pressure and specific threats, but what forms these differences take.

Consider what appear to be two contrasting answers to this question. Harry Frankfurt asks us to consider this problem (which I condense):

> *The Avalanche Case.* (1) B comes to a fork in the road. A threatens to start an avalanche which will kill B if B takes the left-hand fork. To "satisfy a commanding desire" to live, B goes to the right. (2) B comes to the same fork, and notices that natural conditions will cause a similar avalanche if he goes to the left. Because he is "moved irresistibly by his desire to live," B goes to the right.[55]

Although there are, says Frankfurt, "interesting differences" between the two cases, B is no more free or responsible in (2) than in (1). True, we are more *"resentful* when another person places obstacles in our way than when the environment does . . . ," but this is a matter of "pride" or "injustice," not liberty or moral responsibility—"a man's will may not be his own even when he is not moved by the will of another."[56]

Nozick, on the other hand, suggests that our different psycholog-

<hr />

[52] See Jon Elster, "Exploitation, Freedom, and Justice," 278.

[53] "A Common Law for Labor Relations: A Critique of the New Deal Labor Legislation," 92 *Yale Law Journal* 1357, 1372 (1983).

[54] *Sour Grapes*, 126.

[55] "Coercion and Moral Responsibility," in *Essays on Freedom of Action*, ed. Ted Honderich (London: Routledge and Kegan Paul, 1973), 83.

[56] Ibid. (emphasis added).

ical responses to natural and intentional constraints reflect something deeper.

> Writers on coercion have puzzled over why it is important whether another person intentionally directs your behavior in a certain direction. What is the difference, they wonder, between being kept inside a house by a lightning storm or by another person's playing with electricity outside your house, or by another person's threat to electrocute you if you leave the house . . . isn't one equally coerced in all three?[57]

Apparently contra Frankfurt, Nozick argues that one is not, in fact, equally coerced in all three versions of the Electricity Case, and that this is not just a matter of language. It is, on his view, a matter of voluntariness, a matter of freedom, a matter of will.

> In the lightning situation, *your* will keeps you indoors—no other's motives and intentions are as closely connected to your act . . . in the threat situation, it is *another* person's will that is operative. In the intermediate situation where another person acts but without intending to influence you . . . it is *your* intentions that are operating . . .[58]

How can we best understand the difference between Frankfurt and Nozick? It appears that Frankfurt adopts an *absolute* conception of freedom or voluntariness, one that turns on the psychological state of the agent regardless of its cause. Nozick, on the other hand, appears to adopt a *comparative* account, in which the question is which of several possible wills has the *greatest* connection with the agent's act.[59] It appears, for example, that Frankfurt would hold that there is *no* freedom-based distinction between the versions of Nozick's Electricity Case and that Nozick would hold that there *is* a freedom-based distinction between the two versions of the Avalanche Case.

Here, appearances are, in fact, deceiving. If I understand his view correctly, Frankfurt sees no freedom-based distinction between coercion and circumstantial compulsion in the avalanche cases because, in both cases, B is *psychologically overwhelmed* by his desire to live, he is moved "irresistibly." He is not responsible for his action

---

[57] *Philosophical Explanations* (Cambridge: Harvard University Press, 1981), 49.

[58] Ibid. (emphasis added).

[59] Nozick does not explicitly *defend* what he calls "the closest relative view" of coercion. He uses it to exemplify the "closest relative" theory of personal identity that he develops and defends in detail. The "closest relative view" of coercion is, however, compatible with what he says elsewhere.

because his will is truly overborne. If so, Frankfurt does not have to deny that there is a distinction between coercion and circumstantial pressures in cases of constrained volition. On the other hand, if, as I believe, Nozick understands all versions of the Electricity Case as involving constrained volition, he need not deny that B is not morally responsible if natural or unintentional social forces move B "irresistibly" to act, as in the Avalanche Case.

The question remains, then, whether natural or unintentional forces can undermine freedom or responsibility when B is *not* moved "irresistibly" to act, when B makes a deliberate and rational decision to avoid an unacceptable alternative. Interestingly, at least one of Frankfurt's observations—that there may not (always) be moral distinctions between the cases—still seems to apply. Suppose that B has an obligation to do X, where doing X requires that B leave his house. I assume that B can say, in *all three* versions of Nozick's case, that he was not free to leave, that he was forced to remain inside, and that he therefore should not be held responsible. With respect to *that* moral consequence, circumstantial compulsion seems *equivalent* to coercion.

At the same time, it does not follow that they will also have equivalent moral consequences in *other* contexts. Consider my extension of Nozick's story.

> A has developed an electricity shielding device and proposes to enable B to leave his house for a reasonable fee. B agrees to pay A.

If B is being kept inside by lightning, and agrees to pay A, he is bound to keep his agreement. On the other hand, if B is *threatened* by C with electrocution, B could, in principle, pass the costs along to C.[60] Here, the comparative view seems to work. Why does the comparative view of voluntariness seem to work in some cases but not others? This is, I think, an important question, and it is related to the connection between a moralized theory of coercion and voluntariness. I hope to make a start towards answering it in Chapter 16.

[60] This is similar to the case of Marshall who was hit by Ranne's boar. See p. 61.

FIFTEEN

FROM COERCIVE PROPOSALS
TO COERCION

I have argued that receiving a coercive proposal is a necessary condition of being coerced, and that the distinction between coercive
and noncoercive proposals is defined by B's moral baseline. I have
also suggested that receiving a coercive proposal is not a *sufficient*
condition of being coerced, that some coercive proposals do not
coerce in a way that nullifies B's responsibility for the normal moral
or legal effects of his act. In this chapter, I return to a theme that
emerged both in our discussion of the law and in our discussion of
the claim that a coercive situation is one in which B has "no choice"
or "no acceptable alternative" but to do what A demands. I shall argue that having "no *acceptable* alternative" but to succumb to a coercive proposal is, indeed, a necessary condition of being coerced, but
that it, too, is a moralized criterion. For the sense of having "no acceptable alternative" that is relevant here is not that B finds the
other alternatives unacceptable or that it would be irrational or unreasonable for B not to accept A's proposal, but that B has no obligation to accept the other alternatives, or, what is sometimes more
accurate, that B is entitled to yield to A's proposal and then be released from the normal moral and legal consequences of his act. Receiving a coercive proposal and having no acceptable alternative (in
this special sense) but to succumb to the proposal are each necessary and jointly sufficient to establish that A coerces B.[1]

We can set the problematic of this chapter within the framework
of the two-pronged theory of coercion we found in the law. The
two-pronged theory seemed to work like this. The choice prong
identifies B's *situation* as one in which B is (in some sense) actually
coerced, that is, as one in which B has no choice but to do what A
proposes. The proposal prong determines whether A's proposal is
sufficiently wrong to nullify what would otherwise be the legal con-

---

[1] This assumes, of course, that B *does* X and does it in response to and because of
A's proposal.

sequences of B's act. If my argument is on the right track, this order should be reversed. We do not begin with coercive choice situations and then determine which constitute legally recognizable coercion. On my analysis, proposals which are not wrong under the proposal prong are best understood as offers and therefore do not create coercive situations in the first place.

But regardless of where we begin, it is still the case that only coercive proposals which meet the choice prong actually coerce. I do not think, however, that the law gets the function of the choice prong quite right. In my view, the task of the choice prong is roughly this. Given A's credible coercive proposal, B is sometimes entitled to do what A demands and then be released from the normal legal consequences of his act. At other times, B should either stand his ground, or, if he chooses to yield, he should at least not expect to recover later on.[2] The choice prong attempts to capture the moral distinction between these cases.

There are two ways in which the moral force of the choice prong can be expressed. On one view, A coerces B into doing X if and only if (1) A makes a successful coercive proposal to B and (2) B is entitled to succumb to A's proposal and then be released from the consequences of his act (for purposes of brevity, I shall generally omit the clause "and then be released . . ."). On a second view, we can say A coerces B into doing X just in case A makes a successful coercive proposal to B, and then add that B should or should not be held to the consequences of succumbing to A's proposal. Suppose, in some case, that B should *not* yield to A's proposal. On the first view, we would say that A's coercive proposal does *not* coerce B to do X. On the second view, we must say that B is coerced to do X but is responsible for the consequences of his act nonetheless.

Which way of expressing the point is preferable? On moral grounds, it does not seem to matter. For we could say that B is not coerced (because he should have resisted) and is therefore responsible or that he is coerced but still responsible (because he should

[2] Gerald Dworkin puts the point this way: "It doesn't always follow from the fact that someone did something under compulsion that he was compelled to do it." "Compulsion and Moral Concepts," 78 *Ethics* 227, 229 (1968). We might say that B acts under compulsion, says Dworkin, to recognize the nature of the reasons (i.e., A's threat) for which B acts, but we might simultaneously deny that B is compelled in order to express the view that these reasons are not sufficient to excuse B's conduct. Joseph Raz writes that to be coerced, B's action must be "either justified or excused" and that B's action is justified "if the reasons for it, including the threat of harm if it is not undertaken outweigh the reasons against it . . ." "Liberalism, Autonomy, and the Politics of Neutral Concern," in *Midwest Studies in Philosophy*, vol. VII, ed. Peter French et al. (Minneapolis: University of Minnesota Press, 1982), 110.

have resisted). Both expressions would have—or could have—the same moral force. David Zimmerman chooses the second approach, because he sees that the first approach would preclude a nonmoral account of coercion.[3] I believe that the first approach is distinctly preferable, in part because it is more consistent with both linguistic intuitions and the law, and more importantly, because it preserves the traditional link between coercion claims and ascriptions of responsibility. But whichever linguistic approach we adopt, the point is to understand how the choice prong works and what it can add to our general understanding of coercion.

Coercion, Excuse, and Justification

Here, once again, we can learn from the law. H.L.A. Hart argues that there is an important parallel between "invalidating conditions" in the civil law, such as fraud and mistake, and "excusing conditions" in the criminal law, such as insanity. On Hart's view, both sets of invalidating conditions serve to "render effective the individual's preferences"; they enhance one's ability to shape and plan one's life without fear of legal consequences for actions that are beyond one's control.[4] The parallel between the civil and the criminal law is, I think, quite helpful. Understanding the way the choice prong operates in each body of law can deepen our understanding of coercion in the other. At the same time, the parallel is potentially misleading, if, contrary to Hart's intentions, it leads us to think of coercion and duress as having the same *type* of moral force as mistake, accident, and insanity. For I want to argue that whereas the latter sort of invalidating conditions typically *excuse* B's action, the force of coercion and duress is to *justify* it.

Agent Responsibility and Act Responsibility. To see that coercion is best understood as a justification, let us begin with a brief discussion of the distinction between these two questions: (1) Is B an agent who can be held morally responsible for his actions? (2) Should B be held responsible for the normal moral or legal effects of his act? An analogy will help to sharpen the distinction. To be a morally responsible agent is much like having a bank account which can be both debited and credited.[5] Whereas competent adults can have their

---

[3] "Coercive Wage Offers," 10 *Philosophy & Public Affairs* 121, 131 (1981).

[4] *Punishment and Responsibility* (Oxford: Oxford University Press, 1968), 34. Hart draws the parallel in order to defend an account of excusing conditions in the criminal law which is neither utilitarian nor retributive.

[5] I borrow this analogy from Hyman Gross. See *A Theory of Criminal Justice* (New York: Oxford University Press, 1979), 141.

own bank accounts, infants and the severely retarded cannot. And one cannot debit a nonexistent bank account. Similarly, whereas competent adults can have their moral accounts debited and credited, infants and the severely retarded cannot. Unlike competent adults, infants and the severely retarded are not *eligible* for (at least some) ascriptions of moral responsibility.

We can press the analogy a bit further. Just as a particular debit against one's bank account can be wrongly made, a morally responsible agent may claim that he should not be held accountable for the normal moral effects of a particular act. He is *eligible* for blame, but (for certain reasons) he claims that he should not be blamed. When B is *eligible* for blame, I shall say that he is *agent responsible*. When B is agent responsible but should not be held accountable for the normal moral or legal effects of a particular act, I shall say that B is not *act responsible*.

I have argued that coercion *can*, on occasion, so overwhelm B's will that B temporarily loses moral agency, although even this is more complicated than it first appears.[6] Yet despite the frequency with which the law refers to "overborne wills" (or analogues to that phrase), a coercion claim rarely attempts to deny B's moral agency. Consider the restaurant cashier who hands over the money in his till in response to the threat of a gang of armed robbers. We do not blame him for what he does, of course, but not because he lacks moral agency. We do not blame him for what he does because, under the circumstances, he does nothing that is blameworthy.[7] He is agent responsible, but not act responsible.

[6] As our response to drunken drivers suggests, we may properly treat B as a moral agent at Time-2 if his loss of agency at Time-2 is traceable to his agency at Time-1. See Herbert Fingarette and Ann Fingarette Hasse, *Mental Disabilities and Criminal Responsibility* (Berkeley: University of California Press, 1979), 7. Although it presents a more difficult case, we might say something similar about someone who cannot resist a coercive proposal, perhaps because he has failed to shape his character in the right way. Robert M. Adams argues that we can also be responsible for mental states which are not rooted in our voluntary actions. See "Involuntary Sins," 94 *Philosophical Review* 3 (1985).

[7] See Harry Frankfurt, "Three Concepts of Free Action," *Proceedings of the Aristotelian Society*, Supplementary Volume 49 (1975), 123–24. Indeed, we might blame him if he did *not* give up the money and foolishly endangered his life or the lives of others. Precisely because the robbers' threat does not nullify the cashier's moral agency, Frankfurt would deny that the cashier was actually coerced into turning over the money. He maintains that coercion requires more than that A's threat absolves B from blame. It requires that B "is not morally responsible for his submissive action." "Coercion and Moral Responsibility," in *Essays on Freedom of Action*, ed. Ted Honderich (London: Routledge and Kegan Paul, 1973), 77. Frankfurt does not deny that "coercion" has uses which do not entail that B is not agent responsible for his sub-

Duress as Justification in the Law. In Chapter 8, I argued that coercion as a defense in the criminal law is better understood as a justification than as an excuse. What of the civil law? Let us briefly consider a few cases. Recall, for example, the case in which Austin threatened to stop shipments of parts under an existing contract with Loral unless Loral agreed to price increases (and other conditions).[8] When Loral refused and Austin stopped shipment, Loral had essentially two choices: (a) to stand pat, bear the costs, and then attempt to recover for breach of contract; or (b) to agree to the modifications, and then sue. The court held that Loral had had "no choice" but to choose (b). But what did it mean? Surely not that Austin's threat had nullified Loral's moral agency. Surely not that Loral had acted wrongly but excusably. Clearly, the court's view was that given Austin's threat, Loral had had the *right* to prefer (b) to (a), that it had been entitled to succumb first and recover later.

By way of contrast, recall *Meier* v. *Nightingale.*[9] Meier agreed to pay Nightingale for work on his car. Nightingale demanded more than Meier believed they had agreed to, and told Meier that he would not return the car unless he received the additional sum. Meier paid the additional amount, then sued to recover the excess paid on grounds of duress. Given Nightingale's demand, Meier had two choices: (a) to refuse to pay and sue to recover his car; or (b) to pay and recover his car, and then sue to recover the excess paid. Here the court ruled (correctly or incorrectly) that given these alternatives, Meier had *not* been entitled to prefer (b) to (a), and hence there had been no duress.

Or consider *Tidwell* v. *Critz.*[10] Dr. Critz entered into an employment agreement with Dr. Tidwell. When Critz subsequently threatened to break the agreement unless Tidwell agreed to new conditions, the court held that Tidwell had not signed the new agreement under duress. In effect, the court held that as a licensed physician, Tidwell had had these opportunities: (a) to refuse to pay and sue to restore the original agreement; (b) to seek other employment; or (c) to agree to the new conditions, and then sue. The court's view was that because (a) and (b) had been viable options, Tidwell had not been entitled to be released from the agreement—under these con-

---

missive action. He is interested in explaining the conditions under which coercion nullifies agent responsibility, not in explaining the use of a word.

[8] See p. 27.

[9] 46 A.2d 785 (1946).

[10] 282 S.E.2d 104 (1981).

ditions "the threat of losing a job or fear of such loss is not duress which will void a contract."[11]

It is not necessary to retell the story of Part One in more detail. For the general point is, I think, quite clear. In the relatively few civil cases which turn on the application of the choice prong, courts do not argue that B was wrong to succumb to A's coercive proposal but should—for some reason—be excused nonetheless. Rather, the law virtually always seems to say, in effect, that B's agreement should be invalidated only if, given the alternatives, B was justified in succumbing first and then recovering.

Now there is at least one difference between the way coercion serves as a justification in the civil law and the way it does so in the criminal law. In the criminal law, one uses the defense of necessity to advance an agent-neutral justification for what would otherwise be a criminal act, whereas duress can be advanced as an agent-relative justification.[12] The civil law has no analogue to the defense of necessity, and there duress is typically an agent-neutral justification instead.[13] But this qualification aside, if coercion is best understood as a justification in the civil law, and if, as I have argued in Chapter 8, there are independent reasons for thinking that duress is best understood as a justification in the criminal law, it seems reasonable to suppose that coercion in the law is, at the broadest level, best understood as a justification. And if this is so in the law, it is likely to be so in morality as well.

The Choice Prong as Moralized

The foregoing suggests that we need *two* moral theories. We need one moral theory to establish whether A's proposal is coercive. We need a second moral theory to determine when B is entitled to succumb to A's coercive proposal, or as P. S. Atiyah puts it, "when it is permissible for a victim of duress to reopen a question which has apparently been closed by his submission to the coercion."[14] Seeing the choice prong as a moralized criterion makes matters both simpler and more complex. It makes matters simpler because it allows us to recast and defuse some of the controversy over the proper

[11] Ibid., 107.

[12] See pp. 165–69.

[13] It is not clear whether the structure of the civil law allows for agent-relative justification. If B has agent-relative but not agent-neutral justification for doing X, it is not clear why A, as opposed to B, should absorb the burden of B's doing X.

[14] "Economic Duress and the 'Overborne Will'," 98 *Law Quarterly Review* 197, 202 (1982).

interpretation and application of the choice prong. It makes matters more complex because it vanquishes the hope that at least one important component of the assessment of coercion would depend on (reasonably) straightforward empirical criteria, and because the moral theory that accounts for B's right to succumb to A's coercive proposal is itself likely to be reasonably involved.

First consider some ways in which things are made simpler. We might wonder, for example, whether A can coerce B to do X if A's threat is not *credible*. We could settle this by linguistic analysis, but I suspect that the linguistic intuition reflects the moral view that if A's threat is not credible, then B is not entitled to act as if it were. Or consider Zimmerman's suggestion that A does not coerce B to do X unless A proposes to make B *"considerably* worse off"* if he does not do X than he would be in his baseline situation.[15] While there is nothing wrong with Zimmerman's stipulation, he provides no motivation for it. On my account, B is not coerced because B may not be entitled to succumb to A's coercive proposal if he would be only marginally worse off if he stood firm.

A moralized account of the choice prong also clarifies (although it does not resolve) the debate between "subjective" or "individualized" and "objective" or "standardized" tests for coercion.[16] It is, for example, often argued that coercion is a matter of degree. That may be true, but it is also of little help—until we know *what* it is a degree of. Some seem to view the problem of choosing between an individualized and a standardized test for duress as akin to a choice between two thermometers, where we know what we want to measure and the only question is just which instrument is more accurate. But here the question is not which test is more accurate, but what we are measuring. And if I am right, we are measuring not the amount of pressure which A's proposal imposes on B, but whether B is entitled to succumb to A's proposal. From this perspective, it is, I think, an open question whether a standardized or an individualized test provides the better answer. We may want to hold B to the standards of the average man, or the courageous man, or the man of "reasonable firmness," or we may want to try to determine what it is reasonable to expect of B—given his individual circumstances and characteristics.

It is not clear which approach is preferable. On the one hand, there may be good reasons not to press individualization too far, in

---

[15] "Coercive Wage Offers," 124 (my emphasis).
[16] See Chapter 8.

part because epistemological difficulties may make it difficult to customize our expectations too exactly without creating more moral errors than we avoid. On the other hand, there is no obvious and principled reason to think that a common standard is morally superior to an individualized one. B's characteristics or circumstances might enter the equation in two ways. First, if A makes a coercive proposal to a B whom he knows is especially susceptible to such proposals, A's proposal is arguably more wrong than it otherwise would be, and therefore may give B more reason to succumb.[17] Second, we can reasonably expect more of some people than of others. A parent may be entitled to risk endangering others in order to save his child, whereas others would lack such an agent-relative reason to do so. Moreover, the burdens that a person should be expected to bear might appropriately vary with age, intelligence, and experience. Just as rescuing a drowning person may be supererogatory for most, but obligatory for a lifeguard, for some resistance is obligatory, whereas for others it is supererogatory.

Two- and Three-Party Cases

In this section I want to probe, a bit more deeply, the way in which the choice prong functions in the civil and criminal law, or, as we might put it, in two- and three-party cases.

I observed in Part One that the proposal prong does most of the work in the civil law. If A proposes to move B below his moral baseline, there is the further question whether B is entitled to succumb to A's proposal and then undo his agreement—but that part of the story is relatively unproblematic. When, as in the case of agreements (or rights waivers), A proposes to violate B's rights unless B benefits A, it is generally quite easy to justify releasing B from the normal consequences of his act. For if B is released, the burden is typically shifted back to A, who has, *ex hypothesi*, acted wrongfully.[18]

In cases of criminal duress, on the other hand, we take for granted that A is not entitled to make his proposal. There the question is whether B is entitled to succumb or has an obligation to re-

[17] When, for example, a company got a woman to sign a mortgage by threatening to prosecute her psychotic son for embezzlement, the court ruled that the agreement was invalid because, in appealing "to natural affection," the company had attacked "the weakest point of human nature." *McCormick Harvesting Co.* v. *Hamilton*, 41 N.W. 727 (1889).

[18] The shifting of the burden in the civil law is analogous to a morally nonproblematic case of self-defense in the criminal law.

sist. In contrast to the civil law, where the proposal prong figures prominently, here the choice prong does most of the work. When, as in the case of crimes, A proposes to violate B's rights unless B harms C, it is comparatively difficult, although not impossible, to justify not holding B responsible for his act. For if B is not held responsible for harming C, the burden of A's proposal is shifted back not to (wrongdoer) A, but to an innocent C.

The distinction between two- and three-party cases helps us to understand situations which can be viewed from *both* perspectives. Recall Harry Frankfurt's observation that the courts may reject, on grounds of coercion, a prisoner's confession which the police obtained by threats, whereas the prisoner's accomplices are less likely to agree that he was coerced.[19] In both cases, the proposal prong is met. There is a coercive proposal. The difference between the cases is this. Viewed as a two-party case between the prisoner and the police, the prisoner is under little *moral* obligation to resist the proposal not to beat him if he confesses.[20] In effect, we can understand the confession as a case of justifiable self-defense against the police. Viewed as a three-party case between the police, the prisoner, and the prisoner's accomplices, the prisoner's situation is (ironically) comparable to situations of criminal duress. If there is morality among thieves, the prisoner's obligations to his accomplices give him somewhat stronger reason to resist.

Two-Party Cases. Let us consider each situation in a bit more detail. Consider first the two-party case. When we say that B is entitled to succumb and then recover because his alternatives are unacceptable, it is important to see that this unacceptability is *not* equivalent to deprivation or desperation. Suppose that an already affluent B is due to inherit $1 million from C. A, the lawyer for C's estate, threatens to tie up the estate in court for years unless B agrees to pay him exorbitantly high legal fees. Should B agree to pay the high legal fees rather than fight it out in court, he remains in his comfortable *status quo ante*. Nonetheless, it is arguable that B's agreement is coerced. Given a choice between (1) paying A now and attempting to recover the excess fees later and (2) refusing to pay A, foregoing the use of his inheritance, and fighting it out in court, B may be entitled to choose (1) over (2).

Yet it would be wrong to assume that B is *always* entitled to succumb to A's coercive proposal and then seek redress later on—

[19] "Coercion and Moral Responsibility," p. 65. See p. 181.
[20] He may have nonmoral self-interested reason to resist.

given the alternatives that might be available to him. The basic idea is this. The legal system is established to settle conflicts. Its availability and adequacy to that task affects our rights and responsibilities if we choose to settle such differences on our own. This is obvious with respect to crimes, where the presence of a reasonably effective criminal justice system makes it wrong to "take the law into one's own hands." And while it is certainly not wrong to settle a civil dispute out of court, the presence of a legal mechanism by which to successfully resolve a dispute weakens one's right to subsequently complain about the result if one chooses not to use it in the first place.

There are several reasons for this. Recall, in this connection, Blackstone's assertion that a fear of battery is no duress, nor are threats to one's property, for in those cases "a man may have satisfaction by recovering equivalent damages: but no suitable atonement can be made for the loss of life or limb."[21] Its specifics aside, the general point is that when B can receive adequate compensation if he does not succumb to A's coercive proposal, the legal system has provided an alternative which it may reasonably expect B to use. As the Supreme Court held in one of its rare discussions of contractual duress, "Before the coercive effect of the threatened action can be inferred, there must be evidence of some probable consequences of it to person or property for which the remedy afforded by the courts is inadequate."[22] Of course compensation is not always possible, and even when it is possible, B may have a reasonable belief that it may not be forthcoming. Recall *Miller* v. *Eisele*, which involved the stock market crash of 1929.[23] When the plaintiff decided to settle first and sue later, the court held that he had done so under duress, that Miller should not have been required to "rely on his questionable remedy against the brokers."[24]

Let us assume, for the sake of argument, that A would be required to compensate B if B refused to succumb to A's proposal. Why must B avail himself of that legal option? Given that A proposes to violate B's rights, why cannot B have a choice between (1) yielding first and then seeking to undo the agreement and (2) refusing to succumb and then suing for compensation? Why *can't* B have it both ways? The answer is, I think, that sometimes he can and

[21] *Commentaries*, bk. I, chap. 1.
[22] *Hartsville Oil Mill* v. *U.S.*, 271 U.S. 44 (1925).
[23] 168 A. 426 (1933). See p. 36.
[24] Ibid., 432.

sometimes he can't. It depends on whether there are good reasons for thinking that B should refuse to succumb and sue instead.

One set of reasons concerns *dispute resolution* and *compromise*. Although A's proposal is coercive only if A proposes to move B below his moral baseline, A and B may genuinely and conscientiously disagree about B's moral baseline. Recall *Meier* v. *Nightingale*.[25] Suppose that Nightingale was not entitled to keep Meier's car until paid what he demanded, but that Nightingale reasonably thought differently—that he was not about to release the car until paid and was prepared to be sued. Given this, is it undesirable for Meier to be able to make a binding agreement to pay Nightingale? Arguably not (though this is a complicated matter). Meier does not know, in advance, just how the situation is going to turn out. If Meier views the situation prospectively, he may well prefer being able to make a *binding* agreement that he is not otherwise obligated to make, for if Nightingale knows that Meier can invalidate the agreement and recover his money if it turns out that Meier is right, Nightingale may refuse to release the car in the first place.

Put in slightly different terms, compromise is often to be valued, and a response to what would (if adjudicated) turn out to have been a coercive proposal may also represent a genuine compromise between parties who have good-faith *ex ante* disagreements. As the court held in *King* v. *Lewis*: "In order for an agreement to be valid, it is not essential that the matter should be really in doubt; but it is sufficient if the parties consider it so far doubtful as to make it the subject of compromise. Such an agreement is valid and binding, not because it is a settlement of a valid claim, but because it is a settlement of a bona fide controversy."[26] When a bona fide controversy occurs, it is not obviously wrong for one to be bound by an agreement that gives one less than one would have been entitled to receive. Parties cannot undertake a genuine compromise if it is relatively easy to attack it, *ex post facto*.[27]

There is another, and related, reason why B might not be entitled to recover if he chooses not to resist A's coercive proposal. When a parent says to quarreling siblings, "I don't care who started it, I want the fighting stopped," he may be claiming, in effect, that tol-

---

[25] See p. 26.

[26] 4 S.E.2d 464, 468 (1939). See p. 38.

[27] For a general discussion of compromise, see Arthur Kuflik, "Morality and Compromise," in *Nomos XXI: Compromise in Ethics, Law and Politics*, ed. J. Roland Pennock and John Chapman (New York: New York University Press, 1979). Also see George Sher, "Subsidized Abortion: Moral Rights and Moral Compromise," 10 *Philosophy & Public Affairs* 361 (1981).

erating an unjust result is preferable to settling the matter, because it is not worth his while to achieve a just settlement. In a similar vein, the law is also concerned to minimize *transaction* costs, a point which is reflected in the maxim *de minimis non curat lex*.[28] Because resolution of disputes in court is costly both to the parties and to society, it is often more desirable for a party to get less (or more) than he deserves than for the case to be litigated—even if litigation would yield a just result.[29] For that reason, the law builds a certain robustness into its processes. It takes the view that some injustices—including agreements made in response to coercive proposals—can and should be tolerated.

There is still another reason for thinking that B should not always be able to recover if he chooses to yield to A's proposal when he could have pressed the matter in court—one which appeals to the old saw that "two wrongs don't make a right." We must be careful here. The claim that two wrongs don't make a right often begs the question of whether the response to the original wrong is, in fact, wrong—given the wrongness of the act to which it is a response.[30] The question is, after all, precisely whether it is wrong for B to seek to undo an agreement made in response to A's coercive proposal. And the answer is, I think, that it might be. For morality is *dynamic*. Just as A's wrongful proposal changes the moral setting in which B's response is evaluated, B's response to A's wrongful proposal can change the moral setting once again. If B succumbs to A's proposal and then seeks to be released from the agreement, B is asking us to ignore that he acted with the deliberate intent that A should rely on his agreement.[31] Sometimes, A's proposal is sufficiently wrong to justify such a response—particularly when B's alternatives are quite limited. But this is not always so. And when it is not so, it is arguable that B should be held to the terms of his agreement with A—despite the coerciveness of A's original proposal.

Three-Party Cases. Despite the strength and ubiquity of the belief that B should offer considerable resistance to A's proposal in the three-party case, its theoretical rationale is not obvious. Suppose that A throws (a nonswimming) B into a pool and that C is in a position to help. To say, as we might, that C has an obligation to save

[28] "The law does not deal in trifles."

[29] In economic terms, a decision to allow a conflict to be settled on arguably unjust terms may be Pareto-superior.

[30] An advocate of capital punishment does not deny that two wrongs don't make a right. He argues (correctly or not) that unlike the killing of an innocent person, killing a guilty person is not wrong.

[31] See p. 35.

278

B, is also to imply that it is not always wrong to shift the burden of A's wrong against B to an innocent C. And if it is not wrong to shift the burden of A's wrong against B to an innocent C, it is not obvious that when A threatens to harm B unless B harms C, it is wrong for B to shift the *harm* to C. We must determine when and why this might be.

To simplify matters, let us assume that B and C are of equal moral innocence and that the harms to B and C are equivalent, as when A threatens to kill B unless B kills (just one) C. For if the harm that A would impose on B is *less* than the harm that B would inflict on C (or several Cs), then, at least on agent-neutral grounds, it is best that B resist. Given the assumption of equality, however, it could be argued that it would be just as bad for B to be harmed by A as it would for C to be harmed by B, and therefore B should not be punished for harming C.

Now one might say, right off, that the two situations would not be equally bad. For when A harms B, one wrong event has occurred, but when A gets B to harm C, two wrong events have occurred: (1) A's coercive proposal to B; and (2) B's harming C.[32] Or we might say that from B's perspective as a moral agent, it is wrong for him to harm C, even though it is also wrong for A to harm B. I think that one or both of these positions, or something close to them, is ultimately correct. As stated, however, they beg the question. For the issue is precisely whether, under these conditions, it *is* wrong for B to harm C.

Why might it be wrong? The answer might turn on compensation. I have noted that if B refuses to yield in the two-party case and A carries out his threat, it is often possible to require A to compensate B, so that B is no worse off, all told. On the other hand, if A coerces B into harming C, it is unlikely that C will ever be adequately compensated. Criminal harms are often less compensable than civil harms.[33] And even if A can, in principle, be identified and sued, A may not have the resources to pay adequate compensation. If, then, it is especially bad for an uncompensated wrong to occur,

[32] For an interesting analysis of the way "agency" can be accommodated in evaluations of states of affairs, see Amartya Sen, "Well-Being, Agency and Freedom," 82 *Journal of Philosophy* 169 (1985).

[33] For a discussion of the distinction between criminal harm and civil harm, see Nozick, *Anarchy, State, and Utopia* (New York: Basic Books, 1974), 65ff. It is an interesting question whether A or A and B would be required to compensate C. I assume it is A, but if B acts wrongly in not resisting A's coercion, then perhaps he, too, must compensate C.

it also becomes particularly important to *deter* such wrongs at the outset rather than let them occur and try to remedy things later.

There is, however, an obvious problem with this explanation of B's obligation not to succumb, namely, that if B does not inflict an uncompensated harm on C, then A will inflict an uncompensated harm on B. And the uncompensated harm to B is, *ex hypothesi*, no less wrong than the uncompensated harm to C. And so it appears that we are back at the beginning. But not quite. For a practice that holds B accountable for harming C may deter such harms more effectively than a practice that allows B to regard himself as a conduit for A's wrong against C. A's primary goal is to harm C. If B refuses to harm C for A, A may have nothing to gain by harming B. If, on the other hand, B succumbs to A's proposal, it is certain that C will be harmed. In addition, detection and evidentiary factors may make it more difficult to hold A accountable than B. If B were permitted to exonerate himself by claiming coercion, it might be all too easy for A to harm C indirectly and get away with it.

Now I think it entirely possible that the interpretation of the choice prong in cases of criminal duress reflects—at some level—precisely this preference for lowering the aggregate probability of harm. Nonetheless, I am inclined to think that the strength of B's obligation to resist A's threat cannot be explained solely through these sorts of consequentialist considerations. Although deterrence is not unimportant, it seems that B should resist A's threat because, if he does not, it is *he* who will be harming C. B's obligation to resist A's proposal is at least partially rooted in considerations of moral agency.

The force of this point can be brought out by reflecting on Bernard Williams's oft-cited example in which Pedro tells Jim that he (Pedro) will kill twenty innocent persons unless Jim is willing to kill one of them.[34] On straightforward consequentialist grounds, Jim has no problem at all. Indeed, as Amartya Sen points out, even on a more sophisticated consequentialist approach, one which takes Jim's moral agency into account, Jim's decision is still clear. Barring some absolute deontological prohibition on killing, Jim should accept Pedro's offer.[35] Yet, as Sen also notes, Williams's example still packs

[34] See "A Critique of Utilitarianism," in J.J.C. Smart and B. Williams, *Utilitarianism: For and Against* (New York: Cambridge University Press, 1973).

[35] "Jim would have to attach an extraordinary degree of importance to the position of not being a killer himself to come to the conclusion that the value difference between one person being killed by Jim rather than by someone else is enough to outweigh the gain of nineteen people being saved from sure death." "Well-Being, Agency and Freedom," 215.

moral punch. And the moral punch derives from the fact that Jim can and should attach *some* weight to his agency, to the fact that if he accepts Pedro's offer, *he* will be killing an innocent person.

There is this contrast between Williams's example and the standard case of coercion. If Jim attaches moral weight to his agency in Williams's case, this may have a harmful effect on others. If B attaches moral weight to his agency in the typical case of coercion, it will have a positive effect on the interests of others. But the common thread remains, namely, that when B harms C, whether at A's invitation or at A's demand, it is still *B* that is harming C. B does, of course, have agent-relative reason to attach considerable weight to his own welfare. And as I have argued in Chapter 8, such considerations may, on occasion, be sufficient to justify B's succumbing to A's threat. Nonetheless, B's responsibility for what *he* does will also give him (some) agent-relative reason to become A's victim rather than A's (reluctant) accomplice. If these reasons are strong enough, we may want to say that despite A's coercive proposal, B is not coerced into harming C.

Coercion, Responsibility, and Policy

It might, at this point, once again be objected that I have endorsed the use of "policy" considerations in the adjudication of coercion claims, contrary to the position I defended in Part One.[36] The problem, once again, is roughly this. Courts sometimes reject B's coercion claim by arguing that it is not in society's interest to accept it. Rather than ask (only) whether factors intrinsic to B's choice situation entitle him to win, courts often ask whether finding in B's favor will have desirable social effects. I have suggested, at various points, that in appealing to these sorts of "policy" or "external" considerations, the courts may have departed from the moral logic of coercion, a logic in which the ascription of responsibility should turn only on factors which are (in some way) *internal* to B's choice situation.

Put slightly differently, it might be objected that the argument of the previous sections conflates two distinct questions: (1) Given A's coercive proposal, *is* B morally responsible for the normal effects of his act? (2) Given A's coercive proposal, is it morally best to *hold* B legally responsible for the normal effects of his act? And, it might be said, the law often seems to say that B *is not* coerced and therefore

[36] See pp. 174–75.

is responsible for his act when it is entitled only to say, at best, that despite A's coercive proposal it is wise to *hold* B responsible for his act.

Metaphysical and Ascriptive Responsibility. The distinction between the *ascription* of responsibility and responsibility *simpliciter* seems intuitively sound. We may, for example, criticize a particular test for insanity on the grounds that it treats as responsible some who are not (or vice versa).[37] Similar claims may be made about juvenile crime. The structure of our moral discourse does seem to presuppose a belief in metaphysical or free-standing moral responsibility, one which holds that people are or are not responsible and that their actual responsibility can be distinguished from its ascription.

This point may be illuminated by a brief consideration of *strict liability* statutes. A strict liability statute holds B liable for a harm even if B is not culpable, that is, even if his action could, in principle, be subsumed under one of the traditional legal excuses (mistake, unintentionality, ignorance, and so forth). A statute may, for example, hold manufacturers liable for harms caused by adulterated foods even if there is no negligence or wrongdoing in the manufacturing process.[38] It may be said that even if strict liability laws were defensible on social policy grounds, that would only show that it makes sense to *hold* people responsible for acts they *are* not responsible for performing. And, it might be added, such laws would still represent an important deviation from the widely accepted principle that responsibility should be ascribed only to those who are—in some sense—morally at fault.[39]

A parallel argument might be made with respect to coercion. Even if there are good utilitarian or policy reasons to *hold* someone responsible to whom a coercive proposal has been made, it does not follow that he is, in fact, responsible for not resisting it. It might, for example, be said that there are good reasons not to allow intimidated witnesses to use duress as a defense for refusing to testify— even though their situation may meet the traditional criteria for du-

---

[37] Daniel Dennett, *Elbow Room* (Cambridge: MIT Press, 1984), 163. I make extensive use in this section of Dennett's very suggestive argument.

[38] Similarly, a statute may make it criminal to serve liquor to minors even if the server has a reasonable belief that the customer is of age. There might be other justifications for such laws. The epistemological difficulties in the way of assessing moral fault may, in some cases, be so great as to make it practically necessary to ignore it.

[39] As Hart puts it, " 'strict liability' is generally viewed with great odium and admitted as an exception to the general rule, with the sense that an important principle has been sacrificed to secure a higher measure of conformity and conviction of offenders." *Punishment and Responsibility*, 20.

ress as a defense to a crime. But even if this were to be the right social policy, it might be said that such reasons have nothing to do
with whether intimidated witnesses are really acting under duress.

I think something close to this line of objection can, in fact, ultimately be sustained, but that it is not correct in its present form. Although courts may appeal to the *wrong* external moral considerations in adjudicating coercion claims, it is not wrong to appeal to
external considerations per se—in the law or in morality. Indeed,
the appeal to *some* external moral considerations is an integral element of the logic of coercion. The basic idea is this. When someone
is morally responsible, it is because there are good moral reasons to
treat him in certain ways. The reasons which justify holding people
morally responsible may not be identical to the reasons which justify holding people legally responsible, but they serve an analogous
function. By "somewhat arbitrarily" holding people *legally* responsible for their actions, as Daniel Dennett puts it, we attempt to chan-
nel their behavior in certain directions. By holding people *morally*
responsible, we induce them to integrate the consequences of their
acts into their original decisions, and, at a deeper level, to shape
their own inclinations and dispositions in certain directions.[40]

It is not my present purpose to deny that a metaphysical defense
of responsibility could be successfully advanced. It is possible that
the behavioral benefits of ascriptions of responsibility are just
happy by-products of our being in some deeper metaphysical sense
responsible for our actions. But whatever our metaphysical view,
this much can be said. When we are dealing with moral and legal
policy, a question of paramount *moral* importance is whether it is
right to *hold* people responsible, and for this purpose ascriptions of
moral responsibility can be interestingly understood in terms of efforts to direct the behavior of others and ourselves. And it is this
idea that I want to play out.

On the view of responsibility I am considering, the key question
is not whether there is metaphysical or free-standing moral responsibility, but the moral acceptability of the grounds for its ascription.
What should those grounds be? Once again, I shall make but a few
general observations. We should not set our standards too low. We
should not let ourselves off the moral hook whenever conditions for
the ascription of responsibility are less than ideal. Ascriptions of responsibility must be appropriately robust. Suppose, for example,
that one is more likely to lose one's temper if one is hungry and that

---

[40] *Elbow Room*, 165.

there are biochemical explanations of this phenomenon. Given that, one could adopt an excusing or justificatory attitude towards one's own behavior. Or one could, as I believe one should, "somewhat arbitrarily" decide to *hold* oneself responsible for losing one's temper regardless of one's blood sugar level. But if one decides to take responsibility when one's blood sugar level is low, it is not just because one believes that one is metaphysically responsible for losing one's temper, although that may be part of the story. It is at least partially because adopting such an attitude makes it less likely that one will lose one's temper when hungry, or because the general disposition to assume responsibility for one's behavior will have desirable effects in other arenas.

At the same time, we should not set our standards too high. Just as we appropriately allow for permanent disabilities (such as severe retardation) that make it difficult for some to exercise self-control virtually all the time, we should also take note of the temporary disabilities that make self-control difficult for virtually everyone some of the time.[41] If, as Barry Goldwater once said,[42] "extremism in the defense of liberty is no vice," I suggest that moral perfectionism in the ascription of responsibility is no virtue.

Ascriptive Responsibility and External Considerations. Let us assume, for the sake of argument, that there is something to the previous argument, that it is at least part of the truth about responsibility, if not the whole truth. Can we say anything more about the moral considerations which support ascriptions of responsibility? I think so. At the most general level, the central point is this. When we ascribe responsibility, we implicitly adopt an external, detached, or impartial perspective towards our own behavior and the behavior of others.[43] We step outside ourselves, and from that point of view, we attempt to determine what we want ourselves (and others) to be like. We then ascribe responsibility in a manner consistent with that conception. In this special sense, the ascription of responsibility is inherently based on external moral considerations.

On the other hand, to adopt a detached or external perspective

---

[41] As Bernard Williams suggests, defensible ascriptions cannot be made in ignorance of human capacities. See "The Idea of Equality," in *Problems of the Self* (Cambridge: Cambridge University Press, 1973), 235.

[42] At the 1964 Republican Convention.

[43] To further our desire for self-control, we must, as Dennett suggests, have the ability to represent our "beliefs, desires, intentions, and policies in a detached way, as objects for evaluation." *Elbow Room*, 86. For an extended discussion of what is entailed by an objective perspective, see Thomas Nagel, *The View from Nowhere* (New York: Oxford University Press, 1986).

for the ascription of responsibility is not to say that all external reasons are equally appropriate when deciding whether to hold people responsible for their acts when they face considerable pressure to behave otherwise. Roughly stated, some external reasons are grounded in considerations of justice and rights, or, in slightly different terms, in the relative claims of one's own interests and the interests of others. Other external reasons are primarily grounded in considerations of social utility, for example, the sorts of epistemological factors used to justify strict liability laws or precedential factors used to bar a duress defense to prison escape.

To establish stipulative placeholders (and no more than that), let us say that when we ascribe responsibility on grounds of justice (or rights), we have ascribed *responsibility*, and that when we ascribe responsibility primarily on grounds of utility, we have ascribed *liability*.[44] Given this distinction, we can say that responsibility may be ascribed on the basis of external reasons but simultaneously exclude certain sorts of external reasons as justificatory bases for its ascription. When we ascribe responsibility to ourselves or others it is because we understand our (and their) actions from a "detached point of view," a point of view which requires that our actions be based, in part, on the relative claims of those directly affected by them. On the other hand, even from this detached point of view, B need not take into account the utilitarian reasons that have figured so prominently in some judicial opinions and that may appropriately figure in the ascription of liability. On this view, the moral *force* of the earlier distinction between internal and external reasons for holding someone responsible still holds, but it emerges in a different way.

More specifically, I suggest that in deciding whether A's coercive proposal "really" coerces B to harm C, the courts are right to weigh C's interests in avoiding harm against B's interests in avoiding harm. The relative claims of those affected by B's actions are the sorts of factors which should tell for any agent who is capable of viewing his decision from a detached point of view. If, for example, B kills C to avoid having his finger broken by A, B cannot reasonably claim that he was coerced into doing so. For it seems reasonable to suppose that, from a sufficiently detached perspective, even B would want B to resist. On the other hand, in deciding whether B has escaped prison under duress, there are no comparable harms which it is reasonable to expect *B* to factor into his decision. It is, I

---

[44] It is, for example, plausible to speak of strict *liability* without fault, but it seems odder to speak of strict *responsibility* without fault.

suppose, not unreasonable for *lawmakers* to worry about the social costs of encouraging prison escape and the epistemological difficulties in the way of distinguishing false from genuine claims of duress. But it is, I think, a bit much to ask *B* to worry about such consequences. A morally required level of detachment must stop somewhere.

The conclusion is this. We may, on occasion, be justified in ascribing *liability* to persons to whom it would be wrong to ascribe *responsibility*. We may, on occasion, be justified in punishing someone who was (at least on agent-relative grounds) justified in acting as he did and therefore acted under duress. For the fact is that it is not always wrong to punish someone who was justified in acting as he did. Moreover, this is not as problematic as it might seem. That it may be permissible for the state to punish one who was justified in disobeying the law is a claim that is frequently and, I think, correctly made with respect to civil disobedience.

SIXTEEN

COERCION AND VOLUNTARINESS

The Problem

If the account of coercion developed in the previous chapters is roughly correct, it explains a lot. By translating moral threats into offers, the moral baseline account of coercive proposals explains why it is (ordinarily) not legally recognizable coercion to threaten to do something one has a right to do. The account of the choice prong as a justification explains how a proposal could constitute contractual duress, while a similar proposal would not establish duress as a defense to a crime. At the broadest level, the moralized account of coercion does much to explain the underlying logic (if not the actual reasoning process) by which courts determine whether an allegedly coercive proposal bars the ascription of legal responsibility for an act.[1] And if I am right in believing that the logic of coercion claims in moral discourse substantially parallels the logic of coercion in the law, my account of coercion does much to explain the ascription of moral responsibility as well.

But, as I have already noted, it threatens to do all this at a price. For on the moralized theory I have advanced, whether one is held to the normal consequences of one's acts in the face of putatively coercive proposals is largely determined by moral criteria that seem to have little to do with the preanalytic sense of coercion, that is, with the amount of "pressure" to which B is subject or with pressure that overwhelms the "will." And, the objection goes, the point of a coercion claim is that A's proposal gets B to act *involuntarily*, and not that (1) A acts wrongly in making his proposal to B and (2) B is entitled to succumb to A's proposal. We have seen that, precisely for this reason, some have advanced nonmoral theories of coercion which, among other things, claim to preserve the idea that coercion is wrong because it "undermines freedom."[2] Yet, as we have also

---

[1] This is not, of course, to say that I have given a complete account of the *criteria* which are properly utilized within the framework of that logic.

[2] See David Zimmerman, "Coercive Wage Offers," 10 *Philosophy & Public Affairs* 121, 122–23 (1981), and my discussion of Zimmerman's argument in Chapter 14.

seen, nonmoralized theories also have their price. For nonmoral theories of coercion seem to either collapse into moralized theories or be unable to distinguish the coercion that bars the ascription of responsibility from the coercion that does not.

While the desire to explain the relation between coercion and voluntariness may motivate some to seek nonmoral theories of coercion, others prefer to jettison the concern with voluntariness. The view that duress involves an "overborne will," says Patrick Atiyah, should be "consigned to the historical scrapheap."[3] George Fletcher puts the point this way. It is true, he says, that we use the *term* "involuntary" to describe nonvolitional acts and also to describe standard (constrained-volition) coercion in which A's threat justifies or excuses B's action. For present purposes, call these Type-1 acts and Type-2 acts.[4] At the same time, says Fletcher, Type-1 and Type-2 acts have nothing important in common with respect to their *voluntariness*. The common terminology is merely a linguistic device for expressing the *moral* view that one should not be held *responsible* for Type-2 acts just as one should not be held *responsible* for Type-1 acts, and has nothing to do with the *will*.[5] Because we are linguistically committed (for whatever reason) to a reasonably tight connection between voluntariness and the ascription of responsibility, we *say* that B acts involuntarily whenever we conclude that B should not be held responsible. But, the argument goes, we don't really mean it.

J. L. Mackie takes this argument a bit further. He maintains both that criminal acts performed under duress are normally fully voluntary and, more importantly, that nothing objectionable about responsibility follows from this view. Consider, he suggests, a case in which a tyrant proposes to torture or kill B's relatives if B does not perform an (otherwise) evil act. B must choose between (1) performing an evil act and saving his relatives and (2) defying the tyrant and

---

[3] "Economic Duress and the 'Overborne Will'," 98 *Law Quarterly Review* 197 (1982). We saw similar thinking at work in the discussion of coerced confessions. See Chapter 8. Michael Philips has argued that coerced agreements are *not*, in fact, involuntary and that there is no important connection between the voluntariness of an agreement and its bindingness. "Are Coerced Agreements Involuntary?" 3 *Law and Philosophy* 133 (1984).

[4] Jeffrie Murphy makes a similar, though not identical, distinction in "Consent, Coercion, and Hard Choices," 67 *Virginia Law Review* 79, 87 (1981).

[5] "There is a rhetorical point in this confusion: assimilating normative involuntariness [duress] to the paradigm of physical involuntariness, we express the conclusion that the actor should not be held accountable for an "involuntary' act." *Rethinking Criminal Law* (Boston: Little, Brown, 1978), 803.

having his relatives tortured or killed. If B chooses (1), says Mackie, B does so entirely voluntarily.

> Though his being confined to just these alternatives was not voluntary, the agent's choosing one of these complex alternatives rather than the other was wholly voluntary and intentional. And to hold him responsible for his intentional act, *adequately described*, is appropriate and has no undesirable implications. Even if X is in itself morally wrong or dishonourable or illegal, it does not follow that X-rather-than-Y must be so.[6]

Mackie acknowledges that referring to such acts as involuntary is the "colloquially natural way of speaking." But, he maintains, such expressions are philosophically mistaken. It would, he says, be "more accurate" to regard them as voluntary complex acts than as involuntary simple acts.

I indicated at the outset of this book that I would speak of voluntariness in an admittedly rough or colloquial way so as not to prematurely beg the question of whether an act could be both involuntary and volitional. It might now be said that even if that strategy made sense at the start, the time has come to concede that the colloquial expression is, in fact, just that. It might be said that I should be satisfied to have given (assuming I have done so) even a roughly accurate account of the way coercion claims work in the ascription of legal and moral responsibility, even if that account fails to explain the (putative) link between coercion and involuntariness. For, it may be claimed, there is no link to be explained. I suppose that I would be *satisfied*. Nonetheless, I would be even more satisfied if I were able to show that, at the bottom of all this, there remains an important connection between coercion and involuntariness.

My aim, then, is to provide an explanation of the connection between coercion and involuntariness that both explains how coercion undermines voluntariness and preserves the moral force of coercion claims. The problem, once again, is this. If we say (narrowly) that B acts involuntarily only when his will is literally overborne, we give up the chance to say that constrained-volition coercion undermines voluntariness. If we say (broadly) that B acts involuntarily whenever he stands to suffer for his choice or when-

---

[6] "The Grounds of Responsibility," in *Law, Morality, and Society: Essays in Honour of H.L.A. Hart*, ed. P.M.S. Hacker and J. Raz (Oxford: Clarendon Press, 1977), 181 (my emphasis).

ever he acts under great psychic strain, then the involuntariness of B's act will be stripped of its moral force.

I could try to make the link by arguing that just as coercion claims are contextual, so is voluntariness. As I noted in Chapter 11, one can use "voluntary" as a placemarker by which to note that a certain *sort* of pressure is absent. From this contextual perspective, I could argue that while coercion may not undermine voluntariness in one (strong) sense, it may do so in another (weaker) sense. But I do not want to make this move. For I want to show more than that we can *say* that coercion undermines voluntariness on some attenuated account of that term. I want to show that what Mackie describes as the "colloquially natural way of speaking" reflects something deeper about the relation between a moralized theory of coercion and the will.

One thing is clear. *If* there is a connection between coercion and voluntariness, it does not lie on the surface. If, as I suspect, the preanalytic sense of voluntariness has to do with "brute facts" about B's psychic states, and if we examine cases in which, on a moralized theory, B is and is not coerced, looking for the presence (and absence) of these sorts of facts, we are bound to come up empty. If a satisfactory account of the way coercion undermines voluntariness must turn on identifiable and reasonably straightforward *psychological* phenomena, I must concede right off that I cannot give such an account. At the same time, I see no reason, a priori, to accept such a restriction on what might count as an interesting explanation of this connection. My strategy, then, will be to offer a set of interrelated philosophical explanations of how coerced acts can be properly described as involuntary. The main point will be this. Even if, as I have argued, coerced acts are rarely *un*willed, that leaves open the question whether a coerced choice can be said to be involuntary in the sense that it is *against* one's will—in a way that will prove interesting. The purpose of this chapter is to show how this might be possible.

Motivations

If the distinction between the voluntary and the involuntary is to reflect anything more than the distinction between the volitional and the nonvolitional, its *locus* must first be determined. There are two related possibilities. Both rely on a spatial metaphor. And both have long and respectable philosophical pedigrees. The first strategy has to do with the relation between one's behavior and one's self. It turns on the distinction between *internal* causes of behavior, which are said not to compromise voluntariness, and *external* causes of behavior, which do. The second strategy focuses on the nature of one's preferences and the way those preferences are connected to one's actions. On this view, preferences are not all of a piece. They can be hierarchically ordered. And the claim is that although there is a (putatively trivial) sense in which we always do what we prefer, there is another (allegedly more important) sense in which voluntary acts are compatible with our more reflective (higher or underlying) preferences whereas involuntary acts are not. The two strategies may turn out to be different ways of putting the same point. But since that point may be clearer on one approach than the other, I propose to consider each in turn.

Internal and External. In one of the earliest accounts of involuntary action, Aristotle says this: "Those things, then, are thought involuntary, which take place under compulsion . . . and that is compulsory of which the moving principle is outside, being a principle in which *nothing* is contributed by the person who is acting."[7] Here Aristotle has in mind a case of pure external and physical causation, as when A literally forces B's hand to sign a confession. While we are no longer apt to say, with Aristotle, that involuntariness precludes *all* internal causation, his basic view retains much of its appeal. We say, in effect, that one acts voluntarily only when one's motivations are internal to the *self* or internal to the self in a certain way.

Recall two examples in the law. In our discussion of the law of wills, we saw that A may exercise undue influence over (a testator) B if, as a result of A's actions, B is motivated by fear of harmful interventions by A. On the other hand, A does not exercise undue influence over B if B is motivated by the desire to please A. In our discussion of confessions, we saw that even uncontroversially voluntary confessions generally occur only after the police have originated the legal process, that voluntariness does not require that a "guilty person gives himself up to the law and becomes his own accuser."[8]

What do these examples show? First, they show what is obvious, but nonetheless needs to be said, namely, that uncontroversially voluntary acts are *motivated*, and that even those motivations that are paradigmatically consistent with acting voluntarily (whatever

---

[7] *Nicomachean Ethics*, bk. III, sec. 1110a (trans. Ross; emphasis added).
[8] *Ashcraft* v. *Tenn.*, 322 U.S. 143, 160, 161 (1944).

those turn out to be) may cause a person to do something he would otherwise not have done. More broadly, they indicate that *any* account of the distinction between the voluntary and the involuntary which is not parasitic on the distinction between the volitional and the nonvolitional must explain why some motivations are compatible with acting voluntarily whereas others are not. These examples also show that the crucial question is not where the motivation begins in physiospatial terms, for virtually all internal motivations have some external precipitant—nor is it crucial where they end up, for they all operate through internal mental processes. The question is how these motivations are to be *understood*. The view that external causes render action involuntary depends less on this protean spatial metaphor than on the significance attributed to placing a certain cause under the internal or external rubric. Internality, as it were, is not a locational feature of a motivation. It is part of its *description*.[9]

Forms of Power. To bring the relation between motivation and voluntariness into sharper relief, I want to consider some of the ways in which A may exercise power over B, A's power being understood (for present purposes) as A's ability to get B to do X, where B would otherwise *not* do X. Having distinguished between these forms of power, we can then ask whether the voluntariness of B's action is compromised by a particular form of power and go on to see what we can learn from our answer to that question.[10]

Consider first the distinction between persuasion and manipulation. Say that A *persuades* B to do X by giving B reasons to do X. The reasons may appeal to B's interests, as when A persuades B to see a movie or invest in bonds, or to B's moral principles, as when A persuades B to give blood or engage in political activity. Say that A *manipulates* B by altering B's environment in a way that makes it more likely that B will do X, where there is no mutually recognized interaction *between* A and B. In a benign case of manipulation, A might leave a review of a movie (which A wants B to see) where B is likely to find it. Or, perhaps less benignly, A may attempt to get B to want to do X by appealing to B's "unconscious" preference for certain colors or shapes, as when A packages a product in a certain way.

There are important commonalities between persuasion and ma-

---

[9] As Julius Kovesi remarks in a related context, the voluntariness of acts depends not on "the recognition of any empirical similarities" between voluntary acts, but on our "recognition of what it is for an act to be" voluntary. *Moral Notions* (London: Routledge and Kegan Paul, 1967), 17.

[10] See, for example, Anthony de Crespigny, "Power and Its Forms," 16 *Political Studies* 192 (1968).

nipulation. Both can get B to do something he would otherwise not have done. And both originate externally to B. At the same time, it seems that persuasion and manipulation may have different effects on the voluntariness of B's action. It is, I believe, entirely uncontroversial that B acts voluntarily if he is persuaded by A's reasons (whether those reasons appeal to B's interests or to his moral principles). On the other hand, things may be different with respect to manipulation. I do not suggest that B *always* acts involuntarily when A manipulates him, for, as in the case of the movie review, B's act may be perfectly voluntary. All I want to suggest, and all I think I need to suggest, is that when A manipulates B—particularly by working through B's unconscious motivations—we think that the voluntariness of B's actions is debatable or at least of a different sort than when A persuades B.

The point might be put this way. When A *persuades* B to do X, B's action is not only voluntary with respect to B's *doing X*, it is also voluntary with respect to *A's getting B to do X*.[11] What begins as an external force becomes thoroughly internalized, in a way that B knows about and to which he has given his direct and informed consent. When A *manipulates* B into doing X, B may not mind doing X, but he might, if he knew, mind doing X because A wants him to do X. B does not give his informed consent to that fully described action. A's manipulation compromises the voluntariness of B's action because it is not fully and accurately internalized.

Consider now the distinction between threats and offers. Because the distinction between threats and offers clearly does not turn on a difference in their originating locations, the distinction presents a problem for Aristotle's account of voluntariness. For if all external causation were to compromise the voluntariness of one's act, one's response to an inducement as well as one's response to a threat would be involuntary. And that is a view Aristotle wants to reject: "if some one were to say that pleasant and noble objects have a compelling power, forcing us from without, all acts would be for him compulsory; for it is for these objects that all men do everything they do."[12]

Given that actions performed in response to external inducements are both volitional and voluntary, that leaves open the question of how to characterize volitional responses to external threats.

---

[11] Precisely for this reason, we often do not think of persuasion as a form of *power* at all. But if A exercises power over B when A gets B to do something that B would otherwise not have done, persuasion is a form of power.

[12] *Nicomachean Ethics*, bk. III, sec. 1110b.

On that, Aristotle is explicitly ambivalent: "But with regard to the things that are done from fear of greater evils . . . it may be debated whether such actions are involuntary or voluntary . . . the man acts voluntarily; for the principle that moves the instrumental parts of the body in such actions is in him . . . [yet] such actions . . . are . . . perhaps involuntary; for no one would choose any such act in itself."[13] How does Aristotle resolve his ambivalence? Aristotle argues that threats render one's action involuntary if they would motivate a person with the proper character to perform an (otherwise) evil act. Employing what I have called a standardized test of coercion, Aristotle says that pardon should be bestowed "when one does what he ought not under pressure which overstrains human nature and which *no one* could withstand."[14] At the same time, says Aristotle, there are some acts which "we *cannot* be forced to do, but ought rather to face death after the most fearful sufferings . . ."[15]

It seems, then, that Aristotle has actually introduced two versions of the distinction between the voluntary and the involuntary. He argues that the distinction can be understood in terms of the contrast between internal and external causation. He also argues that the distinction can be understood in terms of the contrast between actions that we are justified and actions that we are not justified in performing. He suggests, in effect, that if B is entitled to yield to A's threat, B acts for external reasons and therefore acts involuntarily, but that if B is not entitled to yield, B's motivations are internal, and therefore B acts voluntarily. This is a complicated notion, and more needs to be said about it. But before returning to it, I want to consider what the "hierarchical" model might contribute to the analysis of voluntariness.

Preferences

Momentary and Stable Preferences. There are several ways to make distinctions among one's preferences. As we saw in our discussion of psychological seduction, we may find it useful to distinguish between momentary preferences, on the one hand, and our more considered or stable preferences on the other.[16] On this view, one may have a momentary preference to have a drink or commit adultery

---

[13] Ibid., sec. 1110a.

[14] Ibid. (emphasis added).

[15] Ibid. (emphasis added). This is, of course, a moral and not a psychological "cannot."

[16] See pp. 222–24.

(or, perhaps more accurately, to do that which would constitute an act of adultery) and yet have an underlying or stable preference not to do so. It is true, as is often noted, that the notion of "underlying" preferences is fraught with danger, especially in cases where it is argued that we should ignore, as originating in "false consciousness," those allegedly momentary preferences which do not represent what some may *take* another's "real" underlying preferences to be. Despite these dangers, the notion that a person's momentary preferences can fail to reflect his more considered or stable preferences is clear from introspection and of considerable analytical value.[17]

Given this distinction, we sometimes find it useful to say that B acts involuntarily when his momentary preferences fail to reflect his stable preferences. Such claims are often but colloquial expressions. One may say "I couldn't help myself" when taking a piece of dessert, although one does not wish to be taken literally or believe that the expression has significant moral (excusatory) force. At the same time, there are cases in which the disjunction between momentary and stable preferences is of capital importance. Consider the suspect who confesses after being beaten. We might say that the confession is involuntary precisely because the suspect has a stabler and stronger aversion to spending his life behind bars than to continued physical pain, though his momentary preference to end the physical pain overrides that stabler preference. Interestingly, those who equate the volitional and the voluntary may object to describing even torture-induced confessions as involuntary, because, after all, even those confessions flow from the suspect's will. But whatever we want to call such confessions, they are arguably importantly analogous to the case in which there is *no* correspondence between B's preferences and his bodily movements, as when B's hand is literally forced to sign a confession.

The question now is this. If the disjunction between momentary and stable preferences contributes to an account of involuntariness, how does it connect with the moralized theory of coercion? Even if one acts involuntarily when one's momentary preferences do not reflect one's stable, underlying preferences, why does one act involuntarily when one's response to a morally unjustifiable proposal ("Your money or your life") is consistent with one's stable and long-term preference (to live)? Or why does one act voluntarily when one yields to a proposal one should resist ("Kill him or I'll break your

---

[17] See Albert O. Hirschman, "Against Parsimony," 1 *Economics and Philosophy* 7 (1985).

arm") but act involuntarily when one is entitled to succumb ("Break his arm or I'll kill you")?

Hypothetical Preferences. To answer these questions, we shall, I think, find it useful to extend the analysis beyond the distinction between momentary and stable preferences so as to incorporate the distinction between one's (actual) momentary *or* stable preferences and the *hypothetical* preferences one would have under more ideal conditions. That the hypothetical perspective is, in principle, of some help to the analysis of voluntariness can be seen by its application to cases in which the impairment of voluntariness is primarily cognitive. One very useful way to understand how fraud compromises the voluntariness of B's actual consent is to contrast B's consent with what he *would* have done had he possessed accurate information. This hypothetical perspective seems particularly apt in medical situations, where we may note that B would hypothetically not have consented to a certain procedure had he been adequately informed.

Hypothetical consent also plays an important role in Robert Nozick's attempt to explain how threats undermine voluntariness whereas offers do not. Nozick begins by noting that despite some obvious differences, there are several important commonalities between offer and threat situations: (1) A can get B to do something he otherwise would not do by an offer as well as by a threat; (2) B can refuse to succumb to a threat just as he can refuse to accept an offer; and (3) it may be just as unreasonable for B to refuse an offer as it is for him not to succumb to a threat.[18] Given these commonalities, it is, says Nozick, extremely difficult to show why B voluntarily accepts an offer but involuntarily succumbs to a threat, why threats involve the imposition of another's will whereas offers do not.

If, then, we are to understand how threats undermine voluntariness whereas offers do not, we cannot, says Nozick, "attend only to the choice confronting the person in the threat and offer situations."[19] Instead, we must look to the *hypothetical* choices a rational man would make in a *preproposal* stage. From this perspective, the distinction between threats and offers is roughly this. In the preproposal stage, a "Rational Man" (one who has the psychological capacity to reject offers he thinks he should not accept and not succumb to threats he thinks he should resist) would welcome credible

[18] "Coercion," in *Philosophy, Science and Method*, ed. Sidney Morgenbesser et al. (New York: St. Martin's, 1969), 460.

[19] Ibid., 464.

offers but not credible threats.[20] Whereas he normally would be willing to go from the *preoffer* stage to the offer stage, he would *not* be willing to go from the *prethreat* stage to the the the threat stage.[21] *Given* A's threat, B may be extremely eager to succumb. But B acts involuntarily in response to such threats because it is against B's hypothetical will to receive such a threat in the first place.

Nozick's emphasis on B's hypothetical choices is helpful, but it does not go far enough. The reason is this. On a moralized theory of coercion, whether A's proposal is a threat or an offer depends on whether A has the *right* to make his proposal. While B certainly would not want to receive impermissible proposals ("Your money or your life") in a hypothetical preproposal stage, it seems likely that B would also prefer not to receive a *morally permissible* proposal that would entail a *utility-reducing* move from his nonmoral baseline to his moral baseline ("Settle for $100,000 or I'll sue you for $1,000,000"). So the question arises of whether B's hypothetical choices can be linked to the *morality* as opposed to the *attractiveness* of A's proposal. Although Nozick does not address this question, I think it can be. But we shall have to look a bit deeper.

Hierarchical Preferences

To do so, it will prove useful to consider a third distinction, one which holds considerable promise for our enterprise, because it underlies one of the more important contemporary approaches to the problem of freedom of the will. Following Harry Frankfurt, let us refer to one's actual (momentary or stable) preferences as first-order preferences, and to preferences about one's first-order preferences as second-order preferences.[22] To illustrate, one might have neither a momentary nor a stable first-order preference for classical music, but one might have a second-order preference to have such a first-order preference.[23]

Now it is, argues Frankfurt, a fundamental characteristic of what

[20] Nozick points out that there are some unusual situations in which a Rational Man would welcome a credible threat, but I shall ignore them here.

[21] Ibid., 463.

[22] See Harry Frankfurt, "Freedom of the Will and the Concept of a Person," 68 *Journal of Philosophy* 5 (1971). Whereas the objects of both momentary and stable preferences are actions or states of affairs, the propositional object of a second-order preference is itself a preference.

[23] Amartya Sen argues that it is a defect of much standard economic theory that it ignores precisely this feature of human behavior. See "Rational Fools: A Critique of the Behavioral Foundations of Economic Theory," 6 *Philosophy & Public Affairs* 317 (1977).

it is to be a *person* to have second-order preferences and volitions about our first-order preferences and volitions.[24] In contrast to persons, "wantons" do not have such second-order preferences. A wanton has a will, but unlike a person, a wanton "does not care about his will." But even persons, those who care about their wills, do not always act autonomously. A person's will is autonomous, on Frankfurt's account, when he is motivated by first-order preferences which have been brought into line with his second-order preferences.[25] And extending this view of free will to the nature of free action, we might say that B *acts* freely only if he both has a second-order preference about his first-order preferences and acts from the preferences from which he wants to act. Otherwise, B's act is not *unwilled*, but it is *against* his (second-order) will.

Although second-order preferences need not be moral preferences, the notion does provide us with a way to make the desired link. There is, after all, a long and important philosophical tradition which claims, among other things, that we act voluntarily when we act in accordance with our deepest moral principles.[26] Thus Gary Watson maintains that an agent acts freely when the desires which produce an action are internal to his evaluational system.[27] On this view, the kleptomaniac acts involuntarily because his (compulsive) desires "express themselves independently of his evaluational judgments," because his desires and actions are at variance with his underlying character.[28] So too Gerald Dworkin asks us to consider a case in which one issues a dinner invitation to a boring acquaintance only because one wants to reciprocate his previous invitation. One does so freely, says Dworkin, because one does not mind acting for reasons of reciprocity, even though one would otherwise prefer not to issue the invitation.[29] The point of Dworkin's example, and it is an important point, is that great reluctance and voluntari-

[24] "Freedom of the Will and the Concept of a Person." Also see Gerald Dworkin, "Acting Freely," 4 *Nous* 367 (1970); Gary Watson, "Free Agency," 72 *Journal of Philosophy* 205 (1975); and Wright Neely, "Freedom and Desire," 83 *Philosophical Review* 32 (1974).

[25] "Freedom of the Will and the Concept of a Person," 11. For a discussion of this notion with particular regard to feminism, see George Sher, "Our Preferences, Ourselves," 12 *Philosophy & Public Affairs* 34, 47 (1983).

[26] The tradition ranges from Plato to Rousseau to Kant to Frankfurt to Rawls—to mention but a few. Indeed, on some views in this tradition, a fully autonomous person must be motivated by such second-order moral preference.

[27] "Free Agency."

[28] Ibid., 220.

[29] "Acting Freely," 377.

ness are eminently compatible when our actions flow from what we take to be the right sorts of reasons.

Proposals from an Original Position

Let us assume, for the sake of argument, that there is something to the notion that the voluntariness of one's actions can be connected with the principles one accepts (or should accept). What might those principles be? We might find it useful to consider this question from a Rawlsian perspective, in part because that perspective may enable us to better understand the motivation for and reinforce our confidence in the principles involved in a moralized theory of coercion, and also because Rawls himself suggests that there is a connection between the principles of *justice* (that is, the principles that are chosen in an original position) and the *voluntariness* of one's action. While Rawls acknowledges that society is not, in fact, based on a voluntary scheme of cooperation, he applies to the political realm the general notion that one acts autonomously when one acts from the right sorts of motivations: "a society satisfying the principles of justice as fairness comes as close as a society can to being a voluntary scheme, for it meets the principles which free and equal persons would assent to under circumstances that are fair. In this sense its members are autonomous and the obligations they recognize self-imposed."[30] Putting the point in hierarchical terms, citizens in a well-ordered society, says Rawls, have a "highest order" desire to act from the principles of justice. By acting from the principles of justice, they "express their full autonomy."[31]

Let us play the Rawlsian scheme out just a bit, although I do not think that much turns on whether we accept its entire apparatus or the specific principles Rawls endorses. Let us assume something close to Rawls's conception of an original position, that is, a hypothetical choice situation in which free and equal persons, deprived of knowledge about their specific characteristics (race, gender, class, intelligence, bargaining ability, and so forth), are to choose the principles by which they are prepared to live and be bound.[32] Let us also assume, for the sake of argument, that those in an original position have settled on a package of basic rights. It is possible that those in the original position may have reason to treat a small

[30] *A Theory of Justice* (Cambridge: Harvard University Press, 1971), 13.
[31] "Kantian Constructivism in Moral Theory," 77 *Journal of Philosophy* 515, 532 (1980).
[32] *A Theory of Justice*, 11–12.

class of rights as (technically) inalienable, but they will, I think, generally want to be able to waive their rights and make binding commitments if, by doing so, they expect to be better off by their own lights. Rational and self-interested persons would, of course, prefer being able to reap the benefits of agreements without bearing the costs, but they see that this is impossible. Being unable to anticipate which side of an agreement they will be on, they will prefer principles (and appropriate institutional embodiments of those principles) which hold both parties to the terms of most agreements.

Now within this general structure, those in the original position anticipate that they may be the makers and recipients of various proposals. They anticipate that qua makers of proposals, it will be in their interests to minimize the limits on the proposals allowed, but that qua recipients of proposals, it will be in their interests to establish some restrictions. We can, then, expect them to ask something like this question: Under what conditions should one be held accountable for acts performed in response to proposals that do not conform with the principles of justice or that are made under background conditions that are less than fully just?

It is not my present purpose to show that some version of the two-pronged theory of coercion would be generated from an original position, although I think it distinctly possible that it would. But given this question, it seems likely that those in the original position will decide that agreements secured in response to proposals to violate one's rights (for example, "Your money or your life") should not be enforceable. Although there might be occasional benefits—even to the recipient—from a policy of enforcing such agreements, such a policy would seriously threaten the stability of the basic package of rights and liberties that serves as the framework within which social life (including agreements) takes place. Similar considerations may motivate a decision to restrict the sort of wrongful proposals for which blackmail serves as a model. On the other hand, those in the original position also understand that they are choosing principles for a real world, that illness, accident, and even unjust background conditions may place them in disagreeable, sometimes unavoidable, but importantly improvable, choice situations. For that reason, they may well adopt something like the distinction between intentional and circumstantial forcings we have seen in the law and have defended in some detail. They may be prepared not to enforce agreements made in response to intentional threats, but to enforce agreements that arise out of circumstantial forcings. Indeed, from this perspective, they may even be inclined to make the sort of distinction captured in Nozick's "comparative" or "closest relative view" of coercion, namely, that one is especially concerned to ensure that one's own will is more closely tied to one's actions than the will of anyone else—other pressures notwithstanding.[33]

In addition to circumscribing the sorts of proposals that will be judged an acceptable basis for enforceable agreements, those in an original position may also arrive at the sorts of principles captured by the choice prong, the force of which is to hold B accountable for some acts performed in response to proposals that are otherwise wrongful and that they would disapprove of. For the "detached perspective" that motivates the choice prong is, after all, just another way of putting the point of the original position, which is, as Rawls suggests, simply to "make vivid" the constraints of impartiality to which (at least some) moral principles must conform.[34]

Morality and Voluntariness

If I am right in believing that the connection between a moralized theory of coercion and voluntariness cannot be explained (if it is to be explained at all), in terms of straightforward psychological criteria, any account of that connection is going to look *something* like the one I have discussed. We can probably do without the explicitly Rawlsian perspective, but the argument will be that one acts voluntarily when one acts (or should act) from certain motives or that one acts voluntarily when the factors that define one's choice situation stand in a certain relation to the principles that one does (or should) accept.

As we have seen, two kinds of moral considerations are relevant here. The first sort of moral consideration is captured in the proposal prong. On this view, B acts voluntarily when B succumbs to a proposal that A has a right to make, even if it is one which B finds unattractive and would prefer not to receive. Why? Because B *himself* is committed to the principles which grant A the right to make the proposal. On the other hand, B acts *in*voluntarily when A makes an immoral proposal (a moral baseline threat) because A's proposal attempts to get B to act contrary to his deep preference that he *not* be made to act in response to immoral proposals.

Recall, in this connection, Aristotle's ambivalence about the voluntariness of acts performed in response to threats—they are voluntary because the moving force is in the agent, but involuntary be-

---

[33] See p. 265.
[34] *A Theory of Justice*, 18.

cause "no one would choose any such act in itself."[35] Or recall Mackie's observation that while the action taken within a coercive choice situation is perfectly voluntary, the agent's "being confined to just these alternatives was not voluntary."[36] We can, I think, reformulate Aristotle's and Mackie's common point so as to accommodate the present line of argument. Both Aristotle and Mackie can be understood as arguing that one acts involuntarily when one must choose between alternatives that are contrary to the range of alternatives one's moral will would permit. One does not act involuntarily merely because one does not *like* the available alternatives. For as we have seen, reluctance and voluntariness can well go hand in hand. One acts involuntarily because one has a deep aversion to having to choose in response to immoral proposals. Coerced choices are not unwilled, but they are, it may be said, *against* one's will.

This analysis can also be brought to bear on the moral considerations contained in the choice prong, although here our task is more difficult. We want to explain why B acts *in*voluntarily when he is *entitled* to succumb to A's immoral proposal, but acts voluntarily when he is *not entitled* to succumb to A's immoral proposal. Since it is against B's moral will to be the recipient of such proposals in the first place, it is not clear why he acts voluntarily when he is not entitled to succumb to such proposals.

The explanation may go something like this. Receiving A's immoral proposal is contrary to B's will that he be treated correctly. If there is no countervailing moral reason for B to resist, A's immoral proposal goes, as it were, against B's will through to B's action. On the other hand, B's own moral principles acknowledge that the moral world in which he operates is not perfect, that he has *moral* choices to make under nonoptimal moral conditions. If B has moral reasons to resist A's wrongful proposal, B's action is voluntary because B himself is committed to acting on those moral reasons. Voluntariness turns, as it were, on the last operative moral reasons upon which B acts. In the first case, the last moral reason allows B to yield; in the second case, the last moral reasons require him to resist.

It is important to note that it is the moral principles to which B is committed that determine the voluntariness of B's action and *not* the way in which B understands or interprets them in a particular

[35] See quotation at note 13 above.
[36] See quotation at note 6 above.

case. B may, for example, believe that A is not entitled to make a proposal that A is, in fact, entitled to make—on B's own principles. Or B may think he is entitled to succumb to A's proposal when, on his own principles, he is actually required to stand firm. Because B could be mistaken in this way, he may think that his action is involuntary when it is not. But given that I have argued, all along, that coercion is not radically subjective, that is an implication I am happy to accept.

There are, however, at least two other sorts of cases which create more serious problems for this account of voluntariness. First, it might be objected that my strategy works only for those persons who accept the moral principles which are required by my account of coercion. What can we say of the "wanton" or the egoist? Suppose that A is morally entitled to make his proposal, but that B does not care whether this is the case, that it is part of his *character* to think this way. Or suppose, as in a case of criminal duress, that A's wrongful proposal is one that B should resist, but that (an amoral) B is quite prepared to harm C if that is necessary to protect himself.

There are, at the broadest level, two views we could adopt. We could say, in both cases, that B is acting voluntarily (and wrongly) because A's proposal has not gotten B to act contrary to his moral principles—for he has no such moral principles. This, however, is problematic, since A's proposal has gotten B to act contrary to his deepest (amoral) preferences as to how he should be treated, even if his deepest preferences are not very deep. For that reason we might prefer a second view, on which B acts *in*voluntarily in these cases. We would, then, have two further options. We might treat wantons or egoists in the way we treat the culpable drunk, as a case in which B is held *responsible* for his *in*voluntary acts because they can be traced to prior voluntary acts, or, as in the present case, to B's responsibility for his bad character. Or we could simply concede that B is acting involuntarily *and* that B should be neither treated as a responsible moral agent nor held (act) responsible for what he does. Would this entail the arguably unacceptable consequence that B is beyond our moral clutches? I think not. For to say that an agent is not responsible is not to say that he is beyond the range of legal or moral responses to his actions. Just as we must decide how to deal with sociopaths or psychopaths (who may not be responsible agents), we would still have to determine how to treat nonresponsible wantons and egoists.

Weakness of the will creates a more difficult problem. Suppose, for example, that A gets B to succumb to his proposal even though the principles which B accepts would require that he resist. Does B succumb voluntarily or involuntarily? We could say that B acts involuntarily because he is, in fact, acting contrary to his moral will, and we could proceed to treat (at least some of) these cases as ones in which we hold B responsible for his involuntary act. On the other hand, we could say that B acts voluntarily, in part, because he has shaped his character in a way that renders him less able to act in accordance with his more abstract moral beliefs. I am not sure which of these alternatives is preferable. Fortunately, it can also be said that weakness of the will creates a problem about voluntariness for virtually any theory of the ascription of responsibility—and not just for the theory that I have advanced.

But suppose I concede that B sometimes does act involuntarily even though he acts in ways he is not justified in acting. Could I still claim to have shown a connection between a moralized theory of coercion and voluntariness? That depends on what I take my task to be. If I had to show that one *always* acts voluntarily when complying with moral proposals (and with immoral proposals that one should resist), my account would be inadequate. On the other hand, I see no reason to assume such an ambitious conception of my theoretical task. If, as I believe, it is of value to show how it is *possible* for one to act voluntarily while yielding to moral but unattractive proposals or to immoral and unattractive proposals that one should resist, this account may contribute to that project.

Conclusion

The previous argument has, I fear, been largely defensive. I have argued, in effect, that we can make *sense* of the notion that one acts voluntarily when one acts reluctantly but in accordance with one's moral principles. Yet in doing so, I have sometimes proceeded as if it were more natural to assume some contrary view, as if there were a relatively uncontroversial account of voluntariness against which this more contentious view should be judged. I do not know of any such account. As I have suggested, *any* account of voluntariness on which the distinction between the involuntary and the voluntary is not equivalent to the distinction between the nonvolitional and the volitional must distinguish motivations that are compatible with acting voluntarily from those that are not. And there is no standard or nonproblematic nonmoral view of what the distinction between these motivations might be.

Suppose that we start from the beginning. Assume that it is an *open question* just what sorts of motivations are compatible with voluntariness. What are our options? There are many; I shall note but two. First, we *could* distinguish the voluntary from the involuntary in terms of the "willingness" or sense of reluctance with which an act is performed. The advantage of this view is that it has some linguistic and phenomenological support. The disadvantage is that, on this view, the voluntariness of actions would be morally insignificant. For the moral question is whether B is responsible for his action and not whether he is *happy* about it. We could, on the other hand, adopt something like the "moral will" theory that I have discussed. The advantage of this view is that it preserves the moral force of voluntariness claims. The disadvantage is that it threatens to preserve that moral force by detaching voluntariness from the will, from its psychological referents.

Recall, in this connection, Rawls's claim that people express their (moral) *autonomy* by acting from the principles of justice. Rawls does not say—in so many words—that they act *voluntarily*. While it is not clear how much Rawls would want to make of this distinction, it may be objected that (moral) autonomy and voluntariness are certainly not identical and that I have wrongly proceeded as if they were. And so, it may be claimed, we are right back where we started.

But I do not think that this objection is correct or that the linguistic and phenomenological cards are all stacked against me. The fact is that one's moral will is *not* radically detached from one's phenomenal will. There is something psychologically special about being treated in impermissible as opposed to merely unpleasant ways. We *dislike* unfavorable treatment; we *object* to unjust treatment. We prefer attractive proposals, but we do not typically *complain* about agreements made in response to morally permissible but unattractive proposals. Why? Because we understand that we have no valid complaint.

The point might be put this way. It is uncontroversial that B acts freely and voluntarily when A's proposal increases B's options. But, as we have seen, options can only be increased (or decreased) when compared to a standard or baseline. We could, I suppose, assess the voluntariness of B's action in terms of the baseline that B would *prefer* us to assume, but I see no reason why we should do so. A might claim, after all, that we should use the baseline that A would prefer. Rather than attempt to determine whose favored baseline should be adopted, it is at least plausible to suggest that B's moral baseline is the best perspective from which to evaluate the range of B's options. And on this view, morally permissible (and hence noncoercive) proposals do not compromise the voluntariness of one's actions.

In the final analysis, the most important point is also the most general. Simply put, the distinction between the voluntary and the involuntary must start somewhere. I have argued that there are good reasons to start from a moralized account of B's situation. Perhaps there are reasons to start somewhere else. But that view, too, would have to be defended.

S E V E N T E E N

CONCLUSION

An old chestnut in jurisprudence concerns a statute that prohibits the use of vehicles in a public park. The following question arises: does this statute apply to roller skates (or bicycles or toy automobiles)?[1] What would answering this question involve? We know what it does not involve. Certainly, we do not need additional factual information about roller skates. We know all that we need to know. Nor do we need a conceptual analysis of "vehicle." The question is not whether roller skates are "vehicles" in *some* plausible sense of that term (surely they are), but how this statute should be understood. There are, of course, different theories as to how such laws should be interpreted.[2] But on virtually any such theory, the primary question is not what roller skates are like, but whether roller skates are to be banned.

I have argued, in effect, that whether a coercion claim is true is akin to whether roller skates are vehicles. The interesting question is not whether a given choice situation *can* be understood as coercive, any more than the interesting question with regard to the above statute is whether roller skates can be described as vehicles. The interesting issue is whether A's alleged coercion nullifies B's responsibility for the normal moral or legal effects of his act. I have argued that to ascribe such responsibility in the face of A's alleged coercion of B, we must answer two moral questions: (1) Has A made a coercive proposal as defined by B's moral baseline? (2) Is B entitled to succumb to A's proposal? Although I have tried to say something about what might go into answering these questions, I have only

---

[1] The example was originally designed to criticize a deductive or formalistic model of the law. See H.L.A. Hart, "Positivism and the Separation of Law and Morals," 71 *Harvard Law Review* 593 (1958), and Lon L. Fuller, "Positivism and Fidelity to Law— A Reply to Professor Hart," 71 *Harvard Law Review* 630 (1958).

[2] We might, for example, consider the intentions of those who wrote the statute, or we might ask what is the most sensible construction of its purpose. For a discussion of this point, see Ronald Dworkin, *Law's Empire* (Cambridge: Harvard University Press, 1985).

scratched the surface. The principal burden of the argument is that it is these moral questions that must be answered.

The argument for a moralized theory of coercion proceeded in two stages. In Part One, I argued that a "two-pronged theory of coercion" offers the best interpretation of the way the law has adjudicated coercion claims, and that both the proposal prong and the choice prong explicitly or implicitly advance moral tests. In Part Two, I argued that the two-pronged theory is philosophically defensible and that each prong captures an important dimension of coercion. I believe that the legal and philosophical analyses serve to make each argument stronger than either would be by itself. My account of coercion in the law is, I think, strengthened by the argument that the legal theory is philosophically defensible. The case for the philosophical theory is, I think, strengthened by its consistency with what the best legal thinkers have said about coercion. To elaborate on the latter point, let us suppose that we wanted to *reject* the moralized theory of coercion that I have advanced in Part Two. I maintain that we would still have to deal with the sorts of legal controversies that motivate the moralized theory of coercion we find in the law. And it is by no means clear how or if that could be done in any other way.

Given that I have emphasized the connections between the legal and philosophical analyses of coercion, it might be said that I have wrongly assumed that issues concerning coercion, duress, and responsibility are substantially unaffected by whether we are thinking about them in a "purely" moral context or in a legal context, where concerns about general rules, publicity, conformity to rules, and enforcement seem to have a special place.[3] True; and unlike morality, the law typically requires us to make a binary decision (B is or is not coerced) and uses different mechanisms of enforcement. Nonetheless, I am inclined to think that there is not much difference between the way coercion claims function in legal and in moral contexts. If, for example, we presuppose something like what Rawls calls the "constraints of the concept of right," there is much less to the difference between law and morality than might be supposed. For if Rawls is correct, any conception of right (and that would, I think, include conceptions of coercion and duress) must be general, universal, public, and final. In other words, it must exhibit precisely those characteristics which are properly regarded as essential characteristics of the law.[4]

---

[3] I thank Richard Wasserstrom for pressing me on this point.

[4] *A Theory of Justice* (Cambridge: Harvard University Press, 1971), 130ff. As Rawls himself notes, there is a parallel between his constraints on the concept of right and

If this much can be said for my theory, there are four related objections to that theory that I want briefly to (re)consider. First, it may be objected that my theory lacks the right intuitive feel. It may be said that despite everything I have argued, coercion has to do with the degree of "pressure" on an individual and that the coerciveness of the pressure is independent of moral questions, even if it is important to answering them. I do not have an entirely adequate answer to this objection. I am inclined to take intuitions seriously, and if my theory were clearly counterintuitive, I would be reluctant (although not entirely unprepared) to say so much the worse for our intuitions. I can say this. The circumstances in which, on my theory, B will be coerced will generally be circumstances in which B is also subject to great psychological pressure, even if such pressure is not *sufficient* to establish coercion. Moreover, as I have argued at some length, some of our intuitions are not only eminently *compatible* with my theory, but can only be *explained* by the sort of theory I have advanced. For the fact is that when making coercion claims in the context of ascriptions of responsibility, we do *not* say that B is coerced whenever he is subject to great pressure. Indeed, we often deny it.

Second, it may be objected that my theory misconceives the proper role of coercion claims. On my view, the truth of a coercion claim is largely the *result* of a moral inquiry rather than the *ground* for a moral conclusion. We typically say that B should not be held responsible *because* B has been coerced, and yet, on my account, we can determine that B has been coerced only when we have, in effect, already determined that B should not be held responsible. My response to this objection has been anticipated above.[5] Briefly stated, I believe that the objection is correct, but unimportantly correct. The objection rests, to a considerable extent, on a false hope that precise conceptual analysis and careful empirical investigation will resolve important moral issues that ostensibly turn on coercion claims.

(Re)consider two such substantive issues: Should experiments with prisoners in exchange for rewards be prohibited on the grounds that, given the conditions of incarceration, such blandishments constitute coercion? Should the sale of bodily organs by the poor be prohibited on the grounds that poverty coerces? The form of these questions implies that we can first determine whether such rewards constitute coercion and then go on to say whether the practice should be prohibited. On my view, however, the interesting

Lon Fuller's conception of law. See *The Morality of Law* (New Haven: Yale University Press, 1964).

[5] See p. 243.

question is not whether the offers are, in some sense, coercive. The interesting questions are these: Can persons in such conditions make intelligent judgments about their interests? Does society have an obligation to provide them with better alternatives? If society has not provided better alternatives, should such persons be allowed to improve their positions anyway? And, I suggest, *no* account of coercion could begin to determine whether these practices should be prohibited without answering just these (sorts of) questions.

Third, it might be objected that I have offered a *reductionist*, albeit a *moral* reductionist, account of coercion. I began by noting that a range of important legal, political, and moral questions seem to turn on what it means for someone to coerce someone else. And yet, on my account, whether A coerces B is equivalent to whether A has made an immoral proposal to which B is entitled to succumb. To use Parfit's phrase, no "further facts," and in particular no further psychological facts about B, are necessary to the adjudication of a coercion claim.[6] Indeed, it may be argued that "coercion" has dropped out of the picture.

Is this sort of reductionism to be avoided? I do not think so. As Nozick suggests, we tend to describe as reductionist only explanations which reduce what is thought to be more valuable (or interesting) to what is thought to be less valuable (or interesting) and do so in a way which is false.[7] On those criteria, I do not think that my theory is reductionist. First, I believe that my theory is true. Second, I do not think that the questions to which coercion is reduced are, in fact, less interesting than the simpler preanalytic sense of coercion. If they are not, my account of coercion is not reductionist in an eliminative sense. It does not analyze *away* the concern with coercion. It is reductionist only in that it disaggregates coercion claims into more specific moral claims. To this (presumably benign) form of reductionism, I plead guilty.

A fourth objection (or the previous objection restated) is essentially aesthetic. It might be thought that, on my account, the preanalytic sense of coercion turns out to be much less interesting than it first seemed. This observation is, I think, substantially correct. There is not much of interest left to the preanalytic sense of coercion. But there is this compensation. The moral issues that take its place are very interesting indeed.

[6] *Reasons and Persons* (New York: Oxford University Press, 1984), 210ff.

[7] "A reductionist view sees something as less valuable than it is, not simply as less valuable than it once might falsely have been thought to be." *Philosophical Explanations* (Cambridge: Harvard University Press, 1981), 628.

INDEX

Abbott v. *Regina*, 156
Abrams, Howard, 136n
act responsibility. *See* agent responsibility
Adams, Robert Merrihew, 270n
adoption, 77–84, 235
agent-neutral reasons, 167–69, 279
agent-relative reasons, 167–69, 274
agent responsibility, 269–70
Alexander, Larry, 247n
Allen v. *Morgan*, 81
Alschuler, Albert, 123n, 124n, 125, 129, 130, 141n, 142n, 143
alternatives, acceptability of. *See* no reasonable alternative
Aristotle, 3, 291–94, 302
Arnolds, Edward, 146n, 150n
Ashcraft v. *Tennessee*, 106–7, 291n
assumed risk, 55–61
Atiyah, P. S., 19n, 21n, 23n, 29n, 47n, 50n, 272, 289
Atkinson, Thomas, 85n, 86n, 87n, 88n
Austin v. *Loral*, 27, 35, 201, 271
autonomy, 54, 298–99; and agreements, 20; and deliberation, 195–96; and hard choices, 233; and voluntariness, 305

Bacon, Francis, 146
Barnett, Randy, 19n
Barry, Brian, 185n
Barwin v. *Reidy*, 78n
baselines, 204–5; and employment, 60, 219; moralized, 206–21, 228–29, 242–43, 253, 255; nonmoral, 206–17; phenomenological, 207, 210–11; and plea bargaining, 136–37; statistical, 207, 210–11, 213
Bayles, Michael, 225n
Beauchamp, Tom, 62n
Becker, Lawrence, 100n
Beitz, Charles, 48n

Benditt, Theodore, 10n, 205n, 229n
Benny, Jack, 6n
Bentham, Jeremy, 148–49
Berlin, Isaiah, 259–60
B.I.C. v. *Sony*, 41n, 215n, 249, 250
Black, Hugo, 114–15
blackmail, 90–103; external theories of, 92, 93–96; internal theories of, 92, 96–102
Blackmun, Harry, 133n, 161n
Blackstone, William, 23, 30, 147, 148, 155, 161, 276
Bohlen, Francis, 54n, 60n
Bond, James, 123n, 134n
Bordenkircher v. *Hayes*, 133, 137, 140n, 216n
Brady v. *United States*, 127n, 131, 134, 137, 139n
Bram v. *United States*, 105n
Branson, Roy, 66n
Brenkert, George, 260n, 261n
Brennan, William, 114n, 131–32, 135
Brown, L. Neville, 72n, 73n, 74n, 75n
Brown, Robert, 72n, 73n, 76n
Brown v. *Mississippi*, 106
Brownfield v. *Brownfield*, 85n
Brunk, Conrad, 136n
Buchanan v. *Prall*, 84n
Buckland v. *Buckland*, 75n
Bumper v. *North Carolina*, 114–15
Burger, Warren, 133
Burton v. *State*, 153n
Butterfield v. *State*, 151n

Caivano v. *Brill*, 25, 33, 40, 230n, 232n
Calameri, John, 23
Campbell v. *Parker*, 42n
Cannon v. *Cannon*, 72n
Canterbury v. *Spence*, 62–63
capital punishment, 183
capitalism, 4–5, 210, 246, 251, 253–55, 264

311

Library of Congress Cataloging-in-Publication Data

Wertheimer, Alan.
Coercion / Alan Wertheimer.
p. cm.—(Studies in moral, political, and legal philosophy)
Includes index.
ISBN 0-691-07759-2
1. Duress (Law)—United States. 2. Duress (Law)
I. Title. II. Series.
KF450.D85W47 1987   340'.11—dc19   87-21744

Alan Wertheimer is Professor of Political Science
at the University of Vermont.

ABX 8807

5/8/89

KF
450
D85
W47
1987